New Developments in Worker Training: A Legacy for the 1990s

AUTHORS

ANTHONY P. CARNEVALE

JOEL CUTCHER-GERSHENFELD

LOUIS A. FERMAN

JOHN A. FOSSUM

FRANK GALLO

HAROLD GOLDSTEIN

LOIS S. GRAY

JUDITH M. GUERON

GARY HANSEN

MICHELE HOYMAN

JOYCE L. KORNBLUH

SAR A. LEVITAN

DAVID A. LONG

GARTH MANGUM

STEPHEN MANGUM

DAVID MARSDEN

NOAH M. MELTZ

PAUL OSTERMAN

PAUL RYAN

ERNEST J. SAVOIE

EDITORIAL BOARD

LOUIS A. FERMAN

MICHELE HOYMAN

JOEL CUTCHER-GERSHENFELD

ERNEST J. SAVOIE

First edition

Library of Congress Catalog Card Number: 50-13564

ISBN 0-913447-48-X

PRICE $20.00

INDUSTRIAL RELATIONS RESEARCH ASSOCIATION SERIES
        Proceedings of the Annual Meeting (Spring publication)
        Proceedings of the Spring Meeting (Fall publication)
        Annual Research Volume
        Membership Directory (every third year)
IRRA Newsletter (published quarterly)

Inquiries and other communications regarding membership, meetings, publications, and general affairs of the Association, as well as orders for publications, copyright requests on publications prior to 1978, and notice of address change should be addressed to the IRRA publication office: David R. Zimmerman, Secretary-Treasurer; Marion J. Leifer, Executive Assistant.

INDUSTRIAL RELATIONS RESEARCH ASSOCIATION
7226 Social Science Building, University of Wisconsin, 1180 Observatory Drive, Madison, WI 53706 U.S.A.   Telephone 608/262-2762

CONTENTS

Chapter 1

Editors' Introduction

Louis A. Ferman
University of Michigan

Michele Hoyman
University of Missouri, St. Louis

Joel Cutcher-Gershenfeld
Michigan State University

Ernest J. Savoie
Ford Motor Company

Broad changes in the economy and in society in the United States during the 1980s elevated the importance of training for firms, unions, employees, and policymakers. Traditional training efforts were strengthened and a variety of new experiments were undertaken, some driven by employers, some structured as union-management initiatives, some originating within the labor movement, and some established as public-private partnerships. In this volume we explore many of the themes that emerged from these developments of the past decade. Although the focus is primarily on the United States, in Chapters 9, 10, and 11 we adopt a comparative perspective by examining public policies and approaches to training in Canada and Europe that are specifically relevant to the U.S. The core thesis that ultimately emerges is that the many new developments of the 1980s will leave a powerful legacy for the 1990s.

In organizing this volume it has been helpful to think of training in many different spheres, some overlapping and some separate. The government sphere, for example, includes at the federal level the Job Training Partnership Act (JTPA) and other legislation, such as the Occupational Safety and Health Act, that has training implications. Also within the government sphere are state and local programs that either administer federal funds, support training with other funds, or provide technical assistance in the area of training. In the private sphere there is, first, the internal training efforts within firms (skills training, organizational/management development training, and training in specialized topics such as safety, employee assistance, AIDS, etc.). There are a host of private training providers as well—consulting firms and equipment providers. A third sphere encompasses the training offered through professional associations and unions. Finally, the educational community (primary and secondary schools, community colleges, and universities) represent a fourth sphere of training activity.

Training in the United States historically has been highly segmented. Employers usually provided the training for managerial and professional employees, unions supported apprenticeships for work in the skilled trades, and training for the disadvantaged or the dislocated was the province of federal and state governments. There were few systematic links between the education community and the workplace, and most workers received only some form of on-the-job training. There was not (and still is not) a unified United States policy on training, nor is there a consensus on what would constitute a good training policy.

This fragmentation reflects the different interests and different levels associated with training. For firms, training has traditionally been seen at an organizational level where the focus is on organizational performance. For a union or workers, training has traditionally been seen at an individual level where the focus is on skill acquisition, often with an eye toward upgrading or job security. Government training has traditionally been seen at a macroeconomic level where the focus is on reducing unemployment or fostering economic development. Thus, not only has training been fragmented, but each fragment has been quite distinctly unique and marked by different concerns.

Another characteristic of traditional approaches to training is the "fighting the brushfire" mentality. That is, there has been little long-term planning and little coordination among actors and programs providing training. This has led to a duplication of efforts across programs. With programs organized along categorical lines— around a targeted group such as the disadvantaged, for example— it was harder to recognize common elements in the training process.

A final characteristic of U.S. training is its notable absence, traditionally. Training for most workers has been informal and received on the job (Mincer, 1962). Moreover, the overall level of training has been far lower than that of any of the United States' major trading partners (Osterman, 1989).

Forces Driving Changes in Training

Beginning in the 1980s the distinctions among types of training began to blur, the scope of training expanded, and connections grew among the parties—employers, unions, workers, educators, and governments. Driving the shifts in training are a broad range of social, economic, technical, and organizational forces that include: (1) globalization and specialization in world markets; (2) changes in the structure and identity of corporations; (3) new ways of organizing work; (4) strategic choices of the firm; (5) changes in the labor force; (6) new technology; (7) new recognition of literacy problems; (8) deindustrialization and the concomitant displacement of workers; (9) skill inflation for entry-level positions; and (10) public realization of the connections among training, economic development, and competitiveness. Each development will be examined below.

1. *Globalization and Specialization in World Markets.* At the same time that national markets are becoming more closely connected, there is increasing specialization of the mass markets. In this context, Piore and Sabel (1984) have identified flexible specialization as an alternative to mass production. This calls for high levels of worker skills.

2. *Changes in the Structure and Identity of Corporations.* The business environment in the 1980s was turbulent, as evidenced by the business closings, mergers, and leveraged buyouts. Although some firms retain their "brand name label," they often are gutted internally, necessitating layoffs, severances, and retraining for the survivors. The recent emphasis of firms on quality and on changing the corporate culture both imply extensive training efforts.

3. *New Ways of Organizing Work.* During the 1980s we have seen the development or extension of many innovations in the organization of work—employee participation, team-based work organization, job redesign, statistical process control, and just-in-time delivery. Each of these initiatives involves training in the content and interpersonal skills associated with the innovation.

4. *Strategic Choices of the Firm.* Some strategic choices of the firm have training implications because workers are dislocated. These choices include plant closings and the relocation of production (for example, the "Southern strategy" of relocating a plant in the South where there is cheap nonunion labor). Other strategic choices have training implications because workers become more important to firm goals. This approach is vividly illustrated by the extensive training used in Japanese transplants or U.S. "greenfield" facilities.

5. *Changes in the Labor Force.* Major changes in the labor force are already occurring and will be exacerbated in the 1990s, the consequences being greater diversity, decreasing labor supply, and a raft of retirements (raising the issue of intergenerational transfer of corporate values). Training will be central to addressing the resulting skill-level gaps between workforce entrants and the jobs available (Carnevale and Goldstein, 1990).

6. *New Technology.* New technology is being introduced with lightning-like speed—in telecommunications, for example. Thus, some jobs are becoming obsolete almost overnight and new skills must be acquired by those displaced workers if they are to have any possibility of retaining any position with the same employer or within the same industry. Training enters the debates over new technology in two ways. First, where technology leads to higher-skill jobs (rather than deskilling jobs), training is central to developing those skills. Second, where work is deskilled, viable alternatives will likely require training.

The chief technological change impacting the current workforce has been computerization or mechanization of jobs in every sector of the economy. For instance, employers increasingly expect entry-level clericals to have sufficient computer literacy to master a word-processing package. In manufacturing, training is needed not just for the highly visible robots, but also for numerical control machines, manufacturing inventory programs, and many other functions. Even in the sales and retail sector, the computer has become omnipresent and related training essential.

7. *New Recognition of Literacy Problems.* The 1980s have seen the surfacing of startling figures on the amount of illiteracy among U.S. workers, even some who are high school graduates (Sultan, 1989; Carnevale and Goldstein, 1990). The implications for training are two-fold. First, such deficiencies are an impediment to

advancement and even regular organizational operations. Second, these deficiencies are typically identified at the worksite. For these two reasons, employers (or employers and unions jointly) are offering basic skills as part of a battery of skills prerequisite to vocational training and career counseling. Sometimes a university, community college, or secondary school is the vendor of these services; sometimes it is a private enterprise. Sometimes the classes are held on-site, although it is more usual to have the students take the classes on the campus of the relevant school.

8. *Deindustrialization and the Concomitant Displacement of Workers.* Deindustrialization refers to a shrinking of the traditional manufacturing industry base, often accompanied by a corresponding shift to the service sector. This phenomenon has been well documented elsewhere,[1] but it is important to note here the training implications that accompany such worker dislocation.

The service sector is composed of jobs at the two extremes—the low-skill jobs such as pumping gas or working in a fast-food restaurant, and the high-skill jobs like computer programmer, accountant, lawyer, or stockbroker. The low-skill jobs pay only a fraction of what a unionized auto or steel worker earned, and the skills of an unemployed auto worker are usually not transferable to the high-skill jobs. Thus, the legacy of deindustrialization for training is to build "transferable skills" for displaced workers and to prevent displacement by equipping employees with other skills so that they might be able to stay with the same company or industry even if there is a retrenchment. This concern has been the impetus behind the Economic Dislocation and Worker Assistance Act, the Worker Adjustment and Retraining Notification Act, and other federal requirements of plant closing notifications which oblige the states to take action. Similarly, this concern for the displaced industrial worker also spawned the development of many joint labor-management training programs. Thus, the human tragedy that followed deindustrialization has led to a set of training needs and responses.

9. *Skill Inflation for Entry-Level Positions.* By skill inflation, we are referring to the escalation in the entry-level skills required for many jobs over the past ten to twenty years. Whereas in the 1950s

---

[1] See, for example, Bluestone and Harrison, 1986; Fedrau, 1984; Flaim and Sehgal, 1985; Hansen, 1984 and 1986; Kulik and Bloom, 1986; and Root, 1984.

and 1960s neither a high school diploma nor a baccalaureate degree were necessary for clerking, light accounting or business positions, now the entry-level degree is at least a baccalaureate and perhaps a master's. Similarly, firms are increasingly employing extensive screening of the skills of entry-level manufacturing employees—all of which point to training issues for new workforce entrants.

10. *Public Realization of the Connections Among Training, Economic Development, and Competitiveness.* There has been some public acknowledgement that successful training may be linked to two other goals of importance to communities and nations: economic development and competition. The declining status of the U.S. in world competition has kept this debate in the forefront.

Emerging Themes in Worker Training

The broad mix of social, technical, economic, and organizational changes has dramatically expanded the scope and shifted the structure of training. As a result, a range of new themes are emerging, including (1) the expansion of training to cover active workers in ways that go far beyond on-the-job training; (2) attention to training as a component of career planning for individual workers; (3) the connection of training to economic development and competitiveness; (4) the emergence of a set of governance issues for labor and management as a result of the many stakeholders involved in training; (5) a related development—the increasing use of joint structures for unionized settings; (6) a second related development—the expansion of training providers to a new set of actors: educational institutions, social service agencies, independent vendors of educational services, equipment manufacturers, and funding agencies (federal, state, and local); (7) displaced worker training, with its multiple complexities; (8) wider acknowledgement of the need for basic skills training due to the literacy problem in the U.S.; (9) the extension to all workers of training modes traditionally reserved for professional, managerial, and technical employees (for example, the UAW-GM Paid Educational Leave Program and similar personal development programs); (10) the role of new technology as a determinant of training needs, especially regarding computer-related training; (11) recent attention to whether there should be a federal policy shift, from its historic orientation toward the disadvantaged and the difficult to employ, to displaced workers in Rustbelt regions of the country; and (12) new training initiatives at the state level. Each of these themes will be addressed briefly.

1. *Training of All Workers.* The group of employees who receive training was greatly expanded during the 1980s, the most notable and dramatic inclusion being blue-collar workers (Carnevale and Goldstein, 1990). Historically, the professional employee received the most before-hiring and upgrading training, followed closely by technicians and executive/administrative employees. Precision production and craft workers were less than half as likely to receive either type of training (Carnevale and Goldstein, 1990). The trend, however, is pointing toward blue-collar worker training, in technical skills and organizational development, becoming a core element of a business's overall program.

2. *Training as Essential for Individual Career Opportunities.* Workers, unions, and employers are increasingly giving attention to the way training contributes to planning for career job opportunities. In the past, the primary reason to train was an immediate change— either an impending promotion or layoff or transfer. These were largely reasons imposed by the employer. Now there is a notion of a career rather than just a job, which then involves life-long planning. The motivation is not so much the necessity of a change, but to achieve some greater degree of fulfillment and efficacy.

3. *Training as Integral to Economic Development and to a Better Competitive Status.* For years the question of who benefits from training centered on the interests of the employee or the firm. Now there is greater realization that if you train a worker so that he or she is able to retain a job, benefits accrue to the community, the state, and the country. Many state economic development programs are directly premised on this link—with training being one of the primary inducements associated with industrial attraction and retention (Gerhart, Morgan, and Schenkenberger, 1990; Cleveland, Murray, and Schippani, 1989; Hewitt, Wells, and Marx, 1990).

4. *A General Set of Governance Issues.* As the mix of parties involved in training becomes more varied and complex, the governance arrangements by which multiple interests come together around training issues take on a new significance. For example, as decisionmaking becomes less unilateral and increasingly either bilateral or multilateral, changes may be seen in the content of training, its location, the selection of trainers, the selection of trainees, and the evaluation of outcomes.

5. *The Specific Case of Union-Management Governance of Training.* Since the provision of training has historically been unilateral, with the exception of apprenticeship programs, a new set of challenges and opportunities arise when employers and unions establish joint programs. First, the training content becomes reflective of union as well as management priorities. Second, the service delivery involves more hourly workers as trainers. Third, training becomes embedded with the politics of the rest of the union-management relationship (Ferman and Hoyman, 1987; Savoie and Cutcher-Gershenfeld, 1991).

6. *Expanded Role for New Actors.* Educational institutions, social service agencies, equipment vendors, and private trainers have long had important roles in training, each in its own sphere. However, secondary schools and community colleges are now working more closely with employers in the development of customized training programs. Similarly, equipment vendors and private trainers are entering into long-term training arrangements. The result is both a more integrated service delivery system and a more complex process of administration and decisionmaking.

7. *Displaced Worker Training, with its Multiple Complexities.* Addressing the problems of the displaced is a core function of training. The problem, simply put, is to provide these workers with a set of transferable skills. However, there is often very little notice, considering the shock of a plant closing even with the federal plant-closing requirement, and almost no notice of large-scale layoffs, which can be just as disruptive. There is also a reluctance on the part of many workers to face up to these possibilities, even individuals who have access to joint training programs. In other words, even though they are informed of the general financial status of their industry, they cling to the hope that it "won't be my plant."

8. *Wider Acknowledgement of the Need to Upgrade Basic Skills.* There is a literacy problem in the United States. The implications for the firm is that private industry (sometimes jointly with unions) is taking a stronger role in improving public education—and in some cases direct training for basic skills. There is a particular need to encourage individuals to come forward for this training since they are often unwilling to admit that they have trouble with reading or basic math.

9. *Extension to All Workers of Modes of Training Traditionally Reserved for Professional, Managerial, and Technical Employees.* Innovative programs are now being established which transmit to blue-collar workers the same type of information given to white-collar, managerial, and executive employees. An example would be the UAW-GM Paid Educational Leave Programs, which include training in strategic planning, the state of the economy, and the state of the industry (Schurman, Hugentobler, and Stack, 1991). Indeed, in many cases workers and managers are being trained alongside one another. As well, programs for the disadvantaged are increasingly using state-of-the-art personnel practices in training individuals in job search and other skills.

10. *New Technology as a Determinant of Training.* Training for a broad array of skills needed society-wide is driven by computerization. Thus, entry-level clerical and secretarial jobs now require word-processing and computer skills. Auto workers now must have some knowledge about robotics and other aspects of programmable technology. Much training also takes advantage of the new technology. For instance, computer-learning modules are becoming popular service delivery systems, and both corporate training and labor education now include computer courses.

11. *Potential Shifts in Federal Policy, Historically Oriented Toward the Disadvantaged and Hard-to-Employ.* Now that some of the nation's cream-of-the-crop workers in Rustbelt regions face displacement, government faces challenges to come up with a coherent federal policy that balances these new training needs with traditional training concerns for the disadvantaged.

12. *New Training Initiatives at the State Level.* Inspired by the goals of economic development and/or full employment, a number of states have established economic development agencies. In their efforts to prevent companies from closing and to attract new companies to the area, they offer technical assistance in training.[2]

The Important Themes from Each Chapter

The themes outlined above cut across many chapters in this volume. In an effort to aid the reader, we will review the distinctive focus of each chapter.

---

[2] See Hewitt, Wells, and Marx, 1990; Gerhart, Morgan, and Schenkenberger, 1990; Baker, 1990; and Cutcher-Gershenfeld, forthcoming.

Chapter 2: Carnevale and Goldstein, "Schooling and Training for Work in America: An Overview"

This chapter presents an overview of both the current structure of training in America as well as the demographic makeup of those who are being trained. According to these authors, one of the main challenges to U.S. society is that not enough skilled workers will be available to meet future demand, a circumstance resulting from the transformation in markets and technology.

The authors give us a very vivid and complete picture of the amount of current training. Two out of three Americans have had some education/training for the jobs they hold. Employers pay for 41 percent of the education used for upgrading, as compared to 8 percent of that used to qualify for positions. They also have some figures on the distribution of training across occupational categories: 59 percent of professionals receive training; 45 percent of technicians receive training; 38 percent of executive, administrative, and managerial employees receive training; and 24 percent of precision production and craft workers receive training. These occupational groups that receive training to qualify are also the ones who get it to improve skills.

The role of schools is discussed fully in this chapter. Carnevale and Goldstein maintain that of the 55 percent of the workforce that is trained, 29 percent of the qualifying training is done in schools, as contrasted to 10 percent done by companies and 24 percent which is informal and on the job. They caution, however, that the role of schools may be understated by these statistics, since schools are as valuable for the transmission of values of citizenship and work habits as they are for specific technical training.

Current demographics of the people being trained are in line with previous profiles: fewer blacks, fewer women, and a concentration of middle-aged people. It would appear that a continuing problem in the training fields is that those who require training most (minority group members, younger and older workers) participate least in training efforts.

Chapter 3: Mangum, Mangum and Hansen, "Assessing the Returns to Training"

In Chapter 3, Mangum, Mangum, and Hansen examine the rates of return to investment for both government-provided and corporate-provided training programs. At the outset, the authors note that there has been a dearth of systematic research assessing training outcomes. Most evaluation research has been focused on the relatively minor amounts of taxpayer-supported vocational education and skill training targeted for the disadvantaged, even though it represents only a small part of the whole training and education picture. They also make the point—as does Fossum in Chapter 5—that this limited amount of evaluation has been restricted to the individual level of analysis.

Evaluation studies of cost effectiveness are reviewed in six categories of training programs: vocational education, post-school occupational training, military training, government employment and training programs for the disadvantaged, displaced worker training, and employer-sponsored training. Returns from investment varied both within and across these six categories:

Several key findings are highlighted: (1) Managerial training on the whole is effective. (2) Female students in commercial vocational education fare better than males in other vocational specialties. The results for males in all education programs are quite mixed. (3) In employer-sponsored training, there has been little attempt to measure increases in trainee income or employer profits from training expenditures. (4) Displaced workers after training experience a loss of earnings on post-training jobs compared to earnings on pre-displacement jobs, but such earnings exceed those of workers who did not participate in training.

The authors conclude that measuring the returns to training is difficult. Three sets of obstacles are apparent: (1) developing measurement specific to objectives that may vary from constituency to constituency, (2) overcoming interdisciplinary differences in perspectives and scope of evaluation, and (3) measurement obstacles, particularly in developing quasi-experimental designs when all variables cannot be controlled.

Chapter 4: Gray and Kornbluh, "New Directions in Labor Education"

Gray and Kornbluh present the results of a survey from dominant educators and institutions in the field of labor education. What are the significant trends in labor education that indicated a response to the developments in the 1980s? Four major changes are reported: (1) the rise of new constituencies (top union leaders, women, minorities, immigrants, workers' families, and secondary school teachers); (2) curriculum changes with the introduction of new subjects such as technological change, strategic planning, safety and health issues, special concerns of minority groups, and computer literacy; (3) new and sophisticated approaches to teaching and service delivery such as study circles and video feedback, college degree programs, teleconferencing and broadcasts; and (4) the emergence of new educational providers since 1968 such as the George Meany Center in Washington, the residential education centers of some international unions, and national and regional conferences cosponsored by the AFL-CIO Education Department and the University and College Labor Education Association (UCLEA). The authors also identify new sources of funding for labor education and a broader set of educational providers in addition to the industrial unions that have traditionally been the principal sponsors.

Certain conflicts have become inherent in the role of the labor educator. Should certain topics and courses be taught that challenge the dominant thinking of union leaders? To what extent should traditional topics such as collective bargaining and grievance handling be set aside in favor of new topics that may be controversial?

Since many of the changes in the 1980s were controversial, becoming the basis for internal fights within unions, it is not always easy to introduce information and programming on new developments without the provider becoming a lightning rod for controversy and causing the labor educator to lose his/her effectiveness.

Chapter 5: Fossum, "New Dimensions in the Design and Delivery of Corporate Training Programs"

The author presents an overview of innovations and changes in corporate training programs in the 1980s. He asserts that these changes have resulted from the changing demography of the workforce, the restructuring of organizations due to foreign competition, deregulation, and mergers and acquisitions, and modifications in the design and delivery of T&D activities. Training decisions have also been increasingly influenced by the characteristics of the labor supply (for example, the level of literacy) as well as by the introduction of quality circles, statistical process control, and *kanban* (just in time) in production processes.

Fossum calls for a broader look at the measurement of outcomes than has been customary in the past. He argues that such outcomes evaluations should move beyond the individual level and address results in the performance of work units or the firm. He also asserts that the method of training should be considered in any evaluation of training performance, and that there should be a long-run perspective on training (developmental) rather than a short-run perspective (problem-solving) where the emphasis is on immediate identifiable needs.

Several key points on corporate training are highlighted: (1) While new training techniques have developed rapidly during the 1980s, the prevalence of use has changed only slightly. (2) New technology (video presentations, for example) has come into vogue and has resulted in a decline in role-playing in training. (3) There has been little or no change in the structure or curriculum of supervisor training. (4) Vendor-based training programs have increased.

The author foresees that these trends in corporate training in the 1980s will become even more pronounced in the 1990s.

Chapter 6: Ferman, Hoyman, and Cutcher-Gershenfeld, "Joint Union-Management Training Programs: A Synthesis in the Evolution of Jointism and Training"

In this chapter the authors examine one of the innovations in training service delivery, joint union-management training programs. The basic features of such programs are: (1) Both displaced and active workers of a company are targeted. (2) Such training goes beyond enhancing technical skills and can include personal development skills. (3) These programs are underpinned by an ideology that stresses joint decisionmaking by union and management personnel as well as being participant-driven in choices. (4) Control of the program is typically at the grassroots level of the plant through a series of local joint committees made up of equal numbers of union and management personnel. (5) Use is made of a local community network of educational resources to deliver services.

The authors discuss the scope and extent of such programs, the peculiar structure of service delivery, and the special industrial relations efforts that have become institutionalized as a result of these programs. There is also some discussion of issues that unite the parties in the program and issues that divide.

The major theses in this chapter are: joint union-management training programs result in new institutional arrangements between the parties, such programs are a result of trends in both jointism and training, and specific adjustments in governance and service delivery are required to sustain such programs.

Chapter 7: Gueron and Long, "Welfare Employment Policy in the 1980s"

Chapter 7 gives the reader an overview of welfare employment training programs, including current and historic policy alternatives. The authors trace the evolution of welfare programs from WIN (Work Incentive Program) and its state equivalents of community work-experience programs, to "workfare" programs among the states—and the gradual decentralization of welfare policy. The dominant policy innovation of the 1980s, the addition of a workfare requirement for eligibility for welfare payments, did not fundamentally change the welfare system. Some innovative programs were developed in the 1980s: (1) the Employment and Training (ET) choices program in Massachusetts with a distinctive philosophy of client choice; (2) Greater Avenues for Independence (GAIN) in California that requires participation by AFDC recipients and places an emphasis on education; and (3) Realizing Economic Achievement (REACH) in New Jersey that requires participation by single parents with children aged 2 or above. The main focus of these programs is job-search assistance.

Gueron and Long maintain that one factor inhibiting greater emphasis on training and leading to a lack of innovation in welfare programs is resource constraints, but they expect that the Family Support Act will provide an adequate federal match to make training efforts more attractive. The authors also discuss issues of targeting and participation requirements, contending that the principal design issue is not whether programs are voluntary or mandatory, but the expectations of participants and the enforcement of requirements.

Chapter 8: Levitan and Gallo, "Uncle Sam's Helping Hand: Educating, Training, and Employing the Disadvantaged"

Levitan and Gallo give us an overview of federal employment and training programs aimed at the disadvantaged. They identify a number of cirumstances and training needs for this segment of the population: the increasing proportion who are unemployed or employed part-time, increasing numbers who earn at the minimum wage level, those who are single parents, and those who are displaced by plant shutdowns. The gap between the poor and the nonpoor is indeed substantial (for example, heads of poor families are from three to thirty times as likely as nonpoor family heads to face quantifiable obstacles to self-sufficiency). Characteristic problems with being poor are joblessness, disabilities, and a deficient education.

In this chapter the authors examine a variety of government programs designed to give educational access and training to the disadvantaged. These programs include: Headstart, guaranteed student loans, GI Bill for veterans, summer youth employment, and the Job Training Partnership Act (JTPA). Although there are many programs, their implementation suffers from inadequate funding, sharp swings in funding, a lack of coordination, and a question of "who is in charge." These authors provide rich detail on who are the disadvantaged and the programs designed to help them become economically viable.

Levitan and Gallo also discuss the tension that exists between assisting the most needy and the least needy job-seekers. Reviewing the current JTPA programs, the authors assert that in every case there was evidence of "creaming," which is the local practice of selecting the most employable individuals for training. They also are critical of OJT subsidies to employers who would have trained employees at their own expense.

The authors propose needed reforms in training programs for the poor; the main reforms center on an increase in funding and better coordination. Specific recommendations include: more and adequate support services, consolidation of employment programs into a comprehensive family investment initiative, more monitoring of service programs to upgrade quality, and the targeting of the most disadvantaged clientele for support and services.

Chapter 9: Osterman, "Elements of a National Training Policy"

In this chapter the author presents a critical appraisal of the U.S. training system and discusses what the function of training should be in our society. He contends that the resources for training are inadequate and that many of these components perform well below expectations—points also made by Levitan and Gallo in Chapter 8.

Osterman advances three major theses: (1) America undertrains its labor force compared to other nations, particularly those with whom we compete in the international economy. (2) Demographics are shifting in a direction which makes renewed investment in training more important. (3) The current system for serving the disadvantaged is outside the mainstream of the labor market and tends to stigmatize its clients.

The author suggests that, at the moment, the U.S. has no comprehensive national policy on training. With regard to the current delivery system and its deficiencies, he advises against a strategy of merely increasing resources and argues instead for a structural reform in the training system. He also compares U.S. training efforts, government and corporate, to those of Germany and Japan. His general conclusion is that qualitative differences in philosophy, design, and types of training in these countries contribute to their competitiveness and their relative economic position.

For U.S. training policy to be effective, according to Osterman, there should be a coordinated system of entry-level training and deepening skill training as the worker progresses on the job.

Three policy initiatives are set forth by the author: (1) For those who do not go on to college, there should be a post-high-school graduation year of vocational training and apprenticeship. (2) There should be a system to deepen training based in the internal labor market of the firm. (3) An agency should be created with sufficient resources to provide basic remedial training in the context of local job-creation and development efforts.

Chapter 10: Meltz, "The Evolution of Worker Training: The Canadian Experience"

Meltz presents an overview of the Canadian training experience over the past two decades. During those 20 years, a number of important changes in government funding occurred, culminating in the Canadian Jobs Strategy (a shift away from pure training to a combination of training and work experience). He highlights two issues on the Canadian training scene: (1) the role of training in the effort to achieve economic growth, equity, and stability, and (2) the relative merits of institutional versus industrial training.

Although running parallel to the U.S. economy, the strategies to handle instances of growth and recession differ in Canada. More emphasis is placed on recruiting foreign immigrants to fill skills needs in times of growth. There is also more emphasis on federal-provincial partnerships in developing training programs. More of a focus is placed in recessionary times on job-creation and work experience/training programs. Over time there has been a shift away from institutional training programs to industrial training programs. The federal government through legislation and funding plays the major role in training with the state of the economy being the major influencing factor.

Employer-sponsored training has a limited role in national training programs, being confined to short-term programs or their utility for operating businesses. Federal and provincial tensions seem to be endemic in negotiating partnerships (particularly in funding) for training.

The Canadian experience may have limited application to the U.S. economy because of: (1) the nature of federal-provincial relations in funding; (2) the focus on recruiting large numbers of immigrants to fill skilled and professional jobs; and (3) the shift from pure training to a focus on job creation and/or work experience/training to deal with unemployment and recessions. Furthermore, the economies of the two countries have exhibited different problems in recent years, with Canadian employment at a higher level and job growth declining.

Chapter 11: Marsden and Ryan, "Intermediate Level Vocational Training and the Structure of Labour Markets in Western Europe in the 1980s"

In the final chapter of our volume, Marsden and Ryan tackle two interrelated tasks: first, to provide the interested reader with an overview of the structure in Western Europe of what they term "intermediate level vocational training," and second, to organize that information around a core thesis, which is that the delivery of training interacts with the structure of labor markets.

The overview of practices in Western Europe is extremely important. It is too easy, in the United States, to be caught up in debates over details of training practices here and to lose sight of the many different models to be found elsewhere. Marsden and Ryan distinguish three broad categories of training which are used in varying degrees in different nations: (1) off-the-job training in specialized vocational schools (used extensively in France); (2) mixed on-the-job and off-the-job training in the form of apprenticeships (used extensively in Germany); and (3) simple on-the-job training (used extensively in Italy). While these three models can be found in the U.S., the scale on which the different forms of training operate in various nations is what stands in sharp contrast. For example, the vast majority of workers entering the labor force in Germany undergo a formal vocational apprenticeship for another two years after they complete their high school education.

The second aspect of the Marsden and Ryan chapter represents an important contribution to theory. They trace links between the structure of training practices in Western Europe in the 1980s and the changing structure of labor markets during that decade. Three types of labor markets are distinguished—occupational, internal, and unstructured—and each is vulnerable in different ways to issues of substitution and free-riders. With increased international competition and new technology, the mix of labor market structures is shifting in various Western European countries, and Marsden and Ryan trace the consequent implications for training. They conclude their chapter with a look at the training implications of the single market in 1992.

Implications for Training Practice, Research, and Policy

Underlying this volume has been the core thesis that events of the 1980s will serve as a legacy for training in the 1990s. In this concluding portion of the introduction, we will briefly trace what we see as the legacy for practice, research, and policy. In each case the legacy will be posed as a set of questions since the ultimate outcomes are still very much indeterminate.

Implications for Practice

The 1980s have brought expanded and increasingly overlapping roles for various actors in the design and delivery of training. With these new roles have come formal and informal governance arrangements through which decisionmaking can be channeled. One question posed by this experience concerns the extent to which the new union-management, public-private, or customer-supplier linkages will be institutionalized in the years to come.

During the past decade we have begun to see the workforce becoming increasingly diverse and increasingly concerned with protecting career job opportunities. These two developments on the labor supply side are behind a range of innovations in service delivery, including the use of peer trainers, workplace career counseling, and multimedia delivery vehicles. The diversity and the concerns over job security are only likely to increase, so the next question concerns the degree to which the training innovations in the 1980s are sufficient to meet the task in the years to come.

A final issue in the area of practice concerns the integration of training with other aspects of business operations. We have seen increased attention to such linkages in the 1980s, particularly with respect to strategic planning, but the mechanisms for the integration are still nascent. The question that remains, then, concerns the extent to which the potential for tighter linkages will indeed be realized.

Implications for Research

A baseline research challenge posed by the training developments of the 1980s is one of classification. We have seen the emergence of multiple models for service delivery, the targeting of new populations, the creation of alternative governance structures, and the intermingling of funds from a variety of sources. In this introductory chapter we have distinguished different spheres that were once separate, but that are now overlapping in various ways. This has been a useful organizational tool, but there is a need for a system of classification that is more explicitly rooted in theory around new developments in training.

Within such a framework, it would become clear that the focus of research to date has been disproportionately in certain cells. We know quite a bit, for example, about certain government-funded training programs for disadvantaged youths. Yet we know very little about employer-specific training designed by community colleges. Similarly, much of the research has been at the individual level of analysis, while important developments are occurring at organizational and macroeconomic levels of analysis.

A third issue for researchers concerns outcome measures. The new developments in training make clear that multiple outcomes are valued by different stakeholders. The challenge, then, is to conduct research on training effectiveness that is attentive to these many interests.

Finally, important theory issues are beginning to emerge about understanding training in context. That is, how does the structure of training interact with organizational structure, a firm's competitive strategies, internal union politics, the structure of the labor markets, or macroeconomic policy priorities? In each domain we have seen some work in the 1980s that has begun to expand theory, but much work remains to be done. Any one of these topics would require a long-term research commitment and would, therefore, be promising for a PhD dissertation, a book-length undertaking, or the creation of a multidisciplinary research team.

Implications for Policy

The roles of federal, state, and local government in training have expanded considerably during the 1980s, and the legacy of these new developments for the 1990s will likely be some form of taking stock of the many experiences and the codification of the most successful ones. Such a process raises many questions, however.

A core question for policymakers posed by the developments of the 1980s concerns the extent to which government support of private training initiatives serves as a substitute for or a complement to what would have happened in the absence of such funding. Such questions are never easy to answer, but policy formulation depends on some deeper understanding of this core question. Further, even if government funds do substitute for what the private sector would have done, are the alternative uses of private capital serving public goals?

A second training issue for policymakers involves attending to the mix of public-supported training that goes for firm-specific skills as compared to general skills. The former may more directly contribute to a firm's competitiveness, while the latter may increase the base-line skill level in society. Both are important, but there are policy issues around how this balance is struck.

A final issue facing policymakers concerns the extent to which training policy is driven by the logic of competitiveness rather than other criteria (such as smoothly functioning labor markets, quality of life, standard of living, etc.). During the 1980s competitiveness became a major factor and the question to ask now is what this means for society.

References

Ashenfelter, Orley, and David Card. "Using the Longitudinal Structure of Earnings to Estimate the Effect of Training Programs." *Review of Economics and Statistics* 67 (November 1985), pp. 648–60.

Bailey, Thomas. "Changes in the Nature and Structure of Work: Implications for Skill Demand." New York: Columbia University Center for the Conservation of Human Resources, November 1988. Mimeo.

Baker, Richard. "State Government Partnerships With Employers and Unions in the Training of Dislocated Workers." In *Joint Programs for the Training and Personal Development of Workers: New Initiatives in Union-Management Relations*, eds. Louis A. Ferman, Michele Hoyman, Joel Cutcher-Gershenfeld, and Ernest J. Savoie. Ithaca, NY: ILR Press, 1991.

Bluestone, Barry, and Bennett Harrison. *De-Industrialization of America: Plant Closings, Community Abandonment, and the Dismantling of Basic Industry.* New York: Basic Books, 1988.

Carnevale, Anthony P., and Harold Goldstein. "Schooling and Training for Work in America: An Overview." Chapter 2 in *New Developments in Worker Training: A Legacy for the 1990s*, eds. Louis A. Ferman, Michele Hoyman, Joel Cutcher-Gershenfeld, and Ernest J. Savoie. Madison, WI: Industrial Relations Research Association, 1990.

Cleveland, John, Mark Murray, and Michael Schippani. "Labor Market Strategies: Thoughts on the Michigan Experience." Paper presented at the 42nd Annual Meeting, Industrial Relations Research Association, Atlanta, 1989.

Cross, Patricia. *Adults as Learners.* San Francisco: Jossey-Bass, 1981.

Cutcher-Gershenfeld, Joel. "Constructing a New Social Contract: The Role of Community and State-Level Initiatives in the Transformation of U.S. Industrial Relations." In *New Trends in Industrial Relations in the USA and Italy.* Rome: ENI-ISVET, forthcoming.

————. "Tracing a Transformation in Industrial Relations." Washington: Bureau of Labor-Management Relations and Cooperative Programs, BLMR 123, 1988.

Cutcher-Gershenfeld, Joel, Robert McKersie, and Kirsten Weaver. "The Changing Role of Union Leaders." Washington: Bureau of Labor-Management Relations and Cooperative Programs, BLMR 127, 1988.

Fedrau, Ruth H. "Responses to Plant Closures and Major Reductions in Force: Private Sector and Community Based Models." *The Annals* of the American Academy of Political and Social Science 475 (September 1984), pp. 80–95.

Ferman, Louis, and Michele Hoyman. *The UAW-Ford Joint Labor-Management Training Report: A Report to the National Center.* Prepared for the National Center for Employee Development and Education, Dearborn, MI, Fall 1987.

Flaim, Paul O., and Ellen Sehgal. "Displaced Workers of 1979-1983: How Have They Fared?" *Monthly Labor Review* 108 (June 1985), pp. 3–16.

Gerhart, Paul F., William Morgan, and Miriam Schenkenberger. "Ohio Economic Development: The Effects of State Intervention to Improve the Labor-Management Climate." *Proceedings* of the 42nd Annual Meeting, Industrial Relations Research Association, Atlanta, 1989. Madison, WI: IRRA, 1990.

Hansen, Gary B. "Ford and the UAW Have a Better Idea: A Joint Labor-Management Approach to Plant Closings and Worker Retraining." *The Annals* of the American Academy of Political and Social Science 475 (September 1984), pp. 158–74.

————. *Two Years Later: A Followup Survey of Labor Market Status and Adjustment of Workers Displaced by the San Jose Assembly Plant Closure.* Logan: Business and Economic Development Services, Utah State University, 1986.

Hewitt, Arnold M., John Calhoun Wells, and Stacey S. Marx. "A National Overview of State Labor-Management Cooperation Programs." *Proceedings* of the 42nd Annual Meeting, Industrial Relations Research Association, Atlanta, 1989. Madison, WI: IRRA, 1990.

Hirschhorn, Larry. "The Post-Industrial Economy: Labor, Skills, and the New Mode of Production." *The Service Industries Journal* (Spring 1988), pp. 19–38.

Horvath, Francis W. "The Pulse of Economic Change: Dislocated Workers of 1981-1985." *Monthly Labor Review* 110 (June 1987), pp. 3-12.

Ichniowski, Casey, John Delaney, and David Lewin. "The New Human Resource Management in the U.S. Workplace: Is It Really New or Is It Nonunion?" *Relations Industrielles* 44, 1 (1989).

Katz, Harry, Thomas Kochan, and Jeffrey Keefe. "The Impact of Industrial Relations on Productivity: Evidence from the Automobile Industry." *Brookings Papers on Economic Activity*, 1988.

Katz, Harry C., Thomas A. Kochan, and Kenneth R. Gobrielle. "Industrial Relations Performance, Economic Performance and QWL Programs: An Interplant Analysis." *Industrial and Labor Relations Review* 37 (October 1983), pp. 3-17.

Kochan, Thomas A., Harry Katz, and Robert McKersie. *The Transformation of American Industrial Relations*. New York: Basic Books, 1987.

Kochan, Thomas, and Joel Cutcher-Gershenfeld. "Institutionalizing and Diffusing Innovations in Industrial Relations." Washington: Bureau of Labor-Management Relations and Cooperative Programs, BLMR 128, 1988.

Kochan, Thomas, Joel Cutcher-Gershenfeld, and John Paul MacDuffie. "Employee Participation, Work Re-Design, and New Technology: Implications for Public Policy in the 1990's." Prepared for U.S. Department of Labor Commission on Workforce Quality and Labor Market Efficiency, Washington, 1989.

Kulik, J., D. Smith, and Ernst Stromsdorfer. *The Downriver Community Conference Economic Adjustment Program: Final Evaluation Report*. Cambridge, MA: Abt Associates, September 30, 1984.

Kulik, J., and H. Bloom. *The Worker Adjustment Demonstration Evaluation: Preliminary Impact Report*. Cambridge, MA: Abt Associates, March 11, 1986.

Kulik, J., and Linda Sharpe. *The Worker Adjustment Demonstration Projects: A Comparative Evaluation Report*. Cambridge, MA: Abt Associates, 1985.

Levine, David, and George Strauss. "Employee Participation and Involvement." Report prepared for the U.S. Department of Labor, Washington, 1989.

Mangum, Stephen, Garth Mangum, and Gary Hansen. "Assessing the Returns to Training." Chapter 3 in *New Developments in Worker Training: A Legacy for the 1990s*, eds. Louis A. Ferman, Michele Hoyman, Joel Cutcher-Gershenfeld, and Ernest J. Savoie. Madison, WI: Industrial Relations Research Association, 1990.

Mincer, Jacob. "On-the-Job Training: Costs, Returns, and Some Implications." *Journal of Political Economy* 70 (Supp. October 1962), pp. 50-79.

New York Stock Exchange, Office of Economic Research. *People and Productivity: A Challenge to Corporate America*. New York: New York Stock Exchange, 1982.

Osterman, Paul. *Employment Futures: Reorganization, Dislocation, and Public Policy*. New York: Oxford University Press, 1988.

Piore, Michael J., and Charles F. Sabel. *The Second Industrial Divide*. New York: Basic Books, 1984.

Rogin, Larry, and Marjorie Rachlin. *Survey of Adult Education Opportunities for Labor: Labor Education in the United States*. Washington: National Institute of Labor Education, 1968.

Root, Kenneth. "The Human Response to Plant Closures." *The Annals* of the American Academy of Political and Social Science 475 (September 1984), pp. 52-65.

Savoie, Ernest J., and Joel Cutcher-Gershenfeld. "Reflections on the Government of Joint Training Initiatives." In *Joint Programs for Training and Personal Development of Workers: New Initiatives in Union-Management Relations*, eds. Louis A. Ferman, Michele Hoyman, Joel Cutcher-Gershenfeld, and Ernest J. Savoie. Ithaca, NY: ILR Press, 1991.

Schurman, Susan, Margrit Hugentobler, and Hal Stack. "Creating Educational Partnerships for a Changing Economy: Lessons from the UAW-GM Paid Educational Leave Program." In *Joint Programs for Training and Personal Development of Workers: New Initiatives in Union-Management Relations*, eds. Louis A. Ferman, Michele Hoyman, Joel Cutcher-Gershenfeld, and Ernest J. Savoie. Ithaca, NY: ILR Press, 1991.

Stalk, George. "Time—The Next Source of Competitive Advantage." *Harvard Business Review* (July-August 1988), pp. 44-55.
Sultan, Paul. "Literacy in the Workplace." Paper presented at the Industrial Relations Research Association Gateway (St. Louis) Chapter Spring Meeting, Southern Illinois University, Edwardsville, May 19, 1989.

CHAPTER 2

Schooling and Training for Work in America: An Overview

ANTHONY P. CARNEVALE
American Society for Training and Development

HAROLD GOLDSTEIN
Consultant

The American work training system has been shaped by a turbulent history. This century saw a transformation from a farm to a nonfarm economy, the rapid growth of service-providing industries, increasing use of technology in work, and the attainment of world preeminence by American industry followed by an increasingly successful challenge by other countries. Throughout, the United States absorbed floods of immigrants, a mid-century baby boom, migration of a disadvantaged black minority from rural to urban areas, and an unprecedented shift of women to the workplace—all of which intensified the needs for skill development.

These changes dramatically affected the ways in which people learned to work. On the farm they had learned from their parents. With the advance of industry, workers needed more formal preparation for the workplace. The shifting fortunes of industries and the constant development of new technologies also required people to change occupations frequently, to find ways of updating their technical knowledge, and to develop new work skills on the job.

All this had to be accomplished in an economy in which market forces are major engines of motivation. The returns to skill motivated workers to attain it, just as the returns to industry and society from having a skilled workforce motivated the building of educational and training institutions outside and inside the work-place.

As we approach the end of this stressful century, we face new challenges: The market for mass-produced goods and services is saturated in many industries. There are two major causes. First, low-cost products and many services are generally available as global production and increased productivity outstrip current demand. Second, rising incomes have shifted tastes away from mass-produced goods and services. The new competition has, in part, caused the utilization of more flexible technologies that allow for more variety and customization in products and services (Piore and Sabel, 1984, pp. 165–94; Office of Technology Assessment, 1988, pp. 61–89).

Changes in markets and technology have resulted in equally profound changes in competitive strategies. The basis for competition has shifted from an exclusive focus on cost—the characteristic signature of competition in mass production industry—to quality, variety, customization, service, and timeliness (Bailey, 1988; Hirschhorn, 1988; Stalk, 1988). The new strategies also put a premium on learning in the workplace. Major innovations have little value in and of themselves. The lion's share of competitive advantage lies in the ability to:

- get innovations off the drawing board and on the street quickly (Stalk, 1988; Vernon, 1987), and
- capture incremental cost efficiencies, quality improvements, and new applications in the process of making the product, delivering the service, or interacting with the customer (Ergas, 1987).

The new competition and the new technology that accompanies it have also in turn created new institutional formats that are both more decentralized and more integrated. In order to encourage faster turn-around, customization and customer service as well as incremental learning on the job in institutions have become more decentralized. In the interest of flexibility, the new institutional structures are driving resources and authority toward the point of production, service delivery, and sale. The new, more decentralized structures are also more tightly integrated internally and externally. Internal integration is fostered by flatter structures, more general and overlapping job design, and shared information. The new institutional format is also more integrated upstream with suppliers and downstream with customers in order to improve the competitiveness of the whole network that ultimately delivers the final product or service to the customer (Johnston and Laurence, 1988; Office of Technology Assessment, 1988).

The strategic shift from an exclusive reliance on cost-based competition to more complex competitive strategies ultimately changes institutional formats, job design, and skill requirements for employees. On balance, skill requirements both deepen and broaden. Employees need better grounding in the three Rs and whole new kinds of interpersonal, learning, and problem-solving skills to be successful in the new institutional and technical environment. In addition to more and better generic skills, employees require more and better job and institutionally specific knowledge of the diverse and fast-changing products, processes, and strategic goals (Adler, 1986; Bailey and Noyelle, 1988; Hirschhorn, 1988; Baran and Parsons, 1986; Blackburn, Coombs, and Green, 1985; Carnevale, Gainer, and Meltzer, 1988).

Skill requirements will be driven by more than the needs of employers. As employers organize to increase their own flexibility, they will demand a more flexible workforce. Most employers will minimize the numbers of workers with permanent job security by utilizing suppliers, temporary employees, and part-timers to the extent possible (Abraham, 1987). In general, the commitment between employers and employees will decline. Employees will have to be more loyal to their skills than to their employers if they hope to sustain their own employment security. Employees will need access to more training to maintain and upgrade their skills in order to sustain and improve employment and earnings prospects (Bailey, 1988; Bailey and Noyelle, 1988). They will also need other tools, such as portable pensions, health care, parental leave, and day care, if they are to become truly flexible workers in a change-oriented economy.

Demographic trends will make it more difficult to find the skilled workers we need. As we approach the end of this century, it becomes ever more apparent that the demand for more skilled workers is on a collision course with the quantity and quality of the labor supply. Our current workforce is not suited to the new work requirements. As a nation, we have done well in the education and training of our white-collar and technical elites. Yet, the other half of our high school graduating classes—the noncollege youth—and our nonsupervisory workers are poorly educated and badly trained. Moreover, a dwindling supply of new workers is made worse by the fact that more and more of the new job-seekers come from populations in which our previous human capital investments have been woefully inadequate (Kutscher, 1987; Johnston, 1988).

As a result, the nation's job-training system will be increasingly critical to the employers' ability to deliver efficiencies and quality in products and services and the ability of the nation to provide economic independence and opportunity for the citizenry. Our job-training structure will be critical to our ability to match new skill requirements on the job and the available labor supply. If we are to improve the performance of the nation's job-training institutions, we will need a careful map of the labyrinth of trainers and trainees to tell us where to intervene and to guide our progress.

In the following paragraphs, we will attempt to map the nation's job-related learning structure. We will first discuss the effects of job-related learning on competitiveness and opportunity. We will then examine the three major modes of delivery for job-related learning: schooling, formal on-the-job training, and informal on-the-job training. We will follow with a description of who gets and who pays for job-related learning. The next section of the chapter is a discussion of the roles of the major institutional providers of job-related learning, with an emphasis on the role of employers—large and small. The chapter concludes with recommendations for the improvements in the quantity and quality of job-related learning as well as in the linkages between external providers of job-related learning and the workplace.

What Are the Effects of Job-Related Learning?

Job-related learning has two important economic uses: it leverages individual choices and earnings, and it improves institutional performance. The effect of job-related learning on opportunity, individual earnings, and choice is powerful. On average, about half of one's lifetime earnings are driven by learning in school and on the job. The other half is affected by career and locational choices and by dumb luck. A person with skill can trade earnings for a preferred occupation or employer. People with low skills have less to bargain with; thus their choices are limited and their earnings are low (Lillard and Tan, 1986).

Education has an important effect on opportunity. Returns to investments in education appeared to be falling in the 1970s, probably because of the large number of baby-boomers entering the workforce. The returns to education have increased in the 1980s, however, as the baby-boomers were finally absorbed into the workplace and educational requirements for work shifted upward. In 1979, for instance, a college graduate earned 24 percent more than a high school graduate, but in 1985 college graduates were earning 38 percent more than high school graduates (U.S. Department of Education, 1988, Table 2:3).

Most studies show that, among Americans, 10 percent of the differences in earnings over a lifetime can be attributed to preemployment learning in school (Lillard and Tan, 1986). But that small figure masks big differences in the importance of education in determining earning potential. For instance, education is more important in determining earnings in high-tech industries than elsewhere. In high-tech industries, education is a particularly good investment because it prepares employees for the highly skilled jobs those industries generate, and because it produces adaptable employees who can cope with rapid technical change. The earnings of a high school graduate in high-tech industries are twice those of a dropout; the earnings of a college graduate are twice those of a high school graduate; and earnings of someone with a postgraduate education are 30 percent higher than those of a college graduate (Lillard and Tan, 1986).

Education also improves earnings because it leverages further learning on the job. Skills learned in school and skills learned on the job are complementary. For instance, compared with persons who have only high school diplomas, those with two years of formal education beyond high school have a 20 percent greater chance of getting training on the job. College graduates have a 50 percent greater chance of getting training on the job than do high school graduates. And in most American industries, workers with education beyond four years of college have a 30 percent greater chance than college graduates of getting training on the job. In high-tech industries, postgraduate education increases the probability of receiving training on the job by almost twice as much as does a college degree (Lillard and Tan, 1986).

Although educational attainment certainly influences earnings, learning on the job has the most powerful and substantial effect on earnings. Studies by Lillard and Tan (1986), Bishop and Stephenson (1983), and others consistently show that people who receive formal training on the job enjoy an earnings advantage of 25 percent or more over those who do not receive formal training in the workplace.

Training in the workplace has effects on productivity and earnings beyond the current job. Most people, after all, use what they learn on their current jobs to get new and better jobs. Employees who have had some formal training at a prior job earn 18 percent more in their current jobs than those who have not. Those who have had informal training at a prior job earn 20 percent more than those who have not (Lillard and Tan, 1986; Bishop and Stephenson, 1983).

Available data also suggest that the best way to leverage learning on the job is to stay with a single employer. In a study based on the Panel Study of Income Dynamics, Jacob Mincer (1988) concludes that job mobility accounts for only 15 percent of improvements in lifetime earnings, while duration on the job with individual employers accounts for 55 percent of earnings over a lifetime.

Workplace training also seems to have a more durable influence on earnings than does education or training from other sources. The positive effect of workplace learning on earnings lasts 13 years, compared with eight years in the case of learning in schools (Lillard and Tan, 1986).

How training affects earnings depends on the subject matter as well as the provider. Management training and professional and technical training increase earnings more than do other kinds of training (16 and 14 percent more, respectively) (Lillard and Tan, 1986).

Skills and Competitiveness

Education and training are critical not only to individual opportunity, but to the productivity and competitive advantage of employers and the whole nation. Learning in school and learning on the job are by far the most important factors behind American economic growth and productivity in this century and will determine the nation's economic prospects in the next.

In fact, both formal education and learning on the job have been consistently more important than machine capital in expanding the nation's productive capacity throughout this century. Between 1929 and 1982, education prior to work was responsible for 26 percent of the expansion in the nation's productive capacity. Over the same period, learning on the job, including both training and process improvements, contributed to 55 percent of all the positive improvements in the nation's productive capacity (Denison, 1984). Recent work by Mincer (1988) shows that the productivity returns to training are roughly twice wage increases that result from a better trained workforce.

How Much Training Is Done?

Two out of three American workers have had some education or training for the jobs they hold (Table 1). Looking in another way at

TABLE 1

Training Reported by Workers, by Occupation

Occupation	Percent of All Employed 1983	Percent of All Employed Reporting Training			
		Total	Training to Qualify for Job	Training to Improve Skills	Both (included in previous 2 columns)
All workers	100.0	65	55	35	25
Professional specialty	12.7	95	93	61	59
Technicians and related support	3.0	92	85	52	45
Executive, administrative, and managerial	10.7	80	71	47	38
Precision production, craft, and repair	12.2	76	65	35	24
Clerical and administrative support	16.3	69	57	32	20
Sales workers	11.7	55	43	32	20
Service workers (excluding household)	12.8	47	36	25	14
Machine operators, assemblers, and inspectors	7.7	50	37	22	9
Transportation and materials moving	4.2	45	36	18	9
Farming, forestry, and fishing	3.7	35	28	16	9
Handlers, equip. cleaners, helpers, and laborers	4.1	26	16	14	4
Private household workers	1.0	10	8	3	1

Source: Carey (1985). The second and last columns are based on a special tabulation provided by the Bureau of Labor Statistics.

the question of how much training is done, we can estimate that in a single year at least one adult worker in eight takes formal work-related training.[1]

How Do We Provide Job-Related Learning?

The workplace and the schools, in that order, are the principal providers of job-related learning. Of the 55 percent of American workers who had some training to qualify for their jobs, 29 percent said they had received some or all of their qualifying training from schools, while 10 and 28 percent, respectively, said they had received some or all of their qualifying training from formal or informal employer-provided programs (Table 2).[2]

In the same survey, 35 percent of American workers said they had received some training to improve skills while they were on the job. Twelve percent said they got this training in schools, while 11 and 14 percent, respectively, said they were upgraded through employer-provided formal or informal training.

It is likely that the contribution of informal learning on the job is even greater than these workers reported. All workers, even those with advanced professional education, learn while working—from the instructions of supervisors, by watching fellow workers, and by experience in doing the work. Such informal learning is a major factor in skill improvement, but it is not always identified as "training" by workers reporting to surveys.

Further enhancing the relative contribution of the workplace is

---

[1] U.S. Department of Education, *Trends in Adult Education, 1969–1984*. In a series of surveys conducted every three years from 1969 to 1984, special questions on participation in adult education in the previous 12 months were asked in the national sample of 58,000 households used for the Current Population Survey. By asking about courses and other training activities taken, the survey got information on the more formal, identifiable courses rather than informal learning. The May 1984 survey estimates that 23 million adults took 41 million courses, of which 26 million were work-related (i.e., to improve job skills or train for a new job); 25 million of the work-related courses were taken by persons in the labor force. Allowing for the average of 1.75 courses taken per participant in the age range of 25–54, when most work-related courses are taken, we can estimate that the 25 million courses were taken by about 14.2 million persons—12.5 percent of the 113.5 million in the labor force. There is some evidence of underreporting in this survey, based on comparing survey data with enrollment data for some institutions published by the Center for Education Statistics. Some of the tables we will use were based on unpublished tabulations.

[2] Carey, 1985. Information was obtained by adding questions to the Current Population Survey national sample of 60,000 households in January 1983. Some of the data cited in this chapter are from unpublished tabulations provided by the Bureau of Labor Statistics.

TABLE 2
Sources of Qualifying and Upgrading Training: All Employees (%)

Occupational Group	Percentage of Employees With Qualifying Training				Percentage of Employees With Upgrading Training			
	Total	From School	Employer-Based Formal	Employer-Based Informal	Total	From School	Employer-Based Formal	Employer-Based Informal
All employees	55	29	10	28	35	12	11	14
Professional specialty	93	82	9	22	61	34	15	14
Executive, admin., managerial	71	43	12	39	47	18	17	16
Technicians and related	85	58	14	32	52	20	18	19
Clerical	57	33	7	31	32	10	10	15
Sales	43	15	12	28	32	7	13	15
Service, excluding private household	36	13	9	18	25	7	8	12
Transportation and materials moving	36	2	8	26	18	2	6	9
Machine operators	37	6	6	26	22	3	4	16
Handlers, equip. cleaners, helpers, laborers	16	2	2	13	14	2	2	10
Farming, forestry, and fishing	28	8	1	16	16	5	2	7
Precision products, craft and repair	65	16	17	40	35	7	14	16
Private household workers	8	2	1	4	3	1	1	1

Source: Max L. Carey, "How Workers Get Their Training," BLS Bull. No. 2226 (Washington: U.S. Government Printing Office, 1985).

Note: Individual percentages can add up to more than the totals because some employees received training from more than one source.

the fact that employers pay for a substantial share of the upgrading training that is given in the schools. The same survey shows that employers paid for 41 percent of the education courses used for upgrading and 8 percent of those used to qualify for jobs.

The three modes of job-related learning interact in a dynamic whereby incremental changes in skill requirements accumulate, first requiring informal on-the-job training, then formal on-the-job training, then schooling. Skills are constantly broadening from the specific to the general and shifting in provision from employers to the schools (Carnevale and Gainer, 1989). Employers shift from informal to more formal on-the-job training in order to assure quality and consistency in learning as well as to import new skills unknown to current workers.

Ultimately, skill changes accumulate until they change occupational skill requirements and even basic educational requirements, at which point the provision of skills can be offloaded into the schools. As a result of this dynamic, the dominant trend in work training in the United States over the past century has been the extension of formal education to the population. This is dramatically shown by changes in the schooling attained by people aged 25 to 29, when nearly all have finished school and entered the workforce. Before World War II, less than two-fifths of new workers had a high school education and only a small elite, about 6 percent, had finished college, while now more than 80 percent of Americans build their work skills on a foundation of 12 years or more of schooling and one out of four completes college or graduate education (U.S. Department of Education, 1987).

Who Gets Job-Related Learning?

The fact that only two workers in three had some education or training for the jobs they hold reflects the wide disparity in skill requirements among occupations. As Table 1 shows, more than three-quarters of professional, managerial, technical, and precision production workers—groups representing almost 40 percent of all workers—get some kind of schooling or training. More than two-thirds of clerical and other administrative-support workers get training; these employees represent about 16 percent of American workers. Roughly half of all sales, service, machine operating, and transportation workers get training; these groups comprise more than one-third of the workforce.

At the far end of the job-related learning queue, receiving the least preparation or upgrading for their work, we find workers in the classifications of handlers, cleaners, and laborers, farming, forestry, and fishing, and private household. These groups comprise less than 10 percent of the workforce.

From the last column of Table 1, it is apparent that workers in the occupations receiving the most training are also those most likely to be double-dippers in the training pot—getting both qualifying training and skill-improvement training.

As the reader can see from Table 2, there are also distinctive differences among occupations in the sources of training, depending partly on whether the learning is used to qualify for a job or for upgrading skills once on the job.

- Every occupational grouping received more job-related learning to qualify for their jobs than for upgrading once they are on those jobs.

- Schooling and informal learning on the job drop off dramatically after people qualify for their jobs, while formal employer programs tend to hold steady or increase in importance.

- In general, white-collar and technical employees tend to rely more on schooling and formal employer programs, while blue-collar and service workers rely more on informal on-the-job training.

Who Pays for Job-Related Learning for Adult Americans?

Table 3 shows how participants in adult education reported the sources of funding for the 26 million work-related courses they took in the 12 months preceding May 1984. The participant's employer (including business firms and government agencies) paid all or part of the cost for 14.8 million courses—more than half the total. The participant or his/her family paid for more than one-third of the courses, business and industry paid the cost of nearly two-fifths, and one out of six courses were paid for entirely by public sources. Other sources, including private organizations, paid for 6 percent, and for another 5 percent the funding was shared between the participant and another funding source.

The Training Establishment

Training is provided by a great variety of institutions, using

TABLE 3

Work-Related Courses by Source of Funding

Source of Funding	Percent of Total
Total number (000)	26,159
Percent	100.0
Self or family only	35.0
Public funding only	16.7
Business or industry only	37.0
Private organization only	3.5
Other sources	2.5
More than one source:	
Self or family and other	(4.5)
Public and other	(1.8)
Business or industry and other	(2.6)
Private organization and other	(0.5)
Other source and a source specified above	(0.3)
Total (more than one source)	(9.7)
Omitting duplication (total divided by 2)	(4.9)
Did not know and not available	0.4
Employer was source of funding[a]	56.6

Source: U.S. Bureau of the Census, *Survey of Participation in Adult Education* (Washington: U.S. Government Printing Office, 1984). Special tabulations provided by the National Center for Education Statistics to the American Society for Training and Development.

[a] Information provided in response to a separate question.

different methods, serving different constituencies, sometimes complementing each other, frequently competing with each other—an establishment that has many of the characteristics of a free market. We will first discuss schools, then nonschool training institutions.

Schools

The *elementary and secondary schools* have important roles in addition to direct development of work skills: passing on the culture and values of society, developing citizenship and life skills, and teaching the tools by which people learn, including language, mathematics, and science. Secondary schools have traditionally prepared four out of ten students who are on the academic track to go on to college and have been groping for ways to serve the others. About one in five students enrolls in vocational education courses; 5 percent of American workers qualified for their jobs by skills learned in high school vocational education programs, according to the Bureau of Labor Statistics (BLS) survey referred to earlier. The most notable success of vocational education is in training for office occupations; they trained more than one-third of the secretaries and typists and many others in clerical jobs, as well as one-quarter of those in drafting and between one-tenth and one-sixth of tool and die makers, machinists, automobile mechanics, and printers.

The two out of five high school students who are not bound for college or who cannot compete on the academic track and who are not attracted to the vocational courses fall between stools into the "general" track, which provides over 60 percent of the dropouts. Meeting the work training needs of these students is a major gap in the system (Carnevale and Gainer, 1989).

Noncollegiate post-secondary vocational schools serve high school graduates who are not bound for college, but go directly into full- or part-time study to get a vocational credential, such as a certificate or occupational license. They also serve adults who return to school part time for skill improvement or to develop new job skills. About 7600 such schools were listed by the Department of Education in 1982, 78 percent of which were private proprietary schools and the remainder equally divided between public and nonprofit institutions. They enrolled 1.7 million students in 1980-81. Most schools specialized in a single subject (U.S. Department of Education, 1987, p. 253).

These schools provided training that enabled 4 percent of American workers to qualify for their jobs; they had trained about half of the cosmetologists and barbers, two-fifths of the practical nurses, one-fifth of the personnel clerks and radiology technicians, one-sixth of the registered nurses and real estate salespersons, and one-seventh of the stenographers reporting to the BLS survey. They have flexibility to respond to community needs, maintain close contact with employers, and can use teachers with practical experience even though without academic credentials.

Two-year community colleges and technical institutes are the rapidly proliferating descendants of the junior colleges of the early 20th century. In the past two decades they have expanded more than twice as fast as the four-year colleges, aggressively seeking to serve new needs in their communities. They perform multiple roles, providing the first two years of college for students who then go on to four-year schools, terminal liberal education for some who do not go on, vocational preparation for a variety of occupations, and avocational courses for adults. Sometimes the multiple roles make the schools ambivalent in focusing their curricula and standards. Average age of the student body is 29, reflecting the attraction of these schools to adults as a result of low tuition, liberal admissions policies, accessibility, a wide range of course offerings, and flexible class scheduling. The 1300 institutions enrolled 4.5 million students, mostly part-time, in 1985, 94 percent of them in publicly supported schools. They enrolled about as many freshmen in programs creditable towards a bachelor's degree as did the four-year colleges (U.S. Department of Education, 1987, pp. 122, 126, 130, 167, 216).

They also enable 5 percent of American workers to qualify for their jobs, according to the BLS training survey, including one-quarter of the health-treating occupations, notably registered nurses and health technicians; one-fifth of the engineering technicians, computer programmers, graphic artists, real estate salespersons, sales engineers, computer and office-machine repairers, and barbers; and one out of six secretaries, stenographers, computer operators, and aircraft engine mechanics.

The 2000 *four-year colleges and universities* provide liberal education as well as the professional, managerial, and technical skills that give dynamic leadership to society and the economy. Historically, they antedated high school vocational education, post-secondary vocational schools, and community colleges. They enrolled nearly 8 million students in 1985, of which one-third were in private institutions—a larger proportion than in the two-year schools. Despite their traditionalism, they have been responsive to the training needs of adult workers, organizing ad hoc and off-campus courses. They are increasing their services to adults as the "college-age" population declines (U.S. Department of Education, 1987, pp. 122, 167). They provided the qualifying training for 17 percent of all workers—70 percent of professional specialty workers, 34 percent of managerial workers, 24 percent of technicians, and about one-fourth of all securities salespersons and sales engineers.

In summary, schools provided the training used by 29 percent of American workers to qualify for their jobs. In the American school system, occupational preparation for youth going to college has been the oldest and best established mode of training. As increasing proportions of youths completed high school without planning to go to college, a variety of institutions developed—vocational education in the high schools, post-secondary vocational schools, community colleges, and technical institutes—each seeking to stake out a role and develop curricula in a group of occupations. They do not meet all the needs, and nonschool providers of training try to fill the gaps.

Nonschool Training Institutions

A major role of the *Armed Forces* in peacetime is as training institutions, moving a substantial proportion of the youth population through programs preparing them for military tasks. Some of the skills they impart have civilian applications. Two percent of American workers qualified for their jobs with the help of this training, including nearly half of civilian aircraft mechanics, one-fifth of electrical and electronic technicians, and significant numbers of airplane pilots, electrical and electronics repairers, motor vehicle repairers, and workers in health occupations.

Apprenticeship could be included in this section under either schools, unions, or employers since all these participate. Programs meeting standards laid down by State Apprenticeship Councils or the Board of Apprenticeship and Training, U.S. Department of Labor, are registered; there are, in addition, many unregistered programs run mostly by employers alone. Training is most commonly three to four years, including a minimum of 2000 hours of on-the-job experience phased through all aspects of the craft and at least 144 hours a year of related technical instruction given in vocational schools or community colleges.

Apprenticeship has met only part of the training needs for craft workers; annual completions averaged only 0.4 percent of the number employed in craft occupations in the 1970s. This flow of trainees was supplemented by dropouts, trainees in unregistered programs, and workers who picked up the skills informally or with vocational school training.

Data from the Bureau of Apprenticeship and Training in the U.S. Department of Labor indicate that there were 243,000 registered apprentices receiving training in 1987, 19,000 more than in the previous year, but 77,000 less than in 1980. In 1987, more than 38,000 apprentices completed required training, while 100,400 were newly indentured (i.e., formally accepted as apprentices). The building trades have been the largest users of apprenticeship, mainly in the unionized sector. Programs in three construction areas—carpentry, electrical work, and the pipe trades—enrolled almost 40 percent of all registered apprentices.

Vendors, business firms that provide training to employees of other companies, include both firms that are solely in the business of selling training, and firms that are primarily in the business of selling equipment, but provide training to employees of their customers. The former design training programs for companies or sell them generic programs; they run training programs attended by employees of many companies; and they sell training equipment, materials, and manuals.

Professional associations serve their members by professional meetings and journals as well as by running courses and training programs in their fields. Societies in professions in which continuing education is required for maintaining licenses are particularly active. Prominent in training activity are medical, scientific, engineering, financial, management, and real estate associations. They provided 8 percent of all work-related courses taken by adults.

Unions, through their educational departments and such institutions as the George Meany Center for Labor Studies, provide training in the history and philosophy of unions and in the work of unions—for example, shop-steward training—but also in the substance of their trades, such as courses in electronics for electricians. The union involvement in apprenticeship training sometimes includes running training programs.

Unions have also begun to participate in training through joint training agreements with management. The Mine Workers, Communications Workers, and Auto Workers, among others, have set up new institutions that provide training for dislocated workers and for the general development of workers as well as job-specific training. During 1989 their joint training programs accounted for more than $300 million in spending and benefited over 700,000 workers.

A wide variety of *community organizations*, such as Ys, religious, social and service organizations, fraternal and ethnic organizations, and neighborhood associations provide training, mostly nonvocational, but sometimes vocationally oriented, including preparing people for paid work in the organizations. They provided 3 percent of all work-related courses taken by adults.

Tutors and private instructors provided 2 percent of work-related courses taken by adults and contributed significantly to the teaching of such work skills as music, arts, sports, and languages.

Correspondence schools developed when a large proportion of the population lived in rural areas and towns too small to have vocational schools, and they still teach widely dispersed occupations as well as meeting the needs of home-bound persons, military personnel, prisoners, and those who prefer to work at their own pace. The correspondence method is also used by other providers of training, including colleges, professional societies, and postsecondary vocational schools. Some, as in programs training truck drivers, supplement the mails with brief periods of residential instruction. About 1 percent of workers credit correspondence courses for the training that qualified them for their jobs.

Informal nonwork-related learning includes learning at home or on the farm and from hobbies. It accounts for the training needed to qualify for work by 3 percent of workers, including significant proportions of musicians, photographers, athletes, farmers, auto and other mechanics, construction craftsmen, dressmakers, fishers, hunters, and trappers.

Employers play the major role in developing the skills of the adult workforce—those whose regular schooling has ended. They are credited with providing formal training or informal learning opportunities by 38 of the 55 percent of workers who needed training to qualify for their jobs, and by 25 of the 35 percent of workers who received training to improve their skills. Because of its importance, the employers' role in training is discussed more fully below.

Summary Map of the Training Establishment

An overview of how the task of training was divided among the different institutions is presented in Table 4, which looks separately at two aspects of training—that designed to qualify workers for their jobs and that designed to upgrade their skills on the jobs.

Among the 55 percent of workers who needed qualifying training, two sources of training were the most frequently mentioned—schools and informal on-the-job training or experience in earlier jobs. Since the latter is likely to have been underreported, it was probably the major source of skill acquisition. Among schools, the colleges were the largest providers. Formal company-based training (which includes apprenticeship) was listed by 10 percent, and other providers—the Armed Forces, correspondence

TABLE 4

Sources of Training Reported by Workers

Source of Training	Employed Workers Who Received:	
	Training to Qualify for Present Job	Training to Improve Skills on the Job
Total	55	35
Schools, total	29	12
High school vocational courses	5	c
Post-secondary vocational school		
Private	2	1
Public	2	1
Community college, technical institute	5	3
Four-year college or university	17	6
Formal company training[a]	10	11
Informal on-the-job training[b]	28	14
Training in Armed Forces	2	—
Other		
Correspondence courses	1 ⎫	
	⎬	4
Training by friend or relative or other nonwork experience	3 ⎭	

Source: Bureau of Labor Statistics training survey, 1983.

[a] Includes apprenticeship or other types of training with an instructor and a planned program.

[b] In case of training needed to qualify for present job, includes experience in previously held jobs.

[c] Less than 0.5 percent.

courses, and other sources such as learning from friends, relatives, and other experiences not related to work—were reported by no more than 3 percent each. (Since a worker could report more than one source of training, the components add to more than the sum of those who reported any training.)

Sources of training differed widely among occupations. Schools were listed by 82 percent of professional specialty workers, 58 percent of technicians, 43 percent of managerial workers, and one-third of administrative-support workers (mainly clerical), but only 16 percent of craft workers and smaller proportions in the other occupations. Among types of schools, four-year colleges and universities were the major training ground for professional specialty, managerial, and technical workers (with two-year colleges and technical institutes also important for technicians). High school vocational education was the major training source for office workers and the same, plus two-year colleges, were important for precision metal workers.

Training designed to upgrade skills on the job, reported by 35 percent of all workers, was acquired mostly by informal methods (reported by 14 percent of workers but, as noted earlier, probably received by many more who did not report this experience as "training"). Among formal training modes of skill improvement, schools were listed as the major provider by 12 percent, followed closely by formal company training programs (11 percent). Again, there were differences among occupations following the same patterns as were found in training to qualify for jobs.

Formal Training by Employers

Employers are strongly motivated to increase productivity, reduce labor costs, introduce new technologies quickly, cut down waste, and innovate in a competitive market. When expensive new equipment is introduced, employers have special reasons to train their workers to use it with maximum efficiency and avoid costly accidents. They are in the best position to know what each worker needs to learn, what new technology is being introduced, what the lines of promotion are in the firm, and what prospective expansions or changes in business practices have to be staffed. While most skill acquisition on the job is through informal learning, employers can identify needs for formal programs and either provide them (sometimes with their own training staff, sometimes by contracting with a vendor) or send the employees outside to schools, professional societies, or other providers in the community.

General vs. Job-Specific Training

Employers always face the possibility that the workers they have trained may quit and go to other firms, including competitors. Human capital theory argues that employers should freely give "job-specific" training that applies solely to work in their companies, but should give "general" training that may be used in other firms only if the worker pays for such training through wage rates that are below their productivity (Becker, 1963, Ch. 2). The distinction between "job-specific" and "general" training in this sense is often difficult to make, however, and when firms pay tuition for workers in colleges and other training institutions, it is not clear that they adjust their pay when the content of the training is general.

Indeed, the distinction between general and job-specific training is often quite blurred. Schools and other institutions outside the workplace do supply training that tends to be more general in the three Rs and academic subject matters that are only tangentially useful on the job. Moreover, the central tendency over time is for new skills created in the workplace to be offloaded into the schools as they become more generic. At the same time, however, there are a variety of reasons why employers do provide general training:

- Wages are driven by a variety of forces other than training. As a result, contrary to human capital theory, there is very little direct relationship between the employer's decision to train and the wages of the trainee (Baran and Parsons, 1986).

- There is always a hiatus between the time the skills are required on the job and the time when the schools are ready to include the skills in occupational or general curricula. Historically, this has been particularly true for technical subject matters (Lillard and Tan, 1986). The recent history of manufacturing engineering is a case in point. Manufacturing engineering was an occupational discipline with a full-blown curriculum in industry long before it was accepted by academics as a legitimate engineering field. Much the same is now true with a whole new set of skills associated with flexible, team-based work organization and new information-based technologies. These new skills, including interpersonal skills, problem-solving skills, and others, are not yet generally taught outside the workplace.

- Schooling is often inefficient in its curriculum development and delivery. Schooling is usually provided in abstract formats when it is generally recognized that more applied formats are more efficient and more effective for teaching most skills. The state of the art in workplace learning is generally more advanced than curriculum design and delivery in schools (Carnevale and Johnston, 1989).

Available data tend to confirm the view that the traditional distinction between general and job-specific learning is simplistic. Recent advances in learning theory tend to assert that specific applications are at least as effective as more abstract formats in teaching general principles (Carnevale and Johnston, 1989). This probably explains the powerful impacts of learning on the job on long-term productivity and the career earnings of individuals cited above.

Common sense provides some help on this question. Learning on the job is nothing new. Most people learn their jobs on the job. Most get ahead by leveraging what they learn in the current job into a new and better job. Moreover, for many people, a job is the best teacher. Relatively few people excel in academic settings, but almost everyone is able to learn on the job, either by doing the job, by being coached by peers or bosses, or by attending formal courses provided by the employer. Applied learning, done in the context of a task, has inherent advantages as a pedagogy for both employers and employees. Applied learning is, by nature, more flexible than the academic format. Individuals can learn at their own paces on the job. Applied learning encourages the learner to use, rather than lose, new knowledge. Finally, individuals are motivated to learn on the job because increased proficiency brings immediate rewards in terms of achievement, status, and earnings.

Organization and Delivery

Workplace training is organized into three major domains: (1) management—including executive and management development as well as supervisory training; (2) technical—including the training of scientists, engineers, technologists, technicians, and skilled workers as well as safety and other regulatory training; and (3) sales and marketing training.

The current organization and delivery of learning in the workplace reflects its roots at the worksite. Most learning on the job is still located as closely as possible to the job itself. Even in large organizations, centralized training departments supply less than half of the formal training and development the employees receive. There are exceptions to this rule, however. Training intended to provide skills beyond those required by the current job is often centralized at corporate or divisional levels, as are developmental programs for scientists, engineers, and executives. Training required by strategic changes and major innovations in technology also tend to be centralized until the new knowledge is embedded in institutional cultures and workforces. Once innovations are installed, incremental changes tend to be learned in a more decentralized fashion. The recent shift to quality is an example of a strategic change that has gone through the cycle from central to decentralized training. The introduction of flexible manufacturing is an example of a technical change and team-based production is an example of an organizational change that has followed a similar pattern.

Training and Development

As a rule, supervisory training and technical training for technicians, technologists, and craft and skilled workers have been less developmental, more job-specific, and more decentralized. However, as discussed above, flexible, team-based production, new information-based technologies, and flatter institutional structures are driving new skill requirements, greater autonomy, and responsibility down the line towards the point of production and the point of sale. The resultant more general and abstract skill requirements for nonsupervisory workers are adding a developmental aspect to training requirements and could result in greater centralization of training functions in these occupational areas.

Formal Employer Training by Industry

The extent of training activity varies greatly among industries, since each faces a unique technology and competitive situation. We can get a picture of this from Table 5. This table shows the industries which provided the 14.8 million courses delivered or paid for, in whole or in part, by the participant's employer. Employers include not only business firms, but also government agencies, schools, and nonprofit organizations. Sectors that did much more than their proportionate share of training include health, educational, and other professional services, utilities, communications, and such high-tech manufacturing industries as machinery, electrical equipment, aircraft, automobiles, chemicals, and petroleum products. The table also shows that employers did 69 percent of the formal training they paid for inside the establishments and sent the workers outside for the remainder. Most industries did between 60 and 80 percent inside.

Training Suppliers

Employers buy 31 percent of their formal training courses from outside suppliers (Carnevale and Gainer, 1989). The institutions to

TABLE 5

Employer-Paid Training Courses, by Industry, 1984

Industry	Percent of Total Courses	Training Intensity Index[a]	Percent of Training Done Inside
Total number of courses (000)	14,800	—	—
Total percent	100.0	—	69
Agriculture	.7	.2	62
Mining	1.6	1.8	77
Construction	2.2	.4	59
Manufacturing	18.5	.9	66
Lumber, furniture, stone, clay, glass	.8	.4	56
Primary metals, fabricated metal products	1.4	.7	68
Machinery, except electrical	4.2	1.7	70
Electrical machinery	3.2	1.5	65
Motor vehicles	1.4	1.3	71
Aircraft	.8	1.4	78
Other transportation equip. instruments, toys	1.9	1.1	62
Food, tobacco	1.0	.6	82
Textiles, apparel, paper, printing, rubber, plastics, leather	1.9	.4	55
Chemicals, petroleum products	2.0	1.5	61
Transportation, communications, utilities	7.9	1.1	75
Transportation	2.4	.7	74
Communications	2.6	1.8	79
Utilities	2.8	2.0	74
Trade	8.6	.4	74
Wholesale	2.9	.7	74
Retail	5.6	.3	73
Finance, insurance, real estate	9.4	1.5	63
Banking, finance	5.2	1.8	59
Insurance, real estate	4.2	1.2	68
Services	41.4	1.3	69
Business	2.7	.7	60
Repair, personal, private household, entertainment, recreational	2.3	.4	74
Medical, except hospitals	5.7	1.6	67
Hospitals	10.9	2.7	76
Welfare, religious	2.8	1.3	67
Educational	10.8	1.4	71
Other professional	6.0	2.1	54
Forestry, fisheries	.2	1.5	95
Public administration	9.7	2.1	78

Source: U.S. Bureau of the Census, *Survey of Participation in Adult Education* (Washington: U.S. Government Printing Office, 1984). In combining industries with large relative sampling errors, only those with similar training intensity indexes were combined.

[a] Training intensity index is computed by dividing the percent of total courses taken by employees in each industry (first column) by the industry's percent of total employment, as reported by the Bureau of Labor Statistics.

TABLE 6

Courses Bought by Employers, by Provider

Provider	Percent of Courses Bought by Employers
Total number of courses (000)	4,436
Percent of total	100.0
Schools, total	56.4
Elementary and secondary schools	1.5
Community colleges and technical institutes	15.5
Colleges and universities	31.2
Post-secondary vocational schools	7.0
Other schools	1.2
Professional, trade, and labor organizations	14.2
Business firms[a]	15.7
Community organizations	3.0
Government	5.6
Tutors and private instructors	1.2
Other, or no information on provider	3.8

Source: U.S. Bureau of the Census, Survey of Participation in Adult Education (Washington: U.S. Government Printing Office, 1984).

[a] In the case of courses bought by employers, these firms are vendors.

which the employees went for this outside training are shown in Table 6. Schools got more than half the trainees; most went to four-year colleges and universities. One-sixth went to vendors. The other major supplier of training programs was professional associations. (Unions, tabulated with professional associations, provided a relatively small part of the total in this category.)

Large firms do proportionately more training than small ones; the latter are more likely to try to hire trained workers or send their employees outside for training. A survey of company training in 1974-75 found that 96 percent of firms with 10,000 or more employees gave courses during work hours, with the percentage decreasing in each successively smaller size class to only 55 percent among firms with 500 to 999 employees (Lusterman, 1977).

Formal Employer Training by Recipient Sex, Race, and Age

Who gets training paid for by employers? Women workers received slightly more than their proportionate share of the training, reflecting the massive flow of women into the workforce in recent years and their greater need for training (Table 7). White workers received a more than proportionate share, despite the widespread concern about the inadequate work skills of minorities. As would be

TABLE 7

Employer-Paid Training Courses,
By Characteristics of Participants

Characteristic	Share of Training (%)	Share of Employment (%)
Sex		
Male	53.3	56.3
Female	46.7	43.7
Race		
White	92.2	87.7
Black	5.8	9.6
Other (Asian, Native American, Pacific Islanders, etc.)	1.9	2.6
Ethnicity		
Hispanics	2.7	5.4
Age		
16–17	0.2	2.3
18–19	0.5	3.8
20–24	8.8	13.5
25–34	38.8	28.9
35–44	28.8	22.5
45–54	14.8	15.4
55–59	4.5	6.6
60–64	2.6	4.3
65 and over	1.0	2.7
Occupation		
Executive, managerial	22.0	11.0
Professional specialty	29.8	12.7
Technical and related support	6.4	3.0
Sales	7.3	12.0
Clerical and other administrative support	14.1	15.9
Private household service	0.1	0.9
Protective service	2.9	1.6
Other service	5.1	10.9
Farming, forestry, fishing	0.8	3.4
Precision products, craft, repair	7.6	12.4
Machine operators, assemblers, etc.	2.0	7.6
Transportation, materials moving	1.1	4.3
Handlers, helpers, laborers, etc.	0.8	4.2

Source: Training data from U.S. Bureau of the Census, *Survey of Participation in Adult Education* (Washington: U.S. Government Printing Office, 1984). Employment data from Bureau of Labor Statistics.

expected, the greatest emphasis was put on training young workers and those in the prime skill development years (ages 25–44). Finally, the most skilled and educated workers, those in professional specialty, managerial, and technical occupations, received more than their proportionate share of training.

Small Employers

Small employers (less than 500 employees) account for roughly half of all jobs in the American economy and almost 40 percent of new jobs. While most new jobs and a growing share of the output of products and services are coming from large employers or establishments owned by larger enterprises, small employers are important trainers in the American economy (Office of Technology Assessment, 1988, pp. 177–90). Small employers tend to provide formative work experience. Employees in small businesses tend to be younger and less well educated, and they include more Hispanics, although fewer blacks.

Small employers operate in relatively small markets and, therefore, have jobs characterized by broad assignments of responsibilities. Technologies also are less specialized than in larger businesses. The lack of specialization makes both the employees and the employers flexible and provides a generalized learning experience that aids in career transitions. At the same time, small employers do not have enough employees to afford the time away from work that is required for training during working hours. As a result, employees in small businesses get less training than employees in larger businesses, and the training they receive is more concentrated in informal categories.

According to a survey by the U.S. Small Business Administration (SBA), almost half of the employees in companies with 500 or more employees received some kind of training from their current or former employers. By comparison, only 27 percent of employees in companies with fewer than 25 employees received any kind of training from current or former employers (Carnevale and Gainer, 1989). A study by John Bishop showed that employers with more than 500 employees provided almost three times as much formal training in the first three months of employment as firms with fewer than 500 employees (Carnevale and Gainer, 1989). People who work for small employers get their training off the job. Data from the SBA show that in firms with fewer than 100 employees, 75 percent of employees who receive training are trained off the job, compared to 58 percent of employees in larger firms (Carnevale and Gainer, 1989).

Large employers also tend to pay for more of the employee training done outside the workplace. Data indicate that employers with fewer than 100 workers pay for 23 percent of training done outside the workplace, while employers with more than 100 workers pay for 32 percent of that training (Carnevale and Gainer, 1989).

Conclusions

With two out of three workers getting some training for their jobs, and one out of eight adults receiving formal work-related training each year, the question arises whether the training establishment is doing as much as is needed. In a market-driven economy, it is plausible that workers will take advantage of training opportunities and employers will provide the investment in terms of increased income or productivity. However, disadvantaged and unemployed workers have little access to training opportunities without the intervention of public funding. Moreover, when many corporate managers emphasize current profitability at the expense of long-run investment or when companies are bought and sold, assembled, or dismantled for short-run financial considerations by fast operators without abiding interest in an industry, investment in human—as well as inanimate—capital is likely to be skimped. Finally, perceptions of skill requirements may be subject to cultural lag at a time when rapid changes are taking place in the way work is done. The recent slowdown in productivity growth in the United States may reflect these factors. For all these reasons, we think the training being given is lacking in quantity and quality.

Where should we add quantity? Probably in the institutions that provide job-related learning after high school. We are already graduating upwards of 85 percent of our young people from high school. The two-year and four-year colleges, the military, and especially the workplace are where most work-related learning occurs and where there is most room for increasing overall quantities of training.

We could increase employer commitments to make or buy training through investment incentives. This demand-side strategy has the virtues of market-driven forces that come from putting money in the hands of the customer. A cheaper strategy would be research and development (R&D) to reduce development costs and improve quality, making training a more attractive and certain investment for employers of all sizes (Carnevale and Johnston, 1989). As an alternative or complement to an employer-based strategy, we could provide funding and R&D for training suppliers outside the workplace.

The second conclusion that comes to mind is that the overall quality of the job-related learning system is not up to snuff either. As high school graduation approaches 90 percent, we are not going to get much more quantity improvements from elementary and secondary education. If elementary and secondary education is to continue to make an economic contribution, it will have to be through the quality of its offerings which has been seriously questioned in recent years. The post-secondary education system also needs to improve its flexibility and quality. Post-secondary learning needs to be more flexible if it is to be used by Americans with job and family responsibilities. In addition, post-secondary schooling needs to develop more applied curricula because learning in functional contexts is more efficient and more useful for people with specific career goals in mind.

The most radical challenges for quality improvements fall to American employers. Learning has insufficient standing in the American workplace. Selection, appraisal, and reward systems need to encourage learning of two kinds: skill aquisition and institutional learning that results in new efficiencies, quality improvements, and new applications.

The third conclusion evident in the statistical map above is that job-related learning is maldistributed. In an era when skill requirements of jobs are changing rapidly and when higher skill requirements are being driven down the line toward the point of production, service delivery, and customer contact, our elitest learning system is inappropriate. We need to provide more job-related learning experiences in school and on the job for the other half of the high school graduating class that does not go on to college and for nonsupervisory workers on the job. As a nation, we are pretty good at preparing white-collar and technical elites, but not nearly as good at preparing our nonsupervisory workforce. The need to provide more job-related learning for the other half of our workforce is especially relevant at a time when increasing skill requirements are on a collision course with an entry-level workforce that is declining in size and increasingly drawn from populations in whom our prior human capital investments are insufficient.

A fourth conclusion is that we need to improve the overall performance of the nation's job-related learning network. As skills become more generic, employers need to offload training to external suppliers more quickly. Correspondingly, suppliers need to be more responsive to employers' training needs. Similarly, there needs to be a greater exchange of applied learning derived from incremental innovations in the workplace and basic research in external R&D institutions.

References

Abraham, Katharine G. "Restructuring the Employment Relationship: The Growth of Market-Mediated Work Arrangements." Washington: Brookings Institution, 1987. Mimeo.

Adler, Paul. "New Technologies, New Skills." *California Management Review* 29, 1 (Fall 1986), pp. 9–28.

Bailey, Thomas. "Changes in the Nature and Structure of Work: Implications for Skill Demand." New York: Columbia University Center for the Conservation of Human Resources, November 1988. Mimeo.

Bailey, Thomas, and Thierry Noyelle. "New Technology and Skill Formation: Issues and Hypotheses." Technical Paper No. 1. New York: National Center on Education and Employment, Teachers College, Columbia University, 1988.

Baran, Barbara, and Carol Parsons. "Technology and Skill: A Literature Review." Prepared for the Carnegie Forum on Education and the Economy, January 1986.

Becker, Gary S. *Human Capital.* New York: Columbia University Press, 1963.

Bishop, John, and S. Stephenson. "Productivity Growth and Tenure: A Test of OJT Theories of Wage and Productivity Growth." Columbus: National Center for Research in Vocational Education, Ohio State University, 1983.

Blackburn, Phil, Rod Combs, and Kenneth Green. *Technology, Economic Growth, and the Labor Process.* New York: St. Martin's Press, 1985.

Carey, Max L. *How Workers Get Their Training.* U.S. Bureau of Labor Statistics Bull. No. 2226. Washington: U.S. Government Printing Office, 1985.

Carnevale, Anthony P., and Leila J. Gainer. *The Learning Enterprise.* Washington: U.S. Government Printing Office, 1989.

Carnevale, Anthony P., Leila J. Gainer, and Ann S. Meltzer. *Workplace Basics: The Skills Employers Want.* Washington: U.S. Government Printing Office, 1988.

Carnevale, Anthony P., and Janet Johnston. *Job-Related Learning: Private Strategies and Public Policies.* Washington: U.S. Government Printing Office, 1989.

Denison, Edward. *Trends in American Economic Growth, 1929–1982.* Washington: Brookings Institution, 1984.

Ergas, Henry. "Does Technology Matter?" In *Technology and Global Industry: Companies and Nations in the World Economy,* eds. Bruce R. Guile and Harvey Brooks. Washington: National Academy of Engineering Press, 1987. Pp. 191–246.

Hirschhorn, Larry. "The Post-Industrial Economy: Labor, Skills, and the New Mode of Production." *The Service Industries Journal* (Spring 1988), pp. 19–38.

Johnston, Bill. *Workforce 2000.* Washington: U.S. Government Printing Office. 1988.

Johnston, Russell, and Paul R. Laurence. "Beyond Vertical Integration—The Rise of the Value Added Partnership." *Harvard Business Review* (July-August 1988), pp. 94–101.

Kutscher, Ronald E. "Projections 2000—Overview and Implications of Projections to 2000." *Monthly Labor Review* 110 (September 1987), pp. 3–9.

Lillard, Lee A., and Hong W. Tan. "Private Sector Training: Who Gets It and What Are Its Effects?" R-3331-DOL-RC. Santa Monica, CA: Rand Corporation, March 1986.

Lusterman, Seymour. *Education in Industry.* New York: The Conference Board, 1977.

Mincer, Jacob. "Labor Market Effects of Human Capital and of Its Adjustment to Technological Change." Economics Department, Columbia University, 1988. Preliminary draft of paper for presentation at a Conference on Employer-Provided Training, Washington, sponsored by the Institute on Education and the Economy, Teachers College, Columbia University, and the National Assessment of Vocational Education.

Office of Technology Assessment. *Technology and the American Economic Transition: Choices for the Future.* Washington: U.S. Government Printing Office, 1988.

Piore, Michael J., and Charles F. Sabel. *The Second Industrial Divide.* New York: Basic Books, 1984.

Stalk, George. "Time—The Next Source of Competitive Advantage." *Harvard Business Review* (July-August 1988), pp. 44-55.

U.S. Department of Education, Center for Education Statistics. *The Condition of Education.* Washington: U.S. Government Printing Office, 1988.

_____. *Digest of Education Statistics.* Washington: U.S. Government Printing Office, 1987.

_____. *Trends in Adult Education, 1969-1984.* Washington: The Department, 1987.

Vernon, Raymond. "Coping With Technological Change: U.S. Problems and Prospects." In *Technology and Global Industry: Companies and Nations in the World Economy,* eds. Bruce R. Guile and Harvey Brooks. Washington: National Academy of Engineering Press, 1987. Pp. 119-60.

Chapter 3

Assessing the Returns to Training

Stephen Mangum
Ohio State University

Garth Mangum
University of Utah

Gary Hansen
Utah State University

Considering the massive volume of training ongoing in the U.S. economy and the constant advocacy for more, it may be surprising how little is actually known about the results. This is not true of the relatively minor amounts of taxpayer-supported vocational education and skill training on behalf of those from low-income and minority backgrounds. Perhaps the fact that they are not perceived as contributing to the costs of their own occupational preparation accounts for the repeated demands for evaluation of the results. Substantial effort has been directed to such evaluation over the years, even though the results remain almost as controversial as the justification for the training.

For general and academic education, even that which is directly occupational in its purpose, the evaluative output has been restricted to the return to the individual, not to the society paying most of the bills. Training and development experts in private industry are only beginning to discuss the efficacy and the methodology for outcome evaluations to determine the rate of that return. Those within public-sector employment, including the military, seem even less likely to raise the issue. Perhaps the fact that training exists and persists should be taken as prima facie evidence that, at least in the minds of those who make the training decisions, the benefits exceed the costs. But perhaps, if the oft-expressed opinion that America underinvests in its human resources is true, more concrete evidence of positive returns might enhance the willingness to invest. On the other hand, the limitations for determination of rates of return may have more practical origins. The objectives of training proposals are often unduly murky and the rate of return cannot be measured if the meaning of "return" cannot be defined in quantifiable terms. Psychologists and economists have both claimed the evaluation turf and their conceptions of desired outcome and their consequent measurement tools are so conflicting as to confuse the customer—the training decisionmaker. Technical debates over such important but esoteric issues as selectivity bias also cast doubts on the reliability of the results and therefore discourage further investments in evaluation.

This chapter is a review of the literature on the rates of return to in-school and post-school occupational training, military training, publicly sponsored training for the economically disadvantaged and displaced, and employer-sponsored training. It explores methodological obstacles, including clarification of objectives, interdisciplinary conflicts, and measurement obstacles including selectivity bias. We then attempt to draw some useful conclusions including the researchers' usual recommendations for further research.

Reviewing the Literature

The roster of training of interest to the members of the Industrial Relations Research Association would include such subjects as supervisory and safety training as well as exotic topics such as stress management and self-awareness. It could also include all aspects of education which ultimately contribute to the ability to function in the workplace. However, for purposes of this review, we restrict ourselves to the provision of job skills, though at managerial as well as maintenance and production levels. Such training might be divided between that supported at public expense and that provided by employers. The public programs reviewed here involve the provision of vocational and technical education to the general public, training within the military, and the training programs provided to improve the lot of the economically disadvantaged and those displaced by economic forces beyond their control. Studies of those programs constitute the bulk of the available literature on the return to training, perhaps because they are supported by the public purse and must be defended to the taxpayers. Employers actually provide most of the training, but, being privately supported as well as privately decided, it has made limited contributions to the evaluation literature.

Vocational Education

A strong inverse correlation appears to exist between the extent to which an educational program enrolls the children of opinion-makers and the intensity of demand for its evaluation. There was no demand for evaluation of vocational education until the advent of federally sponsored training for the economically disadvantaged, most of which occurs in vocational education institutions. However, the initiation of such programs, starting with the Manpower Development and Training Act of 1962, was coincident with the passage of the Vocational Education Act of 1963 which multiplied federal vocational education expenditures. It is not clear whether the socioeconomic status of the enrollees, the expansion of expenditures, or the fact that it costs more per capita to teach students to handle tools and operate machines than it does to seat them at desks was the primary impetus for demands to evaluate. At any rate, there was a rapid acceleration of evaluations of vocational education beginning in the 1960s. We restrict ourselves here primarily to evaluations of the past 10 years, the findings of which do not differ appreciably from those of earlier studies.

Evaluations of occupational training received in high school have typically found that commercial training has had significant positive earnings effects for females (in the 16 to 17 percent range), while technical or home economics programs have recorded zero or negative effects (Grasso and Shea, 1979; Meyer, 1982; Gustman and Steinmeier, 1982). Results have been more mixed for males. The evidence is inconclusive as to whether male vocational education high school graduates earn more than similar nonvocationally trained graduates (Campbell et al., 1986; Kang and Bishop, 1986; Meyer, 1982). The literature implies that this ambivalence may result from failure to distinguish whether or not the vocational training is used on the job. Estimates of the extent of training-related placement range from 25 to 45 percent, depending upon occupation (Campbell et al., 1987; Daymont and Rumsberger, 1982; Feltschausen, 1973; Conroy and Diamond, 1976). That ambivalence disappears when the comparison is limited to those with training-related placements. Campbell et al. (1986) found that, when employment matched the training received, high school vocational graduates had significantly higher labor force participation rates, three percentage points lower unemployment rates, and 7 to 8 percent higher median earnings than the nonvocationally trained comparison group. No economic benefits accrued if a training-related job was not obtained. Bishop's work (1982) supports these findings. He uses data, collected from multiple employers, pairing recently hired workers in identical jobs, one worker having vocational education training relevant to the job and the other without vocational training. Bishop documents 7.3 percent lower on-the-job training time, 8.6 percent greater productivity in the first two weeks of employment, and 6.6 percent more productivity after one year of employment for the employee with vocationally relevant high school training.

Research effort has been expended exploring the usefulness of vocational education in serving minority youth. The evidence suggests Hispanics receive higher benefits from vocational programs than do non-Hispanics and that results for blacks are comparable to those for whites (Meyer, 1982; Daymont and Rumsberger, 1982; Campbell et al., 1986). Studies by Mertens, Seitz, and Cox (1982) suggest that participation in vocational education is associated with lower high school dropout rates among dropout-prone youth. They find that completion of one vocational course per year during the ninth to eleventh grades is associated with a six percentage point lower dropout rate for such individuals.

Post-School Occupational Training

No one seems to have done an evaluation of the returns of post-secondary vocational education in recent years. Of course, three-quarters of vocational enrollments occur at the high school level. But, as already demonstrated, few high school students have yet decided on their life's work. Most do not end up in the occupations for which they took training. Vocational education in high school usually involves only two or three hours per day in a six- or seven-course curriculum. The opportunity cost of vocational education at that level is equivalent to the same amount of time in the academic classroom. In contrast, those engaged in post-secondary occupational training typically have made an occupational choice, are forgoing employment and earnings, and are generally devoting most of their in-class hours to their occupational training or to related instruction.

Even though no recent evaluation of the returns to post-secondary vocational education seems to have been undertaken, there are data concerning the returns to post-school occupational training more broadly defined. Data from the Survey of Participation in Adult Education suggest extensive investment in post-school occupational training to the tune of 40 to 45 million participants annually at total estimated annual expenditures of $30 to $50 million (Fraser, 1980; Cross, 1981). The institutions providing such training are diverse and include proprietary business and technical schools, correspondence schools, area vocational schools, company-provided training, apprenticeships, night schools, community agencies, the military, and so forth. The occupations in which training can be received are equally diverse, including professional, technical, managerial, clerical, and skilled manual training. Our knowledge of the returns to post-school occupational training is more extensive in the case of some institutional providers of training than others. The sections that follow present more detailed information where it is available, while this section summarizes our knowledge more generally.

There is basic agreement among studies investigating the returns to post-school occupational training in general. These studies have used data from data bases such as the Current Population Survey, the Panel Study of Income Dynamics, the Employment Opportunities Pilot Projects Survey, and different cohorts of the National Longitudinal Studies of Labor Market Experience.

The literature suggests earnings impacts in the 14 to 20 percent range for participants in professional, technical, or managerial training in comparison to similar individuals not participating in training (Lillard and Tan, 1986; Rumsberger, 1984; Mangum and Adams, 1987). Skilled manual training carries a 5 to 9 percent rate of return (Lillard and Tan, 1986), while the returns to clerical training have often appeared as a lower probability of experiencing unemployment and a higher level of occupational prestige rather than significantly higher wage rates (Mangum and Adams, 1987), in comparison to nonparticipants in post-school training. Participation in professional, technical, and managerial training has been associated with higher occupational prestige and lower incidences and durations of unemployment in many of these studies. In contrast, participants in skilled manual training have often been found to have higher probabilities of experiencing unemployment than individuals receiving no formal training beyond mandatory education (Mangum and Adams, 1987). This may reflect seasonality or the recent displacement sensitivity of many such jobs. Conversely, studies that have sought to look at the duration of the earnings impacts associated with participation in post-school occupational training suggest impacts lasting 11 to 12 years for professional, technical, and managerial training, 15 years for skilled manual training, and about seven years for clerical and other training (Lillard and Tan, 1986).

When the providers of such training are considered, company-based training is uniformly identified as having the greatest effect in terms of increased earnings relative to nonparticipants in training. These earnings impacts have been documented to be in the range of 10 to 30 percent and to persist over about 13 to 14 years, depending on the data base employed, the controls used, and the dependent variable analyzed (Bishop, 1982; Bishop et al., 1985; Lillard and Tan, 1986; Mangum and Adams, 1987; Rumsberger, 1984). Barron, Black, and Loewenstein (1989) are able to analyze company training in several forms (formal on-the-job training, informal OJT with supervisors, informal OJT with coworkers, learning by watching, etc.). On average, their findings suggest a 1.5 percent wage growth impact related to a 10 percent increase in OJT. Lillard and Tan (1986) associate informal on-the-job training with wage effects of 0 to 5 percent. Completion of company-provided training has been associated, in many of these studies, with enhanced occupational prestige and lower probabilities of unemployment than experienced by the comparison group. Given that employers are unlikely to invest in their workers unless they have specific plans to recoup their investment over time, the existence of sizeable earnings effects of such training is hardly surprising.

Results have been mixed concerning other training providers. Findings on nondegree training from academic institutions have shown earnings effects of 0 to 8 percent with a duration of positive earnings effects of about eight years (Lillard and Tan, 1986). Results concerning participation in correspondence schools have been equally mixed, with returns more frequently recorded when hourly wage rather than annual earnings is used as a dependent variable (Mangum and Adams, 1987). Participation in training provided by business and technical institutes resulted in earnings effects in the 8 to 12 percent range, with impacts continuing over approximately a nine- to ten-year horizon (Lillard and Tan, 1986; Freeman, 1974; Mangum and Adams, 1987). There tends to be less variability in all of these findings when investigation focuses on training's impact on increasing occupational prestige or decreasing the probability of unemployment.

Earnings effects associated with participation in training vary markedly by race. Similarly, rates of participation in training across alternative providers vary significantly by race and sex. Adams, Mangum, and Wirtz (1987) find black males to be significantly less likely than white males to participate in training. Lynch (1988) finds women and nonwhites to have significantly lower probabilities of receiving on-the-job training than white males. These results are generally supported elsewhere for nonwhites, but are occasionally questioned for women (Lillard and Tan, 1986; Rumsberger, 1984; Flanagan, 1974). In addition, racial differences in training participation appear by occupational area and by institutional provider of training. For example, nonwhite males have been found to have a lower probability of participation in managerial or professional training and in company-provided training than their white counterparts, controlling for other factors (Lillard and Tan, 1986; Adams, Mangum, and Wirtz, 1987). These differences have held up even when fairly sophisticated controls for selection bias have been used and consequently raise complex but important issues about differential access to post-school occupational training (Adams, Mangum and Wirtz, 1987; Lillard and Tan, 1986; Rumsberger, 1983).

Military Training

The military is both the nation's single largest employer and largest single provider of vocational training. The military offers more than 600 different skill-training courses in subjects ranging from baking to nuclear propulsion, from public speaking to data processing. In addition, the military is heavily committed to professional and managerial training and development. The price tag of this training effort is in the billions of dollars annually (U.S. Department of Defense, 1989).

Like other employers, the military makes up its own mind about whether training is worthwhile for its own internal purposes. Outside evaluators have been more interested in assessing the impact of military training on the external economy and workforce.

A number of studies have examined the impact of military training on post-service labor market outcomes. A first group of studies focused on the labor market experience of military retirees (20-year veterans) in comparison to noncareer veterans (Danzon, 1980; Cooper, 1981; Borjas and Welch, 1984). The findings of Borjas and Welch are representative of these studies. They document 22 percent lower earnings among military retirees than noncareer veterans at the entry of the former into civilian employment and a convergence of earnings profiles at about age 65, with military retirees earning 14 to 25 percent less in total earnings than noncareer veterans over the post-service period.

A second group of studies focused on military nonretirees, but examined the post-service experience of only those who served in the military (Weinstein et al., 1969; Kassing, 1970; Hanushek, 1972; Mason, 1970; McCall and Wallace, 1967; Norrblum, 1976; O'Neill, Ross, and Warner, 1976; Massell and Nelson, 1974). These have been consistent in stressing the importance of training transferability. Norrblum found that an additional year of military service contributed 11.8 percent to post-service wages when the individual found civilian employment in an occupation similar to that held in the military. O'Neill et al. found a similar premium to a military/civilian occupational match and concluded that "the value of alternative types of military occupational training depends primarily upon whether the training is used in the civilian sector" (p. 359).

A third group of studies compared the post-service earnings of individuals who served in the military to individuals who did not experience military service. The finds of these studies are best summarized according to the era analyzed. Studies using pre-Vietnam era data have typically indicated an earnings premium to the magnitude of 3 to 12 percent associated with veteran status (Fredland and Little, 1980; Villemez and Kasarda, 1976; Martindale and Poston, 1979; DeTray, 1982). A number of these studies find the positive earnings impact of military service to be limited to individuals with less than 12 years of education (Knapp, 1976; Rosen and Taubman, 1982; Berger and Hirsch, 1983).

In contrast, studies using data on Vietnam era veterans suggest largely nonpositive returns to military service. Using a matched sample of Social Security and CPS records, Rosen and Taubman (1982) found Vietnam era veterans earning approximately 19 percent less than nonveterans. Villemez and Kasarda (1975), Martindale and Poston (1979), DeTray (1982), and Schwartz (1986) found similar earnings disadvantages among Vietnam era white veterans using data from the 1970 Census. Berger and Hirsch (1983) made adjustments to the earlier Rosen and Taubman study and found few significant earnings differences, with only veterans with less than a high school education realizing an earnings premium to military service during the era. Daymont and Andrisani (1986) found earnings differences between veterans and nonveterans comparable to those of Berger and Hirsh early in the sample's post-military career, but, with the advantage of a longitudinal data set, they document a sharp rise in the veterans' earnings profiles. They find veteran earnings overtaking the earnings of those who never served and the differential persisting over a period of about 20 years after high school. This suggests that the largely negative or nonsignificant findings concerning military training during the Vietnam era may reflect the unpopularity of that war and the associated transitional labor market problems encountered by its participants.

Studies focusing on the post-Vietnam, post-draft era have documented returns to military service comparable to those of earlier studies using data on World War II and Korean War era veterans (Daymont and Andrisani, 1986; Mangum and Ball, 1989).

Government Employment and Training Programs for the Disadvantaged

Over three decades of federal involvement in providing training programs for the disadvantaged, decreed by legislation such as the Area Redevelopment Act of 1961, the Manpower Development and Training Act of 1962 (MDTA), the Comprehensive Employment and Training Act of 1973 (CETA), and the Job Training Partnership Act of 1982 (JTPA), a large number of impact studies have been completed assessing the effectiveness of such programs in influencing the employment and income of participants relative to comparison or control groups. While the literature is rich with evaluative efforts on earlier programs, comparatively little by way of multivariate studies have yet appeared concerning JTPA (see Levitan and Gallo [1988] for a review of the JTPA experience to date). Despite diversity in the findings of pre-JTPA literature, there are also areas of general agreement. Program participants usually experience small but significant earnings increases, earning $200 to $600 more annually in 1985 dollars than do members of the comparison groups (Westat, 1982; Geraci, 1984; Bassi, 1983; Bloom and McLaughlin, 1982; Ashenfelter and Card, 1985).

Throughout the entire quarter-century of such experience, the greatest earnings gains from training have gone to those with the lowest pre-training earnings. There are perhaps two reasons for this. Individuals with high pre-training earnings enter these programs having generally been displaced and consequently are starting over without seniority and usually in lower status jobs. Second, the occupations in which training is typically offered have generally been those where training could be provided in relatively short time periods (usually less than a year) and for which job openings were frequent because of high turnover.

Larger earnings gains have been recorded for women than for men. Females who participate average $1000 to $1800 more in annual earnings than nonparticipants (Bloom 1987), while estimates of the earnings differential for men cluster at $200 to $400. Further, women tend to gain from all strategies—classroom training, on-the-job training, and work experience. Very few studies indicate gains to participation in work experience programs for men. For women, estimated gains are generally equal for blacks and for whites. As alluded to earlier, earnings gains have generally been positively correlated with the degree of participant disadvantage, earnings gains to the marginally disadvantaged being less than those to the very disadvantaged. These findings are consistent with the perception that these programs are more successful in increasing labor force participation rates and hours worked among participants than in significantly altering hourly wage rates.

The duration of training has been shown to be important with respect to earnings impacts. In general, six to nine months on the job or in classroom training programs have been associated with the largest earnings effects. Benefits have been shown to rise with the length of training over this range, with training participation beyond 40 weeks in duration having little or no additional payoff (Taggart, 1981; Bryant and Rupp, 1987).

The areas of greatest disagreement across studies have been over whether adult men benefited at all in terms of net earnings gains and whether there have been positive earnings gains for youth (Barnow, 1987; Bloom, 1987; Bassi et al., 1984). Estimates for adult men have ranged from a $2000 increase in annual earnings to a $3000 decrease in earnings associated with program participation. For youth the estimates range from a $1000 increase to a $1900 decrease in annualized earnings (LaLonde and Maynard, 1987). However, for youth it is critical to know whether the program content involved basic education, skill training, or mere work experience and whether the youth settled down to steady employment or chose some other post-program path.

Exposure to this literature raises the obvious question as to reasons for the wide range of estimates observed. Barnow (1987) suggests several explanations for the variance in estimates in perhaps the best summary of this field to date. He notes that the studies differ dramatically in the range of age groups included in the respective analyses and that since labor market behavior varies widely by age, the resulting diversity in estimates is understandable. Further, the studies differ significantly in the enrollment periods analyzed, in how participants exiting a program before completion are treated econometrically, in how individuals with participation in multiple program components are categorized, and in the prevailing macroeconomic conditions of the time period. These are representative factors possibly accounting for the differences in findings. Beyond these are issues of methodology employed in estimating returns to training, a topic addressed in a later section of this chapter.

Displaced Workers

Declining employment, massive layoffs, and plant closings in "smokestack" industries in the latter 1970s and the first half of the 1980s generated political demand for assistance to displaced workers, including training. A number of demonstration projects preceded passage of Title III of the Job Training Partnership Act. Evaluations of some of the experimental projects are available, but results from the JTPA displaced workers' title are only beginning to emerge.

Beginning in 1980, a group of communities downriver from Detroit, experiencing a series of plant closings, undertook what became known as the Downriver Demonstration Project. Some 2100 workers laid off by suppliers to the automobile industry were tested, assessed, and provided with vocational training and job placement services. The first set of participants experienced a 13 to

20 percent higher placement rate than nonparticipants and earned an average of $77 per week more (Kulik, Smith, and Stromsdorfer, 1984). However, a subsequent group had a much less positive experience as the unemployment rate in the area jumped from 12 to 20 percent (Kulik and Bloom, 1986). The comparison group for the evaluation consisted of workers laid off from other plants, without an attempt to match personal characteristics. The long training times also had nonparticipants taking advantage of whatever alternative jobs were available while participants confronted the job market only after it had substantially worsened. A final conclusion was that job-search training at $628 per participant had a higher payoff than vocational training at $1700 apiece.

Attempts to replicate the Downriver experiment at six other sites were tainted by use of controlled followup at only one site— Buffalo, New York. Emphasis was again placed on job-search training, with placements ranging from 9 to 81 percent among the sites (Kulik and Sharpe, 1985; Corson, Long, and Maynard, 1985).

A more rigorous evaluation in Texas randomly assigned 2250 displaced petroleum and apparel workers among three options: job-search training and placement, classroom training followed by placement services, and a control group. The conclusion was that all gains came from job-search assistance in the form of earlier reemployment and that women gained more than men (Bloom and Kulik, 1986).

In a comparative reassessment of the Downriver, Buffalo, and Texas experiments, Bowman (1986) concluded that, as a result of participation, the men's reemployment rates were increased from 10 to 30 percent with an increase in working time of from 5 to 20 percent. Among women, participants were 15 percent more likely to be reemployed than nonparticipants. The average weekly earnings of male participants climbed $100 compared to nonparticipants, while the women gained $50 in average weekly earnings. The review also concluded that job-search training was preferable to skill training and that those helped within the first year after layoff had 25 to 30 percent better reemployment rates and $100 to $150 higher earnings per week than those later assisted.

Subsequent studies of displaced autoworkers have lacked randomly assigned control groups, though there have been comparisons with nonparticipants. Hansen (1984, 1986) found that workers displaced by closure of a San Jose, California, Ford plant gained in reduced unemployment and increased wages as a result of basic education and skill retraining, with pre-layoff training especially helpful.

Eighteen new questions on worker displacement were added to the Current Population Survey in January 1984. The results of these surveys were presented in 1985 (Flaim and Sehgal, 1985) and in 1987 (Horvath, 1987), but a recent analysis of the survey data by Podgursky and Swaim (1987) suggests that a higher level of general education is associated with an increased likelihood of reemployment and reduced earnings losses, and that higher investment in specific training such as on-the-job training does not appear to protect displaced workers. Further, Podgursky and Swaim suggest that general education and remedial programs should be targeted to groups with educational problems, particularly women and minorities. Finally, their study suggests that prompt adjustment assistance may be important if protracted unemployment indicates greater difficulty in reentering the labor force.

A recently completed follow-up of Utah's 1984-85 JTPA Title III participants may serve as an example of the kinds of results to be found as more of these studies become available (Bowman, 1988). Their earnings on the post-training jobs averaged only one-half the pay of the jobs from which they were displaced. Nevertheless, when compared to those displaced but not participating and controlled for self-selection bias, interventions with costs ranging from $500 for job-search assistance to $2000 for classroom training had net earnings impacts averaging $600 per month for the first 18 months following training. However, the gains were primarily for more hours of employment rather than higher wages.

Employer-Sponsored Training

Contrasted with the volume of studies emanating from publicly supported programs, the literature discussing the returns to employer-sponsored training is remarkably sparse. While hundreds of millions are spent annually on employee development and training (Mangum, 1989), a review of the academic practitioner-oriented literature reveals little attempt to measure increases in trainee income or employer profits from training expenditures.

There have been attempts to compare pre- and post-training performance of specific tasks, reduction in scrap rates and customer complaints, and individual output (Rae, 1986). Managerial or departmental objectives have been established and progress toward these objectives have been measured before and after training (Salemme, 1987). Superiors, peers, and subordinates have been interviewed for their assessment of changes following performance training (Mirabile, Caldwell, and O'Reilly, 1987). Kirkpatrick (1978), after surveying 100 sizeable firms, reported "significant" efforts to evaluate their managerial training, but found that while over 75 percent measured participant reaction to training, less than 50 percent measured knowledge or skills learned, only 20 percent sought information on behavioral changes resulting from training, and less than 15 percent assessed on-the-job results.

The subjectivity and lack of standardization of most of the evaluation measures employed are recognized in the literature (Dixon, 1987). Further, since the usual approach is before-and-after comparison with no use of any kind of control group, critics frequently point to the inability to attribute causation to the training (Cook and Panza, 1987). Although firm-level training experts may recognize these limitations, they frequently do not consider controlled rate-of-return studies possible or worth the cost. While training departments must justify the contribution of their activities to the "bottom line" of profitability, the prevailing opinion is that too many variables enter into profit determination to single out the impact of any incremental training expenditure. Therefore, trainers more frequently seek to defend their activities as cutting costs, increasing revenues, or supporting the corporate business plan (Gordon, 1987). In fact, trainers complain that being forced to scrounge for evidence of financial contributions often diverts them from their assigned tasks of assessing needs and creating innovative training programs. Mining for dollars-and-cents credit can result in a training department being reluctant to prepare and recommend training programs which are obviously needed but lack a certifiable bottom-line payoff (Dixon, 1987). The huge surge in literacy concern is cited as an area of growing training need that is difficult to justify by financial measures alone (Zenke, 1987).

Others argue, however, that profitability is the language of business and the training department which does not at least claim bottom-line results is unlikely to grow (Gordon, 1987). Hence, the pursuit of a return-on-investment measure continues, but the consensus appears to be that "training's exact contribution in terms of dollars and cents is unknown" (Gordon, 1987, p. 32).

Upon reviewing the literature on managerial training as of 1970, Campbell (1971, p. 565) concluded: "The training development literature is voluminous, nonempirical, nontheoretical, poorly written and dull." This sentiment is reflected in more recent major reviews of this literature (Goldstein, 1980; Wexley, 1984). Campbell concluded an earlier (1970) review of practices in major firms with the comment (p. 232): "The major question at this point concerns how long organizations will follow a policy that is best character-ized as spending millions for training but not one penny for training evaluation."

There is some reason for hope, however. The frequency of pleas for rigorous evaluation of managerial training appears to be increasing. A proliferation of books, manuals, and articles presenting alternative methodologies for evaluating training effectiveness and written for practitioners have appeared (Rae, 1986; Phelps, 1983).

In the meantime, all too little is known about the returns to managerial training and the relative effectiveness of alternative types of training and methods of instruction. That which is known is largely the result of academicians gaining entrance to firms as sites for theory testing or validation (see Frayne and Latham, 1987; Frost, 1986; Meyer and Raich, 1983; Scandura and Graen, 1984; Campion and Campion, 1987, as examples). As an overall assessment of such studies, Burke and Day recently (1986) completed a meta-analysis of the effectiveness of managerial training based on some 70 empirical studies appearing in the literature. They conclude that managerial training is, on the average, effective. Their findings relative to specific training technologies and methods is beyond the scope of this current review. Despite shortcomings, recent efforts in managerial training evaluation have won praise from recognized experts. Latham (1988, p. 574) states:

> First, these training programs [those evaluated since 1980] are grounded in theory; second, the training programs have been subjected to repeated investigations; and third, the training has been evaluated empirically. Many of the evaluations include follow-up data collected from three months to five years subsequent to the training. Moreover, the dependent variables for evaluating the training

programs included observable behaviors. Campbell, Goldstein and Wexley should be pleased.

Apprenticeship is another form of at least partially employer-sponsored training which has largely escaped evaluation. As far as we have been able to ascertain, no recent evaluative study has attempted to measure the returns from apprenticeship. There have been studies concluding that apprentice-trained workers have superior skills (Horowitz and Herrnstadt, 1969; Marshall, Glover, and Franklin, 1974) and that apprentices were more likely to become supervisors and employers than those in less formal training systems (Levitan, Mangum, and Marshall, 1981). Apprenticeship has also proved to be an access route to nontraditional employment for women under equal employment opportunity enforcement pressures (Marshall and Briggs, 1967, 1968; Levitan, Mangum, and Marshall, 1981). But none of these gains has been quantified into rates of return.

Much of the same can be said about on-the-job training, other than that subsidized by government-sponsored employment and training programs. Levitan and Mangum (1981) and Taggart (1981) found on-the-job training under the Comprehensive Employment and Training Act (CETA) to return $2.18 in increased earnings of participants for every public dollar invested. However, so few employers participated that only 4 percent of all CETA enrollees were in OJT.

Measuring the Returns to Training

That rate-of-return studies are almost entirely limited to the $5 billion per year spent on publicly supported vocational education and training programs for the economically disadvantaged, while little is done to measure the results of private industry training (variously estimated to cost from $30 billion per year [*Business Week*, 1988] to $210 billion per year [National Alliance of Business, 1988]), is a phenomenon worthy of note. Involved is a tendency to take training on faith. But more important is undoubtedly the confusion in identifying the objectives of training and the technical difficulty of measuring progress toward those objectives. In the face of such difficulties, it is perhaps easier to trust than to measure. There is also interdisciplinary conflict over what to measure and what measurement means. The case for training and its magnitude would likely be greater if these difficulties were resolved.

Identifying the Objectives of Training

Training may be instigated by trainees, employers, training institutions, employee organizations, or public officials, each with different motives. The trainee seeks training in hopes of obtaining greater job security, steadier employment, higher income, or accelerated career advancement. Training is obtained by enrollment in a training institution or by seeking employment with an employer who provides it. The employer initiates training, either externally by making it an entry requirement or by paying its costs on behalf of employees, or internally through on-the-job training or classroom training within the establishment. The employer's motives are either to make production possible or to enhance productivity. The training institution instigates training either for profit or for justification of its existence. Employee organizations—both unions and professional associations—may undertake or sponsor training to make their members more attractive to employers, to make their organizations the preferred recruiting source, or to enhance the incomes and job security of their members. The public interest in training may be to better the income of citizens, to meet the demands of the labor market, or to enhance economic growth and development.

The critical test of training's worth is whether the benefits exceed the costs. But the costs are often paid and the benefits received by different people and measured by sharply diverging values. The trainee may pay for off-the-job training through tuition, other fees, and forgone earnings. On-the-job training may involve acceptance of wages lower than productivity. The employer may support training by paying the tuition and fees for employees sent for off-the-job training, by bearing the instructional and equipment costs of on-the-job training, or by paying trainees beyond their productivity. The employee association can support training only through its dues income or by selling its services to employers or public agencies. The public may pay for training by providing tax-supported training institutions, by paying tuition and stipends for trainees attending private institutions, or by subsidizing employer training efforts, either by direct cost reimbursement or through tax incentives.

Somewhat paradoxically, only the public has overtly demanded quantitative evidence of the excess of benefits over costs. The other actors have been satisfied to exercise their own qualitative judgments. In part that may be because many public objectives are more easily measured than some of the private ones. But more importantly, the private payers are the direct recipients of the returns. If they cannot measure the relationship between costs and benefits, they can at least feel it. They only need to reassure themselves of the validity of their own judgment. In the public-policy case, resources are being extracted from taxpayers on behalf of specific recipients who can receive explicit gains, whereas the taxpayers can share only in the widely disseminated social gain. The taxpayer has to both keep the political decisionmaker honest and be assured that the direct recipient is worthy of the sacrifice.

A trainee never knows whether the returns to the training exceeded its costs. The decision to invest can be made only by observing the results for predecessors or by accepting the foresight of prognosticators. Looking backward down the career path in the years after training, the trainee knows what has happened, but cannot know what would have happened had other choices been made. Nor can what would have happened despite the training be separated from what has happened because of it.

The employer's plight is similar. Where the skills involved are firm-specific, the only alternative to training is some technological change bypassing the skill. A large employer who dominates a labor market may be able to persuade public institutions to provide even firm-specific training. If the skills required are generic, an employer will have a choice between recruiting people who already have some degree of skill or selecting people with only the potential, then providing the training, with the risk of having them attracted away to other employers. Even with generic skills there may be special attitudes an employer may want to inculcate in employees which may necessitate providing some training. If the employer has the alternatives to persuade public institutions to train or to recruit workers trained or experienced elsewhere, the only returns to training can be some added productivity or advantage of firm loyalty emanating from that training.

Beyond job skills and company loyalty, an employer may prefer employees with a sufficiently broad foundation of general education, basic preparation, and problem-solving skills to adapt quickly to new technologies, processes, and situations. But that is frequently a product too long in development for employer-provided training. Consequently, the employer will generally rely on the external education system for such training. The employer will contribute through taxes and will profit from the adaptability, but will have no way to measure the return or compare it to the cost. Like most private training decisions, it is again an act of faith.

Apprenticeship began in an era without training institutions so that craft skills could be learned only from those already practicing the arts. The process was taken over by craft unions having a strong incentive to become the only source for those scarce skills within each labor market. Today, there are multiple sources for almost every skill. Rarely do employee organizations now provide training at their own dues payers' expense. However, they often negotiate apprenticeship funds from the employers or contract with public agencies to provide training for the disadvantaged or displaced. Such returns can never be quantified, but the costs to the organization are purely administrative. The only limitation is the energy of the negotiator or administrator, the resistance of the employer, and the limited availability of public funding.

Only in the public sector can there be quantification of the returns to training and then only in a narrow arena. Everything in education is in some sense preparation for work as well as preparation for life outside the workplace. Yet returns to it can be measured only by comparing the subsequent incomes of people who have various amounts or kinds of it. The faith in general and academic education in the United States is so strong that rarely is its worth challenged and a rate of return required to justify its existence.

Of public training expenditures in the United States, only two aspects lack that general level of approval and constantly have to defend their existence. Those are vocational education and second-chance training programs on behalf of the economically disadvantaged. Evaluation has seldom been attempted of scholarship, school subsidy, and grant programs to accelerate the output of scientists, engineers, medical personnel, and others thought from time to time to be critical to national defense or other purposes. Increasingly, education and training are perceived as critical contributors to economic growth and development in both international and interregional competition. But that is probably the most difficult of objectives toward which to define and measure progression. Much of this literature measures returns by putting a human capital label on an unexplained residual of economic growth. Even that is after the fact, and so the questions remain: Do economies become prosperous because they spend on education and training, or do they spend because they are prosperous and can afford it? Can an area, a region, or a nation invest its way to growth by spending on education and training? Can it predetermine its economic future by spending on the types of education needed to produce the skills required by the industries it does not yet have but hopes to attract?

Custom-fit training offering to produce the skills newly locating or expanding employers request has produced no evidence that the jobs would not have emerged but for the training expenditures. Yet backward economies are clearly without human capital investment. Who is to take the risk of not educating and training just because the returns cannot be unchallengeably quantified? Unlike training for the disadvantaged, for the objectives of economic growth, policymakers will often make the leap of faith and train without evidence.

Interdisciplinary Conflicts

Psychology and economics have been predominant disciplines in the literature of training program evaluation. While psychologists focus on changes in employee behavior as the focal point for evaluating training, economists tend to focus on outcome measures such as employment stability or earnings as the appropriate criteria (Latham, 1988). Latham summarizes the psychologist's view of the economist's focus by saying ". . . such variables are so highly contaminated that they usually preclude meaningful conclusions." Economists argue that outcome measures are appropriate in that the motivation behind investment in training is defined by the "bottom line." That is, an individual contemplating a training investment decision is interested in its probable impact on individual earnings; a company is interested in impacts of training on profitability; a nation is interested in expected impacts on social welfare.

Neither focus is incorrect; they are simply different. Both are part of training evaluation. This is perhaps best demonstrated in the evaluation scheme often credited to Kirkpatrick (1976). Kirkpatrick divides evaluation into four steps: reaction, learning, behavior, results. "Reaction" refers to determination of how well the trainees liked a particular training program. Such information is typically collected through questionnaires composed of ratings, scales, and open-ended questions.

"Learning" is the "principles, facts, and skills understood and absorbed by participants." It is most easily assessed when skills training is involved and demonstration of learning is possible. Where principles and facts are taught, learning is typically measured by paper and pencil tests. "Behavior" refers to observed changes in on-the-job performance. Again, this has historically been the focal point of evaluation in the psychology tradition.

In the Kirkpatrick framework, "results" refers to the bottom line—outcomes such as increased productivity, reduced costs, reduced turnover, increased production, better morale, increased earnings, and improved employment stability. This has traditionally been the domain of the economic approach to training evaluation. Valuable, therefore, in Kirkpatrick's work is recognition that focal points of psychology and economics in evaluation efforts are complementary rather than at odds with one another and that both endeavors are integral parts to the full investigation of the returns to any training effort.

Some reasons for the difference in focus between the two disciplines appear obvious. Economists have focused on the evaluation of large-scale training programs, primarily governmental programs in aid of the disadvantaged. These programs typically cut across organizations and the training is often in an off-the-job setting. This makes changes in on-the-job behavior difficult to assess. Further, the cost/benefit analysis sought is fairly global in dimension. In the absence of an organizational context in which to assess impacts on the bottom line, the impact of training on individual earnings becomes a primary outcome measure. Moreover, economics has a strong tradition of viewing wages as reflecting productivity and consequently economists tend to view observed wage gains as a reasonable proxy for the productivity gains and changes in the on-the-job behavior that psychologists attempt to measure.

There is some evidence that economic and psychological approaches to training evaluation are converging. An example is the emphasis on youth competencies among the JTPA performance standards. Immediate placement is not necessarily the most desirable outcome for youthful enrollees. A return to school or even enrollment in the military may have more desirable long-range impacts. Hence the use of these and improvements in basic skills such as reading and math as alternative measures of program success.

Measurement Obstacles

Whatever the differences in focal points, the economics and psychology traditions agree that the primary goal and chief concern of efforts to quantify the results of training is to isolate the outcomes attributable to training from those that would have occurred in the absence of training. Maturation effects, impacts attributable to the ebbs and flows of the macroeconomy, and so forth are potential examples of forces the effects of which must be taken into account. Hence, both groups argue strongly for estimation of returns to training through experimental designs.

Basic experimental design involves pretraining measurement, the occurrence of training, and post-training measurement—with the difference between post- and pre-training measurements being attributable to the training intervention. This type of procedure is frequently referred to as gross impact analysis. It relies on gross program outcome measures and descriptive statistics to describe how many and what kinds of individuals are being served, what services are received, and whether the program is being operated efficiently in a managerial sense relative to budgetary costs and predetermined program objectives.

While a useful form of evaluation design for managerial purposes, this design yields no knowledge as to the impacts of the training intervention in that it reveals nothing about what would have occurred in the absence of the program. Consequently, the program impacts cannot be isolated from other effects. Isolation of program effects involves construction of a control group design in which one group (the experimental group) receives the training intervention, while the second group (the control group) does not. When the drawing of the sample of subjects and the assignment to treatment and control groups are random, observed differences in outcome variables (behaviors, on-the-job performance, earnings, etc.) between the two groups are currently attributable to the training intervention. Concern over whether pretraining measurement of the groups may produce a "Hawthorne effect" in relation to the results of the experimental group gives rise to experimental designs involving two control groups (Parker, 1976) or the three control groups of the Solomon (1949) four-group design.

While pure experimental designs are the preferred methodology of psychologists and economists alike, quasi-experimental designs have received great attention recently. This is particularly true among economists. These designs involve construction of comparison groups by careful selection of a sample of individuals from a population as a whole with measurable characteristics matching the characteristics of the training participants. Alternatively, there is the use of a sample from the population and the development of an econometric model accounting for differences between the earnings of the training participants and the comparison group. Quasi-experimental designs are often employed because of the high cost of pure experimental designs for large-scale social program evaluation, the frequency of after-the-fact demands for program evaluation, and the questionable ethics of assigning individuals desperately needing services to nontreatment groups for purposes of scientific investigation. That may be acceptable in the medical world, but not in the politicized goldfish bowl of publicly financed training efforts.

Because experimental design with random assignments is difficult to achieve, particularly outside the confines of a controlled laboratory experiment and because of the growth of quasi-experimental designs, selectivity bias is perhaps the major methodological concern in the estimation of the returns to any type of intervention strategy. Selectivity or selection bias is concerned with the presence of characteristics associated with both the probability of being drawn from the population or assigned to a particular group and with the outcome. When this condition exists, false indications of causality between the treatment and the outcomes arise and the estimated impacts of the training intervention are biased. As such, selectivity is classed among the omitted variable problems of econometric modeling (Barnow, Cain, and Goldberger, 1981). Selectivity or selection bias is a concern any time that the draw from the population or the assignment to treatment or control groups is not random.

Selectivity bias can enter at various levels of analysis (Maddala, 1986). The first is where the decision of whether to participate in a program is nonrandom. Take the example of a cohort of young people facing the decision of whether or not to enlist in the armed forces. The decision to enlist is an individual one. The individual decides on a course of action on the basis of weighing alternatives—

the benefits and costs of alternative actions. We expect those deciding to enlist to be those perceiving that option to offer them the greatest net benefits. Similarly, in the case of employment and training programs for the disadvantaged, some in the population apply to the program, others do not. We have no a priori reason to expect that the decision of who seeks participation (and who does not) is randomly determined.

A second potential source of selectivity bias is involved in the decision as to who is accepted into a particular program. In the military example, there are basic qualifications that must be met—as determined by background checks, medical examinations, mental aptitude testing, etc.—before enlistment proceeds. Such selection criteria are clearly nonrandom. In the example of employment and training programs for the disadvantaged, eligibility determination is a fundamental programmatic step. Those determined to not meet the regulations are denied participation. Frequently the numbers meeting eligibility restrictions greatly outstrip the number of available program slots and a program administrator must select among the eligibles on the basis of some criteria, uniformly applied or otherwise. Again, the chance of random selection is often slim.

The third potential source of selectivity bias is the one most commonly identified as such—the process of assignment to treatment or control group by a program administrator or evaluator. One example is the case of evaluation after the fact, where selection of a predetermined control group is impossible and comparison groups are constructed by characteristic matching and through econometric modeling. Bias occurs any time the two groups differ on unmeasurable characteristics related to earnings or the probability of participation and these differences are not captured in the regression-adjusted earnings comparison. Similarly, where programmatic decision rules are involved in the assignment to control versus treatment group, the potential for bias is also introduced.

A fourth potential source of selectivity bias occurs after the assignment of subjects to the treatment or control group. Attrition from the sample and the corresponding loss of information may introduce selection bias whenever the resulting truncation of the sample is nonrandom in nature.

Where the rules governing assignment or selection are known or the causes of attrition are understood, the problem of selectivity bias may be at least partially retractable. The problem is manageable if these rules or processes can be accounted for and proxied in the estimation equations through the introduction of control variables. Bias arises to the extent that the control variables are less than perfect proxies for the rules governing the selection or assignment mechanism at work in the phenomena being studied (Goldberger, 1972).

A number of econometrically sophisticated techniques have been developed to control for selectivity bias in its various forms. The most widely applied technique is perhaps that developed by Heckman (1974, 1979), the technique often referred to as "Heckman's Lambda." Detailed review of this and other techniques (Olsen, 1980; Griliches, Hall, and Hausman, 1978; Lee, 1982) is beyond the scope of the current piece. Most troubling about selectivity is that, because it is an omitted/unobservable variables problem, the analyst is never certain of to what degree the influence of unobservables has been successfully captured. Similarly, one is never certain as to whether decision rules known to govern nonrandom assignment processes are correctly proxied.

These problems are perhaps best summarized by comments from two nationally recognized experts in program evaluation:

> If there were agreement on the functional form and arguments [variables] that belong in an earnings function and if all the required variables were available without measurement error, there would be no controversy about how to estimate the impact of CETA programs. . . . Unfortunately, such a simple procedure is not available for estimating the impact of training programs. (Barnow, 1987, p. 179)

> A complete set of measurable variables, to adjust statistically for population differences, does not exist. Therefore program effects are known to be estimated with statistical bias and to varying and unknown degree do not reflect true program effects. (Stromsdorfer, 1988, p. 35)

The problems of quasi-experimental research designs (involving matched comparison groups as opposed to randomly assigned control groups) have recently been demonstrated in a series of studies commissioned by the Job Training Longitudinal Survey

Research Advisory Panel. This effort involved some seven individual studies by independent researchers of data on programs offered under the Comprehensive Employment and Training Act (CETA). Using different estimation techniques and alternative comparison group designs, the studies indicate a high sensitivity of estimated impacts to the type of evaluation designs and techniques employed (Dickinson, Corcoran, and West, 1987) and stress the difficulties of developing matched comparison groups (LaLonde and Maynard, 1987).

While some of the studies in this effort are more hopeful of possibilities to develop unbiased econometric estimators for nonexperimental program evaluation (Heckman, Hotz, and Dabos, 1987), the overall assessment seems to be that there is no econometric substitute for random assignment (Bryant and Rupp, 1987; LaLonde and Maynard, 1987; also see Fraker and Maynard, 1987). In any other evaluation design one can never be certain that the program participants and the comparison group come from the same population.

For example, a study by LaLonde (1986) compares the results obtained from a field experiment including random assignment to the range of estimates that would be obtained from evaluation of the same program using comparison groups and modern econometric techniques in the absence of a randomly selected control group. He clearly documents the failure of the standard selection controls to replicate the experimentally determined results. The findings of these and other studies has prompted the JTPA Advisory group to the U.S. Department of Labor to recommend use of classical experimental design for evaluating JTPA, while continuing to "analyze and resolve" the problems of selection bias (Stromsdorfer, 1987). Given the past track record, one would not want to forgo training program evaluation awaiting that millenial day.

What Does It All Mean?

Our knowledge of the rate of return on skill training is largely limited to publicly supported vocational education and training programs for the disadvantaged. Evaluation of vocational education suffers from one issue of objective identification and one of neglect. Studies of secondary-level vocational education usually show, as noted, a low rate of training-related placement and therefore a low rate of return. But if the purpose were identified as career exploration rather than career preparation, the return might appear entirely different. The issue would then shift to: How does this compare with other alternative means for giving the young the exposure necessary to make an informed occupational choice? The neglect is the focus on evaluation of secondary programs when the real skill training from vocational education occurs at the post-secondary level. For programs for the economically disadvantaged, the neglect and the need is for evaluation of training occurring under the Job Training Partnership Act. Decisions are being made about JTPA's results when the only solid data relate back to the results of MDTA and CETA. Who is enrolled and how many are placed provide little useful information without means of comparison to what would have happened in the program's absence. Employment and training programs, which were the targets of considerable evaluative effort in the 1970s and have been largely neglected since, need to be readdressed.

Relying on the earlier studies, the rate of return literature is characterized by general agreement as to the level of returns, though there is more information on some types of training than on others. Relatedly, there is or should be increasing concern with issues of access. These issues include who participates in what kind of training, what mechanisms govern selection of or assignment to various types and providers of training, and how returns vary by demographic group. These issues are of particular concern inasmuch as demographic trends suggest future decades character-ized by an older, more minority laden, less English proficient labor force involved in more human capital reliant work. There is also greater need than in the past to probe the interaction between skill training and literacy deficiencies, family disorganization, substance abuse, and other social maladies.

Properly measuring the returns to training is difficult. Among the reasons for this is the confusion and frustration inherent in identifying training objectives common to the variety of actors involved in training decisions. Second, there have been inter-disciplinary conflicts as to what to measure and how. Third, there are a number of technical difficulties involved in producing rate-of-return estimates. A fourth problem is one of motivation. For some involved in training decisions, the value of sophisticated rate-of-return information may be overshadowed by the costs of obtaining such information.

The objectives issue can be resolved by clear thinking and careful statement. Interdisciplinary conflict will undoubtedly continue, but there appears to be more common ground today than in years past. There is basic agreement on the importance of experimental designs with randomly assigned control groups and the limitations of various selectivity controls. There is also growing recognition of the validity of alternative disciplinary approaches. For example, economists are beginning to look beyond wages as proxies for productivity and to measure productivity more directly. Interdisciplinary research can be an effective solution to interdisciplinary conflict. Both sets of focus and methodology are valid and can be mutually reinforcing. The technical difficulties will be resolved by qualified people chipping away at them. The need is for a return to the research and evaluative funding of the 1970s which attracted that talent. The evaluation of employer-sponsored training will occur only as employers perceive the need to know. The academic mentors of those who become training specialists for industry must share the blame for this lack of perception.

There are obvious reasons to seek improvement in our methodology for evaluating the benefits and costs of training activities. But at its root, training is an act of faith. Its promised or hoped-for payoff lies largely in an immeasurable and unpredictable future. That current commitment to training is strong is evidenced by the fact that private training expenditures are increasing and did not decline in the 1981-82 recession. Further, training is increasingly extolled by the popular press. Its value is apparently assumed to be self-evident. For example, *Business Week* entitled its September 19, 1988, special report "Needed: Human Capital." No place in its 21 pages is the payoff to training questioned. Greater functional literacy is touted as the key to Japan's manufacturing superiority. The $150 billion yearly U.S. trade deficit is attributed to the inability of a large percentage of the American workforce to compete successfully. The *Business Week* article reports that "much of the success of Japan stems from the fact that its blue collar workers can interpret advanced mathematics, read complex engineering blueprints and perform sophisticated tasks on the factory floor far better than blue collar workers in the U.S." (p. 101). The authors charge that "while Washington has been hell-bent on throwing incentives at business to increase spending on plant and equipment, outlays for human capital . . . have lagged behind" and that "those cuts [in the Labor Department's manpower training programs] could not have been timed worse" (p. 103). Further, "The productivity of the unskilled [U.S. labor force] is plummeting, while worker productivity abroad is soaring" (p. 103). The conclusion is that "investments in education and training will yield sure-fire returns we can't afford to ignore" (p. 140). Economic salvation is achievable by:

- instilling the habits of learning and working in kids at an early age,
- paying teachers more, and perhaps transforming the whole teaching process,
- adopting new incentives to train and retrain workers, and
- tailoring the workplace to the new labor force.

  Too frequently, managers have looked at workers as a cost rather than as a resource and every extra dollar spent on workers was viewed as that much more of a burden, whereas it could be, if wisely spent, a means to empower workers to do better. Hundreds of companies now recognize this to be true with respect to training. Investments in training yield tangible rewards . . . without strong leadership and new spending priorities, America's most precious resource will be neglected. In the words of a familiar advertisement: A mind is a terrible thing to waste. (*Business Week*, 1988, p. 141.)

That spirit can carry training budgets through the crunch of international competition. Quantitative evidence of a positive rate of return will be needed when the heat is off or when enthusiasm flags. Then we may begin to ask ourselves for the evidence of underinvestment in human resources. Beyond the time lag as market demand changes more rapidly than institutional programs can adjust, it is difficult to identify an occupation in persistent shortage. What employers appear to be complaining about is the quality of the raw material available for their internal training efforts. What are the means available for creating a self-disciplined, motivated population possessed of the basic skills upon which skill training can be founded? What would be the costs and rate of return from such investment? That appears to be the priority research challenge at this juncture.

References

Adams, Arvil V. "The Stock of Human Capital and Differences in Post-School Formal Occupational Training for Middle Aged Men." *Southern Economic Journal* (April 1978).

Adams, Arvil V., Stephen L. Mangum, and Philip W. Wirtz. "Postschool Education and Training: Accessible to All?" *Review of Black Political Economy* 15, 3 (Winter 1987).

Ashenfelter, Orley, and David Card. "Using the Longitudinal Structure of Earnings to Estimate the Effect of Training Programs." *Review of Economics and Statistics* 67, 4 (1985).

Barnow, Burt S. "The Impact of CETA Programs on Earnings." *Journal of Human Resources* 22, 2 (Spring 1987), pp. 157–93.

Barnow, Burt S., Glen G. Cain, and Arthur S. Goldberger. "Issues in the Analysis of Selectivity Bias." In *Evaluation Review Studies*, Vol. 5, eds. E. W. Stromsdorfer and G. Farkas. Beverly Hills, CA: Sage, 1981.

Barron, J. M., D. A. Black, and M. A. Loewenstein. "Job Matching and On-the-Job Training." *Journal of Labor Economics* 7, 1 (1989).

Bassi, Laurie J. "The Effect of CETA on the Postprogram Earnings of Participants." *Journal of Human Resources* 18, 4 (Fall 1983), pp. 539–56.

Bassi, Laurie J., et al. "Measuring the Effect of CETA on Youth and the Economically Disadvantaged." Washington: Urban Institute, 1984.

Berger, Mark C., and Barry T. Hirsch. "The Civilian Earnings Experience of Viet Nam Era Veterans." *Journal of Human Resources* 18, 4 (Fall 1983), pp. 455–79.

Bishop, John H. *The Social Payoff for Occupationally Specific Training: The Employers' Point of View*. Columbus: National Center for Research in Vocational Education, Ohio State University, November 1982.

Bishop, J. H., K. Hollenbeck, S. Kang, and R. Willke. "Training and Human Capital Formation." Columbus: National Center for Research in Vocational Education, Ohio State University, July 1985.

Blaug, Mark. "Human Capital Theory: A Slightly Jaundiced Survey." *Journal of Economic Literature* 14, 3 (September 1976).

Bloom, Howard, and Jane Kulik. *Evaluation of the Worker Adjustment Demonstration, Final Report*. Cambridge, MA: Abt Associates, July 1986.

Bloom, Howard S. "What Works for Whom: CETA Impacts for Adult Participants." *Evaluation Review* 11, 4 (August 1987).

Bloom, Howard S., and Maureen A. McLaughlin. "CETA Training Programs—Do They Work for Adults?" Washington: Joint Congressional Budget Office/National Commission for Employment Policy Report, 1982.

Borjas, George J., and Finis Welch. "The Post-Service Earnings of Military Retirees." Los Angeles: Unicon Research Corp., 1984.

Bowman, William R. *Do Displaced Worker Programs "Work"? Final Report*. Annapolis, MD: Annapolis Economic Research, July 22, 1986.

————. *Net Impact Estimates, Utah Job Training Partnership Act Title III, Program Year 1984-85*. Annapolis, MD: Annapolis Economic Research, September 1988.

Bryant, Edward C., and Kalman Rupp. "Evaluating the Impact of CETA on Participant Earnings." *Evaluation Review* 11, 4 (August 1987).

Burke, Michael J., and Russell R. Day. "A Cumulative Study of the Effectiveness of Managerial Training." *Journal of Applied Psychology* 71, 2 (1986).

Business Week. "Needed: Human Capital." September 19, 1988, pp. 100–141.

Campbell, J. P. "Personnel Training and Development." *Annual Review of Psychology* 22 (1971).

Campbell, J. P., M. D. Dunnette, E. E. Lawler, and K. E. Weick, Jr. *Managerial Behavior, Performance and Effectiveness*. New York: McGraw-Hill, 1970.

Campbell, Paul B., Karen S. Basiner, Mary Beth Dauner, and Marie A. Parks. "Outcomes of Vocational Education for Women, Minorities, the Handicapped and the Poor." Columbus: National Center for Research in Vocational Education, Ohio State University, 1986.

Campbell, Paul B., Jack Elliot, Suzanne Laughlin, and Ellen Seusy. "The Dynamics of Vocational Education Effects on Labor Market Outcomes." Columbus: National Center for Research in Vocational Education, Ohio State University, 1987.

Campion, Michael A., and James E. Campion. "Evaluation of an Interviewee Skills Training Program in a Natural Field Experiment." *Personnel Psychology* 40 (1987).

Card, David, and Daniel Sullivan. "Measuring the Effect of Subsidized Training Programs on Movements In and Out of Employment." NBER Working Paper Series #2173, February 1987.

Conroy, William A., Jr., and Daniel E. Diamond. *The Impact of Secondary School Occupational Education in Massachusetts.* Lowell, MA: University of Lowell, College of Management Series, Spring 1976.

Cook, James R., and Carol M. Panza. "ROI, What Should Training Take Credit For?" *Training* (January 1987), pp. 59–68.

Cooper, Richard V. L. "Military Retirees' Post-Service Earnings and Employment." Santa Monica, CA: Rand Corporation, 1981.

Corson, W., S. Long, and R. Maynard. *An Impact Evaluation of the Buffalo Dislocated Worker Demonstration Program.* Princeton, NJ: Mathematica Policy Research, Inc., March 12, 1985.

Cross, Patricia. *Adults as Learners.* San Francisco: Jossey-Bass, 1981.

Danzon, Patricia Munch. "Civilian Earnings of Military Retirees." Santa Monica, CA: Rand Corporation, 1980.

Daymont, Thomas N., and Paul J. Andrisani. "Military Service and Civilian Labor Market Success." Paper presented at the Eastern Economics Association Meetings, Philadelphia, April 1986.

Daymont, Thomas, and Russell Rumsberger. "Impact of High School Curriculum on the Earnings and Employment of Youth." In *Job Training for Youth*, ed. Robert Taylor. Columbus: National Center for Research in Vocational Education, Ohio State University, 1982.

DeTray, Dennis. "Veteran Status as a Screening Device." *American Economic Review* 72, 1 (1982), pp. 133–42.

Dickinson, Katherine P., Terry R. Johnson, and Richard W. West. "An Analysis of the Sensitivity of Quasi-Experimental Net Impact Estimates of CETA Programs." *Evaluation Review* 11, 4 (August 1987).

Dixon, Nancy M. "Meeting Training's Goals Without Reaction Forms." *Personnel Journal* (August 1987), pp. 108–15.

Felstchausen, Joyce L., et al. *Followup Report on Illinois "Class of 71" Occupational Program Alumni, Final Report.* Charleston: Eastern Illinois University Center for Educational Studies, June 1973.

Flaim, Paul O., and Ellen Sehgal. "Displaced Workers of 1979–83: How Have They Fared?" *Monthly Labor Review* 108 (June 1985), pp. 3–6.

Flanagan, Robert J. "Labor Force Experience, Job Turnover, and Racial Wage Differentials." *Review of Economics and Statistics* 56 (November 1974).

Fraker, Thomas, and Rebecca Maynard. "Evaluating Comparison Group Designs with Employment-Related Programs." *Journal of Human Resources* 22, 2 (Spring 1987), pp. 194–227.

Fraser, Bryan S. "The Structure of Adult Learning, Education and Training Opportunity in the United States." Washington: National Institute for Work and Learning, 1980.

Frayne, Colette A., and Gary P. Latham. "Application of Social Learning Theory to Employee Self Management of Attendance." *Journal of Applied Psychology* 72, 3 (1987).

Fredland, John E., and Roger D. Little. "Long Term Returns to Vocational Training: Evidence from Military Sources." *Journal of Human Resources* 15, 1 (Winter 1980), pp. 49–66.

Freeman, Robert B. "Occupational Training in Proprietary Schools and Technical Institutes." *Review of Economics and Statistics* 56 (August 1974).

Frost, Dean A. "A Test of Situational Engineering for Training Leaders." *Psychological Reports* 59 (1986).

Geraci, Vincent J. "Short Term Indicators of Job Training Program Effects on Long Term Participant Earnings." Report prepared for U.S. Department of Labor Contract 20-48-82-16, 1984.

Goldberger, A. S. "Selection Bias in Evaluating Treatment Effects: Some Formal Illustrations." Discussion Paper 123-72, Institute for Research on Poverty, University of Wisconsin, 1972.

Goldstein, I. L. "Training in Work Organizations." *Annual Review of Psychology* 31 (1980).

Goldstein, Mark L. "Tomorrow's Workforce Today." *Industry Week*, August 15, 1988.

Gordon, Jack. "Romancing the Bottom Line." *Training* (June 1987), pp. 31-42.

Gordus, Jeanne P. *Labor Force Status, Program Participation and Economic Adjustment of Displaced Autoworkers.* University of Michigan Report to the U.S. Department of Commerce, Office of Automotive Industry Affairs, 1985.

Gordus, Jeanne P., et al. *Retraining Experiences and Outcomes: The Case of Displaced Automakers.* Ann Arbor: University of Michigan, Institute of Science and Technology, Industrial Development Division, forthcoming.

Grasso, J. T., and J. R. Shea. *Vocational Education and Training: Impact on Youth.* Berkeley, CA: Carnegie Council on Policy Studies in Higher Education, 1979.

Griliches, Z., B. H. Hall, and J. A. Hausman. "Missing Data and Self Selection in Large Panels." *Annals de l'INSEE* 30-31 (1978).

Gustman, A. L., and T. L. Steinmeier. "The Relation Between Vocational Training in High School and Economic Outcomes." *Industrial and Labor Relations Review* 36, 1 (October 1982).

Hansen, G. B. "Ford and the UAW Have a Better Idea: A Joint Labor-Management Approach to Plant Closings and Worker Retraining." *Annals of the American Academy* 475 (September 1984), pp. 158-74.

_____. *Two Years Later: A Followup Survey of Labor Market Status and Adjustment of Workers Displaced by the San Jose Assembly Plant Closure.* Logan: Business and Economic Development Services, Utah State University, 1986.

Hanushek, Eric A. "Regional Differences in the Structure of Earnings." Washington: Office of Economic Research, Economic Development Administration, U.S. Department of Commerce, 1972.

Heckman, James J. "Shadow Prices, Market Wages and Labor Supply." *Econometrica* 42 (1974).

_____. "Sample Selection Bias as a Specification Error." *Econometrica* 47 (1979).

Heckman, James J., Joseph Hotz, and Marcelo Dabos. "Do We Need Experimental Data to Evaluate the Impact of Manpower Training on Earnings?" *Evaluation Review* 11, 4 (August 1987).

Horowitz, Morris, and Irwin Herrnstadt. *The Training of Tool and Die Makers.* Boston: Department of Economics, Northeastern University, 1969.

Horvath, Francis W. "The Pulse of Economic Change: Displaced Workers of 1981-85." *Monthly Labor Review* 110 (June 1987), pp. 3-12.

Kang, Suk, and John H. Bishop. "The Effect of Curriculum on Labor Market Success Immediately After High School." *Journal of Industrial Teacher Education* (Spring 1986).

Kessing, David B. "Military Experience as a Determinant of Veterans' Earnings." In *Studies Prepared for the President's Commission on an All Volunteer Armed Force*, Vol. 2, Part 3, No. 8. Washington: 1970.

Kirkpatrick, D. L. "Evaluation of Training." In *Training and Development Handbook*, ed. Robert L. Craig. New York: McGraw-Hill, 1976. Ch. 18.

_____. "Evaluating In House Training Programs." *Training and Development Journal* (September 6-9. 1978).

Knapp, Charles B. "The Effect of Military Experience on Post-Service Earnings Without the Draft." In *Defense Manpower Policy*, ed. R. V. L. Cooper. Santa Monica, CA: Rand Corporation, 1976.

Kulik, J., and H. Bloom. *The Worker Adjustment Demonstration Evaluation: Preliminary Impact Report.* Cambridge, MA: Abt Associates, March 11, 1986.

Kulik, Jane, and Linda Sharpe. *The Worker Adjustment Demonstration Projects: A Comparative Evaluation Report.* Cambridge, MA: Abt Associates, 1985.

Kulik, J., D. Smith, and E. Stromsdorfer. *The Downriver Community Conference Economic Readjustment Program: Final Evaluation Report.* Cambridge, MA: Abt Associates, September 30, 1984.

LaLonde, Robert J. "Evaluating the Econometric Evaluations of Training with Experimental Data." *American Economic Review* 76, 4 (September 1986).

LaLonde, Robert, and Rebecca Maynard. "How Precise Are Evaluations of Employment and Training Programs: Evidence from a Field Experiment." *Evaluation Review* 11, 4 (August 1987).

Latham, Gary P. "Human Resource Training and Development." *Annual Review of Psychology* 39 (1988).

Lee, L. T. "Some Approaches to the Correction of Selectivity Bias." *Review of Economic Studies* 49 (1982).

Levitan, Sar A., Peter A. Carlson, and Isaac Shapiro. *Protecting American Workers.* Washington: Bureau of National Affairs, 1987.

Levitan, Sar A., and Frank Gallo. *A Second Chance: Training for Jobs.* Kalamazoo, MI: W. E. Upjohn Institute for Employment Research, 1988.

Levitan, Sar A., and Garth L. Mangum, eds. *The T in CETA.* Kalamazoo, MI: W. E. Upjohn Institute for Employment Research, 1981.

Levitan, Sar A., Garth L. Mangum, and Ray Marshall. *Human Resources and Labor Markets.* New York: Harper & Row, 1981.

Lillard, Lee A., and Hong W. Tan. "Private Sector Training: Who Gets It and What Are Its Effects?" Santa Monica, CA: Rand Corporation, 1986.

Lynch, Lisa M. "Race and Gender Differences in Private Sector Training for Young Workers." Working Paper Series. Cambridge, MA: Sloan School of Management, MIT, 1988.

Maddala, G. S. *Limited-Dependent and Qualitative Variables in Econometrics.* New York: Cambridge University Press, 1986.

Mangum, Stephen L. "Evidence on Private Sector Training." Paper written for the Commission on Workforce Quality and Labor Market Efficiency, U.S. Department of Labor, June 1989.

Mangum, Stephen L., and Arvil V. Adams. "The Labor Market Impacts of Post-School Occupational Training for Young Men." *Growth and Change* 18, 4 (Fall 1987).

Mangum, Stephen L., and David E. Ball. "The Transferability of Military-Provided Occupational Training in the Post-Draft Era." *Industrial and Labor Relations Review* 42, 2 (January 1989).

Marshall, Ray, Robert Glover, and William F. Franklin. *Training and Entry into Union Construction.* Washington: U.S. Government Printing Office, 1974.

Marshall, Ray, and Vernon M. Briggs, Jr. *The Negro and Apprenticeship.* Baltimore: Johns Hopkins Press, 1967.

————. *Equal Apprenticeship Opportunity.* Ann Arbor and Detroit: National Manpower Policy Task Force and Institute of Labor and Industrial Relations, University of Michigan–Wayne State University, 1968.

Martindale, Melanie, and Dudley L. Poston, Jr. "Variations in Veteran/Nonveteran Earnings Patterns Among World War II, Korea and Vietnam War Cohorts." *Armed Forces and Society* 5, 2 (1979), pp. 219–42.

Mason, William. "On the Socioeconomic Effects of Military Service." Ph.D. dissertation, University of Chicago, 1970.

Massell, Adele P., and Gary R. Nelson. "The Estimation of Training Premiums for U.S. Military Personnel." Santa Monica, CA: Rand Corporation, 1974.

McCall, John, and Neil Wallace. "Training and Retention of Air Force Airmen: An Economic Analysis." Santa Monica, CA: Rand Corporation, 1967.

McMillan, John D., and Claire O. Waters. "Dominating the Dollars." *Personnel Administrator* (August 1988), p. 30.

Mertens, Donna M., Patricia Seitz, and Sterling Cox. "Vocational Education and the High School Dropout." Columbus: National Center for Research in Vocational Education, Ohio State University, September 1982.

Meyer, Herbert H., and Michael S. Raich. "An Objective Evaluation of a Behavior Modeling Training Program." *Personnel Psychology* 36 (1983).

Meyer, R. "Job Training in the Schools." In *Job Training for Youth*, eds. R. Taylor, H. Rosen, and F. Pratzner. Columbus: National Center for Research in Vocational Education, Ohio State University, 1982.

Mirabile, Richard, David Caldwell, and Charles O'Reilly. "Soft Skills, Hard Numbers." *Training* (August 1987), pp. 53–56.

National Alliance of Business. "Business and Education: The Demand for Partnership." *Business Week*, May 2, 1988, pp. 123–35.

Norrblum, Eva. "The Returns to Military and Civilian Training." Santa Monica, CA: Rand Corporation, 1976.

Nussbaum, Bruce. "Needed: Human Capital." *Business Week*, September 19, 1988, pp. 102–103.

Olsen, R. J. "A Least Squares Correction for Selectivity Bias." *Econometrica* 48, 7 (1980).

O'Neill, David M., Sue G. Ross, and John T. Warner. "Military Occupation, GI Bill Training, and Human Capital." In *Defense Manpower Policy*, ed. Richard V. L. Cooper. Santa Monica, CA: Rand Corporation, 1976.

Parker, T. V. "Statistical Methods for Measuring Training Results." In *Training and Development Handbook*, ed. Robert L. Craig. New York: McGraw-Hill, 1976. Ch. 19.

Pergamit, Michael R., and Janice Shack-Marquez. "Earnings and Different Types of Training." BLS Working Paper #165, June 1987.

Phelps, Jack. *Handbook of Training Evaluation and Measurement Methods.* Houston: Gulf Publisher, 1983.

Podgursky, Michael, and Paul Swaim. "Job Displacement and Earnings Loss: Evidence from the Displaced Worker Study." *Industrial and Labor Relations Review* 41, 1 (October 1987), pp. 17–29.

Rae, Leslie. *How to Measure Training Effectiveness.* New York: Nichols Publishing Co., 1986.

Rosen, Sherwin, and Paul Taubman. "Changes in Life-Cycle Earnings: What Do Social Security Data Show?" *Journal of Human Resources* 17, 3 (Summer 1982), pp. 321–38.

Rumsberger, R. W. "The Intensity of Occupational Training and Its Effect on Earnings." In *Market Defenses: Early Work Decisions of Today's Middle Aged Men*, ed. Stephen M. Hills. Columbus: Center for Human Resource Research, Ohio State University, 1983. Ch. 7.

_____. "The Incidence and Wage Effects of Occupational Training Among Young Men." *Social Science Quarterly* (September 1984).

Rumsberger, R. W., and T. N. Daymont. "The Impact of High School Curriculum on the Earnings and Employability of Youth." In *Job Training for Youth*, eds. R. Taylor, H. Rosen, and F. Pratzner. Columbus: National Center for Research in Vocational Education, Ohio State University, 1982.

Salemme, Tom. "Measuring White-Collar Work." *Training* (July 1987), pp. 33–35.

Scandura, Terri A., and George B. Graen. "Moderating Effects of Initial Leader-Member Exchange Status on the Effects of a Leadership Intervention." *Journal of Applied Psychology* 69, 3 (1984).

Schwarz, Saul. "The Relative Earnings of Vietnam and Korean-Era Veterans." *Industrial and Labor Relations Review* 39, 4 (1986), pp. 564–73.

Solomon, R. "Extension of Control Group Design." *Psychological Bulletin* 46 (1949).

Stromsdorfer, Ernst. "Economic Evaluation of the Comprehensive Employment and Training Act: An Overview." *Evaluation Review* 11, 4 (August 1987).

_____. "Evaluating CETA: An Overview of Recent Findings and Advances in Evaluation Methods." *Evaluation Forum*, Issue 3, 1988.

Taggart, Robert. *A Fisherman's Guide: An Assessment of Training and Remediation Strategies.* Kalamazoo, MI: W.E. Upjohn Institute for Employment Research, 1981.

U.S. Department of Defense. Military Manpower Training Report for FY 1984. Washington: March 1989.

Villemez, Wayne J., and John Kasarda. "Veteran Status and Socioeconomic Attainment." *Armed Forces and Society* 2, 3 (1976), pp. 407–20.
Weinstein, Paul A., et al. "Final Report of the Military Training Study. Labor Market Activity of Veterans: Some Aspects of Military Spillover." College Park: University of Maryland, 1969.
Westat, Inc. "Net Impact No. 1, The Impact of CETA on 1978 Earnings: Participants in Selected Program Activities Who Entered CETA During FY 1976." Report prepared for the U.S. Department of Labor under Contract 23-25-75-07, 1982.
Wexley, K. N. "Personnel Training." *Annual Review of Psychology* 35 (1984).
Zenke, Ron. "Training in the 1990s." *Training* (January 1987).

Chapter 4

New Directions in Labor Education*

Lois S. Gray
Cornell University

Joyce L. Kornbluh
University of Michigan

For more than 100 years the field of labor education in the United States has encompassed a wide range of educational offerings for working people under a variety of institutional auspices (Dwyer, 1977). These programs developed and evolved over the years, with unions and university labor education centers emerging after World War II as the principal providers of education programs, most of them on union-building and labor-management relations.

Twenty-five years ago, veteran labor educators Larry Rogin and Marjorie Rachlin published a survey of labor education in the United States, based on data they had collected for the years 1965 and 1966 (Rogin and Rachlin, 1968). In the most extensive review of the field to that date, they reported on programs offered by approximately 40 unions, 24 university labor education centers, 10 Catholic labor colleges, the national AFL-CIO Education Department, and AFL-CIO state and city councils.

Their survey revealed that labor education at that time was funded primarily by the unions themselves, and the objective underlying all of the reported programs continued to be union-building. These programs, on such topics as union administration, collective bargaining, leadership skills, and political action, were usually attended by staff, elected officers, and activists from blue-collar unions.

*Data collection for this chapter was made possible, in part, through travel support provided by Rudy Oswald, Director of Economic Research, and Dorothy Shields, Director of Education, AFL-CIO.

Most of the noncredit educational offerings of the mid-sixties were conferences, one-week residential schools, and seven- to ten-week evening classes. By 1966 several universities were sponsoring two-year programs on a noncredit basis. Rogin and Rachlin found no "typical" labor education program and no national network of labor education providers.

The Rogin and Rachlin volume was the point of departure for our study in which we chose to focus on new trends and innovations in the field rather than to attempt a comprehensive documentation of the extent and content of labor education in the U.S. today. Our sources of information, collected in 1988 and 1989, were a survey questionnaire, correspondence and interviews, written reports, and a feedback session during a national meeting of union and university labor educators in March 1988.

We received 51 responses to the questionnaire that we mailed to 51 university and college labor programs affiliated with the University and College Labor Education Association (UCLEA) and to the 79 unions on the mailing list of the AFL-CIO Education Department. The response rate was 34 percent. In addition, we interviewed 21 labor educators and analyzed material from university and community college programs, union education departments (including national, state, and local), and "independent" labor education organizations. It should be noted that we relied on self-evaluations: what labor educators themselves considered new and innovative themes and methods as well as new approaches to traditional labor education subjects.

Highlights of Our Survey

From our data and information sources, we were able to identify a number of major changes in labor education that will be discussed in later sections of this chapter.

Labor education today is reaching *new constituencies* that range from top union leaders to rank-and-file workers, including white-collar and service employees, women, minorities, immigrants, workers' families, disabled workers, and secondary school teachers and students. Second, reflecting workplace changes and these new constituencies, *new content areas* are being addressed in labor education programs: labor-management approaches to workplace issues and workplace organization; technological change and strategic planning; health and safety in the workplace; substance abuse; special concerns of women, minorities, and immigrant workers; economic and technological trends in specific industries; and workers' culture. Other additions to curricula include language and computer literacy, teaching about labor in the schools, and training for full-time union staff.

A third change is the use of *more sophisticated approaches* to labor education curricula. Subject matter coverage has been broadened, drawing from the social and behavioral sciences. Included under these new approaches are new techniques: one-on-one interactions, study circles, video feedback, games, and the use of computers. Fourth, there are a variety of *new delivery systems* such as college degree programs, teleconferencing, and television broadcasts.

A fifth change is the emergence of *new labor education providers.* These include the George Meany Center for Labor Studies, community colleges, coalitions for occupational safety and health (COSH), and commercial consultants. Several national unions have established resident education centers. In addition to the education departments of the AFL-CIO and national unions, other union departments such as organizing, civil rights, community services, legislation, and women's affairs have joined the ranks of labor education providers.

Although there is still no national system of labor education, annual national and regional conferences co-sponsored by the AFL-CIO Education Department and the University and College Labor Education Association (UCLEA) have developed a degree of collaboration among union and university labor education staffs in recent years (MacKenzie, 1984). Current UCLEA institutional membership consists of 51 programs in 29 states and the District of Columbia (UCLEA, 1989). Other professional developments include such publications as the quarterly *Labor Studies Journal*, the "AFL-CIO Education Update" and UCLEA's "Labor Education Forum," research and technical assistance services within university labor education centers, and a number of national task forces and committees on labor education program directions.

New sources of funding for labor education, in addition to traditional support from unions and from state-supported public universities, are private foundations, national and state government agencies, and employers through collectively bargained, jointly administered training and education programs for employee development.

New Providers of Labor Education

It may be useful at this point to discuss in detail the new providers of labor education. The mix of educational institutions providing labor education has changed in recent years. Union-sponsored education programs have been expanded by the year-round, one-week and weekend courses for full-time union staff in the influential AFL-CIO-sponsored George Meany Center for Labor Studies in suburban Washington, D.C. Increasingly, unions of building trades, white-collar, and service workers have initiated educational programs, thus broadening the range of union sponsors beyond those industrial unions (auto, steel, electrical, garment, communications) that Rogin and Rachlin (1968) identified as the principal providers in the mid-sixties. Also, educational activities are increasingly being sponsored by the AFL-CIO and the national union departments responsible for organizing, collective bargaining, legislation, community services, and public relations. This support supplements the on-going work of the education departments that have been primarily responsible for union education activities in the past.

University labor education centers have been joined, and in some cases rivaled, by community colleges that entered the labor education field in response to the demand for college credit courses (Brickner, 1975; Gray, 1976). Many community colleges now offer "traditional" noncredit labor education services similar to those provided by university labor education centers.

In only one state is there a coordinated institutional approach. California has developed a three-tier system in which the university provides instructor training and labor education materials, four-year colleges offer bachelor degrees, and community colleges provide two-year associate degrees in labor studies that are transferable, if desired, to four-year programs.

Coalitions for occupational safety and health (COSH) groups, now numbering 24 around the country, have been an important source of education and training for the past 15 years. These independent, nonprofit, volunteer coalitions of union and community activists are supported by per capita union dues, foundation grants, and grass-roots fund-raising, and they provide technical assistance, education materials, and training on specific health and safety workplace hazards (Levenstein et al., 1984).

New to the labor education field are several independent, nonprofit agencies offering education, materials, research, and skill-building programs to union members, and a growing number of profit-making consultants who provide specialized programs on request. Newest of all are the joint labor-management structures in the auto industry. These were originally inspired by plant shutdowns and the need for worker retraining, but currently they are sponsoring workers' education on a wide range of subjects.[1]

New and Broader Constituencies

As in the mid-sixties, local union officers and activists continue to be the main participants in labor education progams. However, reflecting changing workplace structures, demographics, legislation, and labor-management relations, labor education in unions and universities is reaching out to top union leaders, union staff, women and minorities, union family members, high school teachers and students, and disabled workers.

Union Officers

Rarely did labor education in the past involve the leaders of international unions until a highly successful series of Brookings Institution seminars in the early 1960s for national union presidents led to the establishment of the George Meany Center for Labor Studies by the AFL-CIO in 1968 (Hoehler, 1988). Center programs focus almost exclusively on full-time union staff—for example, the recent programs for secretary-treasurers and administrative directors of national unions. Universities are beginning to offer seminars for top union leaders in their geographic areas.

Union Staff

Informal, experiential-based learning has long been part of the training of union staff representatives, but it is only in recent years that there has been a major focus by unions on more formal staff training (Gray, 1981).

Most of our surveyed unions reported that they are involved in some form of staff training (see Appendix Table). Those that are

---

[1]See Hugentobler, Robins, and Schurman, 1989; Ferman and Hoyman, 1991; Ferman, Hoyman, Cutcher-Gershenfeld, and Savoie, 1991; Schurman, Hugentobler, and Stack, 1991; and Savoie and Cutcher-Gershenfeld, 1991.

now send their staff people to courses at the Meany Center and to university labor education programs. In other words, there is a recognition of the need to develop new leadership, of the increased responsibilities assigned to international union staff, and of the growing complexity of industrial relations and, consequently, of staff roles.

What are the subjects offered? Almost all staff training covers such core subjects as collective bargaining, labor law, organizing, legislation, and political action and includes basic training in personal and communication skills and managerial and behavioral effectiveness. New courses, such as strategic planning, are offered in some programs.

Several unions are also conducting specialized staff training in teaching methods. The United Auto Workers, the United Food and Commercial Workers, the American Federation of State, County and Municipal Employees, and the International Brotherhood of Electrical Workers offer this training, and it is also included in the annual one-week introductory and advanced training seminars offered by the AFL-CIO Education Department at the Meany Center.

University and college labor programs play less of a role in staff training than do union departments. The Harvard Trade Union Studies Program, begun in 1942, reaches a relatively small number of international union officers and staff in its 11-week residential program each year. A number of other university labor education programs surveyed in our study reported occasional staff training, most of it in cooperation with a national union or the Meany Center. However, university education programs cite the participation of regional and local union staff in their conferences and workshops on specialized topics.

Rank-and-File Members

Course offerings for union activists and rank-and-file workers have expanded with programs related to workplace interests (apprenticeship, skill training, career planning, safety and health, workplace computer literacy) as well as those developed to meet personal interests and problems (community services, substance abuse, English as a Second Language, preretirement planning, literacy, AIDS education). In some cases these education programs are co-sponsored by unions, or by unions and employers, and are offered on company time.

Apprenticeship Training

Although apprenticeship training is the oldest form of union-sponsored workers' education, dating back to the origins of the U.S. labor movement (Barbash, 1955), new and innovative are the partnerships that have been forged between apprenticeship programs and institutions of higher education, which offer college credit for knowledge acquired through work experience and linkages to college degrees for apprentices when they graduate as journeymen.

Pioneering in the effort to achieve college credit for apprentices was the International Union of Operating Engineers, under a grant from the U.S. Department of Labor in 1972. Dual enrollment agreements under which apprentices engage in on-the-job training and enroll in college for related instruction have spread in the U.S., mainly in two-year community colleges. A number of university labor education centers are also offering courses on labor subjects specially designed for union members who are enrolled in job-site skill training.

Unique is the labor studies degree offered by the Harry Van Arsdale Center for Labor Studies at Empire State College and initiated by Local 3, International Brotherhood of Electrical Workers, and the Joint Industry Board of the Electrical Industry in New York City, which requires all apprentices to complete an associate degree and obtain a background in labor studies in order to become journeymen electricians in construction (Mantsios, 1984). The linkage between labor studies and apprenticeship that this model exemplifies is spreading, offering promising opportunities to inform new entrants to the workforce about unions and labor issues. Recently the U.S. Department of Labor awarded a grant to the AFL-CIO Human Resources Development Institute for an experimental program designed to aid in upgrading of apprenticeship training in an effort to offset displaced worker casualties (McMillan, 1991).

Community Services

Many rank-and-file union members, including a number who are not active in their unions, are engaged in an expanding network of membership services and employee assistance education programs run by unions and university labor education centers in cooperation with community agencies.

Currently, each year some 8000 rank-and-file union members enroll in union counseling courses, learn about community resources, and are trained to provide peer referrals to other union members facing personal or workplace problems. In addition, courses on plant closings, strike support, drug testing, substance abuse, blood banks, preretirement planning, consumer protection, and crime prevention are offered. Many of these programs are coordinated by some 50 Union Counsellor Associations around the country, set up by the AFL-CIO Community Services Department. In addition, a number of university labor education programs, as well as unions such as the American Federation of State, County and Municipal Employees, have developed education, training, and materials on various aspects of employee assistance.

Preretirement courses, started in the mid-sixties, have spread, providing members with information on paid benefits, financial planning, health care, legal issues, leisure activities, and community services (Charner, Fox, and Tractman, 1988). In Minnesota the United Way trains union members to help other workers write wills, get medical care, and process social security claims. The United Auto Workers union has developed audiovisuals and a self-study guide in a preretirement program that has recently been absorbed into its joint labor-management programs with Ford, General Motors, and Chrysler.

Women

Reflecting the expansion of the white-collar and service sectors and the dramatic increase in the numbers of women in the labor force, programs for women workers and union activists have been one of the most significant new developments in labor education in unions and universities. Starting in the mid-seventies with pioneering projects at Cornell University's New York State School of Industrial and Labor Relations and at the Labor Studies Center, University of Michigan (Wertheimer, 1981), these programs for women workers aim to assist them in attaining information, skills, and support for greater involvement in labor organizations and for union leadership and staff positions.

A ten-year report on women's programming at UCLEA-affiliated institutions (Haddad, 1985) indicated that over half the universities and colleges surveyed had conducted noncredit programs offered as one-day conferences and annual four-day weekend and one-week residential "schools," co-sponsored by university and union labor education programs in five regions in the U.S. for the past 15 years. Our survey confirms the continuing expansion of that program direction.

A number of unions—the Communications Workers, International Union of Electrical Workers, AFSCME, UAW, the Service Employees International Union, and the Teamsters, for example— also conduct annual national and regional conferences for women. The Coalition of Labor Union Women (CLUW) adds several days of workshops to their biennial convention. Topics highlighted in union and university programs include union leadership skills and basic "tool" courses, health and safety, new technology, pay equity, labor legislation, sexual harassment, labor history, and women and political issues.

Also included, moreover, are classes on personal issues and growth: time management, stress, substance abuse, career development, sexism and racism, and parenting skills. Many of these courses are co-taught by women members of university and union staffs.

Responding to a changing constituency, union and university labor education programs have increased the proportion of women on their staffs. In her survey of the number of women labor educators on the staffs of UCLEA-affiliated institutions, Anne Nelson (1985) reported a 20 percent increase in women staff members between 1973 and 1985. Currently, almost a third of labor educators on university/college staffs are women.

Minorities

African-American, Hispanic, Asian, and Arab workers and union members are the focus of programs in a number of labor education centers. In Michigan, a unique Title III state grant to a consortium of the university labor education programs, the Union Women/ Minorities Leadership Training Project, has produced full-time staffing and year-round programming for weekend and one-day conferences on workplace, union, family, and community issues for minority workers.

Several West Coast labor education centers (University of California, Los Angeles and Berkeley, and San Francisco Community

College) and Cornell University in New York City have developed workshops focusing on issues of Asian-American workers. Concerns of Hispanic workers and union members have been addressed at university labor centers such as Rutgers, Cornell, Oakland, Florida International, Michigan State, and UCLA.

A unique program in Los Angeles is sponsored by the AFL-CIO Labor Immigrant Assistance Project of the county federation of labor. This 100-hour, 25-week course provides classes in English and U.S. history and government for amnesty applicants who applied for legalization under the Immigration Reform and Control Act of 1986. Classes are offered at union halls, churches, worksites, and government agencies in Los Angeles and Orange counties. Students are also instructed in workplace English (the names of tools), workers' rights, employee benefits, and the labor movement.

English as a second language is also the focus of the program sponsored by the Southeastern Massachusetts University Labor Education Center in cooperation with the Amalgamated Clothing and Textile Workers' Union, the United Electrical Workers, and the International Ladies' Garment Workers' Union as part of a state-financed Workplace Education Project that was selected as an outstanding industry-education partnership by the Massachusetts Department of Education.

Disabled Workers

Classes and education programs for workers with disabilities are a recent development in labor education. Responding to the large numbers of hearing-impaired in the U.S. Postal Service, the American Postal Workers' Union (APWU) has developed regional and national annual conferences on issues of grievance handling, union participation, job mobility, collective bargaining, and employee assistance for these workers. Signers are used at all sessions of the conference programs, which include training workshops to develop an APWU network of hearing-impaired instructors who will teach or co-teach future education programs.

Eastern Michigan University's labor program has developed education and training materials to address the leadership skill-building, legislation, community resources, union participation, and jobsite building-accessibility issues of workers with various disabilities.

Family Members

The United Automobile Workers (UAW) Family Education Center at Black Lake, Michigan, a national residential center, runs year-round programs that involve union members and their families in "learning by doing"—participating in mock local unions "in which they discuss, make decisions and act on administrative problems and economic and social programs similar to those encountered in actual locals." In the years since its establishment in 1970, the Center has involved thousands of members and their families in a two-week experience designed to commit them to union goals and democratic procedures.

While the UAW program is unique, several other unions offer special sessions for spouses and children in connection with their national conventions and their regional summer schools. For example, the American Postal Workers Union sponsors a family-member training program on "Parenting." Recently the UAW-Ford joint program began to extend certain of its paid educational leave program offerings to family members at selected pilot plants.

High School Teachers and Students

High school teachers and students have been targeted by union and university labor educators in a variety of programs aimed to rectify the omission of information about organized labor from textbooks and curricula. Twenty-one states sponsor speakers' bureaus for classroom presentations. Many university labor centers have offered courses and programs to give teachers and students background information, new curricula, and materials.

The number of these programs is steadily increasing, an AFL-CIO Education Department report concludes. The leadership provided by the AFL-CIO Education Department and by unions such as the American Federation of Teachers, the International Ladies' Garment Workers' Union, the United Automobile Workers, the United Food and Commercial Workers, the Communication Workers of America, and the Teamsters has resulted in a range of new materials, publications, and programs.

Three programs stand out for their innovations. In Green Bay, Wisconsin, 46 middle-school classes took part in a 30-hour, 10-session program on labor sponsored by the Labor Agency of the United Way. The Bureau of Labor Education at the University of

Maine received a U.S. Department of Labor grant to increase the number of educators teaching labor law to students in Maine and neighboring states, a project that trained 275 educators and 896 students in 32 demonstration sites. And in a three-year pilot program in the 1980s, the International Brotherhood of Teamsters paid full tuition, travel, and living expenses for approximately 125 high school teachers each summer for two-week, three-credit graduate labor studies seminars at Cornell, University of California, Berkeley, and the University of Wisconsin.

New Delivery Systems for Labor Education

Although the short-term, noncredit course/workshop continues to be the typical form of labor education, college degree programs for union members emerged as the major development during the past 25 years and remains the most pervasive of the new delivery systems. Sparked by financial support provided by union-negoti-ated, tuition-refund benefits, encouraged by union education directors who view these degree-granting programs as advanta-geous for their union officers and staff, and welcomed by colleges seeking adult students, labor-oriented degree programs have expanded in number. According to a survey, in 1975 there were 47 institutions of higher education offering college degrees with a labor studies major (Gray, May 1976). While there have been a number of dropouts, colleges and universities continue to enter this field, bringing the estimated current total to 75.

Credit and degree programs have been developed both in universities with long-established labor education programs and in community colleges with no previous experience in the field (Morrison, 1980). New York City's highly unionized population can now choose among several undergraduate credit programs specifically designed for union members.

College labor studies programs vary in target students. Some design courses for members of a specific union; others recruit union members within a geographic area; still others offer courses to union members along with college-age students. Ranging in level from certificate programs to associate, bachelor, and master degrees, most are delivered in the traditional classroom mode.

Some experimentation is taking place with other forms of delivery. Independent study through correspondence leads to a one-year certificate from Indiana University that can be applied with more course work to a BS in labor studies. Classroom instruction is supplemented with individual mentoring and credit for knowledge acquired through experience in the degree program at Empire State College in New York City. Twice-a-year residential sessions supplemented with individual study leads to a degree from Antioch College in a program for union staff and activists at the George Meany Center. An MA program in labor and public policy at Empire State College recruits students nationally for periodic residential sessions and independent study. And an MA from the University of Massachusetts, designed to prepare participants for careers in the labor movement, includes graduate classroom study and a union internship.

College degree programs for labor union staff and activists parallel the business and public administration degrees required for aspirants to management-level jobs in government and industry. Anticipated by the rising education levels of union officials (Schwartz and Hoyman, 1984) and the increasing complexity of industrial relations, labor studies degree-holders have emerged in a number of union positions.

This trend, however, has sparked considerable discussion and debate (Lieberthal, 1977; Nash, 1978). Questions are raised about appropriate curriculum content (that is, the mix of industrial relations, labor-focused, and liberal arts courses), course materials, and faculty credentials. The proliferation of labor studies degree programs has influenced hiring criteria for university labor education and labor studies staff positions, usually a PhD, together with demonstrated research and publishing productivity. The importance of trade union experience has tended to diminish as the hiring criteria in the field becomes more concerned with academic credentials.

Starting in 1986, the George Meany Center has been testing the use of teleconferencing technology to reach large numbers and geographically dispersed union activists. Three successful teleconferences have been conducted to date—Negotiating Health Care Cost Containment, Right to Know About Workplace Chemicals, and Internal Organizing. The 1988 two-day teleconference was transmitted to 35 university labor education sites throughout the United States, utilizing 100 labor educators to reach about 3500 participants. These programs, conducted in cooperation with the AFL-CIO's Labor Institute for Public Affairs and national departments, involved special materials development and site coordinator training on the technological issues involved.

New Content Areas

Although a wide range of new topics have been introduced in labor education over the past 25 years, responses to our questionnaire and interviews indicate five major new content areas: health and safety, joint labor-management activities, technological change, basic skills instruction, and workers' culture.

Safety and Health

Safety and health issues have become an important focus of union, university, and community labor education programs. Beginning in the late 1960s with the coal miners' agitation for health rights and their organization of the Black Lung Association, and stimulated by the passage of the Occupational Safety and Health Act (OSHA) in 1970, labor educators have been providing a range of progams on workplace hazards. OSHA's "New Directions" grants, started in 1977, prompted a variety of programs to train workers in hazard recognition and control, worker and union legal rights, and labor-management workplace problem-solving of safety and health issues. After federal funds were cut, state funds were forthcoming, enabling many of these projects to continue.

Unions and universities responding to our survey report courses, conferences, and residential workshops on right-to-know laws, health and safety committees, collective bargaining, legal issues, OSHA regulations, workers' compensation, and utilizing community resources. Recent programs include drug-testing in the workplace, AIDS education, health effects of video display terminals, training the trainers on monitoring ergonomic issues, and the impact of the workplace on physical and mental health.

Following the passage of OSHA's Hazard Communication Standard that requires off-site and on-site instruction and refresher courses for workers, managers, and supervisors, a number of union and university programs received grants to train hazardous waste workers. There have also been joint union-management-university programs for systematic training of all employees/union members in hazard recognition.

Some of the most innovative work in this field has been done by the labor education centers at the University of California, Berkeley

and Los Angeles, and the University of Wisconsin where extensive
materials as well as intensive training courses have been developed.
The Michigan State University and University of Michigan labor
programs and the University of Michigan Environmental Health
Department developed a joint labor-management team of four
trainers in each of the 90 Ford plants in the U.S. in a program
sponsored by the UAW-Ford Employee Development Training
Program. An evaluation of the UAW-Ford effort (Hugentobler,
Robins, and Schurman, 1989) indicates that this "train the trainer"
(TTT) program was most successful where there was union
pressure for a systematic in-plant program implementation and
follow-through.

Throughout the country, labor education programs and COSHs
(coalitions of safety and health activists) have developed a variety
of training videos, visual aids, and other instructional materials on
issues, laws, regulations, contract language, and safety and health
grievances.

A concentration of specialty courses in occupational safety and
health constitutes a major in the college degree program offered by
the Center for Labor Studies at Empire State College in New York
City.

Participative Management and New Work Organization

Programming in response to what has been called "the new
industrial relations" has been the most controversial direction in
labor education in recent years (Banks and Metzger, 1989; Parker
and Slaughter, 1988; Cohen-Rosenthal and Burton, 1987). Beginning
in the mid-seventies, joint labor-management structures and
processes and, more recently, programs installing new forms of
work organization (the team concept, sociotechnical systems, and
autonomous workgroups) have created the need to train union
members to more effectively represent their own interests when
called upon to participate in these systems as well as to formulate
union responses and relationships to these developments.

New trends in policymaking, financing, curricula, and the
administration and evaluation of some of these programs are
described and discussed in other chapters of this volume.[2] Many

---

[2]See, in this volume, Chapters 2, 3, 5, 6, 7, 8, and 9 for U.S. trends and Chapters
10 and 11 for the experience in other countries.

university labor centers are being asked to provide educational services for union members and managers in these projects: education and training, new materials, and, in a few cases, technical help in conducting research for specific local unions involved in joint labor-management projects. We describe a few of the most adaptive and innovative of these programs.

In 1986, in conjunction with Wayne State University and the University of Michigan labor programs, and other resource people, the United Auto Workers and General Motors Human Resource Center inaugurated a systematic, four-week residential program, Paid Educational Leave (PEL), for top local union officers and leaders as well as some management officials (Schurman, Hugentobler, and Stack, 1991). Financed by nationally negotiated, jointly administered funds, the PEL curriculum includes courses on critical thinking and strategic planning, with a focus on the economics of the company and the industry in a global market, new developments in industrial relations, and the political context for labor and management. The PEL program has been adapted into a one-week format for local rank-and-file union members and supervisors. In their evaluation, Hugentobler, Schurman, and Stack (1988) reported significant changes in participants' perceptions of issues facing the union and the company and a positive overall assessment of the PEL experience.

The joint UAW-Ford and UAW-Chrysler national training centers have also adopted PEL-type programs, and this model has been adapted in two pilot projects—one on strategic planning for smaller industries and another for the construction industry's unions and contractors in Michigan.

The Labor Center at the University of California, Los Angeles, contracted to train the 5000 workers in the Van Nuys, California, General Motors plant to convert to a team-based work organization. Fifty-four hours of instruction were provided for each group of participants in a TTT delivery system, which included leadership skills, problem-solving, active listening, handling stress, health and safety, and timing jobs.

As in the UAW-Ford hazard recognition program, a need for large-scale union member training has led to a delivery system that identifies and trains unionists to be instructors of others. A concept of labor education that originated in the Pulp, Sulphite and Paper Workers and Papermakers unions a generation ago has now been successfully adapted and diffused in these current programs that are making new demands on labor educators.

Technology

Technological change is another major theme. In the 1950s numerous conferences on automation raised the specter of widespread displacement of workers by robots. Recently, specific attention focuses on union strategies for coping with the impact of actual changes taking place.

Notable is the International Association of Machinists' (IAM) Workers' Technology Bill of Rights, the programmatic theme of a one-week course for local union officers held at IAM's residential education center in Maryland. The Communications Workers developed an instructor's manual for training union activists about "Technological Change: Challenges and Choices." CWA education programs also alert members to the dangers of electronic surveillance with a manual on "Monitoring in Telecommunications." The UAW-GM Paid Education Leave (PEL) program emphasizes technological changes taking place in auto manufacturing.

Unions are negotiating training and retraining agreements for their members who are affected by workplace changes in methods and machinery. Several have established employer-funded programs for transitioning to new occupations. One of the most innovative is the contract negotiated by IAM and the U.S. Naval Research Laboratory in Maryland. It prohibits job displacement by technological changes, time-motion studies, and electronic workplace monitoring. However, it also sets up a comprehensive retraining program that works with management to redesign machines for productivity as well as for worker satisfaction and safety (Deutsch, 1987).

Several universities have played an active role in educating union members about new technology. For example, the University of Illinois, in cooperation with the City of Chicago's Technology Commission, designed a program to enable leaders of the Steelworkers' Union to participate more effectively in technological changes affecting their members.

The Labor and Technology Program of the State of Michigan, with a statewide labor advisory board, assists unions in taking a proactive approach to technology by conducting research on industry trends and technology implementation patterns. The program also provides implementation patterns, makes technology experts available for consultation, and develops training modules.

Basic Skills Instruction

Faced with foreign competition, technological change, job restructuring, and occupational shifts, unions are using their collective bargaining power to negotiate innovative employer-financed programs that upgrade the educational competencies of their members.

Basic skills classes are provided by a variety of sponsors, including unions, labor-management structures, partnerships with boards of education, community volunteer literacy organizations, and state government agencies, such as the Massachusetts Workplace Education Initiative that matched Job Training Partnership Act (JTPA) and other state monies to fund classes at 40 worksites.

Many union and university labor education programs report sponsorship of basic skills activities for union members, and others conduct needs' surveys, train union members to be workplace peer educators or education advisors, and consult on program materials and curricula.

A path-breaking, job-related program was negotiated by the UAW and the Ford Motor Company in 1982—the Employee Development and Training Program (EDTP)—that includes basic skills education for displaced Ford workers at more than 50 learning centers throughout the country. This model, whose negotiated financial support was doubled in 1984, has been emulated in bargaining agreements between the UAW and General Motors and Chrysler. A recent survey revealed a surprising amount of diffusion of this innovation to a full 40 percent of the union-employer pairs (Hoyman and Ferman, 1991).

Other unions that sponsor basic skills and literacy programs for their members, either through collective bargaining or government/ foundation grants, include the American Federation of State, County, and Municipal Employees Hospital and Health Care Workers, the Service Employees, the Seafarers, the Bricklayers, and the Communications Workers.

In New York City, a unique coalition of unions, the Consortium for Worker Literacy, serves approximately 450 union members and their families in a $2 million a year program launched in 1985. Classes at union halls, factories, schools, and housing projects provide information on the labor movement, workplace and family experiences, peer teaching, and a buddy-support system. Also in New York, District Council 37, with city funding, sponsors a comprehensive basic skills program which goes beyond literacy training to high school equivalency and career counseling.

Workers' Culture

An increasing number of cultural and artistic activities have been added to enrich labor education programming. From the innovative rank-and-file workers' theater company, "Workers' Lives/Workers' Stories," at the Labor Studies Center, University of Michigan, to the sponsorship of a rock musical, "Seattle 1919," by the Labor Center at Evergreen State College in Washington, there is renewed interest in using workers' culture as a union-building activity.

Two union programs were pioneers in incorporating workers' culture in labor education. One was ACTWU's THREADS project, funded by the National Endowment for the Humanities. From 1978 to 1982 it developed programs in 20 states for thousands of clothing workers, using labor music, plays, oral histories, and photos to document contributions of union members. The second was the Bread and Roses project of District 1199, National Union of Hospital and Health Care Employees. Aided by grants from public agencies and private foundations, this program developed theater productions, TV documentaries, art and photo exhibits, labor film festivals, and traveling musical theater troupes.

The UAW encourages workers' writing by including members' stories and poems in its publications. The labor program at Pennsylvania State University pioneered in incorporating oral history projects in its labor education programs.

Picking up this theme, several university and college labor studies programs offer credit courses on culture and worklife as well as noncredit workshops on labor history and workers' culture. Following its 1980 national conference on workers' culture, the Labor Studies Center at the University of Michigan initiated weekend workers' culture conferences, exhibits of worker art, and a week-long training course on the art of labor storytelling.

Innovative Approaches to Traditional Content Areas

The dominant focus of labor education for the past 50 years continues as the principal fare of both the unions and the universities today. All of the respondents to our survey reported offering "union-building" courses in collective bargaining and leadership skills for officers and activists, and most indicated that these classes are still the mainstay of their programs. Innovative aspects are to be found in the broad range of subjects covered, the increasing sophistication of teaching materials and methods, and the relatively new emphasis on strategic and policy considerations.

Collective Bargaining

As the content and scope of bargaining has broadened over the years, so has the training of union officials. For example, the George Meany Center, in a series of one-week offerings for union staff and officers, features courses on profit-sharing and employee stock ownership along with a long-term certificate program on employee benefits. National unions build on the Meany Center offerings with additional in-depth coverage of such issues as pay equity, job evaluation and reclassification, plant closing, and contracting out. University-sponsored conferences are briefing bargainers on such topics as the current interest in deregulation, bankruptcy, health care cost containment, and child care, backed up with a variety of published materials.

The current climate of employer demands for givebacks and the declining union bargaining power has inspired a new emphasis on bargaining strategies, including the potential use of corporate campaigns and alternatives to strikes. Examples of written materials relating to this theme include those dealing with corporate finance developed by Pennsylvania State University with funds from the State of Pennsylvania; Cornell University's *Guide to Information on Closely Held Corporations*, which focuses on building construction and other industries characterized by small employers; and the AFL-CIO Food and Allied Service Trades Department's *Manual of Corporate Investigation* for training programs with its affiliates. The many new programs and materials designed to increase the sophistication of bargainers about the economics of the corporations with which they negotiate draw on insights from accounting and finance, which are new subjects for labor education.

Techniques of teaching collective bargaining have been increasingly refined through the infusion of action techniques and psychological applications, many adapted from the more highly developed (and better financed) field of management education.

Role plays and case studies have been elaborated on to become collective bargaining games and simulations. For example, the Indiana University of Pennsylvania course, "How to Negotiate in Seven Hard Days and Nights," aims to build a fiercely competitive atmosphere through an intense one-week bargaining simulation relieved by "self-hypnosis relaxation techniques." Psychology is an important ingredient of the George Meany Center course on "The Art of Negotiation," which builds on concepts widely used in management training.

Video tapes are employed to enhance the effectiveness of collective bargaining training through simulation feedback, and computers are used to cost alternative bargaining strategies.

A recent survey of university educators (Ellinger and Nissen, 1984) reported that two-thirds of the respondents teach courses in steward training—characteristically, stressing technical skills such as investigation, screening and writing grievances, understanding legal responsibilities, and analyzing contract language, with most also adding new components. This traditional emphasis on labor relations has been supplemented with information on health and safety at work and human rights as well as intensive training in problem-solving skills (Broadbent, 1989). These findings are consistent with our survey results on new topics in steward training: "duty of fair representation," affirmative action, and occupational safety and health. Our respondents also reported that stewards are currently treated to psychological insights about their role, including communication and "assertiveness" skills.

Training for handling arbitration cases has proliferated and the program content has become more complex, reflecting new issues such as drug testing and mental health problems. Simulations and computer tracking techniques are new methods used in these courses.

New since 1965 is an emphasis on specialized education for the public sector of the labor movement.

Organizing

Organizing the unorganized has been an important theme of union-sponsored education from the earliest days, constituting the major focus during the 1930s (Rogin and Rachlin, 1968; Dwyer, 1977). Currently, there is renewed emphasis on organizing members as well as potential members.

Facing an increasingly uphill struggle to organize in a climate of sophisticated employer opposition and weak legal protection, unions are updating and improving skills and methods of researching target companies and employees, and of recruiting and training an in-house organizing committee. One-on-one interpersonal communication is emphasized as a concept and technique.

Organizer training has shifted from information-giving (about the law and merits of unionization) to in-depth practice in skills required for effective enlistment of members—speaking, planning, interpersonal and group relationships. How to cope with "union-busters" is another feature. Case studies and simulations immerse trainees in problem-solving and interpersonal skills development. The building and construction trade unions, traditionally exclusive and rarely active in labor education, have stepped up their pace of organizing activity in recent years, emerging as major sponsors and consumers of labor education services. The George Meany Center currently offers special organizing courses for unions in the building trades, adapted to the unique legal and labor relations aspects of the industry.

Another current trend is the training of rank-and-file members to organize, supplementing or replacing staff organizers. For example, the Sheet Metal Workers Union trains apprentices to be organizers on job sites with nonunion contractors. The Amalgamated Clothing and Textile Workers Union and the United Food and Commercial Workers train volunteer organizers by dividing them into management and labor teams and simulating an organizing campaign.

To bridge the gap between classroom and field work, the AFL-CIO Industrial Union Department set up an internship program in which trainees are assigned to work with experienced field organizers and graduates are referred to union organizing departments for full-time job openings. Evergreen State College, one of the most recent entrants to the field of labor education, also sponsors an organizer internship program that combines classroom and field work.

Internal organizing—that is, unionizing the organized—has become a major theme in both union- and university-sponsored programs. Promoted by the AFL-CIO Departments of Education and Organizing and Field Services, the programs stress one-on-one communications techniques. The AFL-CIO Education Department surveyed 7000 participants in their one-on-one training programs in 1987 and 1988 and found that more than half of the respondents (73 out of 131) were implementing some aspect of this program. Our survey confirms this finding, with most respondents including internal organizing and incorporating one-on-one techniques in their ongoing programs.

Union Administration and Leadership

Union leadership training, always popular, has evidenced the most dramatic changes in recent years, in both scope and methodology. What types of skills and knowledge do union leaders need to be effective? Early emphasis on parliamentary procedure and public speaking broadened in the post-World War II period to include training in group process and communications skills (Rogin and Rachlin, 1968). In the 1970s, training began to include more sophisticated approaches to interpersonal relationships.

Several unions have sponsored staff training that incorporates insights from the behavioral sciences and adapts concepts and techniques widely used in managerial training ("Management by Objectives" and "Transactional Analysis," for example) to problems of decisionmaking, problem-solving, and leadership in unions (Gray, 1981). Currently, the George Meany Center and several international unions and universities have elaborated further on organizational behavior for union leaders. Meany Center workshops for union staff include skills-training in communications and conflict resolution and a new course, "Effective Leadership Styles," which was adapted from staff observation of management training programs on this theme.

The Operating Engineers Union reports that all of its international representatives have completed a "systems" approach to organizational planning and management designed for the union by a management consulting firm. Progress of each individual toward acquiring the targeted skills and knowledge is tracked by computer (Israel, 1989). While many of the teaching techniques used in interpersonal and union leadership education have been borrowed from management, a few unions are designing their own. For example, the Service Employees International Union has developed "Power Game," a form of poker, which introduces participants to concepts of power relationships in an organization.

The union leader as manager is the new thrust of some recent programs for full-time staff and officers that are in the formative stage. The traditional union official, despite growing administrative supervisory responsibilities, has eschewed the self-image of being a "boss" (Bok and Dunlop, 1979). A new generation of labor leaders, many with college educations and a few with degrees in business administration, is becoming more aware of the need for training for managerial functions involved in leading large organizations.

Harvard University's 13-week Trade Union Program, the oldest continuous university leadership training program for union executives, has adapted its curriculum to incorporate material and insights from its executive development program for business leaders. It announces that part of its mission is to help union leaders "develop keener analytical, managerial and problem-solving skills." Currently, one of its courses is "Long Range Strategic Planning for Unions."

The University of California, Los Angeles, one of the universities that has ventured into the challenging field of managerial training for union leaders, recently conducted a seminar, "Human Resource Management for Union Chief Executives," with content paralleling executive training for business. Participants developed individual mission statements, analyzed their own organizations, studied and practiced tools for resolving internal organizational conflicts and improving organizational communications, and engaged in a planning and problem-solving exercise in managing organizational change.

These innovations in training for full-time union staff and elected officials are yet to be incorporated in ongoing educational work with local union officers, most of whom are volunteers. An exception is the Bricklayers and Allied Craftsmen, which has introduced a system of local union officer and business agent training based on self-assessments (that is, officers rate their own knowledge and skills in relation to the responsibilities of their union positions), which are translated into learning objectives that guide their selection of subjects to be studied.

At the local level, administrative training tends to be more technical, focusing on the specific responsibilities of the job—for example, record-keeping for local secretary-treasurers. A new thrust is training in the use of computers. The University of Wisconsin and Indiana University have taken the lead in offering training not only in how to use a computer, but how it can be applied to a variety of union functions. Indiana University cooperated with the International Association of Machinists in developing computer software adapted to union administrative and bargaining needs.

Economic Education

Economics, despite its importance to the collective bargaining and political goals of labor unions, has not been a frequently offered subject in labor education since the 1930s (Dwyer, 1977). Only one union, the United Auto Workers, lists this subject among its innovative offerings. The courses for staff and local officers emphasize such union-related economic issues as imports of foreign cars and exports of manufacturing plants to foreign soil (for example, the Maquilidora plants in Mexico), but also encompass broader questions relating to the national economy.

Institutionalizing a commitment to programs of "economic literacy for union members," Boston College, with a grant from the Fund for Improvement of Post-Secondary Education and working with the Massachusetts AFL-CIO, assigned teams of faculty and graduate students to research specific industries, including garment, ship-building, public schools, and hospitals, as a basis for developing curricula for teaching union activists about their own industries (Derber, 1987). Cornell ILR's Institute for Industry Studies grew out of experience with the UAW-PEL program and currently offers similar services to other industries in New York State.

The University of Minnesota has also given major emphasis to economics, designing specialized courses for railroad workers on "The Company's Ability to Pay" and "The Economics of the Railroad Industry," and developing an innovative television series, "Build Minnesota," which deals with the state's economy and its ability to attract jobs. "A Worker's Guide to Collective Bargaining Economics," published by the University of Maine, is designed to equip bargainers with knowledge of economic data sources and how to interpret and use them. The University of California, Berkeley, developed a conference for the International Brotherhood of Teamsters and published a bulletin on "Labor and the New Business Environment: A Guide for Union Representatives."

Labor-oriented resources for programs on economic themes are also available from the independent Labor Education Center for

Popular Economics in Amherst, Massachusetts, and the Center for Labor Education in New York City.

Political Education: Issues and Techniques

With growing union emphasis on political action has come stepped-up efforts to train activists in voter registration, fund-raising, and lobbying. Most of this activity is sponsored by unions, including national COPE departments and state and city central bodies. Nonetheless, many university labor education centers provide supplemental technical training along with course work on the political process and specific political issues.

Few among our respondents mentioned political education as an "innovative" program offering. One exception is Rutgers University, which provides an in-depth exposure to the functions and policies of state government in the form of a six-week internship for unionists, sponsored in cooperation with the New Jersey Department of Labor. The experience encompasses field work observation of state agencies as well as classroom study of the structure and functions of state government and legislative issues. Information acquired through the internship enables participants to advise their membership on a variety of issues and procedures involving state government (Steffen, 1987).

Labor Law

Labor law was rarely mentioned by survey respondents despite the fact that this subject is a staple of the labor education curriculum. The University of Maine is providing leadership in this field, training instructors and publishing texts and manuals for teachers of labor law in several New England states.

Labor History

Labor educators and labor leaders lament the neglect of labor history, but rarely do much about it. Promising developments that may help to fill this gap are the establishment of the George Meany Archives at the George Meany Center and the publication of *Labor Heritage*, a magazine written to appeal to a popular audience of union activists and members. Several universities, such as Pennsylvania State University, are collecting oral histories, helping unions to write their own histories, and publishing histories of labor unions in their states. The University of Minnesota sponsors a television program on this theme. Bus and walking labor history tours developed by the University of Illinois labor program in Chicago and the Illinois Labor History Society have been the models for similar activities in other states.

International Programs

Programs of international exchange mushroomed in the early post-World War II period, funded largely by U.S. government agencies (Agency for International Development and the U.S. Department of Labor). Cutbacks in funding have curtailed this type of interchange between U.S. trade unionists and their counterparts from other countries. The George Meany Center, for example, reports a decline of one-third in programs specially designed for visitors from abroad, and most of the university center international labor programs have been dropped. Nonetheless, interest in international issues and comparative labor practices continues and is reflected in university-sponsored seminars on labor practices in other countries, notably Sweden and Japan.

The International Affairs Department of the AFL-CIO, as well as affiliated regional centers in Asia, Africa, and Latin America, continue an active program of education for union leaders in other countries and conduct periodic conferences on international issues for union activists in the United States.

To broaden the background of union and management leaders, the Rutgers labor program, in conjunction with the Swedish Information Service, sponsored a series of seminars at 12 labor programs around the country on Sweden's approach to labor market questions. The University of Michigan's labor center also sponsored a two-day residential conference on the Swedish Approach to Work Environment and Work Organization, emphasizing the participatory nature and strong union involvement in these areas and using a number of Swedish labor, management, and university resource persons.

New Types of Services: Research and Technical Assistance

With growing professionalization of the education services to labor offered by colleges and universities has come increased interest in research. A recent survey revealed that two out of five labor educators employed by colleges and universities hold doctorate degrees and nine out of ten are currently engaged in some type of research activity (Clark and Gray, 1990). Research by labor educators is applied to classroom teaching, material development, and, in many institutions, new technical assistance services to unions.

Faculty members at the University of Oregon are studying the effect of disinvestment and international trade in cooperation with labor leaders in that state. They also took part in a major state study on comparable worth. Evergreen State University offers a contract service to assist Washington unions in researching corporation finances that impact on their bargaining negotiations. Similar services provided by labor education staff of the University of Missouri-Kansas City and Longview Community College also include information on relevant government regulations. In recognition of the growing research tie between universities and unions, Cornell University and the AFL-CIO Research Department have co-sponsored annual conferences that bring together union and university researchers around common research agendas.

Trends and Directions

Moving into the mainstream from its marginal position of yesteryear, labor education is currently receiving top-level attention and support within the labor movement. The AFL-CIO Committee on the Evolution of Work, in its widely circulated *The Changing Situation of Workers and Their Unions*, underscored its importance: "Unions should devote greater resources to training officers, stewards and rank-and-file members. In a vastly more complicated world, there is an increased need to provide training opportunities for local leadership and potential leaders. Training must encompass the skills local leaders need to function effectively and the information local leaders need to confront the issues of the day" (AFL-CIO, 1985).

Our survey indicates that an increasing number of unions, in compliance with this policy proscription, sponsor their own programs and/or utilize services provided by the George Meany Center and various universities and colleges. Responding to changes in the workplace, union-management relationships, and society, labor education is broadening its scope and outreach.

During the post-World War II years, unions and labor services in universities tended to concentrate on "bread and butter" subjects related to union building. Today the curriculum of offerings has expanded to service the needs of working people as union members and job holders and as individuals with careers, personal development interests, and family and community relationships. In addition, traditional "bread and butter" subjects—collective bargaining, union administration, and organizing, for example—have been transformed in content to reflect the changing realities of today's industrial relations scene.

While leaders and activists continue to be the principal consumers for labor education services, many programs reach rank-and-file workers and their families and even young people in school. Participants are more reflective of the ethnic mix in American society, and women are increasingly represented.

Changes in subject matter and participants that demand in-depth treatment of those subjects have fostered specialization among providers and enhanced professionalization for labor educators. Pedagogical methods that continue to rely on participation of adult learners are increasingly sophisticated in form and design, drawing on available technology and even borrowing techniques from the more extensively financed programs offered by business and industry.

Despite these positive trends, there are many unresolved questions that call for further analysis and study. Most important is an examination of priorities and whether limited resources are being stretched too thin. This is the old question of "Knowledge for What?", as Professor Robert Lynd challenged the UAW's first national education conference in 1955, and one that is periodically reexamined in the *Labor Studies Journal*. Are there long-range goals that go beyond skill training and organizational efficiency (Schachhuber, 1979)?

Labor educators also debate the merits and long-term impacts of "jointness"—that is, co-sponsorship with management in educational and training activities. What are the trade-offs from this type of collaboration? Labor educators question the desirability of training union leaders to "manage" their organizations. And even those who accept the concept of labor leaders as managers express concern about the applicability of concepts and materials and particularly the use of instructors from business administration to the differing environment and goals of unions. Another unknown is the impact of credentialism—degree programs and academic pressures on labor education—on the social commitment that has characterized labor education.

Labor education is increasingly accepted but poorly financed in unions and universities. Still missing is a system of public support and coordination that exists for labor education in a number of West European countries.

Looking ahead to the 1990s, there is an urgent need for a comprehensive analysis of all aspects of labor education on the scale of the two-year Rogin and Rachlin study in 1965-66. Included should be an assessment of the educational needs of the new workforce and an inventory of the most effective programs servicing these needs. Also needed are smaller scale demonstration projects and studies to evaluate alternative approaches to teaching and delivering labor education as well as a survey of the long-term impact of labor education on organizational sponsors and individual participants.

Continuing research and evaluation will assist labor educators in dealing with unresolved issues and providing more effective educational services in the years ahead. It will also help unions develop educational agenda and priorities to better serve their members in rapidly changing workplaces and a global economy.

APPENDIX TABLE

Innovations in Labor Education
(As Reported by Program Directors in 1988 and 1989)

Innovations in Terms of Constituencies	Organizations Reporting
Top Union Officials (national or regional)	GMC, UCLA
Full Time Staff	GMC, UAW, U WISC, IUP, ILGWU, BAC, IBEW, CU, AIW, IAM, CWA, U ILL, UFCW, APWU, IUOE, OPEIU
Local Union Leaders (officers and stewards)	UAW, GCIU, U MA, UCLA, UA, IUP, EMU, U WISC, U ILL, U M-KC, UWV, U MICH, AFSCME, H 1199, U IOWA, IBT, OPEIU
Rank-and-File Workers	UAW, ILGWU, BAC, IUOE, AFSCME 37, AIW, MSU, WSU, CU, NYS AFL-CIO, NYCCLC, U MA, U WISC, U ILL
Families of Members	UAW, ILGWU, NYS AFL-CIO, APWU
High School Students	PWU, U WISC, CU, UCB, UM-KC
Joint Labor-Management	MSU, U MICH, UWV, UAW, PSU, IBT, U WISC, CU, U ILL, U IOWA
Women	OAK U, MSU, WSU, EVSU, UO, MSU, SEMU, RU, UCLA, MASS AFL-CIO, U MICH, CU, AFSCME, SEIU, CWA, IUE, EMU, U MINN, U ILL, U IOWA, U ALA, PSU

APPENDIX TABLE (*Continued*)

Innovations in Labor Education
(As Reported by Program Directors in 1988 and 1989)

Minorities (Blacks, Hispanics, Asians)	MSU, CU, UCLEA, U MICH, EMU, U MINN, U ILL, WSU, UOUCD, OAK U, U MASS, RU, SFSC, SEMU, ILGWU
Differently Abled	EMU, APWU
Themes	*Organizations Reporting*
Work and Family	UO, CU, APWU, ACTWU, OAK U
Work Organization	UCLA, IUP, UO, PSU, UWV, CU, U MICH, U WISC, MSU, U IOWA, U ILL, WSU
Labor's Image	PSU, U MA, WSU
Technology	UCLA, MASS AFL-CIO, CWA, IAM, U IOWA, MSU, RU, CU
Occupational Safety and Health	MSU, OAK U, UO, IUP, U MA, U WISC, AIW, CU, U MICH, UCLA, UCB, U IND, PSU, RU, ESC, NYS AFL-CIO, UWV, U ILL, U IOWA
Computer Training	U MICH, MSU, OAK U, CU, U IND, UAW, IAM, GMC
Health Care Issues	UO, EMU, UCB, PSU, U ILL, MSU, RU, U WISC
Substance Abuse, Drug Testing and AIDS	MSU, AFL-CIO, AFSCME, APWU, U MINN, OAK U, ESU, UO, U WISC, UCB, NYS AFL-CIO, CU, PSU, EMU, U ILL, U MA, SEMU, U MICH, CU
Worker Culture and Multiculture Education	U MICH, SFSC, U IOWA, H 1199, UCLA, ESU, U MASS, SEMU, WSU, UAW, RU, ILGWU, ACTWU
Literacy and Bilingual Education	ILGWU, IBT 237, AFSCME 37, BAC, SE MU, NYCCLC, MASS AFL-CIO, OAK U,U IND, UAW
Approaches to Traditional Themes	*Organizations Reporting*
Collective Bargaining	U ALA, UCLA, IUP, UO, U MASS, PSU, UWV, U IOWA, UAW, EMU, U MI-KC, GMC, SEIU, CU, AFSCME, AIW, IAM, MSU, RU
Community Services	AFL-CIO (national, state and city)
Organizing	UO, U WISC, GMC, AFL-CIO, SEIU, IBEW, CWA, ESU, CU, U MA, U ILL, MSU, RU, UFCW, OPEIU
Union Administration and Leadership	UCLA, IUP, UO, U MA, ILGWU, GMC, IBT, SEIU, IUOE, CU, AFSCME, MSU, UAW, U MICH, UO

APPENDIX TABLE (*Continued*)

Innovations in Labor Education
(As Reported by Program Directors in 1988 and 1989)

Political Education	RU, ESU, SEIU, AFSCME, CU
Labor Law	UCLA, U MA, EMU
Economic Education	PSU, UCB, CU, UAW, U MINN, U ILL, U IOWA, MSU
Labor History	U MA, PSU, WSU
International	AFL-CIO, WSU, RU, U MICH, CU
Methods and Materials	*Organizations Reporting*
Instructor Training	UAW, UCLA, UO, UFCW, U MICH, GMC, IBEW
Video	UAW, IUP, UCLA, GMC, WSU, U MINN
Computer Applications	IAM, UAW, U IND
Simulations and Games	IUP, UO, SEIU, CU
Materials	UAW, IUP, U MA, EMU, AFL-CIO, PSU, EMU, SEIU
Delivery Systems	*Organizations Reporting*
Credit and Degree Programs	GMC, CU, ESC, PSU, RU, SFSU, U IND, U MASS, U MINN, UO, EMU, YU, ESU
Television and Teleconferencing	GMC, AFL-CIO, U MINN, CU, UA, UCB, UCLA, CWA, U ILL, U IND, U IOWA, U MA, RU, PSU, IUP, UWV, U WISC
Study Circles	IUP, BAC
Research and Technical Assistance for Unions	ESU, UO, U MI-KC, U IND, CU, U IOWA, PSU, RU

CODE FOR SURVEY RESPONDENTS

ACTWU	Amalgamated Clothing and Textile Workers Union
AFL-CIO	American Federation of Labor-Congress of Industrial Organizations, Headquarters Staff
AFSCME	American Federation of State, County and Municipal Employees
AFSCME 37	District Council 37
AIW	Allied Industrial Workers
APWU	American Postal Workers
BAC	Bricklayers and Allied Craftsmen
CWA	Communications Workers of America
CU	Cornell University
EMU	Eastern Michigan University
ESC	Empire State College, Harry Van Arsdale School for Labor Studies

CODE FOR SURVEY RESPONDENTS (*Continued*)

ESU	Evergreen State University
GCIU	Graphic Communications International Union
HU	Hospital Union, Local 1199
IAM	International Association of Machinists
IBEW	International Brotherhood of Electrical Workers
IBT	International Brotherhood of Teamsters
IBT 237	International Brotherhood of Teamsters, Local 237
ILGWU	International Ladies Garment Workers Union
IUOE	International Union of Operating Engineers
IUP	Indiana University of Pennsylvania
M. AFL-CIO	Massachusetts AFL-CIO
MSU	Michigan State University
NYCCLC	New York State University
NYS AFL-CIO	New York State AFL-CIO
OAK U	Oakland University
PSU	Pennsylvania State University
OPEIU	Office and Professional Employees International Union
QC	Queens College
RU	Rutgers University
SEIU	Service Employees International Union
SEMU	Southeastern Massachusetts University
SFSU	San Francisco State University
UA	University of Alabama
UAW	United Automobile Workers
UCB	University of California, Berkeley
UCLA	University of California, Los Angeles
UFCW	United Food and Commercial Workers
U ILL	University of Illinois
U IND	University of Indiana
U IOWA	University of Iowa
U MA	University of Maine
U MASS	University of Massachusetts, Boston and Amherst
U MICH	University of Michigan
U MINN	University of Minnesota
U MI-KC	University of Missouri, Kansas City and Longview Community College
UO	University of Oregon
UWV	University of West Virginia
U WISC	University of Wisconsin
YU	Youngstown University
WSU	Wayne State University

References

Abbott, William L. "College Credits: Trend in Apprenticeships." *Worklife* (September 1977), pp. 27–30.

AFL-CIO. *The Future of Work*. Washington: AFL-CIO, 1983.

AFL-CIO Committee on the Evolution of Work. *The Changing Situation of Workers and Their Unions*. Washington: AFL-CIO, 1985.

Aronson, Rondal, and Charles Rooney. "Teaching Them What They Already Know: College Education and Working Class Adults." *Labor Studies Journal* 3 (Spring 1978), pp. 19–30.

Azzan, Cynthia Conway. "A New Beginning: Labor Education in the Graphic Arts Union." *Labor Studies Journal* 7 (Winter 1983), pp. 232–39.

Banks, Andy, and Jack Metzger. "Participating in Management." *Labor Research Review* 7 (Fall 1989).

Barasch, Frances K. "Learning in the Workplace: Stronger Support for the Union." *Change* 13 (April 1985), pp. 42–45.

Barbash, Jack. *Universities and Unions in Workers' Education.* New York: Harper & Bros., 1955.

Beck, John P., and Janet Schneider. "None of Us Alone Knows as Much as All of Us Together: Participatory Learning for Worker Participation." *Labor Studies Journal* 8 (Winter 1983), pp. 287-300.

Bertelsen, P., P. Fordham, and J. London. *Evaluation of the Wayne State University Studies and Weekend College Program.* Paris: UNESCO, 1977.

Bilicic, George William. "An Examination and Analysis of the United Steelworkers Union of America Continuing Education Program in Relation to Responsiveness, Organization and Projection." PhD dissertation, University of Wyoming, 1972.

Bok, Derek, and John Dunlop. "The Administration of Unions." Chapter 5 in *Labor and the American Community.* New York: Simon and Schuster, 1979. Pp. 138-88.

Boyle, George V. "Functions of University Labor Education Programs." *Labor Studies Journal* 2 (Fall 1977), pp. 139-44.

Brickner, Dale. "National Allies—Organized Labor and Community Colleges." *Organized Labor and Community Colleges: Report of the American Association of Community and Junior Colleges.* United Auto Workers and AFL-CIO Assembly, Washington, December 8-10, 1975. Pp. 9-14.

Broadbent, Brooke. "Identifying the Education Needs of Union Stewards." *Labor Studies Journal* 14 (Summer 1989), pp. 46-60.

Brotslaw, Irving. "A Pre-Retirement Education Program." *Labor Studies Journal* 3 (Spring 1978), pp. 41-45.

Burns, Greg, Gene Daniels, and Tony DeAngelis. "Proving Union Leadership Education: For a Change." *Labor Studies Journal* 11 (Winter 1987), pp. 238-57.

Byrd, Barbara, and Clark Everling. "Discovering Working-Class Culture: A Case Study in Curriculum Development." *Labor Studies Journal* 8 (Spring 1983), pp. 18-33.

Catlett, Judi. "After the Goodbyes: A Long-Term Look at the Southern Summer School for Union Women." *Labor Studies Journal* 10 (Winter 1986), pp. 300-11.

_____. "Reaching Workers Off the Job: The Southern Summer School for Union Women." *Lifelong Learning* 9 (April 1986), pp. 4-5.

Charner, C. A., and A. Rolinski, eds. *Responding to the Educational Needs of Today's Workplace, New Dimensions for Continuing Education.* San Francisco: Jossey-Bass, 1987.

Charner, Ivan, Shirley Fox, and Lester Tractman. *After Retirement: Local Union Programs and Services for Retirees.* Washington: National Institute for Work and Learning, 1988.

Clark, Paul, and Lois Gray. "Research Activities Among Labor Educators: Results of a Survey." *Proceedings* of the 42nd Annual Meeting, Industrial Relations Research Association, 1989. Madison, WI: IRRA 1990.

Cohen-Rosenthal, Edward. "Enriching Workers' Lives: Education Programs of the IBEW." *Change* 11 (July 1979).

Cohen-Rosenthal, Edward, and Cynthia E. Burton. *Mutual Gains: A Guide to Union-Management Cooperation.* New York: Praeger, 1987.

Coxon, Dewayne Allen. "A Description of Labor Studies Programs at Michigan Colleges and Universities and a Study of the Attitudes of the Participants." PhD dissertation, Michigan State University, 1978.

Daniels, Gene, Roberta Till-Retz, Larry Casey, and Tony DeAngelis. *Labor Guide to Local Union Leadership.* Englewood Cliffs, NJ: Prentice-Hall, 1986.

Daws, Lee A. "The Development of Interactive Skills." *Labor Education Viewpoints,* undated, pp. 22-25.

Denker, Joel. *Unions and Universities: The Rise of the New Labor Leader.* Montclair, NJ: Allanheld Osmun, 1981.

_____. "Successful Adult Workers' Education Programs." Topic Paper No. 4, Labor Institute for Human Enrichment, Inc., 1982.

Derber, Charles. "Worker Education for a Changing Economy: New Labor Academic Partnerships." *New Directions for Continuing Education* (Spring 1987), pp. 49-57.

Deutsch, Steven. "Successful Worker Training Programs Help Ease Impact of Technology." *Monthly Labor Review* (November 1987), pp. 15-17.

Dwyer, Richard E. "An Examination of the Development of Labor Studies at Rutgers University, 1931-1974: A Study in Union-University Cooperation." EdD dissertation, Rutgers University, 1975.

_____. "Workers' Education, Labor Education, Labor Studies: An Historical Delineation." *Review of Educational Research* 47 (Winter 1977), pp. 179-207.

_____. *Labor Education in the United States: An Annotated Bibliography.* Metuchen, NJ: Scarecrow Press, 1977.

Dwyer, Richard E., Miles Galvin, and Simeon Larson. "Labor Studies: In Quest of Industrial Justice." *Labor Studies Journal* 2 (Fall 1977), pp. 95-131.

Eiger, Norman. "Labor Education—A Past and Future View." *New Jersey Adult Educator* (Winter 1975), pp. 13-15.

Ellinger, Charles, and Bruce Nissen. "A Case Study of a Failed QWL Program: Implications for Labor Education." *Labor Studies Journal* 11 (Winter 1987), pp. 195-219.

_____. "University and College Steward Training Programs: A Report and Evaluation." *Labor Studies Journal* 9 (Spring 1984), pp. 19-45.

Ferman, Louis A., Michele Hoyman, Joel Cutcher-Gershenfeld, and Ernest J. Savoie, eds. *Joint Programs for Training and Personal Development of Workers: New Initiatives in Union-Management Relations.* Ithaca, NY: ILR Press, Cornell University, 1991.

Ferman, Louis, and Michele Hoyman. "Service Delivery in Joint Training Programs." Chapter 9 in *Joint Programs for Training and Personal Development of Workers: New Initiatives in Union-Management Relations*, eds. Louis A. Ferman, Michele Hoyman, Joel Cutcher-Gershenfeld, and Ernest J. Savoie. Ithaca, NY: ILR Press, Cornell University, 1991.

Ferman, Louis A., Michele Hoyman, Joel Cutcher-Gershenfeld, and Ernest J. Savoie. "Editors' Introduction." In *Joint Programs for Training and Personal Development of Workers: New Initiatives in Union-Management Relations*, eds. Louis A. Ferman, Michele Hoyman, Joel Cutcher-Gershenfeld, and Ernest J. Savoie. Ithaca, NY: ILR Press, Cornell University, 1991.

Filippelli, Ronald L. "The Uses of History in the Education of Workers." *Labor Studies Journal* 5 (Spring 1980), pp. 3-12.

Franklin, Barbara Hyes. *Leadership Training for Union Women.* New York: Coalition of Labor Union Women, 1983.

Friedman, Harvey L. "Labor Studies Curricula: The Development of the Professional Labor Specialist." *Proceedings* of the 41st Annual Meeting, Industrial Relations Research Association, 1988. Madison, WI: IRRA, 1989. Pp. 468-73.

Galvin, Miles, and Edward Gonzalez, Jr. "Reaching Out: New York's Hispanic Leadership Training Project." *Labor Studies Journal* 7 (Spring 1982), pp. 3-19.

Glass, Ronald D. "New Life for Labor Studies: Rediscovering America's Working Heritage." *American Educator* (Fall 1982).

Golaszewski, Jean M., and Joyce L. Kornbluh. *Women Workers View Their Learning.* Ann Arbor: Institute of Labor and Industrial Relations, University of Michigan, 1983.

Golatz, Helmut. "Labor Studies: New Kid on Campus." *Labor Studies Journal* 2 (Spring 1977), pp. 15-22.

Gomberg, William. "Education and Leisure: A New Curricula." *Change* 11 (July 1979), pp. 30-34.

Goode, Bill. "Point of View: Liberal Education for Labor." *Labor Studies Journal* 5 (Spring 1980), pp. 62-69.

Gray, Lois S. "The American Way in Labor Education." *Industrial Relations* 5 (February 1966), pp. 53-66.

_____. "Labor Studies Credit and Degree Programs: A Growth Sector of Higher Education." *Labor Studies Journal* 1 (May 1976), pp. 34-51.

_____. "Organized Labor and Community Colleges." *Labor Education* 32 (October 1976), pp. 34-40.

_____. "Academic Degrees for Labor Studies: A New Goal for Unions." *Monthly Labor Review* (June 1977), pp. 15–20.

_____. "Trends in Selection and Training of International Union Staff: Implications for University and College Labor Education." *Labor Studies Journal* 5 (Spring 1980), pp. 13–24.

_____. "Unions Implementing Managerial Techniques." *Monthly Labor Review* (June 1981), pp. 3–13.

Haddad, Carol. "Ten-Year Report on Women's Labor Education at UCLEA-Affiliated Institutions." Lansing, MI: MSU Labor Program Service, March 1985.

Hakken, David. "Impacts of Liberation Pedagogy: The Case of Workers' Education." *Journal of Education* 165 (Winter 1983), pp. 113–29.

Herring, George Surrey. "A Study of an Inter-Institutional Effort for Preparing Minority Trade Union Leaders: A Programmatic Alternative for Higher Education." EdD dissertation, University of California, Berkeley, 1977.

Hoehler, Fred K., Jr. "Labor Education and the Academy." *Liberal Education* 65 (Summer 1979), pp. 234–40.

_____. "Notes from a Special Project." *Labor Studies Journal* 13 (Winter 1988), pp. 3–12.

Hoyman, Michele, and Louis A. Ferman. "The Scope and Extent of Joint Labor-Management Training Programs." Chapter 1 in *Joint Programs for Training and Personal Development of Workers: New Initiatives in Union-Management Relations*, eds. Louis A. Ferman, Michele Hoyman, Joel Cutcher-Gershenfeld, and Ernest J. Savoie. Ithaca, NY: ILR Press, Cornell University, 1991.

Hugentobler, Margrit, Susan Schurman, and Hal Stack. "UAW-GM, Hydramatic Division, Local Paid Education Leave Program." Evaluation Report. Ann Arbor: Institute of Labor and Industrial Relations, University of Michigan, 1988.

Hugentobler, Margrit, Tom Robins, and Susan Schurman. "How Unions Can Improve the Outcomes of Joint Health and Safety Training Programs." 1989. Unpublished.

Israel, Phyllis. "Education and Training Programs of the Operating Engineers Union." Unpublished report to the National Institute of Education, Program for Educational Policy and Organization, June 1989.

Kennedy, Don, ed. *Labor and Reindustrialization: Workers and Corporate Change*. University Park: Pennsylvania State University, Department of Labor Studies, 1984.

Kingery, Lionel Bruce. "Labor Studies as an Academic Field of Study: Establishing an Undergraduate Curriculum for Organized Labor in America's Postsecondary Institutions." EdD dissertation, Wayne State University, 1981.

Knauss, Keith, Judith A. Redwine, and Paul A. Joray. "Improving Labor Studies Courses Through the Use of the Student Evaluation Committee." *Labor Studies Journal* 5 (Winter 1981), pp. 179–85.

Knauss, Keith. "Evaluating Non-Credit Labor Education Programs: Practices and Problems." *Labor Education Viewpoints*, Lincoln, ME, undated, pp. 13–21.

Kochan, Thomas, Harry Katz, and Robert B. McKersie. *The Transformation of American Industrial Relations*. New York: Basic Books, 1986.

Levenstein, Charles, Leslie I. Boden, and David H. Wagman. "COSH: A Grass-Roots Public Health Movement." *American Journal of Public Health* 74 (September 1984), p. 964.

Lieberthal, Mil. "On the Academization of Labor Education." *Labor Studies Journal* 1 (Winter 1977), pp. 235–45.

_____. "Osmotic Process in Labor Education and Labor Studies." *Labor Studies Journal* 5 (Fall 1980), pp. 115–23.

Luxewnberg, S. "Labor Studies Blossom in Community Colleges: Cooperation with Unions." *Change* 11 (July 1979), pp. 57–59.

MacKenzie, John R. "Development and Functions of the University and College Labor Education Association." *Labour Education* 54 (January 1984).

_____. "Education and Training in Labor Unions." 36 pp. 1982.

_____. *Labor Education: New Dimensions, Materials and Methods in Continuing Education.* Kevins Publications, 1976.
Mantsios, Greg. "Educating the Ranks: The First Five Years of Local 3's College Program for Electrical Apprentices." *Labor Studies Journal* 9 (Fall 1984), pp. 151–66.
Marrone, John J. "New Directions for Labor Education." *Proceedings* of the 42nd Annual Meeting, Industrial Relations Research Association, 1989. Madison, WI: IRRA, 1990.
McKean, Ronald L., and Larry D. Terry. "Evaluation of a Minorities Leadership Institute in a Large Labor Union." *Labor Studies Journal* 13 (Spring 1988), pp. 58–67.
McMillan, Michael G. "Fostering Labor-Management Cooperation in Training Dislocated Workers: What Does It Really Take?" Chapter 6 in *Joint Programs for Training and Personal Development of Workers: New Initiatives in Union-Management Relations*, eds. Louis A. Ferman, Michele Hoyman, Joel Cutcher-Gershenfeld, and Ernest J. Savoie. Ithaca, NY: ILR Press, Cornell University, 1991.
Michaelson, Elana. "Labor Studies and the Assessment of Experiential Learning." *Labor Studies Journal* 10 (Fall 1985), pp. 139–52.
Morrison, Walbert. "Community College-Labor Union Cooperation: Program in Labor Studies." EdD dissertation, Teachers College, Columbia University, 1980.
Nash, Al. "The Walter and May Reuther UAW Family Center." *Free Labour World* (May 1973), pp. 14–16.
_____. "Labor College and Its Student Body." *Labor Studies Journal* 1 (Winter 1977), pp. 253–76.
_____. "Labor Education, Labor Studies and the Knowledge Factor." *Labor Studies Journal* 3 (Spring 1978), pp. 5–18.
_____. "The University Labor Education: A Marginal Occupation." *Industrial and Labor Relations Review* 32 (October 1978), pp. 10–38.
National Joint Apprenticeship and Training Committee for Operating Engineers. "Dual Enrollment as an Operating Engineer Apprentice and Associate Degree Candidate." Final Report, December 31, 1975.
Nelson, Anne. "Women's Representation on the Staffs of UCLEA Institutions." New York: NYSSILR, Cornell University, March 1985.
"The New Industrial Relations." *Business Week*, May 11, 1981.
Parker, Mike, and Jane Slaughter. *Choosing Sides: Unions and the Team Concept.* Detroit Labor Notes. South End Press, 1988.
Parsons, Michael D. "Teaching Workers to Deal with Job Stress: A Four Step Model." *Lifelong Learning* 10 (April 1987), pp. 4–6.
Remington, John. "The Impact of Evaluation on Professional Standards." *Labor Studies Forum,* Newsletter of the University and College Labor Education Association 1 (Fall 1988), pp. 1–2.
Repas, Bob. "Methods and Techniques, University Instructor Training Programmes for Teaching Shop Stewards." *Labour Education* 23 (1974), pp. 40–44.
Roberts, Higdon C., Jr. "Labor Education Organizational Participation." *Adult Leadership* 25 (1976), pp. 77–80.
_____. "Notes on a Rank and File Program." *Labor Studies Journal* 1 (Winter 1977), pp. 246–52.
_____. "Problems in Program Development and Implementation in Labor Education." *Adult Leadership* 23 (1975), pp. 197–98.
Rogin, Larry, and Marjorie Rachlin. *Survey of Adult Education Opportunities for Labor: Labor Education in the United States.* Washington: National Institute of Labor Education, 1968.
Ronchi, Don. "A Psychological Parable for Labor Education." *Labor Studies Journal* 4 (Fall 1979), pp. 99–108.
Rundell, Malcolm Ray. "A Survey of the Use and Potential of Non-Traditional Methods of Education Within the U.S. as Exemplified by Labor Education at the Higher Education Level." EdD dissertation, University of Houston, 1975.

Sandver, Marcus Hart, and Harry R. Blaine. "Teaching: The Development and Implementation of a Real-World Collective Bargaining Simulation." *Labor Studies Journal* 5 (Fall 1980), pp. 106-14.

Savoie, Ernest J., and Joel Cutcher-Gershenfeld. "Reflections on the Governance of Joint Training Initiatives." Chapter 10 in *Joint Programs for Training and Personal Development of Workers: New Initiatives in Union-Management Relations*, eds. Louis A. Ferman, Michele Hoyman, Joel Cutcher-Gershenfeld, and Ernest J. Savoie. Ithaca, NY: ILR Press, Cornell University, 1991.

Schachhuber, Dieter. "The Missing Link in Labor Education." *Labor Studies Journal* 4 (Fall 1979), pp. 148-58.

Schurman, Susan, Margrit Hugentobler, and Hal Stack. "Creating Educational Partnerships for a Changing Economy: Lessons from the UAW-GM Paid Educational Leave Program." Chapter 4 in *Joint Programs for Training and Personal Development of Workers: New Initiatives in Union-Management Relations*, eds. Louis A. Ferman, Michele Hoyman, Joel Cutcher-Gershenfeld, and Ernest J. Savoie. Ithaca, NY: ILR Press, Cornell University, 1991.

Schwartz, Arthur R., and Michele M. Hoyman. "The Changing of the Guard: The New American Labor Leader." *The Annals* of the American Academy of Political and Social Science 473 (May 1984), pp. 64-75.

Seeber, Ron. "The Industrial Relations Labor Studies Nexus." *Proceedings* of the 42nd Annual Meeting, Industrial Relations Research Association, 1989. Madison, WI: IRRA. 1990.

Shore, Jane. "Education Fund of District Council 37: A Case Study." *Worker Education and Training Policies Project*, 1979.

Sorcinelli, Gino. "Kohlberg's Theory of Moral Development: Its Implications for Steward Training." *Lifelong Learning: The Adult Years* 5 (December 1981), pp. 14-17.

Sorcinelli, Mary Deane, and Gino Sorcinelli. "Faculty Development in a Labor Studies Credit Program." *Labor Studies Journal* 5 (Winter 1981), pp. 186-98.

Stack, Hal, and Carroll Hutton, eds. *Building New Alliances: Labor Unions and Higher Education*. San Francisco: Jossey-Bass, 1980.

Steffen, Robert A. "On-the-Job Study of State Government: A Unique Internship for Union Leaders." *Labor Studies Journal* 12 (Fall 1987), pp. 65-76.

Stern, James L., and Barbara D. Dennis, eds. *Trade Unionism in the United States: A Symposium in Honor of Jack Barbash*. Madison: University of Wisconsin, Industrial Relations Research Institute, 1981.

Tyler, Gus. "The University and the Labor Union: Educating the Proletariat." *Change* 11 (February 1979), pp. 32-37.

UCLEA. Abstracts of papers/presentations given at the 1987 and 1988 Annual Meetings.

————. *Membership and Resource Directory of Institutions and Professional Staff, 1989-1990*. Cincinnati, OH: UCLEA, 1989.

University of California, Berkeley, Center for Labor Research and Education. "Labor and the New Business Environment: A Guide for Union Representation." June 1980.

Wertheimer, Barbara. "Union Women: A New Focus for Labor Education." *Labor Education Viewpoints*, undated, pp. 31-35.

Wertheimer, Barbara, ed. *Labor Education for Women Workers*. Philadelphia: Temple University Press, 1981.

Wheeler, Hoyt N., and Anthony J. DeAngelis. "Steward Performance: A Behaviorally Anchored Description." *Labor Studies Journal* 6 (Winter 1982), pp. 186-201.

Wirtz, Willard. *Worker Education and Training Policies Project: Tuition Aid Revisited: Tapping the Untapped Resources*. Washington: National Manpower Institute, September 1979.

CHAPTER 5

New Dimensions in the Design and Delivery of Corporate Training Programs

JOHN A. FOSSUM
University of Minnesota

Training and development (T&D) programs and levels of activities have changed dramatically during the 1980s and can be expected to continue evolving rapidly through the 1990s. These changes result from the evolving demography of the workforce, the restructuring of organizations due to foreign competition, deregulation, mergers, and acquisitions, and modifications in the design and delivery of T&D activities. During the 1980s a variety of changes occurred in the focus of T&D activities, toward the explicit enhancement of productivity and entrepreneurship and away from career development and other more personal goals. The 1990s will find major shifts in emphases as the workforce ages markedly, larger proportions of labor force participants are women and minorities, and production technologies increasingly require more cognitively based job designs.

These changes have spawned concern among both employers and policy implementers. The U.S. Department of Labor commissioned a major study, *Workforce 2000* (Johnston and Parker, 1987), to identify the human resource needs and availabilities forecasted for the year 2000. Unlike an issue in the late 1970s which chronicled the excess supply of labor associated with the baby boom (*Business Week*, 1978), *Business Week* (1988) recently devoted an issue to "Human Capital" and cataloged the problems that employers and labor force participants were likely to face in the future as imbalances between the demand for and supply of knowledge, skills, and abilities are likely to be exacerbated.

Literacy is becoming increasingly important as cognitive skill requirements increase. The implementation of various Japanese management techniques such as quality circles, statistical process control, and *kanban* (just-in-time) inventory systems require substantially improved quantitative skills. More concern for the interaction between stakeholders in organizations, particularly between customers, manufacturers, and suppliers, has increased the need to acquaint employees with quality control procedures and techniques to enhance responsiveness to customer needs. These and other changes in management, including the flattening of managerial hierarchies, have increased the need for intensified and broadened management T&D.

There have been several reviews of research on training and development (Campbell, 1971; Goldstein, 1980; Latham, 1988; Wexley, 1984; Wexley and Baldwin, 1986a). Systematic treatments of T&D theories, diagnostic tools, methods, and techniques are also available (Gagne and Briggs, 1979; Goldstein, 1986; McGehee and Thayer, 1961). A cursory examination of the book review section of *Personnel Psychology* indicates new T&D publications for practitioners are generated at a rapid rate. These concentrate generally on the construction of T&D programs and their effectiveness for influencing changes in measured abilities or on-the-job behavior rather than measuring the economic value of T&D activities.

Training and development is intended to create or enhance the knowledge, skills, and abilities of individuals in order to equip them to perform at higher levels in their employment. Demonstration of the acquisition by individuals is reflected through behavior in either ability test situations or on-the-job performance. T&D outcomes are not necessarily the same as educational outcomes. T&D outcomes are, by definition, employment-related, while educational outcomes may consist of immediate consumption (appreciation of what is learned for its own sake) and both indirect and direct human capital building components (e.g., analytical skills and computer programming). This review focuses on T&D theories, practices, and outcomes.

T&D theories and research relevant for industrial relations have evolved in very dissimilar streambeds. Psychological theories are concerned at the molecular level with the primary neurological mechanisms involved in acquisition and memorization of bits of information, with processes by which psychomotor connections are established, and with the interaction between the individual and the environment (Neisser, 1967). These theories are involved primarily with the development of knowledge, skills, and abilities (some of which may be employment-related). Other relevant psychological theories for T&D are involved with the explanation of human motivation. Assuming innate and learned hedonic preferences, motivation theories attempt to explain how individuals make choices to acquire knowledge, skills, and abilities that enable them to behave in ways most closely associated with attaining important ends. Both types of theories, in their more applied versions, have relevance for training and development since they help to explain how various types of potential training vehicles may differ in their efficacy for enhancing learning, given differences in aptitude and motivational variables of potential trainees.

Economic theories are both directly and indirectly related to training and development. Human capital theory (Becker, 1975; Schultz, 1961; Thurow, 1970) seeks to determine returns to investment in education and T&D activities as reflected in future income streams. Individuals are assumed to forgo leisure and employment and may pay fees to be trained in order to maximize their lifetime earnings. Human capital theory distinguishes between types of educational and T&D investments. The two major classes are general human capital, which consists of knowledge, skills, and abilities of value to most employers for the production of goods and services, and specific human capital, which consists of knowledge, skills, and abilities of value to one's present employer but of little or no value to alternative employers. The development and operation of internal labor markets are theoretically closely associated with the concept of specific human capital. Other recent developments in economic theory which have relevance for T&D decisions involve work in transaction cost analysis (Williamson, 1975) and the analysis of principal-agent relationships (Lazear, 1986).

Given that this review examines corporate training programs, the impetus for their training and development activities resides in the expectation that T&D will positively influence firm performance (cf. Kleiner et al., 1987), and that the expenditures of resources on T&D will result in greater returns than will other investments. Until recently there has been little research at the organizational level about the effects of T&D programs on firm performance. An analysis of a new large survey of organizations has found that having a formal training program was related to organizational size, the introduction of new technology, and internal promotion structures. The inclusion of formal training positively influenced labor productivity (Bartel, 1989).

Implicitly, T&D decisions are tied to choices about how the organization's production function should be configured. T&D may be a substitute for or a complement of a current system. Where it is a substitute, the choice to implement, increase, or decrease a T&D program assumes that the marginal rate of technical substitution of labor for other inputs has changed, and if T&D efforts are intensified, that the returns to human capital (labor) have increased relative to returns to materials and/or physical capital. In complementary situations, T&D investments would be employed to the point where their marginal costs equalled the marginal revenue that followed from their use. An example might be a situation in which some T&D would be necessary to enable the implementation of a new production technology or to deal with new materials.

Changes in the use of T&D activities may result from exogenous changes that alter the relative prices of inputs and thus create income and substitution effects among them. For example, if raw materials increase in price, labor intensity involving T&D might be increased by programs to develop skills enabling employees to conserve materials or reduce scrap. On the other hand, if a goods-producing process is automated, T&D might be decreased for certain production jobs as the job design could change from assembler to tender. There may also be endogenous changes that influence T&D activities. Within the labor input, management decisions may be made to reorganize authority relationships or reapportion various tasks, duties, and responsibilities among jobs to enhance efficiency. These create income and substitution effects within the labor input and may require T&D activities for employees to develop the knowledge, skills, and abilities necessary to reach the potential outcomes offered by the new task configurations.

To this point, there have been few attempts to explicitly tie psychological and economic theories. Human capital theory pays little attention to the method of training. In fact, many studies of the returns to human capital use experience (measured in years) and education (measured in years or degree types and levels) as the predictors of future returns. Evaluations of learning theories and techniques generally use short-run behavioral or achievement outcomes as measures of training program effectiveness.

Given the title, the organization of this chapter will emphasize training and development primarily from the standpoint of organizational or work-unit outcomes. However, it will also examine individual outcomes within organizations. Since it focuses on initiatives by the firm, outcomes from training will be assessed in terms of variables of relevance to the organization, such as performance, job capabilities, and attitudes toward work.

Given that labor, capital, and materials are combined interactively to produce products and services for consumption, and given that employees initiate and maintain the conversion process, T&D activities might be divided into those focusing on the operation of capital, efficient utilization of raw materials, and the facilitation of interactions among labor. Employees are assigned to jobs, which are collections of tasks, duties, and responsibilities capable of being performed by a single individual. The ability of employees to perform certain configurations depends on their knowledge, skills, and abilities. These configurations depend not only on capital, but on the knowledge, skills, and also abilities of other employees.

Jobs are frequently organized around production technologies, but are also organized in ways that are idiosyncratic to the firm. In other words, each firm may develop unique or proprietary methods of production in the use of its labor input, thus requiring specific human capital. Much of this involves the interactions that take place between employees across jobs and between employees across organizational levels. Training programs thus also involve enhancement of the labor content of the production function. Thus knowledge and the skills and abilities specific to the firm may become general human capital over time if the organization in which they are utilized consistently outperforms others in the industry.

Employees are not homogeneous in terms of their aptitudes and capacities for learning. This heterogeneity may be related to the aptitude requirements of jobs and to individual differences such as age, experience, and the like. Evidence suggests that learning models may be differentially effective among employees of different age groups (Birren, Cunningham, and Yamamoto, 1983). Further, human capital theorists recognize that outcomes to certain types of training may decline with age if the payoff stream is expected to continue for relatively long periods. Thus, training type may interact with individual differences and the type of production function variable that is being considered.

Short- and long-run training outcomes are also of concern to the individual and the organization. If training were to be distinguished from development, it might be thought of as enhancement of knowledge, skills, and abilities for an immediate, identifiable need. Development, on the other hand, is a longer-run process that is designed to equip the employee for a future role of higher value. Job progression might be thought of as involving a performance component and a development component, particularly when the organization has a defined internal labor market.

T&D programs are designed primarily to create or enhance specific-human-capital knowledge, skills, and abilities. As such, they operate on the ability dimension of employee performance. However, employee performance depends on both ability and motivation. While motivation may be influenced by both external and internal factors, T&D programs may positively influence employees' efficacy beliefs and may provide information that helps them to clarify what performance is defined to be. Further, modules of the training program may address situations in which the motivation of the employees to apply the training could be reduced by situational constraints.

Training-needs analysis is a central concern in corporate training and development programs. The classical needs analysis model (Goldstein, 1986; McGehee and Thayer, 1961) includes three phases. First, the organization must determine where it intends to go in the future. Second, from this determination an analysis evolves of how operations are to be changed. Third, capabilities of a target employee or applicant population are assessed to determine how well their knowledge, skills, and abilities fit the proposed operations. To the extent that deficits occur which will be addressed through T&D programs, the most appropriate designs can be constructed using the information developed from the needs analysis. On a longitudinal basis, needs assessment programs might forecast likely obsolescence of employees and pinpoint appropriate evaluations of behaviors likely to indicate individual obsolescence (Rosen and Jerdee, 1985).

Training and development activities are divided in this review. In the section devoted to training, various theories of learning that influence the design of training programs will be presented. This will be followed by an examination of areas in need of ability or behavior changes of interest to employers. Development activities will be examined through a linkage between the internal labor market and organizational performance requirements. Career development from an individual perspective will not be covered since this review assumes that organizational goals drive the design and delivery of development programs, while career interests rest primarily with the individual. Given that the organization is interested in optimizing its production function, T&D programs will be examined against the component of the production function they are designed to influence. Opportunities for integrative research will be presented last.

T&D Learning Models

Learning within a training and development context represents a permanent change in the job-related knowledge, skills, and abilities of employees. The rate and magnitude of their acquisition depends on a variety of factors such as the material to be learned, the instructional technology to be applied, the timing of delivery in the training program, feedback to the learner, support for the learned behavior in the work environment, and other similar considerations. This knowledge and these skills and abilities, however, might be thought of as labor power. Their value depends on the incremental improvement forecasted for their application in the organization. Their conversion to labor and the rate and speed at which they are acquired are dependent on employees' motivation levels. The efficacy of reward systems tied to T&D programs depends on the accuracy of the identification of desired outcomes of employees and how attainment of these outcomes can be tied to T&D outcomes. The retention of learning and its application in on-the-job situations requires that employees recognize situations, ex ante, that are likely to interfere with the implementation of their learning and develop ways to cope with or overcome those obstacles.

Learning takes place in a variety of environments. Training programs are designed to provide opportunities beyond those acquired through ongoing work experience. They may be an integral part of production activities such as on-the-job training, may be supplemental to production work, or may involve employees in activities away from the production environment.

Activities away from the regular work environment are increasingly appropriate and likely in situations in which the job to be learned has a relatively long cycle time and certain critical elements may occur randomly or at widely spaced time intervals. Learning transfer is an important issue involved in the development and implementation of off-job training programs. Learning transfer is a measure of the degree to which the knowledge, skills, and abilities developed in the training program are applicable to and applied in the work setting. Transfer depends to an extent on the similarity of the training and job situations from a behavioral requirements standpoint and partially on the extent that post-training rewards support rather than punish learned behavior.

The design of training programs from a sequence and timing standpoint is also important. Part vs. whole learning involves situations in which either a part of the desired behaviors is learned before going on to the next module or where all of the behaviors are learned simultaneously. Evidence suggests that learning complex tasks is somewhat easier under part-learning programs except that as the organization necessary between tasks increases, whole learning becomes substantially more effective (Blum and Naylor, 1968). Massed vs. spaced practice has been studied thoroughly. Massed practice results in more fatigue and initially lower performance for psychomotor skills (Holding, 1965). Spaced practice requires more time, and where employees must leave the workplace for training, it costs more and disrupts production. Evidence on overlearning (continued training beyond demonstration of competency) unequivocally points to its efficacy (Goldstein, 1986); however, it might be most efficient where the time required for repeated sessions is relatively small.

A variety of motivation models have been used to construct training programs. These are usually independent of the type of training to be offered. However, expectancy theory (Lawler, 1975; Vroom, 1964) may be more closely related to development programs, while reinforcement (cf. Yukl and Latham, 1975) and social learning models (Bandura, 1977) are probably more often used for training programs. In addition, goal-setting (Locke et al., 1981) has frequently been used as a motivational tool.

Reinforcement models are based on the premise that rewarding appropriate responses to learning stimuli will increase the likelihood that they will occur in similar stimulus situations in the future. To be effective, the rewards must be of value to trainees and seen as following from their responses. As responses to a given stimulus become dependable, as in overlearning, reward schedules may be changed from being given for every success to occurring periodically or randomly. Behavioral persistence is enhanced by random reinforcement.

Social learning theory suggests that learning can take place in the absence of actual behavior. An example of social learning would involve trainees watching trainers assuming certain roles and behaving in work-related situations. As a result of observation, the trainees would be enabled to learn how to behave in similar situations. Since no behavior would actually have been demonstrated by the trainee, no reinforcement could be tied to it. Vicarious learning, however, could have taken place if the trainee values the observed behavior for accomplishing work outcomes. Reinforcement is assumed to occur through the trainee's identification with the success of the trainer which the trainee is interested in achieving as well.

Learning transfer has been a major problem in industrial training programs, particularly for supervisory and managerial training. Many supervisory training programs have been designed to equip trainees with new behavioral skills in negotiating, problem-solving, conflict resolution, and the like. While these may be behaviorally modeled and learning may be reinforced in the training program, there may be infrequent support for the new behavior in the workplace. Subordinates may be the focus of the newly desired behaviors and may resist them, while superiors may neither understand nor support the program. Trainees who are equipped to recognize situations in which their learning will not be supported can be taught to reinforce themselves or get support from other employees. This so-called "relapse training" is a relatively new development (Marx, 1982) and has been applied successfully in supervisory training (Noe, Sears, and Fullenkamp, 1990). Goal-setting also may enhance learning transfer if the goals are tied to expected future job performance improvements (Wexley and Baldwin, 1986b).

From an individual standpoint, training effectiveness and transfer may be related to the trainee's beliefs about the accuracy of his/her individual training needs diagnosis and the ability to master the training material, that mastery is tied to job performance, and that job performance is important for gaining important personal outcomes (Noe, 1986).

Another area of importance to transfer is the similarity of the work environment and reward system to that of the learning situation. Internship and co-op programs are designed to enhance transfer between school and the job. Transfer is enhanced by gradually changing the mix between instruction and work, the amount of interdependency between school and the job, and the application of theory (Bialac and Wallington, 1985).

New Training Techniques

Developments in microcomputing, computer networks, artificial intelligence, video presentation, and satellite communications have all contributed to the creation of new training techniques during the 1980s. Organizations are more frequently developing packaged training modules that may be used by individuals in their T&D. Hardware costs are high, with satellite delivery facilities costing about $20,000. In larger facilities, a learning center may be constructed with all of the required hardware, which will allow multiple users to be trained in different topics simultaneously. While these are expensive to develop, the variable costs are low (Tuck, 1988). Employees may be trained at their worksites rather than having to be transported to a central training facility. Lower variation in the quality and subject matter of training programs also results.

Computer-assisted instruction has developed more rapidly as artificial intelligence has been added. A more reactive environment is enabled with the instructional level and speed tailored to the response of the individual (Gladwin, 1984), Standardization, flexibility, and uniformity in the quality of instruction through tests and debugging make computer-assisted instruction particularly attractive (Wehrenberg, 1985). This approach may be particularly important for learning gains when trainees are of different ages.

Simulations and games have been used increasingly in both computerized and noncomputer environments. Particularly where environments are changing rapidly and managers need an opportunity to identify possible different patterns of behavior, experiment with alternative solutions, test skills in potentially high-cost situations, and see the effects of poor decisions without incurring large costs, simulations and games have high potential for transfer of knowledge at low relative costs and risks (Wehrenberg, 1986).

Training program design for employees of varied age groups is an important consideration (Bove, 1987). Franz (1983) recommends an ecological approach to retraining older adults. Cognitive complexity is usually greater among older adults, while flexibility may not be.

While new training techniques have developed rapidly during the 1980s, the prevalence of use has changed only slightly. In an annual survey (Gordon, 1988), use of training by technique and source indicates that use of videotape methods has increased somewhat, while role-playing has declined. Organizations are somewhat more likely to use both in-house and outside training programs for supervisors, but few changes have been found for training of senior managers and executives. The greater use of videotape methods combined with a reduction in role-playing may suggest that training managers subscribe to vicarious learning as a less intensive and expensive, but equally effective, substitute for requiring actual job-related behavior. This would be consistent with social learning theory and might be particularly appropriate where the demonstrator on the videotape was a person with high salience for trainees.

Knowledge, Skills, and Abilities Desired by Employers

A recent research project (Carnevale, Gainer, and Meltzer, 1988; Carnevale et al., 1988) identified seven hierarchically ordered employee skill groups that are important to employers. These include: learning to learn; reading, writing, and computation; listening and oral communications; creative thinking/problem solving; self-esteem, goal-setting and motivation, personal and career development; interpersonal, negotiation, and teamwork skills; and leadership for organizational effectiveness. This set might be thought of as a global collection of general human capital knowledge, skills, and abilities. Some are skills to be applied (e.g., computation, oral communication, problem-solving, etc.), while others are predispositions to act in certain ways (e.g., self-esteem, career development, leadership, etc.).

At the lowest end, employer desired skills involve basic readiness to learn. In the middle levels, broad skill groups are primarily related to cognitive diagnostic skills for problem-solving in the use of capital, raw materials, and interactions of labor between job groups. At the upper levels, skills are primarily interpersonally oriented, aimed at organizing, motivating, and directing a defined segment of the workforce.

Employers recently have been placing more emphasis on individual differences and their association with trainability. They are more often making selections for training programs on the basis of aptitudes rather than present skill levels (Casey, 1984). This may work to the disadvantage of senior employees if aptitude levels are uncorrelated with skill. Further, senior employees may be less likely to receive training if aptitudes for learning lead to faster promotions. The more senior employees in any given job will be more likely to have lower aptitudes than those who have been promoted.

From the perspectives of employees aged 40 and up, Tucker (1985) found that government managers between 40 and 49 preferred management training, those between 50 and 59 preferred technological training, and employees aged 60 and over were generally uninterested in either. These preferences are probably linked to perceived promotion or employment security probabilities.

Training Applications to Enhance the Use of Capital

Training in the use of new capital equipment is often provided by vendors as part of their sales packages. Some evidence exists that the focus of this training is either misplaced or not wide enough (Ettlie, Vossler, and Klein, 1988). Installers of robotics equipment most frequently train engineers and employees in skilled trades occupations of their customers. However, operator training appears to have a strong relationship with the reduction of problems in implementing robotics.

Where new capital equipment requires a more cognitive job design and greater interaction among employees to operate and monitor the process, supervisors need retraining that emphasizes the new technical skills necessary for operation, supplemented by participatory leadership and human relations training (Hill and Kerr, 1984).

Training Applications to Enhance the Use of Materials

With an increased emphasis on the quality of products, some manufacturers are beginning to require vendors to train their employees in statistical process control as a condition for continued purchase of parts (Heidenreich, 1988).

As the work environment becomes more complex and as the federal Hazard Communication Standard is implemented, hazardous materials used in production or machine loading (chemicals, radioactive components, and the like) require more care, and employees are now being increasingly informed about workplace hazards and trained to reduce the possibility of injury or environmental discharge (Kimmerling, 1985; Olian, 1990).

Training Applications to Enhance the Use of Labor

Management training needs as perceived by employees appear to vary systematically with hierarchical level of the target group. Preferred training topics for first-line supervisors involve information collection and transmission (record-keeping and written communications); for mid-level managers, the primary topic is human resource management; and for upper-level management, it is training emphasizing planning and goal-setting (Bernick, Kindley, and Pettit, 1984).

Assuming that organizations develop specific-human-capital knowledge, skills, and abilities among their employees to facilitate operation of their particular management styles, when reorganization or restructuring occurs, many of the present specific-human-capital knowledge, skills, and abilities become obsolete. Managers and other employees have to learn new patterns of interaction. Previously appropriate behaviors may now be incongruent with the way the organization will be operated. Activities that might have been the responsibilities of staff employees may now be incorporated in line employee responsibilities. Orientation toward customers and markets may reallocate employees from production and staff areas (*Wall Street Journal*, 1987). However, at least in the United Kingdom, top management generally saw little necessity for contemporaneous training and development when strategic emphases changed (Hussey, 1985).

Managerial training does not seem to be particularly different, regardless of the provider. On the average, managers receive about 36 hours of formal training per year. The breakdown between formal and on-the-job training depends to some extent on the organization's needs for specific-human-capital knowledge, skills, and abilities. In 80 percent of the surveyed organizations, executive training is administered centrally, but 60 percent is paid for by the executive's home department. In general, managers are most often trained in human resource management, group and team relationships, and external relations (particularly at higher levels) (Carnevale, 1988).

Japanese Management Systems

Among large companies, training in Japan appears to be different from that employed in the United States. Part of this may be linked to differences in job design and production technology. For example, just-in-time inventory systems, statistical process control quality programs, quality circles, and the like require different types of skills than traditional U.S. production situations where jobs have been structured to require relatively little training. In Japan, production workers receive more training through job rotation, classroom skill development sessions, on-the-job tutoring, and attention to corporate culture (Weber, 1984). An examination of Oriental and Western thinking has suggested that as complexity and interrelatedness of functions increase, Oriental "holistic" approaches to management T&D become increasingly appropriate (Adler, Doktor, and Redding, 1986).

While many employers may stress the training in teamwork and interpersonal skills associated with Japanese management, it is important to realize that the ability to use statistical process control and just-in-time programs requires a higher level of mathematical ability than most U.S. production employees and their supervisors possess. Mathematics training is a central part of Japanese production worker training (Nonaka and Johansson, 1985).

Management and Executive Team Building

Two major developments in higher level team building involve off-site training. The first employs role-playing in a simulated organization. Using structured information about a firm's financial and production situation, participants are required to make decisions to respond to changes in the external environment and create and operate an internal organization to respond to problems. After the simulation is completed, trainers provide feedback to the participants on their observations. Then participants apply what they have learned to a second simulation. While evidence of learning through simulation is abundant (Kaplan, Lombardo, and Mazique, 1985), there is some problem with learning transfer that might require the addition of relapse learning.

Wilderness training has also recently been used for team building. Intact management teams are taken to unfamiliar wilderness areas and, with the help of trainers, confront challenges with which they are not familiar. These involve mountain climbing, rappelling off cliffs, rigging high lines to traverse chasms, and the like. The challenges require teamwork, problem-solving, and trust to accomplish different tasks. The presumption is that the teamwork and acceptance of challenges will transfer to the work situation (Long, 1987).

Training programs for specific managerial teams (such as airline cockpit personnel) involve role plays, group decisionmaking exercises, individual diagnoses of problems with reports to the group, and videotaped presentations (Margerison, Davies, and McCann, 1987). Conflict management is another important substantive area covered in training (Shockley-Zalabek, 1984), with increasing emphasis being placed on identifying organizational as well as interpersonal causes (Chasnoff and Muntz, 1985). The identification of transaction cost issues would be an important area to cover here.

Supervisory-Subordinate Relationship Training

A perennial area for training involves performance appraisal. A good deal of evidence has been developed recently on the evaluation of training programs to increase rater accuracy (Pulakos, 1986). Much of the effectiveness of training depends on the requirements of the rater. If the rater is simply required to observe and record behavior, then training would be different than in situations in which the rater is to make a judgment regarding the performance effect of the behavior. Reliability of measurement is enhanced by the degree to which rater training fits the instruments, observational or evaluative, he/she is asked to use.

An instrumented approach to enhanced workgroup effectiveness has been developed and studied by Graen and his associates (Graen and Scandura, 1986; Graen, Scandura, and Graen, 1986; Scandura and Graen, 1984). The assumption behind their approach is that there are "in" and "out" groups in work units. When supervisors and subordinates are made aware of each other's perceptions, both supervisor support and member availability increases. Productivity and job satisfaction increases for trained groups as compared to control groups. Increases in both areas were higher for employees for whom growth needs were important. If the organization seeks participation by supervisors and subordinates, the quality of leader-member exchange becomes important for both groups, while the subordinate must also be perceived to be a high performer by the supervisor before he or she will initiate and maintain participation (Scandura, Graen, and Novak, 1986).

Initial training for new supervisors appears to occur in about half of the organizations surveyed by the Bureau of National Affairs ("Training and Development Programs," 1985). About one-third of the companies offer training before promoting an individual, following a supervisor's nomination. After promotion, of the half of the firms that offer training, about 80 percent require it. Common content in over half of the programs included coaching, counseling, and discipline, leadership skills, performance appraisal, and equal employment opportunity and affirmative action. Many also covered selection, safety and security, and planning and time management. Larger companies were more likely to train middle managers in interviewing and selection. The majority of surveyed companies augmented supervisory training with tuition assistance, on-the-job coaching, and opportunities to attend outside seminars and professional and/or trade association meetings.

Leadership Training

Increasing attention is being paid to social learning theory (Bandura, 1977) in the design and delivery of leadership training for managers. Evidence suggests that it has become a very pervasive approach to managerial training (Parry and Reich, 1984). One of the key features of social learning theory is that people with strong feelings of self-efficacy should cope with their environments more effectively. Evidence also suggests that people infrequently actively attempt to regulate their own performance (Brief and Hollenbeck, 1985). Active participation in training programs leading to accomplishment appears to enhance perceptions of self-efficacy (Gist, 1987). To the extent that self-efficacy is satisfying, as it increases, the need for external reinforcement to support learning decreases (Bandura, 1986).

To avoid difficulties in the transfer of training where self-efficacy has been enhanced, environments that do not respond to effort and accomplishment will probably be associated with higher turnover among employees who were trained (Bandura, 1982).

Behavior demonstrated by learners is moderated, however, by the types of behavior modeled. Differences exist when the modeler uses punishing or rewarding behavior in the role-play (Manz and Sims, 1986). Besides self-efficacy, goal-setting and task-training appear to influence both the amount of effort put forward and the performance on the task. Specific performance goals lead to task planning (Earley, Wojnaroski, and Prest, 1987).

Management competency training (Cameron and Whetten, 1983) focuses on how to execute managerial behaviors rather than on what they are. Advocates claim that business school training does not prepare future managers to behave as their roles will require. Lean (1985) argues that management is a process that uses little intellectual learning, but rather involves agenda-setting and networking competencies (among others). Critics suggest that the behaviors to be learned are simply an unvalidated theory of managing and may not be representative of how managers actually behave (Vaill, 1983).

Intercultural Training for Expatriate Assignments

It has been suggested that self-orientation, other-orientation, and perceptual and cultural toughness dimensions are all important in expatriate acculturation. Self-orientation has been hypothesized to be dependent on substituting new reinforcers for those of the sending culture, stress reduction, and technical competence. Other-orientation depends on relationship development and a willingness to communicate (Mendenhall and Oddou, 1985). Cultural training would appear to be important to identifying potential new reinforcers in an expatriate's assignment, but over two-thirds of the corporations have no formal training programs (Tung, 1981).

Among a group of male expatriates, performance ratings in foreign assignments were higher for individuals who received either documentary or interpersonal training on the countries to which they were being assigned. Documentary training involved reading about politics, religion, food, male and female roles in that society, and the like. In interpersonal training, role-playing in foreign social situations was done. Both techniques were effective and additive (Earley, 1987).

The Changing Workplace

The 1980s and 1990s have seen and will see a continuing change in the workplace, particularly in the gender composition of jobs. Some organizations are experimenting with training programs to educate their men and women managers to behave more androgynously (Berryman-Fink and Fink, 1985). While there are no significant ability differences between men and women managerial candidates, role conflicts, stereotypes, and lack of role models may require additional support for women trainees (Larwood, Wood, and Inderlied, 1978).

Another area of increasing change is the continually declining opportunities for individuals with mechanical skills and the increasing need for people with electrical, electronic, and cognitive skills. Some companies and their unions, most notably AT&T and the Communications Workers of America, have begun to develop programs in which employees receive training outside of their job classifications to enable them to cope with anticipated changes (*Employee Relations Weekly*, 1987).

Training Applications Involving New Production Functions

As the 1980s revealed an increasing need for organizations to be competitive and profitable, a variety of production technology changes took place that led to training needs. Competitiveness has been enhanced by cost reduction and product quality. More attention to quality at specific points may also contribute to cost reduction through lowered rework requirements. Costs are also reduced by maintaining lower inventories of materials in process. Some advocates of the *kanban* (just-in-time) inventory system also argue that its implementation reveals problems that have previously been dealt with by increasing organizational slack. The reduction of inventory requires that employees know how to diagnose problem causes and to develop mechanisms for anticipating problems (Musselwhite, 1987).

At the heart of quality control are statistical and measurement procedures to determine when a process is running out of control. Since quality problems are probably first noticeable for the producer of a part or the assembler who uses vended parts, his or her ability to identify problems requires computational skills associated with statistical processes. Various training programs have been developed to impart the knowledge necessary to practice statistical quality control and to motivate employees to accept quality control as a primary production goal (Dumas, Cushing, and Laughlin, 1987).

Some companies are developing training programs to acquaint employees with new production technologies. These programs help to identify resistance points in implementing new methods and provide information to trainees to allow them to overcome the barriers. These appear to be particularly appropriate for the introduction of information system technology (Conner, 1985). Divergent thinking frequently is important for recognition of the need to make changes, especially in production technologies. Training to enhance attitudes toward divergent thinking appears to have positive effects, particularly in intact workgroups of manufacturing engineers (Basadur, Graen, and Scandura, 1986). For example, the planned General Motors–Saturn plant and others similar to it have radically different technologies and markedly different job designs. GM and the United Auto Workers have agreed to job security, training, and work-design changes to support the new technology (*Employee Relations Weekly*, 1986).

Developing Managers and Organizational Cultures

Supervisors and lower level managers have a major impact on the implementation of personnel policies and practices in organizations. At General Electric, first-level supervisors manage 50 percent of all exempt employees and make selection decisions for 90 percent of the professional positions that are filled each year. New lower level managers attend formal training courses, 6 to 12 months after their promotion to their new positions, in order to become familiar with upper management's goals and objectives. These courses emphasize communications skill-building, creation and leadership of work teams, candid and effective communication, the planning and design of work, network-building, problem-solving, leadership, creating ownership, appraisal, coaching, and applying corporate values (Komanecky, 1988). One of the messages behind this approach is that fundamental transformation of organizations along lines that are relevant to top management may bypass middle management. This is consistent with the restructuring and reductions in force that have been implemented during the 1980s.

Some organizations have created specific development programs for so-called "high-potential" managers. Many identify the candidates for these programs through assessment centers. Where organizations do not spend much effort on career development planning with individuals, Broszeit (1986) suggests that employees should have a major role in choosing development activities with access based on merit and active involvement from superiors. These programs frequently include rotational assignments through various functions or facilities. However, managers to whom they are assigned may not be motivated to expend time or resources in development, given their other work or budgetary responsibilities. These transaction cost problems have led some companies, including McDonnell Douglas, to transfer these high-potential candidates to a personnel budget, give a replacement to the releasing department, and assign the candidate free to the receiving department (Settle, 1988).

Assessment centers are also used for development activities. Candidates and assessors receive developmental benefits through feedback on performance to candidates, early identification of potential, diagnosis of individual training needs general to management in the organization, development experience as an assessor, and information for the organization for aggregate human resource planning (Boehm, 1985).

Mentoring was an increasingly popular management tool during the 1980s. However, questions have been raised recently about its efficacy. Mentors should not be thought of as comprehensive role models. Emulation in only five work aspects—intellectual sharpness, job skills, career management, social skills, and emotional characteristics—is the usual profile of identified mentors, according to one study. Learning and sponsorship probably do not belong together (Clawson, 1985). Mentoring effectiveness probably follows a social learning model in many instances. Thus, choice of mentors is very important for the organization. The effectiveness of mentoring is generally mixed (Kram, 1985).

With the restructuring and early retirements that have taken place recently, first-line supervisors may frequently have less experience before promotion and may not have an immediate superior with much experience. An example of the areas covered in development programs include technical information, safety, human resource management, administrative systems, and collective bargaining. Goal-setting is included through the creation of a supervisor-mentor learning contract coupled with a productivity improvement project between scheduled training classes (Beaulieu et al., 1988).

Rotational assignments and other mobility opportunities within an organization provide for development. In some structured situations, developing managers are purposely exposed to both good and bad role models in the on-going work situation to learn about effective and problematic practices (Lombardo and McCall, 1983). On-the-job training is a major component of managerial development (Zemke, 1985), partly because the cycle time of managerial job requirements is generally much longer than for other jobs.

Effectiveness of Management Training

Effectiveness in management training has always been a difficult operationalization. From an individual's standpoint, development may be effective to the extent that opportunities are realized and satisfaction is increased. But for the organization, evidence that employee behaviors have changed and that these changes contribute to better performance is necessary to demonstrate effectiveness.

A meta-analysis of managerial training studies found that management training, in general, is effective (Burke and Day, 1986). However, there is less evidence about its cost-effectiveness or the relative efficacy of various methods or their interactions with individual differences. There is a further question of a more normative nature that also must be addressed. At what unit of analysis are training programs effective? There may be situations in which individual effectiveness, as measured by relative income progression of trainees vs. nontrainees, improves, while organizational effectiveness, as measured by work unit performance, does not change. Finally, effectiveness might be measured against whether or not the T&D program accomplished what upper management intended for it to accomplish (Latham, 1988). Thus, its external validation is against their criteria rather than against economic measures. If the T&D effort is not effective for enhancing economic outcomes, it may be that top management had the wrong behaviors in mind as targets for training.

If T&D efforts are beneficial to employees in developing specific-human-capital knowledge, skills, and abilities which enhance their opportunities, then turnover should be lower than for nontrained groups. Ferris and Urban (1984) found that of six professional occupations that received training in a petrochemical operation, five had lower turnover subsequently as compared to controls. On an individual basis, de Meuse (1985) found that participation in an in-house education program was related to increased perceived effectiveness and valued by the person. These perceptions were stronger with shorter tenures in the organization, suggesting that the learned behaviors may not be supported in that environment. Besides their individual aptitudes and motivations, trainees may be influenced by support in their workgroups and situational resources for implementing the behaviors that they have learned (Noe, 1986). These are essentially transfer problems.

The larger the organization, the more formal are its training practices. In a survey of 1000 companies with 1000 or more employees, training needs analysis was associated with company size. Over two-thirds had managerial training, with about equal proportions involved in broadening and specific knowledge, skills, and abilities development activities. Reputation and competitors' enrollment in programs predicted use of external sources by companies. Top-level management selects managers to attend university programs in most cases. This percentage falls as lower managerial levels are considered. Little formal follow-up of the effectiveness of formal training programs, especially those conducted outside the organization, was undertaken (Saari et al., 1988).

Future Research and Applications

This review has suggested that training and development activities should be considered from a production function standpoint as well as from the standpoint of the effects on individual trainees. Most of the T&D activities examined here can be considered as complementary to other changes, and most involve attempts to enhance the operation of interchanges between various levels and roles among the labor input segment of the production function. T&D is usually considered as a substitute only in situations in which the employer is deciding whether to hire new employees who have the requisite knowledge, skills, and abilities required by present tasks, duties, and responsibilities or to train present employees. The answer to this problem depends to some extent on the cost of training new employees for the specific knowledge, skills, and abilities required by the employer.

T&D activities, since they involve primarily the enhancement of interactions within the firm's labor force, are heavily laden with specific human capital. To the extent that internal labor markets are created and operated because of a need to develop and preserve specific human capital, then T&D activities are closely connected with its operation. More emphasis on the study of returns to various types of T&D and when they are available to employees is important. Additionally, more emphasis on the relationship between the firm and its employees with regard to career development might be interesting. For example, companies in the computer industry have markedly different espoused philosophies about career development. Digital Equipment proclaims that employees own their careers. As such, jobs at all levels are posted and employees can bid on them. They are, in essence, creating their own career development programs. On the other hand, at IBM employees may be encouraged to change occupational emphases as the firm restructures to better match its perception of the environment. Substantial retraining opportunities are available for employees who decide to change their interests toward those of the company.

Training and development and its effects should also be examined from a transaction cost perspective. Major differences might be expected in the design, operation, and pervasiveness of various types of T&D activities depending on what area of the organization pays for them. Line managers might not be expected to pay for development when the employee will not use the skills within that budgetary unit or during the present budget period. On the other hand, if T&D is funded through a corporate center, then line managers may not be careful about who is assigned to these activities. The patterns of T&D expenditure control may dictate not only the individuals who might be trained, but also the subjects, the amount of training, and whether or not it is oriented to general or specific human capital.

Other areas that need emphasis include who should be responsible for training, cost accountability, the role and potential bias of experts involved in the training needs analysis, and the choice of an appropriate trainer (Sonnenfeld and Ingols, 1986).

Finally, additional work is necessary in identifying the structure and strategy of the organization in the future and the role of training and development in supporting them. It is quite possible that the restructuring of organizations, the transience of products and the velocity of change, and the decreasing job security seen recently may require organizations to act more as venture capitalists and holding companies (Drucker, 1988). If so, my predictions will be wrong, and the 1990s will be a decade of increasing attention to selection and an offloading of T&D activities to individuals in the labor market. I doubt this will happen, however, as particular management approaches distinguish themselves in light of the performance of the organization in which they are practiced.

References

Adler, N. J., R. Doktor, and S. G. Redding. "From the Atlantic to the Pacific century: Cross-cultural management reviewed." *Journal of Management* 12 (1986), pp. 295–318.

Bandura, A. *Social Learning Theory*. Englewood Cliffs, NJ: Prentice-Hall, 1977.

———. "Self-efficacy mechanism in human agency." *American Psychologist* 37 (1982), pp. 122–47.

———. *Social Foundations of Thought and Action*. Englewood Cliffs, NJ: Prentice-Hall, 1986.

Bartel, A. P. "Formal employee training programs and their impact on labor productivity: Evidence from a human resources survey." National Bureau of Economic Research Working Paper 3026, July 1989.

Basadur, M., G. B. Graen, and T. A. Scandura. "Training effects on attitudes toward divergent thinking among manufacturing engineers." *Journal of Applied Psychology* 71 (1986), pp. 612–17.

Beaulieu, A., T. Turner, J. Levert, and S. LeBel. "Foreman development with a difference." *Training and Development Journal* 42, 4 (1988), pp. 66–69.

Becker, G. S. *Human Capital*, 2nd ed. New York: National Bureau of Economic Research, 1975.

Bernick, E. L., R. Kindley, and K. K. Pettit. "The structure of training courses and the effects of hierarchy." *Public Personnel Management* 13 (1984), pp. 109–19.

Berryman-Fink, C., and C. B. Fink. "Optimal training for opposite sex managers." *Training and Development Journal* 39, 2 (1985), pp. 27–29.

Bialec, D., and C. Wallington. "From backpack to briefcase." *Training and Development Journal* 39, 5 (1985), pp. 66–68.

Birren, J. E., W. R. Cunningham, and M. Yamamoto. "Psychology of adult development and aging." *Annual Review of Psychology* 34 (1983), pp. 543–75.

Blum, M. L., and J. C. Naylor. *Industrial Psychology: Its Theoretical and Social Foundations*. New York: Harper & Row, 1968.

Boehm, V. "Using assessment centres for management development: Five applications." *Journal of Management Development* 4, 4 (1985), pp. 40–53.

Bove, R. "Retraining the older worker." *Training and Development Journal* 41, 3 (1987), pp. 77–78.

Brief, A. P., and J. R. Hollenbeck. "An exploratory study of self-regulating activities and their effects on job performance." *Journal of Occupational Behavior* 6 (1985), pp. 197–208.

Broszeit, R. K. " 'If I had my druthers . . .': A career development program." *Personnel Journal* 65, 10 (1986), pp. 84–90.

Burke, M. J., and R. R. Day. "A cumulative study of the effectiveness of managerial training." *Journal of Applied Psychology* 71 (1986), pp. 232–46.

Business Week. "Americans change: How demographic shifts affect the economy." No. 2522, February 20, 1978, pp. 64–67.

Business Week. "The decline of America's workforce." No. 3070, September 19, 1988, pp. 100–40.

Cameron, K. S., and D. S. Whetten. "A model for teaching management skills." *Organizational Behavior Teaching Journal* 8, 2 (1983), pp. 21–27.

Campbell, J. P. "Personnel training and development." *Annual Review of Psychology* 22 (1971), pp. 565–602.

Campbell, J. P., M. D. Dunnette, E. E. Lawler III, and K. E. Weick, Jr. *Managerial Behavior, Performance, and Effectiveness.* New York: McGraw-Hill, 1970.

Carnevale, A. P. "Management training: Today and tomorrow." *Training and Development Journal* 42, 12 (1988), pp. 18–29.

Carnevale, A. P., L. J. Gainer, and A. S. Meltzer. *Workplace Basics: The Skills Employers Want.* Washington: U. S. Government Printing Office, 1988.

Carnevale, A. P., L. J. Gainer, A. S. Meltzer, and S. L. Holland. "The skills employers want." *Training and Development Journal* 42, 10 (1988), pp. 23–30.

Cascio, W. F. *Costing Human Resources: The Financial Impact of Behavior in Organizations.* Boston: Kent, 1982.

Casey, J. G. "Trainability diagnosis: A humanistic approach to selection." *Training and Development Journal* 38, 12 (1984), pp. 89–91.

Chasnoff, R., and P. Muntz. "Training to manage conflicts." *Training and Development Journal* 39, 1 (1985), pp. 49–53.

Clawson, J. G. "Is mentoring necessary?" *Training and Development Journal* 39, 4 (1985), pp. 36–39.

Connor, D. R. "Introducing new technology humanly." *Training and Development Journal* 39, 5 (1985), pp. 33–36.

de Meuse, K. P. "Employees' responses to participation in an in-house continuing education program: An exploratory study." *Psychological Reports* 57 (1985), pp. 1099–1109.

Drucker, P. F. "The coming of the new organization." *Harvard Business Review* 66, 1 (1988), pp. 45–53.

Dumas, R. A., N. Cushing, and C. Laughlin. "Making quality control theories workable." *Training and Development Journal* 41, 2 (1987), pp. 30–33.

Earley, P. C. "Intercultural training for managers: A comparison of documentary and interpersonal methods." *Academy of Management Journal* 30 (1987), pp. 685–98.

Earley, P. C., P. Wojnaroski, and W. Prest. "Task planning and energy expended: Exploration of how goals influence performance." *Journal of Applied Psychology* 72 (1987), pp. 107–14.

Employee Relations Weekly. "New directions: Saturn-UAW agreement." Washington: Bureau of National Affairs, April 10, 1986.

——————. "Case studies in cooperative training." Washington: Bureau of National Affairs, July 16, 1987.

Ettlie, J., M. Vosser, and J. Klein. "Robotics training." *Training and Development Journal*, 42, 3 (1988), pp. 54–58.

Ferris, G. F., and T. F. Urban. "Supervisory training and employee turnover." *Group and Organization Studies* 9 (1984), pp. 481–90.

Fossum, J. A., R. D. Arvey, C. A. Paradise, and N. E. Robbins. "Modeling the skills obsolescence process: A psychological/economic integration." *Academy of Management Review* 11 (1986), pp. 362–74.

Franz, J. B. "Cognitive development and career retraining in older adults." *Educational Gerontology* 9 (1983), pp. 443–62.

Gagne, R. M., and L. J. Briggs. *Principles of Instructional Design*, 2nd ed. New York: Holt, Rinehart & Winston, 1979.

Gist, M. E. "Self-efficacy: Implications for organizational behavior and human resource management." *Academy of Management Review* 12 (1987), pp. 472–85.

Gladwin, L. A. "The impact of artificial intelligence training." *Training and Development Journal* 38, 12 (1984), pp. 46–47.

Goldstein, I. L. "Training in work organizations." *Annual Review of Psychology* 31 (1980), pp. 229–72.

——————. *Training in Organizations*, 2nd ed. Monterey, CA: Brooks/Cole, 1986.

Gordon, J. "Who is being trained to do what?" *Training* 25, 10 (1988), pp. 51–60.

Graen, G. B., and T. A. Scandura. "Toward a psychology of dyadic organizing." In *Research in Organizational Behavior*, eds. B. M. Staw and L. L. Cummings. Greenwich, CT: JAI Press, 1986.

Graen, G. B., T. A. Scandura, and M. R. Graen. "A field experimental test of the moderating effects of growth need strength on productivity." *Journal of Applied Psychology* 71 (1986), pp. 484–91.

Heidenreich, P. "Supplied SPC training: A model case." *Training and Development Journal* 42, 3 (1988), pp. 60–62.

Hill, K. D., and S. Kerr. "The impact of computer integrated manufacturing systems on the first-line supervisor." *Journal of Organizational Behavior Management* 6, 3-4 (1984), pp. 81–97.

Holding, D. H. *Principles of Training*. London: Pergamon, 1965.

Hussey, D. E. "Implementing corporate strategy: Using management education and training." *Long Range Planning* 18, 5 (1985), pp. 28–37.

Johnston, W. B., and A. H. Packer. *Workforce 2000*. Indianapolis, IN: Hudson Institute, 1987.

Kaplan, R. E., M. M. Lombardo, and M. S. Mazique. "A mirror for managers: Using simulation to develop management teams." *Journal of Applied Behavioral Science* 21 (1985), pp. 241–53.

Kimmerling, G. F. "Warning: Workers at risk: Train effectively." *Training and Development Journal* 39, 4 (1985), pp. 50–55.

Kleiner, M. M., R. N. Block, M. Roomkin, and S. W. Salsburg, eds. *Human Resources and the Performance of the Firm*. Madison, WI: Industrial Relations Research Association, 1987.

Komanecky, A. N. "Developing new managers at GE." *Training and Development Journal* 42, 6 (1988), pp. 62–64.

Kram, K. E. *Mentoring at Work: Developmental Relationships in Organizational Life*. Glenview, IL: Scott, Foresman, 1985.

Larwood, L., M. M. Wood, and S. D. Inderlied. "Training women for management: New problems, new solutions." *Academy of Management Review* 3 (1978), pp. 584–93.

Latham, G. P. "Human resource training and development." *Annual Review of Psychology* 39 (1988), pp. 545–82.

Lawler, E. E. III. *Motivation and Work Behavior*. Monterey, CA: Brooks/Cole, 1975.

Lazear, E. "Incentive contracts." National Bureau of Economic Research Working Paper 1917, 1986.

Lean, E. "No more pencils, no more books." *Training and Development Journal* 39, 4 (1985), pp. 62–67.

Locke, E. A., K. N. Shaw, L. M. Saari, and G. P. Latham. "Goal setting and task performance." *Psychological Bulletin* 90 (1981), pp. 125–52.

Lombardo, M. M., and M. W. McCall. "Great truths that may not be." *Issues and Observations* 5, 2 (1983). Center for Creative Leadership, Greensboro, NC.

Long, J. W. "The wilderness lab comes of age." *Training and Development Journal* 41, 3 (1987), pp. 30–39.

Manz, C. C., and H. P. Sims. "Beyond imitation: Complex behavioral and affective linkages resulting from exposure to leadership training models." *Journal of Applied Psychology* 71 (1986), pp. 571–78.

Margerison, C., R. Davies, and D. McCann. "High-flying management development." *Training and Development Journal* 41, 2 (1987), pp. 38–41.

Marx, R. D. "Relapse prevention for managerial training: A model for maintenance of behavior changes." *Academy of Management Review* 7 (1982), pp. 433–41.

McGehee, W., and P. W. Thayer. *Training in Business and Industry*. New York: Wiley, 1961.

Mendenhall, M., and G. Oddou. "The dimensions of expatriate acculturation: A review." *Academy of Management Review* 10 (1985), pp. 39–47.

Musselwhite, W. C. "The just-in-time production challenge." *Training and Development Journal* 41, 2 (1987), pp. 27–29.

Neisser, U. *Cognitive Psychology*. New York: Appleton-Century-Crofts, 1967.

Noe, R. A. "Trainees' attributes and attitudes: Neglected influences on training effectiveness." *Academy of Management Review* 11 (1986), pp. 736-49.

Noe, R. A., J. Sears, and A. M. Fullenkamp. "Relapse training: Does it influence trainees post training behavior and cognitive strategies?" *Journal of Business and Psychology* (1990).

Nonaka, I., and J. Johansson. "Japanese management: What about the hard skills?" *Academy of Management Review* 10 (1985), pp. 181-91.

Olian, J. D. "The manager's agenda for health and safety: Reasons and strategies." In *Employee and Labor Relations*, Vol. 4 in SHRM Handbook of Personnel and Industrial Relations, ed. J. A. Fossum. 1990, in press.

Parry, S. B., and L. R. Reich. "An uneasy look at behavior modeling." *Training and Development Journal* 38, 3 (1984), pp. 57-62.

Pulakos, E. D. "The development of training programs to increase accuracy with different rating tasks." *Organizational Behavior and Human Decision Processes* 38 (1986), pp. 76-91.

Robinson, J. "Beam me up, Scotty." *Training and Development Journal* 42, 2 (1988), pp. 46-48.

Rosen, B., and T. H. Jerdee. "A model program for combating employee obsolescence." *Personnel Administrator* 30, 3 (1985), pp. 86-92.

Saari, L., T. Johnson, S. McLaughlin, and D. Zimmerle. "A survey of management training and education practices in U. S. companies." *Personnel Psychology* 41 (1988), pp. 731-43.

Scandura, T. A., and G. B. Graen. "Moderating effects of initial leader-member exchange status on the effects of a leadership intervention." *Journal of Applied Psychology* 69 (1984), pp. 429-36.

Scandura, T. A., G. B. Graen, and M. Novak. "When managers decide not to decide autocratically: An investigation of leader-member exchange and decision influence." *Journal of Applied Psychology* 71 (1986), pp. 579-84.

Schultz, T. W. "Investment in human capital." *American Economic Review* 51 (1961), pp. 1-17.

Settle, M. E. "Developing tomorrow's managers." *Training and Development Journal* 42, 4 (1988), pp. 60-64.

Shockley-Zalabek, P. S. "Current conflict management training: An examination of practices in ten large American organizations." *Group and Organization Studies* 9 (1984), pp. 491-507.

Sonnenfeld, J. A., and C. A. Ingols. "Working knowledge: Charting a new course for training." *Organizational Dynamics* 15, 2 (1986), pp. 63-79.

Thurow, L. C. *Investment in Human Capital*. Belmont, CA: Wadsworth, 1970.

"Training and Development Programs." *Personnel Policies Forum*, No. 140. Washington: Bureau of National Affairs, September 1985.

Tuck, J. W. "Professional development through learning centers." *Training and Development Journal* 42, 9 (1988), pp. 76-79.

Tucker, R. D. "A study of the training needs of older workers: Implications for human resources development planning." *Public Personnel Management* 14 (1985), pp. 85-95.

Tung, R. L. "Selection and training of personnel for overseas assignments." *Columbia Journal of World Business* 16, 1 (1981), pp. 68-78.

Vaill, P. "The theory of managing in the managerial competency movement." *Organizational Behavior Training Journal* 8, 2 (1983), pp. 50-54.

Vroom, V. H. *Work and Motivation*. New York: Wiley, 1964.

Wall Street Journal. "Tough choices: Cutting output, IBM tells some workers." 209, 68, April 8, 1987, pp. 1, 16.

Weber, D. E. "An eye to the east: Training in Japan." *Training and Development Journal* 38, 10 (1984), pp. 32-33.

Wehrenberg, S. B. "Is the computer the ultimate training tool?" *Personnel Journal* 64, 4 (1985), pp. 95-98.

_____. "Simulations: Capturing the experience of the real thing." *Personnel Journal* 65, 4 (1986), pp. 101-105.

Wexley, K. N. "Personnel training." *Annual Review of Psychology* 35 (1984), pp. 519-51.

Wexley, K. N., and T. T. Baldwin. "Management development." *Journal of Management* 12 (1986a), pp. 277-94.

_____. "Strategies for facilitating the positive transfer of training: An empirical exploration." *Academy of Management Journal* 29 (1986b), pp. 503-20.

Williamson, O. E. *Markets and Hierarchies.* New York: Free Press, 1975.

Yukl, G. A., and G. P. Latham. "Consequences of reinforcement schedules and incentive magnitudes for employee performance: Problems encountered in an industrial setting." *Journal of Applied Psychology* 60 (1975), pp. 294-98.

Zemke, R. "The Honeywell studies: How managers learn to manage." *Training* 22, 8 (1985), pp. 46-51.

Chapter 6

Joint Union-Management Training Programs: A Synthesis in the Evolution of Jointism and Training

LOUIS A. FERMAN
University of Michigan

Michele Hoyman
University of Missouri, St. Louis

Joel Cutcher-Gershenfeld
Michigan State University

Joint union-management efforts to provide training in technical skills and personal development not only increased dramatically during the 1980s, but also was a symbol of the emergence of new and innovative arrangements between unions and managements that went beyond earlier initiatives. The new joint programs ranged and continue to range from a relatively narrow focus on on-the-job and workplace training (including apprenticeships, certifications, and licensing) to general worker education. The most advanced of the programs are in the automotive and communications industries, but there are well-established programs in the steel industry, construction, and the public sector.

Current programs vary in the amount of control the union and the employer exert over policy decisions as well as over their day-to-day administration. Our focus in this chapter is on those training programs where there is some degree of joint decisionmaking. Thus, we exclude from our discussion such "set-aside" arrangements as the Stabilization Agreement of the Sheet Metal Industry under which 3 percent of gross payroll for various employment security purposes is deposited in a trust fund that finances training but is not governed on a joint basis. Rather, we chose to focus on large-scale programs, jointly administered (sometimes from an independent fund), which may embody various types of technical training as well as lifetime education and personal development.

Our broad purpose is to describe the emerging set of institutional arrangements that are presently associated with joint training. In the sections that follow we will summarize some of the scholarship that currently exists on this topic, the scholarship that is only beginning to get the attention of the academic community.[1] Hence, the codification of this literature will be less relevant in this chapter than setting the stage for future research.

The Roots of Joint Training Programs

Joint training programs can best be understood as the product of two separate historical trends, the first being the evolution of joint union-management activities. The second involves the expanding scope and importance of training in U.S. workplaces. The trends come together in the context of union-management training programs, and each set of roots is informative in assessing joint training efforts.

Jointism as One Set of Historical Roots

Joint union-management activities (which we will also refer to as "jointism") are distinct from unilateral union or employer activities in that there is some measure of codetermination in decisionmaking and some degree of shared resources. Because activities are jointly administered, however, it does not necessarily mean that they are cooperative. Indeed, given that the interests of labor and management typically include areas of conflict and commonality, we would expect to find both in the context of joint activities.

Jointism has a long history in the United States prior to current joint training activities (Gomberg, 1967; Jacoby, 1983; Cutcher-Gershenfeld, 1985). For example, at the turn of the century, Louis Brandeis's Protocol of Peace was a joint effort aimed at encouraging the use of arbitration as an alternative to strikes. During the 1920s and 1930s, shop floor problem-solving groups were jointly sup-

---

[1] The most complete source to date for this topic is a volume that we have helped to produce: Louis A. Ferman, Michele Hoyman, Joel Cutcher-Gershenfeld, and Ernest J. Savoie, eds., *Joint Programs for the Training and Personal Development of Workers: New Initiatives in Union-Management Relations* (Ithaca, NY: ILR Press, 1991). Reluctantly, given our involvement in the volume, we have drawn extensively on the material in this book for various parts of this chapter.

ported by employers and unions in the railroad and textile industries. Joint committees were an integral part of the wartime production effort during World War II, with more than 5000 labor-management committees established (De Schweinitz, 1949). During the 1950s and 1960s, temporary joint committees were established around a range of special issues, including technological change, grievance administration, displaced worker training, and productivity improvement.

In an analysis of the historical stability of these many joint efforts, Gomberg (1967) concluded that labor-management committees endured only so long as they were a subsidiary adjunct to collective bargaining rather than an alternative to it. In other words, joint committees were seen as of use to unions and employers only when they were either temporary or relatively narrow in focus. Beginning in the 1970s and expanding in the 1980s, however, a set of joint activities has served to call into question Gomberg's thesis. In many workplaces there have emerged a broad array of joint committees responsible for topics such as safety and health, employee assistance programs, health care cost containment, absenteeism, product quality, employee involvement, quality of worklife, and, of course, training. Some of these committees are adjuncts to the collective bargaining process, while others are not. There are even joint committees of top leaders who are responsible for coordinating the activities of the many other joint committees that exist in a given worksite. These joint activities represent an entire domain of contract administration that can sometimes surpass grievances and arbitration in terms of the time and even the importance of the activity for union leaders, which has led some scholars to argue, contrary to Gomberg's thesis, that broad-based joint activities can have a robust, two-way relationship with collective bargaining instead of just serving as a secondary adjunct (Cutcher-Gershenfeld, Kochan, and Verma, 1990).

Among today's joint activities, union-management training programs may stand as among the most comprehensive in terms of scope, funding, staff, and facilities. Because their roots lie, in part, with the history of jointism, the current joint training programs can be assessed relative to the historical experience with union-management committees. That is, will joint training efforts endure only so long as they are either temporary or narrow in focus? Or are they part of a fundamental shift in the status of joint activities relative to collective bargaining and hence understandable as a stable and significant domain for labor-management interactions?

Training as a Second Set of Historical Roots

Historically, the provision of worker training in the United States has been highly segmented. Employers generally supported training for executives, managers, and professional and technical employees. The government generally supported training for the disadvantaged and the hard to employ. Unions supported apprenticeship programs for employees in the skilled trades. And, for the majority of U.S. workers, the dominant mode was on-the-job training.

Not only was training in the U.S. highly segmented, but it was not a top priority issue for labor, management, or the government. In most cases the training function had relatively little status in corporate hierarchies. Similarly, while most unions expended some internal resources on training, they did not see the issue as a bargaining priority. For the government, training programs did take on increasing significance as a component of poverty programs, but the focus was always kept within that context.

Today training has become a high priority issue for unions, employers, government officials, and workers. New technologies require skill training and, as the technologies change work organization, there is a greater need for various forms of organizational development training. Changing world markets are associated not only with new products, which may be associated with new training, but also with a need for greater flexibility in meeting market demands, which may require training in multiple skills. Today's workforce is more educated, more diverse, and more uncertain about the future vitality of many traditional manufacturing jobs. All of these factors are associated with workers' greater interest in personal development training and career planning. With this dramatic expansion in the importance of training, questions arise regarding how well training is integrated into strategic or policy planning by employers, unions, and government (Ford, 1990). In addition, these joint efforts involve partnership arrangements, between employers and government or employers and educational institutions as well as between employers and unions. Certain key questions that arise with these new partnerships are matters of governance (Savoie and Cutcher-Gershenfeld, 1991).

That is, how do the various interests of the stakeholder organizations come together in decisionmaking about training activities? How are conflicts resolved and how are common interests pursued?

Thus, a second set of roots for current joint training activities can be seen in the evolution of U.S. training from a relatively unimportant and highly segmented domain to an issue of top priority and one that involves a broad range of partnerships. Each of these general developments in training has specific implications for union-management training. That is, does a joint structure increase the status of the training function in the respective organizations? What are the new mechanisms for decisionmaking? How do the two parties sort out their common and competing interests around training?

Distinctive Features of Joint Training Programs

We have seen that joint training programs are but one of many forms of jointism. We also have seen that joint training programs are but one of many signs of the increased importance and complexity of training activities in the U.S. Joint training programs are not new in this country, of course. During the 1920s and 1930s, many of the shop-floor problem-solving activities in the railroad and textile industries involved some degree of training and orientation, which was provided by consultants such as Otto Beyer (Jacoby, 1983). During the 1950s and 1960s, there were some highly publicized examples of joint training in the face of technological change and worker displacement (the Armour Automation Committee, for example). During the 1970s, many health and safety efforts had some degree of joint training associated with them. Finally, some apprenticeship programs have been, and still are, administered on a joint basis.

Still, most of the past experience with joint training has been around either narrowly focused, single-issue training or time-bound training efforts. Of particular interest in the 1980s, however, has been the rise of joint training programs that span many areas of training activity, that cover many populations of workers and managers, and that are established as permanent social institutions. These joint training activities truly represent a synthesis of the dual roots of jointism and the increasing importance of training in society. The following are among the distinctive aspects of these emerging joint training programs:

1. Joint training programs have a broader target population than other areas of joint activity in that both displaced and active workers may be targeted for training and education.

2. Joint training goes beyond training for the internal labor market of the company, in that workers may be provided with personal development training that is not directly related to their specific job and they may even receive preparation for employment outside of the firm.

3. Underpinning joint programs is an ideology and process that are distinct from most unilateral training efforts. The ideology centers on participation and involves a process of codetermination in decisionmaking. Thus, these programs are participant-driven (that is, the content and priorities of the local program are often driven from the inputs of workers), and a strong emphasis is put on joint decisionmaking by union and management members responsible for training programs.

4. Although there is a great deal of variation in the structure of joint training programs, a common element of most programs is that they are governed by equal numbers of union and management representatives. This sort of formal structure is common with other joint initiatives, but is distinct from other forms of training.

5. Most joint training programs have a high degree of local control, reflecting the need to administer training at a worksite level. This is similar to some joint activities, but stands in contrast to others. Similarly, this parallels some unilateral training efforts, but, again, stands in contrast to others.

Most of the joint programs make an extensive use of local community educational institutions for training. Thus the programs are closely articulated with education in the broader community.

The Contours of Joint Training Programs

There are, of course, many types of union-management training programs. The most highly publicized have been the national and local joint programs in the automotive and communications industries. Subsequent efforts in the steel industry, larger auto supply firms, and other large firms are modeled on the automotive and communications efforts. In contrast, joint training programs in small and medium-sized firms have their own unique set of characteristics. Training programs in these two contrasting settings (larger and smaller firms) each have their own contours.

The joint training efforts in larger firms are usually first defined at the collective bargaining table where contractual provisions establish the programs, specify governance and coverage, and provide some financial formula to cover the cost of program operations. For example, in the automobile industry, the joint training is funded on the basis of a certain number of cents per hour worked. By contrast, in smaller firms the joint training efforts may not be explicitly defined in the contract and the funding is allocated more on a case-by-case basis, reflecting a reduced degree of slack resources in a smaller firm.

Many of the joint training programs in larger firms were begun in the early 1980s in response to the dislocation of many workers during the first recession of the decade. In time, however, the focus broadened to include active workers as well. Joint training has also been employed as a vehicle to address worker dislocation in smaller firms, often with the assistance of state and federal government (Baker, 1991).

It is particularly in the larger firms that joint training programs often go beyond skill development for specific jobs to encompass personal development skills and long-term career planning. Workers in such settings will generally be eligible for an entire package of services rather than for a single program. This broader focus is reflective of the union's priorities, which are tied to the long-term needs and priorities of the members, and some managers' estimates of the need for a broad education base if a workforce is going to be flexible and adaptive. Smaller firms and unions also support broader training, but it is more likely to be explained by the specific values of a firm's founder and/or owners in combination with the approaches of the local union leadership (Block et al., forthcoming).

In all organizations the control of the program is primarily at the grass roots level. Joint union-management committees at the local plant level determine worker needs, select and organize training resources, set training priorities, and develop contracts with community service vendors. In a larger firm, a national or regional center may provide technical assistance, a coordinated computer data base, model training materials, and other forms of support. As well, where workers are no longer subject to the jurisdiction of a local facility (in the case of a plant closing or a transfer), the regional or national centers may take on certain direct training responsibilities.

An important component of the programs in many larger firms is that the training activities must not replace existing union or company training obligations. Thus, apprenticeship training, technical training for a specific piece of equipment, labor education programs, and other training that would have taken place in the absence of the joint program are to be supported separately by the employer or the union. In practice, such distinctions become increasingly difficult to make. Indeed, as the joint training staff demonstrates a high degree of skill in program administration, there is often an incentive on both sides to bring additional areas of training under the joint umbrella. For example, the previously separate joint health and safety activities of the United Auto Workers and General Motors have now been brought under the auspices of the UAW-GM National Joint Human Resources Center. Further, some larger firms in the steel industry have placed nearly all of their technical, job-specific training under the auspices of joint programs.

In both larger and smaller firms, top-level program responsibilities for joint training activities usually lie with an employer's labor relations officials and a union's top officers and bargaining committee members. There may then be union appointees who work jointly with an employer's training and education staff and/or with organizational development (OD) staff. This arrangement can have the effect of placing certain aspects of a firm's training and OD functions under joint governance.

All these firms may place considerable reliance on local community service networks for counseling, assessment, and training. Both community colleges and secondary schools may contract with the union-management pairs to provide various training-related services. Of interest are the reports of both union and management officials that they can be very effective in negotiating with these service-providers—in effect, jointly turning their well-developed negotiations skills toward a new area.

Thus, the picture that emerges is a training activity characterized by codetermination in decisionmaking, with high degrees of local control, that is providing services to active and displaced workers via a mix of internal worker-trainers and external service providers, all of which may be supported with internal funds and public dollars. It stands as a highly advanced form of jointism and as a distinctive structure for providing training to workers.

The Frequency and Range of Joint Training Programs

Because joint training programs are such a recent phenomenon and because most of the data surrounding the experience are under the control of the parties themselves, there is very little systematic research on the frequency and range of such programs. One survey completed in 1988 does, however, document the joint training activities of 102 labor-management pairs (Hoyman and Ferman, 1991). We report some of the results from this survey to provide a preliminary sketch of the frequency and range of joint training programs in the U.S.

The sample was drawn from lists, compiled by the U.S. Department of Labor, of union-management relationships that had some measure of cooperative activity. Forty percent of the sampled relationships featured joint training programs, covering nearly one million bargaining unit members. The above figures represent a notable amount of diffusion for this innovation, and this diffusion is particularly impressive because joint labor-management training programs involve an extensive commitment of resources.

Most of the joint training programs serve multiple constituencies, often focusing on both active and displaced workers. The substantive focus can range from training in basic skills, such as upgrading of specific skills, to training to fulfill future staffing needs of the company and to training for organizational or personal development. The Hoyman and Ferman study indicates that most of the training efforts have more than one substantive purpose. For instance, many of the 45 efforts identified had two or three purposes simultaneously. This is demonstrated by the figures in Table 1 in which the 45 unique labor-management programs enumerate 152 different purposes.

The purposes of these programs can be divided into the traditional and the nontraditional. Traditional purposes include safety and health policy, upgrading, staffing (manpower), and outplacement. Nontraditional activities include displaced workers, communication skills, personal development, and basic skills training, as well as others. When Hoyman and Ferman examined the

TABLE 1

Purpose of Joint Labor-Management Training Programs

Safety and health	33
Upgrade	26
Communication skills	24
Displaced workers	17
Personal development	15
Basic skills	13
Staffing	13
Outplacement training	7
Other	4
Total number of responses	132

Source: Michele Hoyman and Louis A. Ferman, "The Scope and Extent of Joint Training Programs," in Louis A. Ferman, Michele Hoyman, Joel Cutcher-Gershenfeld, and Ernest J. Savoie, eds., *Joint Programs for the Training and Personal Development of Workers: New Initiatives in Union-Management Relations* (Ithaca, NY: ILR Press, 1991).

distribution of 152 different activities cited in the 45 programs, they found almost as many nontraditional as traditional activities reported—73 as opposed to 79 (Hoyman and Ferman, 1991, p. 11). See Table 2 for details.

The broad mix of traditional and nontraditional training can be understood when the set of reported driving forces behind the training is examined. No single driving force dominates. Instead, all of the following were cited (in order of frequency): jointism, competition, leadership, worker displacement, schools/community colleges, and new technology. Given these various driving forces, it should be no surprise that there is diversity in program focus.

Also of note is the high proportion of programs found in the Middle West and in certain industries, including automotive manufacture, steel, oil refining, rubber, transportation, cement, and the manufacture of writing instruments. All of these industries correlate highly with most of the driving forces noted earlier. That is, most of the industries are characterized by high levels of jointism, extensive competition, a history of innovation in collective bargaining, high levels of worker displacement, and the introduction of new technologies.

Of interest is the observation that just over 40 percent of the respondents with joint training programs were firms with less than 600 employees. This finding suggests that joint training programs are not just a phenomenon limited to a handful of high-profile,

TABLE 2
Traditional Versus Nontraditional Purposes
in Joint Training Programs

Traditional		Nontraditional	
Safety and health	33	Displaced workers	17
Job upgrade	26	Communication skills	24
Staffing	13	Personal development	15
Outplacement	7	Other	4
Total	79	Total	72

Source: Michele Hoyman and Louis A. Ferman, "The Scope and Extent of Joint Training Programs," in Louis A. Ferman, Michele Hoyman, Joel Cutcher-Gershenfeld, and Ernest J. Savoie, eds., *Joint Programs for the Training and Personal Development of Workers: New Initiatives in Union-Management Relations* (Ithaca, NY: ILR Press, 1991).

large-employer settings. It also invites additional research into the distinctive nature of joint programs in larger and smaller firms.

One key research question that arises in the context of joint training programs concerns whether the establishment of such a program is usually accompanied by a corresponding change in either substance or service delivery. Hoyman and Ferman found some preliminary indications that the joint programs tend to have very few eligibility requirements, with only a fraction specifying seniority or managerial discretion as a means for determining access to training. Most rely on member self-selection. In contrast, frequent prerequisites for employer-only programs are a supervisor's recommendation, a certain test score, or other merit-based criteria. Also in employer-sponsored programs there is often an additional requirement that the training or education be job-related. The combination of few or no eligibility requirements, along with the fact that many of the training topics are chosen entirely by the individual employee leads to the description of such programs as "participant driven" (Ross and Treinen, 1991).

The joint programs are characterized by a philosophy of open admissions, but there was typically a requirement of bargaining unit status among almost all respondents. There are a couple of programs in which the person has to be on the permanent seniority list to be eligible. In summary then, the effect of such programs is to democratize access to training (within the union membership) and to let the participants themselves define programmatic content.

Often doing this means that the only criterion for inclusion in a training program is self-actualization or personal development. Thus, the programs are more likely to be oriented toward personal development than toward vocational training.

The marketing techniques are different for joint programs than what we usually conceive of for employer-only training. For example, although newsletters and direct mail are used most frequently as means for disseminating information on joint programs, union bulletin boards and union meetings were the third and fourth devices most frequently mentioned by survey respondents (Hoyman and Ferman, 1991, p. 21). In this sense, there is some evidence that joint programs can give rise to a new division of labor within the training function, with the union handling more of the outreach and recruitment and the company handling the more technical aspects of the training.

The conclusion is inescapable that joint training programs result in a change in who is trained and the type of program that is defined as training, with the emphasis being more on personal development. Further, the change in structure impacts directly on the structure of the training function.

Service Delivery in Joint Training Programs

One useful way to highlight the service delivery features of joint training programs is to compare and contrast some of their salient features with those of other training programs. The primary alternative types of training programs that can be used are (1) the company training program that is plant-based, and (2) the public-based, government employment and training organization. In every large company there is a concern and some provision made at the plant level for training new workers and for upgrading the skills of still other workers. There is also a concern in these programs with keeping the firm competitive by introducing new technology and providing training to workers to operate the technology. Such company training is provided for in the plant's overall operations budget.

The public-based, governmental employment and training programs are supported by tax funds and offer a variety of employment and vocational services to categorical groups in the community (for example, the unemployed, the displaced worker, minority group members, the disabled, and the older worker). Beginning with the United States Employment Service in 1935, extending to include the Comprehensive Employment and Training Act (CETA), and continuing through the current Job Training Partnership Act (JTPA), these programs use a combination of federal and state tax monies to deliver employment and training services to recipients identified by legislative guidelines.

Both private employer and governmental public programs have developed distinctive features that can be contrasted with joint training programs.

Company Training Programs Compared to
Joint Training Programs

Chart 1 presents a contrast between company training programs that are plant-based and joint training programs. While this comparison is highly stylized, it does capture the dominant tendencies of the two domains.

As the chart indicates, company training programs are concerned with the internal labor market and making the company more competitive by increasing the human capital stock of its workers. The goals are to provide for mobility in the internal market by developing and upgrading worker skills to fill existing or future needs of the plant or company. Workers are usually trained within a given line of progression (for example, electricians receive training in electrical skills). There is a training budget that is usually a line item in the total plant operational budget, and training in various forms is extended to both unionized and nonunionized workers.

By way of contrast, joint training programs are participant-driven. The emphasis is on opportunities for career development and lifetime employment, education, and training. The program is structured by the *expressed needs* of the worker and not the job needs of the plant. Besides technical training, there is a focus on personal development, which is seen as an important component of lifetime career development. Costs for the joint training program are negotiated as a company contribution based on worker effort (for example, the number of hours worked). Finally, the joint training program is restricted to union-represented workers.

There are also some differences in how the two types of programs operate. For unionized workers in a company training program, inclusion is a function of seniority, bidding rights, and the recommendation of supervisors. Training is mostly conducted in-house by a company training department, although some training

CHART 1

Comparison Between Company Training Programs
and Joint Training Programs

Company Training Programs	Joint Training Programs
Underlying Assumptions	
Provide opportunity for mobility in internal labor market	Provide an opportunity for career development and lifetime employment training and education
Develop or upgrade worker skills to fill current/future job vacancies or technology demands within the plant or company	Develop an opportunity for lifelong training and personal development of the worker
Enlarge worker skills within a given line of job progression	Enlarge worker skills outside a normal line of job progression
Training costs are a line item in a total plant operating budget	Costs are negotiated (often as a company contribution based on worker effort, such as the number of hours worked)
Training available to both unionized and nonunionized workers in the company (with most union members receiving only on-the-job training)	Training may be restricted to union-represented workers
Operations	
For unionized workers, inclusion in training program is a function of seniority, bidding rights, and supervisor recommendations	All unionized workers (as specified in the contract) are eligible for services and training
Training is mostly conducted by company training department	Training involves more worker trainers and more outside vendors
What to train for is a managerial decision	What to train for is based on joint committee determination of workers' expressed needs and aspirations
Effectiveness of training is based on subsequent job performance	Effectiveness of training is based on career development and satisfaction of the individual worker

Source: Louis A. Ferman and Michele Hoyman, "Service Delivery in Joint Training Programs," in Louis A. Ferman, Michele Hoyman, Joel Cutcher-Gershenfeld, and Ernest J. Savoie, eds., *Joint Programs for the Training and Personal Development of Workers: New Initiatives in Union-Management Relations* (Ithaca, NY: ILR Press, 1991).

may be vendored out. In the last analysis, what to train for is a managerial decision and the effectiveness of the training is mirrored in subsequent job performance. All of these operating features stand in sharp contrast to those in a joint training program where all union-represented workers can elect to receive services and what to train for is based on joint committee determination of workers' expressed needs and aspirations. Training is also usually vendored out, and the effectiveness of training is based on fulfillment of targets set in a personalized employability plan of career development for each participant.

Traditional Employment and Training Programs Compared to Joint Training Programs

Traditional education and training agencies are usually organized around community services for unemployed rather than active workers. The prototype programs of the 1970s and the 1980s are the Comprehensive Employment and Training Act (CETA) of 1973 and the Job Training Partnership Act (JTPA) of 1982. Some characteristics of traditional education and training programs and joint training programs are listed in Chart 2. Again, these characterizations are stylized and intended to capture the dominant tendencies of the two types of programs: underlying assumptions, processing of participants, administration, and operation.

The focus of the assumptions underlying traditional education and training agencies is on identifying job openings in the local labor market and filling those jobs with job-seekers. The emphasis is on *matching* job-seeker to job opening. If the job-seeker lacks requisite skills, an attempt is made to provide him/her with the skills required for the particular job that is open through some specified training program. The skills required for the job dictate what training is available to the job-seeker, thus circumscribing or limiting his/her choices to one of a number of uniform, canned programs. Such programs are developed by "experts" in the higher echelons of the organization and sent on to the local office to be implemented. Local office staff are concerned with interpreting and executing the program in a uniform manner that does not violate organizational guidelines.

By way of contrast, joint training programs focus on employment security (or lifelong job-holding). The emphasis here is often on the combination of personal and technical skills developed over a lifetime, rather than the technical skills associated with a single job. The starting point in joint training programs is, what does each worker need and expect for a lifetime of work? It is the aspirations, desires, and needs of the participant that shape the program rather than the immediate needs of the job market. The objective is to

CHART 2

Selected Characteristics of Traditional
Employment/Training Programs and Joint Training Programs

Traditional Education and Training Programs	Joint Training Programs
Underlying Assumptions	
Emphasis is on job finding and job security	Emphasis is on career development and employment security
Local office implements uniform, canned program developed centrally	Local committee is empowered to initiate, plan, and organize program tailored to needs of local workforce
Program participant is limited in job choices and routed to available job openings	Program participant is to be empowered by giving him/her choices and options for employment development
Emphasis is placed on skill development of program participant	Emphasis is placed on both skill and personal development of program participant
Participant Processing	
Batch processing of program participants	Personalized processing of participants
Relatively little attention to employability	Specific attention to employability, often with targeted outcomes
Fragmented and uncoordinated management	Centralized case management of services, with an emphasis on "one-stop-shopping"
Fixed, uniform services based on existing organizational technology and expertise	Services channeled among many vendors and internal service providers to match participant's needs
Eligibility is legislatively mandated and services based on categorical designation	Eligibility is contractually defined and services based on participant's needs
Recruitment of program participants is largely passive and restricted to formal channels of communication	Recruitment of program participants is active, using both formal and informal channels of communication
Assessment of program participants is based on standard assessment testing	Assessment of program participants is based on work history as well as standardized testing
Routing decisions for services are based on serial recommendations of staff professionals	Routing decisions for services are based on individual employability/career plans
Creaming of program participants for services (that is, only top prospects are processed to improve placement rates)	Each participant has equal access to programs since service to many is a criterion of success
Service providers are primarily training professionals	Peers may serve as service providers

CHART 2—(*Continued*)

Selected Characteristics of Traditional
Employment/Training Programs and Joint Training Programs

Traditional Education and Training Programs	Joint Training Programs
Administration	
Planning and development of local programs is mandated via central rules and regulations	Local committees are empowered to control many aspects of planning and development
Clearly defined hierarchical structure, with rules and authority as vehicles for control	Flattened organizational structure, with union-management check and balance as vehicle for control
Rigid division of labor based on formal qualifications	Collegial organization, with shared responsibilities and job switching based on individual capabilities
Rule-based decisions	Consensus-based decisions
Operations	
Services mostly in-house, with few vendored training programs	A mix of in-house and outside vendors for service providers
Few provisions for relocation assistance in other parts of the country	Relocation assistance for alternative positions in other facilities of a large firm
Local labor market information available	Local labor market information available
Industry and company vacancy surveys to identify local training needs	Worker surveys to identify personal aspirations combined with internal company information on firm's training needs
Program evaluation focuses on staff effort measures (when evaluation is done)	Program evaluation focuses on participant outcome measures (when evaluation is done)

Source: Louis A. Ferman and Michele Hoyman, "Service Delivery in Joint Training Programs," in Louis A. Ferman, Michele Hoyman, Joel Cutcher-Gershenfeld, and Ernest J. Savoie, eds., *Joint Programs for the Training and Personal Development of Workers: New Initiatives in Union-Management Relations* (Ithaca, NY: ILR Press, 1991).

empower the participant and let him/her shape the work future through his/her own choices. For this reason joint programs emphasize *both* personal and skill development, and local committees are assigned the task of planning and organizing programs based on participant needs. In joint programs, the program is participant driven and moves upward in the organization from the grass roots actions of local committees and their worker constituencies.

Traditional education and training agencies rarely personalize or individualize programs for participants. The typical agency has a maze of service stations through which a client is routed and various pathways through this maze. At each station a diagnosis may be made, a service given, or a routing decision made during a fleeting encounter between provider and participant. Consequently, the gatekeeper of the station may learn little about the participant beyond information generated in the encounter. A wide geographical distribution of stations can add to the alienation that workers and the unemployed experience in such a system.

Traditional education and training agencies emphasize batch processing (that is, participants are processed in groups rather than as individuals). The reasons for this are simple: (1) there is a tendency to reduce individual needs to group needs (for example, all unskilled workers need training), and (2) there is an organizational economy of scale to treat participants in groups, particularly where large numbers of people are involved. Processing may be further complicated by the lack of individual employability plans to guide selection of services and the fragmented/uncoordinated management of services that often exists in a multistation service maze.

Other processing problems occur in traditional education and training programs. First, the programs have a fixed, uniform set of service options that represent one aspect of the organizational culture of the past. Traditional service options are considered to be best, and these are reinforced by both technology and the expertise that exists within the organization. Very few new service options are brought in by vendors. The end result is that the participant is shaped to the existing service options rather than the service options being shaped to the participant. Second, eligibility in public education and training programs is legislatively mandated, as are service options that are available to a particular category of participants. Thus, even if certain services are perceived to be needed, the legislative mandates may preclude their acquisition. Third, broad-based assessments are almost nonexistent; assessment is based on standardized assessment testing. The end result is a limited view of the skills and capabilities of the participant. Finally, "professional expertise" is the basis of most decisions in the program, whether they be assessment, service-giving, or routing. This can result in a limitation of possible options for action. For example, "creaming" (considering only the most capable prospects) for program participation may largely result from the fact that college-educated professionals place their bets for success on the more educated participants and ignore others, motivated by evaluation that is based on measures such as worker placements.

Selected Innovations Associated with Joint Training Activities

Joint union-management structures have proved fertile ground for innovation in the development and delivery of worker training. Our focus in this section of the chapter is on documenting selected innovations as illustrations of the distinctive influence that a company and a union can have when they are working together under a joint structure. We will highlight specific training programs that were developed in the 1980s in the context of union-management training structures. These include the use of Life Education Advisors (LEAs) to guide workers in career planning, the establishment of Paid Education Leave (PEL) programs for broad worker education on issues of competitiveness and strategic planning, and the development of joint responses to worker dislocation. For each of these innovative programs we will note the distinctive aspects of their emergence under joint structures.

The Life Education Advisor (LEA)

Career planning has traditionally been the exclusive province of managers and professional employees. But now other workers, as well, have begun to anticipate facing major shifts in the work that they do as a result of new technology, changing markets, and other forces. Too often, however, they lack access to the information or assistance that is required to prepare for such shifts. Perhaps the most far-reaching effort to respond to such worker concerns has emerged in the context of union-management training programs.

A graphic example is the Life Education Advisor (LEA) program established by the United Auto Workers and the Ford Motor Company. Under this program, individuals are selected to serve as career counselors (LEAs) for the entire hourly workforce in a given facility. These individuals will typically have worked as school teachers, social workers, or counselors in other contexts. Sometimes an LEA will be permanently located in a given plant, while in other cases LEAs travel and serve several facilities.

The LEAs are taught about the vast array of Ford/UAW training programs and activities in a given location, and their counseling skills are reinforced and targeted for the unique needs of workers in the automobile industry. With these tools in hand, the LEAs then meet with employees and assist them in the construction of their own life plans.

In a unique, quasi-experimental assessment of the LEA program, Gordus, Kuo, and Yamakawa (1991) found that worker (particularly male worker) participation in training activities increased significantly when LEAs were available. The primary mechanism for this impact was in the way the counselors helped to reduce perceived barriers to participation in educational activities. This study also documented preliminary indications that the LEA concept can be understood only in the context of an employee's broader social support system.

It is both the interests and the resources of the union and the employer that help to explain why such far-reaching career counseling for workers has emerged in the context of joint union-management training efforts. The presence of the union helps to ensure that the career interests of employees are seen as legitimate in their own right, independent of the employer's projected workforce needs. The presence of the employer helps to ensure that such discussions can take place in the workplace, often on worktime, and that they will be at least informed by the firm's future opportunities and threats. Still, there is no reason why such services could not be provided by either the company or the union on a unilateral basis. Thus, out of the joint structure we see emerging a powerful model for establishing career planning for workers that could have applicability in many settings.

The Paid Education Leave (PEL) Program

Given the increasing complexity of world competition—with shifting markets, strategic alliances among firms, changing demographics, new technology, and other developments—education on these issues is of increasing importance to workers and managers. Many firms are investing heavily in management education on these topics, and many unions are working to increase the knowledge base of union leaders in the same areas. Too often, however, the education of workers about matters of competition or workplace change has become a battleground where each side vies for influence. Thus, it is interesting to learn from the way such education takes place under a joint structure.

The leading program in this area was established by the UAW and General Motors in the mid-1980s and is well documented by Schurman, Hugentobler, and Stack (1991). The Paid Educational Leave (PEL) program, as the parties have labeled it, was first designed as a four-week training program in which top union leaders and selected managers would be briefed by outside or internal experts on topics such as basic economic principles, changing world markets, emerging technologies, new patterns of industrial relations, the political and regulatory context, and strategic planning principles. These sessions, which take place in Ann Arbor, Detroit, Boston, and Washington (one week in each) have been well received, particularly for the degree to which they provide the parties with a common language and information base upon which to discuss the specifics of strategic planning in a given location.

One unanticipated feature of the program evolved from the growing appeals from local union leaders who returned to their plants, only to encounter frustration as they tried to communicate all that they had learned to their colleagues in the union and in management. As a result, a local PEL program was designed, which involves a one-week overview of all the issues covered in the four-week program. These local PEL sessions are now being delivered in UAW-GM worksites around the country to groups of approximately 40 workers and supervisors, often with one or two such sessions being held every month in a given facility.

The idea of union leaders and union members being paid for four weeks, or even one week, to learn about economic principles, strategic planning, and other matters is surely a distinctive product of a joint structure. It is only with the union as a party that such training would be made a priority, particularly with outside neutral instructors. On the other hand, without the full support of the employer, the vast investment of time and resources would not be possible.

One important indication of the value of an innovation such as this is the diffusion of the program across workplaces. Not only has it expanded to cover a wide range of GM worksites, but a parallel program established by the UAW and Ford is also now expanding to many settings. Even more significant for the vast majority of workplaces (which cannot necessarily afford to have their own custom-designed PEL-type program) is a current initiative under way by the State of Michigan to make what they have called Strategic Education Programs available for small and medium-sized employers. This state-sponsored program builds directly on the PEL model and educational materials.

All of these joint education efforts are still very much experimental. Indeed, they are something of an experiment in democracy. That is, they can be thought of as an experiment to see how much impact a more educated and informed workforce, union leadership, and lower-level management contingent might have on the relations between labor and management.

Joint Resources to Worker Dislocation

Worker dislocation, whether by plant closing or permanent layoff of a portion of the workforce, can have a devastating effect on individuals and communities. It is also an area in which the interests of the employee and the employer can diverge most sharply. Thus, it is particularly interesting to note the extent to which joint approaches to worker dislocation have been developed and successfully implemented.

Joint approaches to worker dislocation can range from relatively narrowly focused joint provision of relevant information for the affected workers to broad-based programs that involve the coordinated efforts of workers, the union, the employer, the community, and state government. Such joint programs, particularly the more broad-based ones, have been endorsed by the AFL-CIO as a recommended approach to worker dislocation (McMillan, 1991). They have also been identified by the federal government as a preferred model, on the basis of pilot initiatives in Michigan and extensive experience in Canada (Baker, 1991). In fact, Baker found that the participation of workers and union leaders in the planning and administration of worker dislocation programs in their own facility helped build personal skills that were helpful in subsequent job search by these individuals.

What makes joint training in such situations possible? While the interests of a union and workers in assisting in such situations are clear, it may be also often the case that managers at the plant level were opposed to the idea of a plant closing or downsizing and felt concern about the consequences for the workers and the community.

Thus, joint training associated with worker dislocation, like joint support for worker career planning and joint worker education on issues of competitiveness and strategic planning, represents a program area where a union-management partnership has made a distinctive contribution. Each of these innovations represents a combination of the interests of labor and management that contrasts with what would most likely have taken place in the absence of joint activities.

As a final note on the program innovations, it is important to recognize that these are just three of many innovations that might have been selected. Further, there are innovative features of service delivery (as we have noted earlier in this chapter) that also derive from joint structures in distinctive ways. These include more of a demand-driven approach in the provision of training, an increased use of workers as trainers, greater leverage with respect to training providers and public sources of training dollars, and the establishment of systems of checks and balances guiding the administration of training. As such, it is both in the area of program innovation and in advances in service delivery that joint union-management training offers great promise.

Issues that Divide and Unite

At the outset of this chapter we noted that jointism is not the same thing as cooperation since a joint activity would be likely to involve both issues of common concern and points of conflict. In the area of training quite a bit of conflict is conceivable since joint programs are often charting new territory that borders on training issues that were previously jealously guarded by the parties. A high level of cooperation is also likely since there are many aspects of training that, for different reasons, may meet the interests of both labor and management. In order to further capture the mixed-motive nature of joint training activities, it will be helpful to itemize some key issues that have the potential to divide the parties and key issues that can help unite them.

Issues That Divide

The following is a list of potentially divisive issues that may arise in the establishment and administration of a joint training program:

1. *Whose money is it anyway?* There is a strong belief among many union leaders and members that money allocated for joint

training programs is a form of deferred wages. (If the money hadn't gone to training, it would have come to employees in some other form.) In contrast, many managers see joint training funds as a special allocation, over and above wages, which was made only because it was going to pay for training. So long as there is ambiguity about whose money is being allocated to pay for joint training, there will also be ambiguity over whether one party or the other has a greater say in how it is being spent.

2. *How should the money be allocated?* Union representatives will often urge that all available money be spent on services that directly benefit the members, rather than on administration, research, and technical assistance. Managers may be more inclined to spend money on program administration. Training professionals and union and management training appointees may go even further in their interest in program development, program administration, and program evaluation. Thus, a tension emerges between the provision of immediate services, at one extreme, versus the perfecting of program offerings at the other. No joint program lies fully at one extreme or the other, but the relative emphasis can be another issue that divides.

3. *Who should staff the program?* As joint training programs expand, there may be increased pressure to use union members—especially unemployed union members—to staff program activities. This preference is supported by the argument that these individuals know the target population better than anyone else. At the same time, an emphasis on using only union members as staff may be seen by company officials as limiting access to outside professionals, and possibly even as the creation of a vehicle primarily intended for patronage. In fact, there are many domains where worker-trainers make critical contributions to the effectiveness of joint training programs, but there are also instances where appointments by the union seem to be motivated primarily by internal politics.

4. *What facilities will be used for training?* Inevitably, most joint training programs involve an expansion in the scope of training offered at a worksite. This may require an increased commitment of space and facilities. This issue can be divisive if the management personnel feel that productivity needs are being sacrificed for training.

5. *To what extent do jointly funded activities replace prior unilateral efforts by the union or the management?* In many cases, especially where a separate joint training fund is established, union-

management training efforts feature the restriction that the joint initiative not replace any training that either party would have done on their own. Yet there are many gray areas. For example, training and education for union leaders or members and even supervisors or managers on topics such as labor history, management organizational structure, or strategic planning are often seen as very appropriate for joint funds, but these are also activities traditionally handled via internal union or management education funds.

6. *Where will the time come for committee meetings?* Both union and management leaders are increasingly finding themselves serving on a range of joint committees, consuming time that may even exceed that required for administering the grievance procedure. Often, however, one or both sides may conclude that all the time is not well spent, with the result being either a refocusing of joint efforts or a decline in participation by one side or the other.

7. *Does the program serve just the interests of line management or personnel staff, and what of the roles of stewards and bargaining committee members?* Training programs often are established and run by management personnel staff and by union appointees. When workers are brought off the job to participate in training, line management may see a loss in productive capabilities without perceiving any immediate gain in return. Similarly, union stewards and bargaining committee members may see the joint training as a potentially dangerous benefit to the membership that may not fully involve them. A controversial alternative is also possible where training is driven by a coalition between line management and local union leaders, leaving out personnel staff. Where joint training does have the potential to undermine the interests of one party or another, the very stability of the effort may come into question.

8. *Should salaried workers be trained in the same sessions with hourly workers?* Management frequently argues that combining salaried and hourly workers in appropriate training sessions can lead to savings via economies of scale—especially if program slots have not been fully filled by hourly employees. Yet union leaders or members may see the presence of salaried employees as inappropriately taking advantage of "their" training resources. However, over time classes that combine salaried and union personnel have been implemented successfully, provided that it does not occur at the expense of joint training funds reserved for union workers.

9. *Are union leaders perceived as being "too close" to management?* One of the most fundamental dilemmas faced by any union leader involves maintaining both the perception and the reality that they are independent of management while serving on a joint committee.

10. *Are managers giving up control of their hierarchical responsibilities?* One of the most fundamental dilemmas faced by managers involves preserving both the perception and the reality that they have not abandoned their managerial responsibilities by serving on a joint committee.

11. *How will joint training be evaluated?* Training evaluation is too rare in most unilateral programs. Because management and labor each have distinctive interests, agreement on the evaluation of a joint program is even more complicated. Each side has separate political concerns about potential conclusions from an evaluation study, so they often choose a default option of conducting limited forms of assessment (such as counting the number of training participants rather than examining how new skills are applied).

Given the many potentially divisive issues that can arise in the context of a union-management training committee, why are they formed at all? The answer is two-fold. First, as has been noted above, there are mechanisms for resolving some of these issues. Second, the divisive issues are counterbalanced by a number of unifying ones where the interests of labor and management are jointly enhanced.

Issues That Unite

There are a few critical issues that represent the common domain of labor and management when it comes to joint training, and it is these aspects that serve to unite the parties and reinforce their separate commitments to the joint activity. Listed in the following paragraphs are issues that can unite the parties with respect to joint training:

1. *The joint programs may increase the skill potential and the quality of the internal workforce—a shared objective for both parties.* A workforce with increased skills and knowledge is more likely to be productive and flexible, which contributes directly to management's interests in organizational performance. Concurrently, the union gains by contributing to the job security of its membership and by expanding members' skills and knowledge.

2. *Both union and management achieve good public relations among workers for their efforts.* The joint training programs reinforce a dual loyalty between the union and the employer, where neither's claim for loyalty is made at the expense of the other.

3. *The delivery of services is enhanced by a philosophy that emphasizes worker involvement.* Workers may be more likely to be involved both in the identification of training topics and in actual service as trainers. Both forms of worker involvement can lead to a higher quality and more popular training program.

4. *The involvement of both the union and the management serves as a check and balance in the administration of training activities.* Where a joint structure is established for training, the requirement of union and management agreement on a broad range of administrative decisions ensures that more diverse views are considered at early stages of decisionmaking. In contrast, a unilateral program may encounter implementation problems because certain perspectives were not considered in advance.

5. *The union confers a measure of legitimacy on the training efforts.* Workers may be skeptical of participation in managerial training programs for a variety of reasons. They may not be sure that the content is neutral. They may not be sure that they will be able to use what they learn. They may not be sure that the educational experience will be positive. In contrast, when a union places its stamp of approval on a training effort, the members may have a greater degree of confidence that their concerns have been addressed in advance. As well, they have access to a vehicle to raise concerns if they are not satisfied about such issues. Thus, the union brings a distinctive competence to the training effort that extends what management could do on its own.

6. *Management links training to organizational resources and line operations.* When a training program is run just by a union or just by an external training provider (public or private), there may be limitations on the extent to which the training is incorporated into the way the organization operates. By contrast, a joint program ensures that the training is always assessed relative to actual operations.

7. *The joint structure facilitates links between internal and external labor markets.* Because of the mix of interests that labor and management bring to joint training efforts, a worker's career

opportunities both within the firm and external to it are likely to be taken into account. As such, the focus of joint training program bridges between the status and opportunities within and outside the workplace.

The unifying issues associated with joint training represent the glue that holds a program together. To the extent that service delivery is improved, the scope of training broadened, and the interests of each side addressed, the joint training structure will be seen as valuable and something to be reinforced by the parties. Ultimately, these potential upside gains have to be seen also as outweighing the potentially divisive aspects of joint training.

Research and Public Policy Implications of Joint Training

The nexus between research, practice, and public policy has always been at the heart of the Industrial Relations Research Association. The focus of the above sections of this chapter has been on documenting and describing emerging joint training practices. In this concluding section we will sketch some of the research and policy implications of these new practices.

Research Implications

A threshold research question regarding joint training activities is the challenge of classification. We have noted that these activities can be narrowly focused or broadly defined. Further, they can be funded separately or jointly. There can be a fully joint governance structure in every aspect of the program, or there can be only a partial degree of jointness. The joint training can be the most significant undertaking that the parties pursue, or it can be a relatively minor aspect of the labor-management relationship. The program can be highly centralized or highly decentralized.

Although there are many dimensions upon which training programs can be arrayed, the various combinations do not come together randomly. A centralized program, for example, may be more likely to be linked to a separate source of funding and to have full-time staff. Thus, the classification challenge for researchers involves identifying various ideal types that represent meaningful structural tendencies among joint training programs.

With a useful taxonomy of joint training programs, it would then be possible to collect the systemic data needed to assess the level of current practice. Such data collection would be the next research challenge. The survey data reported in this chapter represent an initial effort at taking an inventory of activity.

Once we have an understanding of the scope of joint training activities, it then becomes possible to assess the potential significance of these activities. Here, all the challenges of program evaluation that are associated with assessing any training program apply. For example, simple through-put measures of the numbers of people trained are less informative than measures of the ways that new knowledge and skills are actually used. That is, what is taking place that would not have occurred if it were not for training? Too, there are some special issues associated with joint training programs. For example, the parties will have interests not in any one outcome, but in a range of outcomes including the impact on organizational performance and on job security and career opportunities.

Looking beyond outcomes, we see a number of research issues raised about which specific service delivery practices are unique to joint programs and linked to the outcomes. That is, we need to be even more precise about what aspects of joint programs make substantial contributions to the interests of one party or another. For example, how important is a separate joint fund to support training, as compared to funding training activities on a case-by-case basis?

All of the issues of outcomes and service delivery can then be examined in the context of the broader labor-management relationship, raising another domain for research. How do experiences on joint committees spill over into other aspects of the union-management relationship, and vice versa? Do some types of joint training, such as strategic planning, have greater labor-management implications than do others, such as health and safety training?

A yet broader contextual research issue involves the increased interdependency between the parties and external training providers. Equally, a set of research questions arises regarding the increased interdependency between joint training activities and governmental programs. These broader contextual issues are central to an assessment of the long-term potential for joint training activities.

Finally, a most controversial issue involves the extent to which joint training programs have lessons applicable to training in non-union settings. Does training benefit from a joint oversight structure in which the workers have elected or appointed representatives? Can there be such arrangements within a nonunion facility?

Ultimately, the research questions associated with joint training are all centered on what would have happened in the absence of the effort. These are among the hardest questions to answer since they involve estimating the impact of something that has not occurred.

Policy Implications

Given that training in the United States is becoming a more important policy issue—especially at the state level—and given the increased presence of various partnership structures, we will conclude this chapter with a brief consideration of the policy implications associated with joint labor-management training efforts. The issue can be seen from two perspectives. How do union and management pairs view public policy regarding training, and how do policymakers view joint efforts?

The first key policy area concerns public funding of private training activities. From the perspective of the parties, such funding has been a valuable supplement to the budgets for a number of local union-management pairs. An issue that concerns the parties in such cases involves any constraints on the usage of the money, though there are usually few. For government, however, there are profound policy challenges, including a core question regarding the degree to which such training would have taken place anyway in the absence of such funding. The answer to such a question is difficult since it is always hard to assess what might have happened, but didn't. On an a priori basis, however, we might expect that some forms of training that occurred under joint auspices would not have taken place if the initiative was only from the employer. To the extent that this is true, then a presumption might be made that public funding for joint training may be preferable to unilateral training. A related factor would be that joint training is more likely to encourage the development of general or transferable skills, which are usually seen as more in the public interest than narrower employer-specific skills.

The second policy domain involves the provision of technical services. More specifically, as secondary schools and community colleges are supported in their efforts to provide educational services to the private sector, joint committees will be among the clients contracting for these services. Further, governmental programs around worker displacement will likely count joint structures as being among those they help to establish. For the parties, these interactions raise issues regarding how to assess the relative competence of various public service-providers and how they manage their interactions with them. For public educational institutions and governmental agencies, contracting with a union-management pair may be somewhat more complicated and may involve a somewhat broader range of training activities. Thus, with respect to public providers of service, joint training arrangements add some twists on both sides of the arrangement (service-provider and customer), but these are not fundamentally new issues.

The third policy domain is the most elusive, but also the furthest reaching. This is the issue of governance. As linkages form between union-management training programs and public entities—around either funding or services—both sets of parties will have some measure of interest in the decisionmaking processes of the other. It remains to be seen, however, how unions and employers, on the one hand, and public institutions, on the other, will approach such multilateral public-private partnerships.

It should be noted that all three policy domains highlighted here—funding, technical assistance, and governance—may take on different meanings in the case of joint programs involving large employers as compared with those in smaller firms. In the case of larger employers and larger union locals, the leverage of the employer and the union will be greater vis-à-vis the government, but the need for public assistance will (arguably) be lower. In the case of the smaller employer, there may be less leverage, but the public sector can play a far more critical role in fostering the development of joint training initiatives.

To date there has been very little research on policy development in relation to joint training efforts. Given the diversity of such joint efforts, it is unlikely that research would point to any single model for the relationship between joint training and government. Yet further investigation is clearly called for. There is preliminary evidence to suggest that joint programs may be more complementary with the public purpose than are unilateral programs. Equally, public support has played a critical role in various joint training efforts. The opportunity before us is to better understand the nexus between the two domains.

Conclusion

Joint union-management training has emerged in the 1980s as a distinctive innovation. It stands as an alternative to unilateral training, and it marks an advanced stage in the evolution of jointism. In these ways joint training represents a synthesis between the evolution of jointism and the increased importance of training.

Since there has been relatively little research to date on joint training, this chapter has served to describe the phenomenon as much as it has codified existing scholarship. In the process we have learned that codetermination in decisionmaking is at the core of joint training and that many of its distinctive aspects flow from this joint structure. Decisions emerge on a consensus basis rather than via a top-down hierarchy, though there is as much conflict as there is cooperation between the parties. Target populations frequently include active and displaced workers. Worker trainers can play key roles in service delivery, as can public funds and public educational institutions. There are often high degrees of local control, but training structures still vary greatly with firm size, industry structure, and other factors. Ultimately, we see that unions can bring a certain degree of legitimacy and access to the training, but they insist on more of a long-term career focus in training content. Employers make it possible for the training to take place on a vast scale, but bring a set of firm interests into the situation. It remains to be seen whether nonunion analogues will emerge, where employees have direct representation in training policy decisions. But at least in the unionized sector, joint training stands as a distinctive innovation of the 1980s that is sure to have a far-reaching legacy for the 1990s.

References

Baker, Richard. "Joint Labor-Management Responses to Worker Dislocation Under the Auspices of State Government." In *Joint Programs for the Training and Personal Development of Workers: New Initiatives in Union-Management Relations*, eds. Louis A. Ferman, Michele Hoyman, Joel Cutcher-Gershenfeld, and Ernest J. Savoie. Ithaca, NY: ILR Press, 1991.

Block, Richard, Joel Cutcher-Gershenfeld, Ellen Kossek, Michael Moore, Debra Gash, Patrick McHugh, and Almira Gilles. *Innovative Labor-Management Practices in Small Firms*. Washington: U.S. Department of Labor, forthcoming.

Cutcher-Gershenfeld, Joel. "Reconceiving the Web of Labor-Management Relations." *Labor Law Journal* 36, 8 (August 1985), pp. 637-45.

Cutcher-Gershenfeld, Joel, Thomas Kochan, and Anil Verma. "Recent Developments in U.S. Employee Involvement Initiatives: Erosion or Transformation?" In *Advances in Industrial Relations*, forthcoming 1990.

De Schweinitz, Dorothea. *Labor and Management in a Common Enterprise*. Cambridge, MA: Harvard University Press, 1949.

Ferman, Louis A., and Michele Hoyman. "Service Delivery in Joint Training Programs." In *Joint Programs for the Training and Personal Development of Workers: New Initiatives in Union-Management Relations*, eds. Louis A. Ferman, Michele Hoyman, Joel Cutcher-Gershenfeld, and Ernest J. Savoie. Ithaca, NY: ILR Press, 1991.

Ford, Kevin. "Training and Strategic Planning in Michigan Firms." Social Science Research Bureau Seminar, Michigan State University. East Lansing, May 1990.

Gomberg, William. "Special Study Committees." In *Frontiers of Collective Bargaining*, eds. John T. Dunlop and Neil W. Chamberlain. New York: Harper & Row, 1967.

Gordus, Jeanne, Cheng Kuo, and Karen Yamakawa. "A Joint Employee Development Program for Lifelong Learning: Creating Educational Opportunity and Support Structure." In *Joint Programs for the Training and Personal Development of Workers: New Initiatives in Union-Management Relations*, eds. Louis A. Ferman, Michele Hoyman, Joel Cutcher-Gershenfeld, and Ernest J. Savoie. Ithaca, NY: ILR Press, 1991.

Hoyman, Michele, and Louis Ferman. "The Scope and Extent of Joint Labor-Management Training Programs." In *Joint Programs for the Training and Personal Development of Workers: New Initiatives in Union-Management Relations*, eds. Louis A. Ferman, Michele Hoyman, Joel Cutcher-Gershenfeld, and Ernest J. Savoie. Ithaca, NY: ILR Press, 1991.

Jacoby, Sanford M. "Union-Management Cooperation in the United States: Lessons from the 1920s." *Industrial and Labor Relations Review* 37, 1 (October 1983), pp. 18–33.

McMillan, Michael. "Fostering Labor-Management Cooperation in Training Dislocated Workers: What Does It Really Take?" In *Joint Programs for the Training and Personal Development of Workers: New Initiatives in Union-Management Relations*, eds. Louis A. Ferman, Michele Hoyman, Joel Cutcher-Gershenfeld, and Ernest J. Savoie. Ithaca, NY: ILR Press, 1991.

Ross, Kenneth, and Donald Treinen. "The Emergence of a Union-Management Training Program: The Case of CAW, IBEW, and AT&T." In *Joint Programs for the Training and Personal Development of Workers: New Initiatives in Union-Management Relations*, eds. Louis A. Ferman, Michele Hoyman, Joel Cutcher-Gershenfeld, and Ernest J. Savoie. Ithaca, NY: ILR Press, 1991.

Savoie, Ernest J., and Joel Cutcher-Gershenfeld. "Reflections on the Governance of Joint Training Initiatives." In *Joint Programs for the Training and Personal Development of Workers: New Initiatives in Union-Management Relations*, eds. Louis A. Ferman, Michele Hoyman, Joel Cutcher-Gershenfeld, and Ernest J. Savoie. Ithaca, NY: ILR Press, 1991.

Schurman, Susan, Margrit Hugentobler, and Hal Stack. "Creating Educational Partnerships for a Changing Economy: Lessons from the UAW-GM Paid Educational Leave Program." In *Joint Programs for the Training and Personal Development of Workers: New Initiatives in Union-Management Relations*, eds. Louis A. Ferman, Michele Hoyman, Joel Cutcher-Gershenfeld, and Ernest J. Savoie. Ithaca, NY: ILR Press, 1991.

CHAPTER 7

Welfare Employment Policy in the 1980s*

JUDITH M. GUERON AND DAVID A. LONG
Manpower Demonstration Research Corporation

The decade of the 1980s was important in the evolution of employment and training policy for welfare recipients. Major federal legislative and budgetary changes, culminating in the Family Support Act (FSA) of 1988, set overall policy direction. But it was at the state and local levels, where programs were actually designed and implemented, that a surge of new interest and initiatives pushed this program area into the domestic-policy limelight.

In this chapter we discuss what we have learned about designing and implementing these programs. We begin with an overview of policy issues and changes during the eighties and describe the competing objectives policymakers grappled with in designing welfare employment programs. We explain why, their high visibility notwithstanding, these initiatives had limited resources and consequently stressed low-cost services rather than intensive education or training. We then summarize the available evidence on program implementation and effectiveness by drawing on findings from a series of studies of state initiatives, and we conclude by identifying a number of important unanswered questions.

* Partial funding for this chapter was provided by the Ford Foundation. The research summarized was supported by the Ford, Winthrop Rockefeller, and Claude Worthington Benedum Foundations; the Congressional Research Service of the Library of Congress; the Office of the Assistant Secretary for Planning and Evaluation and the Office of Family Assistance, U.S. Department of Health and Human Services; and the states of Arkansas, California, Illinois, Maryland, Virginia, and West Virginia. The conclusions reached by the authors, however, do not necessarily reflect the official positions of the funders.

In preparing this chapter, the authors drew on the work of their colleagues at MDRC, in particular Michael Bangser, Barbara Goldman, and Daniel Friedlander.

Federal Policy and State Programs

Providing employment and training services to the welfare caseload is different from providing them to other populations because of the particular needs of welfare recipients and the interplay of the services with welfare policy. Compared to most other groups served by schools and training programs, welfare recipients have far more limited skills and employment histories. Further, because most recipients are single parents and all are poor, they have family obligations and crises but do not have the resources of other parents for handling them. These two factors create serious obstacles to successful participation in education and training.

Finally, employment and training programs for this population are often mandatory, with participation being a requirement for continued receipt of public assistance. State welfare programs have frequently included work requirements, but Congress first introduced the concept in 1971 for the federally assisted Aid to Families with Dependent Children (AFDC) program, which supports primarily single mothers and their children. Starting that year, all adult recipients in single-parent households with school-age children (AFDC cases)—and one adult in two-parent families (AFDC-UP, or "Unemployed Parent," cases)—were required to register and participate in a welfare employment program, the federal Work Incentive (WIN) program, or risk grant reductions. Because of resource constraints, however, participation was often limited to registration, and the program gradually lost credibility as it failed to meet its operational objectives and could provide no reliable findings on cost-effectiveness. During this period, a number of small-scale tests of voluntary employment, training, and job-search programs showed that services for women on AFDC could be cost-effective and produce long-term benefits (Manpower Demonstration Research Corporation, 1980; Wolfhagen with Goldman, 1983). But research on large-scale state programs during the 1970s yielded more questions than answers and, given the increasing perception of poor WIN performance, welfare employment policy failed to generate much excitement.[1] During the 1980s, however, many states initiated new welfare employment programs and many others altered their existing programs.

---

[1] See Gueron and Nathan (1985) for a summary of the lessons from pre-1980 state demonstrations.

At the opening of the decade, state welfare employment programs were relatively homogeneous, since almost all the funding came from WIN and other federal funding sources and federal rules were attached to the funds.[2] All state WIN programs had essentially the same administrative structure, used federal definitions of who was required to participate, and were judged according to federal performance standards. States generally followed the "WIN model" in providing services; it emphasized short-duration assistance and prescribed program processes in detail. For example, employability development plans had to be completed by one group of WIN counselors, while support-services needs had to be identified by a separate unit.[3]

This environment changed with passage of the Omnibus Budget Reconciliation Act (OBRA) of 1981, which cut total domestic spending by more than $50 billion and reduced federal WIN funding in fiscal year 1982 by more than $80 million. With this and other cuts during the decade, federal WIN expenditures dropped from $365 million in 1980 to $93 million in 1988. In constant dollars, federal support for WIN at the end of the decade was less than a fifth of what it was at the start. Confronted with their loss of core funding, many states eliminated WIN altogether in some of their counties; others dropped relatively expensive training and support services in favor of limited job-search and placement assistance (Nightingale, 1985).

But there was another side to this story. Under OBRA and other legislation, the reduced WIN funding was provided as a block grant, which states were freer to use as they wished. Further, most federal WIN reporting requirements were eliminated. States could now run Community Work Experience Programs (CWEP)—popularly known as "workfare"—in which AFDC recipients are required to work in community agencies in exchange for their welfare

---

[2] Ninety percent of the cost of WIN, the primary employment and training program for the welfare population, was paid for by the federal government under Title IV-C of the Social Security Act, and 10 percent was paid for by state and local governments (the required "match" of federal funding). Fifty percent of certain related costs was covered by the federal government under Title IV-A of the act (the state and local match was the remaining 50 percent). In addition, welfare recipients were served by programs funded under the Comprehensive Employment and Training Act (CETA), the costs of which were borne largely by the federal government.

[3] For a discussion of this model, see Mitchell (1979), especially Chapter 1. See Mead (1986) and Rein (1982) for different views of the WIN program.

benefits, mandatory-participation job search programs for new AFDC applicants (previously states would operate these programs only for people who were already on the AFDC rolls), and AFDC grant diversion to pay for on-the-job training programs.[4] In addition, states were given WIN Demonstration authorization to reorganize their welfare employment programs institutionally. States were allowed, but not required, to make any or all of these changes.

Most states responded to these options. For example, about half the states created CWEP within two years of OBRA's passage, and most established new administrative arrangements, typically assigning full responsibility for welfare employment activities to the same agency that was responsible for welfare (Nightingale, 1985, Table 4:1). But state and local officials were prudent and cautious in experimenting with new program approaches during the first few years after OBRA, limiting the extent of their initial changes and relying heavily on the federal "reform" options they had been given. Legislators and administrators in some states, however, became increasingly interested in more ambitious change, especially as publicity about new state initiatives grew and evidence of their potential effectiveness mounted. Thus, the decentralization of welfare employment policymaking that occurred during the decade, which can be traced to OBRA and other federal legislation, gathered momentum as state and local officials got involved in new policymaking efforts.

Virtually all programs implemented in the early and mid-1980s can be thought of as the "first generation" of welfare employment programs developed during the decade. Although they frequently included innovations and practical features tailored to their local environments, these programs characteristically entailed modest overall changes from what went on before them. They usually sought to improve on WIN by implementing a single mandate for part of the welfare caseload to participate in one or two work-related activities lasting at most three or four months—based on federal actions, such as the OBRA provision to permit CWEP, and supported primarily by federal funding.

A number of "second-generation" initiatives instituted more far-reaching changes in welfare employment policy. These programs

---

[4] Under grant diversion, all or part of a person's AFDC benefits can be offered to an employer as a subsidy to encourage the hiring of the welfare recipient.

relied more heavily on both state ideas and state funding. The Employment and Training (ET) Choices program in Massachusetts, inaugurated in 1983, was particularly influential in persuading other states to consider more ambitious initiatives. The ET program had a distinctive philosophy, which contrasted with both the WIN model and the OBRA options. Although it required AFDC recipients to register for the program (consistent with federal WIN requirements), ET urged rather than required participation in training activities, and it "marketed" the value of the program in actively recruiting participants. Unlike most WIN programs that preceded it, in which enrollees had no choice in the activities they attended, ET clients made their own decisions about whether to participate in the program and which of its services to use. Importantly, the state's investment in the program—taking enough funds from its own treasury to put together a budget of more than $45 million in fiscal year 1989—has allowed ET to offer services to all welfare recipients who want them.

ET demonstrated how states, in a newly decentralized policy-making environment, could make their mark in welfare employment policy by developing their own programs. Publicity about the ET program, as well as favorable findings from studies of several new initiatives in other states, helped stimulate the development of second-generation programs in much the same way that OBRA stimulated the first-generation programs. Two of these second-generation programs have been statewide initiatives involving funding commitments comparable to that of ET. One is California's Greater Avenues for Independence (GAIN) program, which had a budget of more than $370 million for fiscal year 1989. Unlike ET, however, GAIN requires participation by AFDC recipients (except single parents with very young children) until they leave welfare, and it places greater emphasis on education. And almost $52 million was budgeted for the same year in New Jersey, where the Realizing Economic Achievement (REACH) program intends to require participation by single parents with children as young as 2 years of age.

Many states, however, made no major changes in their welfare employment policies other than those necessitated by federal budget cuts. Typically, these states reduced the scope of WIN activities early in the decade and did not subsequently increase it, relying entirely or almost entirely on declining WIN funds. For example, 12 states and the District of Columbia received only regular WIN funding from the federal government in 1986. Moreover, only 19 states operated WIN in all of their counties in late 1986, so part of the welfare caseload in the remaining 31 states was not covered by a welfare employment program of any kind. These uncovered cases amounted to 20 percent of the AFDC cases nationwide (Nightingale and Burbridge, 1987).

Thus, the homogeneous welfare employment conditions of 1980 gave way to highly variable conditions by 1989, a situation likely to continue in the nineties. The Family Support Act of 1988, which provides additional federal funding to states willing to spend their own money to develop and extend welfare employment programs, will expand education and training activities in some states more than in others. This variation in programs, it should be noted, provides a natural laboratory in which to study the design, implementation, and effectiveness of welfare employment policy.

Designing Programs

The variation in state programs reflected choices among competing uses of limited resources. These choices generally fell into three categories: service delivery, caseload targeting, and participation requirements. In simple terms, states faced competing pressures to allocate their limited resources to high-cost services, to reach a large share of the caseload, and to manage the caseload to ensure participation in programs.

Service Delivery

Some programs, including many first-generation initiatives, emphasized immediate employment. These programs relied on job-search assistance as the primary service offered to welfare recipients. This kind of assistance, which is geared to increasing and improving job-seeking efforts, is given in a group or an individual setting. When provided to a group, it usually is a structured activity including instruction in résumé writing, job interviewing, and other job-search skills, followed by telephoning employers to obtain specific job leads. When provided on an individual basis, a single caseworker gives guidance and specific job-placement assistance to an individual recipient. In both cases, the program was intended to provide short-duration, low-cost help—offering the shortest distance between two points, welfare dependence and jobs.

Other programs put more emphasis on providing skills so as to increase an individual's human capital. These programs included various forms of education (adult basic education, GED or high school classes, vocational education, and English as a second language) and vocational training (both in the classroom and on the job). Increased human capital improves an individual's potential for obtaining high wages and a "good" job (although, of course, there are no guarantees of either). This, in turn, increases the probability of job retention and self-sufficiency and reduces the chance that someone will return to welfare. This was an explicit goal of programs such as ET.

To a large extent, however, state decisions in this area were driven by resource constraints, which severely limited most states' ability to provide higher-cost services, especially education and training. All state policymakers faced the same fundamental conflict between what they ideally wanted to do and what their resources permitted them to do. Some were particularly constrained, especially those in states that relied primarily on declining federal WIN funds. Others were less restricted because supplemental funds—usually at least some federal Title IV-A funds, which must be matched 50-50 by states—were obtained. Funding from other federal sources, such as the Job Training Partnership Act (JTPA) system, has sometimes been earmarked for welfare employment programs as well. "Second-generation" programs such as ET and GAIN were generally developed with sufficient resources so that WIN funding constituted a small fraction of total funding. But this was true of very few programs operated during the eighties, even at the decade's end. As noted above, the Family Support Act offers increased federal funding for welfare employment initiatives. Because it provides a more generous federal match, it makes commitment of state monies to these efforts more attractive.[5]

---

[5] Federal funding for the Job Opportunities and Basic Skills Training (JOBS) program of the Family Support Act of 1988 was $600 million for fiscal year 1989 ($800 million for fiscal year 1990). Because only 15 states started JOBS in fiscal year 1989, and those states were not allowed to begin their JOBS programs until the fourth quarter of the year, actual expenditures were substantially less than $600 million.

Of the JOBS annual entitlement, $126 million requires only a 10 percent match by the states (compared to the $93 million federal WIN allocation that was subject to the same matching requirement in 1988); the remainder requires matches of between 20 and 50 percent, depending on the state and the activity. (Title IV-A funding in 1988 covered a much more limited range of activities and required a 50 percent match.) Also, the Family Support Act places no limit on the amount of federal funds available to match state funds to pay for child-care services.

Further complicating the states' decisionmaking was the absence of reliable information on the key assumption underlying programmatic choices. In particular, there was uncertainty about whether low-cost job-search programs had only short-term effects and whether human capital investment strategies would deliver on their promise of greater long-term effects.

Caseload Targeting

Operating a statewide welfare employment program for the entire AFDC caseload is an expensive proposition, especially if education and training are prominent among the services offered. Hence, most welfare employment programs focused on only part of the caseload. Their targeting fell into two categories. Geographic targeting directed a program's limited resources to selected areas. For example, many states excluded their most rural counties from WIN programs, and many targeted new welfare employment initiatives to particular counties or offices within a county.

Targeting according to the characteristics of welfare recipients was also common. For example, most states concentrated services on women with school-age children (the traditional WIN-mandatory group), some provided services to new welfare applicants only, and others emphasized the relatively small number of two-parent welfare families (AFDC-UPs).

Participation Requirements

How did policymakers ensure that the targeted population participated in the program? A voluntary-participation program could recruit participants. But given the recipient-obligations philosophy of most welfare employment programs during the 1980s, participation was usually sought through participation requirements. This approach—which involved sanctions that reduced grants for individuals who did not meet the requirements—was attractive to programs that sought broad caseload coverage. It was generally less appropriate for very narrowly targeted programs, however, because fairness issues would have arisen if particular groups were singled out for participation obligations.

Much of the controversy surrounding welfare employment programs has centered on the question of whether participation should be voluntary or mandatory. An ideological debate on this issue continues between those who believe that the poor are entitled to income support without work or other requirements and those who believe that obligations have to be imposed on those who receive support; the latter group has gained the upper hand in most states.

However, the program-design issue was not whether a program should be "voluntary" or "mandatory," terms that convey little about either a program's requirements or its message. Rather, the issue was the extent to which programs imposed and enforced obligations. All programs were mandatory to some degree, because federal WIN rules required that program registration be mandatory. Beyond this, several design decisions affected the nature of the participation requirement:

- *What were individuals required to do?* Typically, welfare recipients in the first-generation programs were required to look for a job for two to four weeks (often in a group job-search setting); if unsuccessful, they were frequently assigned to a work-experience position for up to three months. In contrast, GAIN has required recipients to participate in a sequence of activities determined by their characteristics (such as educational deficiencies) and preferences. Also, in some programs, the welfare recipient has been allowed to choose the activity in which he or she has been required to participate.

- *For how long?* Most programs imposed short-term participation requirements. For example, required job search followed by work experience ordinarily lasted less than four months. However, several programs required individuals to participate as long as they remained on welfare.

- *How were requirements enforced?* Federal WIN rules called for individuals to be sanctioned when a local program found them to be out of compliance with locally set participation requirements. Sanctions eliminated grants to two-parent cases and reduced them to single-parent cases. However, programs had latitude in setting their own requirements and determining what constituted noncompliance. Enforcement, therefore, entailed any amount of persuasion (efforts to communicate requirements, solve individual problems preventing compliance, and promote participation) and sanctioning that state and local policymakers deemed appropriate.

Thus, a wide range of "mandatory" programs were designed. Most first-generation programs imposed relatively simple, short-duration requirements, while programs such as GAIN have adopted complicated rules that have been difficult and expensive to enforce.

Program Experience

While many states initiated new welfare employment programs during the 1980s, much of what is reliably known about program implementation and effectiveness came from evaluations conducted by the Manpower Demonstration Research Corporation (MDRC) of programs started between 1982 and 1985. Because of the absence of similar data for other locations, the remainder of this chapter draws heavily on seven of those evaluations. These initiatives, the main features of which are summarized in Table 1, covered a range of designs and environments.[6] All were mandatory programs serving about 40 percent or less of the AFDC caseload, in most cases applicants and recipients with school-age children. Most were first-generation initiatives that provided short-term services—primarily job-search assistance followed by three months in an unpaid work experience or workfare position for those who did not find jobs. In some instances, education and vocational training were also part of the program model, notably in two initiatives (Baltimore and San Diego II), where welfare recipients were referred to other programs for such services. Only the second program in San Diego—which provided multiple services to a large share of the AFDC caseload and required ongoing participation by recipients in these services—can be considered a second-generation program. Program costs were low to moderate, ranging from under $200 in Cook County (Illinois) and Arkansas to around $1000 in Baltimore and $1100 in San Diego II, calculated as the average cost per eligible (that is, per welfare applicant or recipient targeted by the initiative, including those contacted by a program but receiving no direct services).

---

[6] The programs were implemented in all counties in West Virginia and Virginia, and in selected counties in Arkansas. In these three states, MDRC's evaluation covered a subset of these counties. The first San Diego demonstration operated between 1982 and 1985 and provided short-term job search and work experience. The second operated between 1985 and 1987 and imposed an ongoing participation requirement in a sequence of services, including education or training. See Gueron (1987) for further discussion of these studies.

TABLE 1

Dimensions of Seven Welfare Employment Programs

Location	Duration of Obligation	Target Group	Primary Program Services	Extent of Enforcement
Arkansas	Limited	WIN-Mandatory AFDC Applicants and Recipients[a]	Job Search/ Work Experience Sequence	Moderate
Baltimore	Limited	WIN-Mandatory AFDC and AFDC-UP Applicants and New Recipients	Job Search, Education, Training, OJT, Work Experience Options	Moderate
Cook County	Limited	WIN-Mandatory AFDC Applicants and Recipients	Job Search/ Work Experience Sequence	Strong
San Diego I[b]	Limited	WIN-Mandatory AFDC and AFDC-UP Applicants	Job Search/ Work Experience Sequence	Strong
San Diego II[b]	Ongoing	WIN-Mandatory AFDC and AFDC-UP Applicants and Recipients	Job Search/ Work Experience/ Education or Training Sequence	Strong
Virginia	Limited	WIN-Mandatory AFDC Applicants and Recipients	Job Search/ Work Experience Sequence	Moderate
West Virginia	Ongoing	WIN-Mandatory AFDC and AFDC-UP Applicants and Recipients	Work Experience	Moderate for AFDC; Strong for AFDC-UP

Note: The "WIN-mandatory" portion of the caseload consists of single heads of households with children age 6 or older (referred to as AFDC cases) and, in most states, case heads of two-parent households (AFDC-UP, or "Unemployed Parent," cases). Most AFDCs are females; most AFDC-UPs are males.

[a] Includes women whose youngest child is 3 years of age or older.

[b] The first San Diego demonstration operated between 1982 and 1985. The San Diego II demonstration operated between 1985 and 1986.

Delivering Program Services

In most of the initiatives studied by MDRC, the new service delivery systems were similar to their predecessors, making planning and implementation of the new systems relatively easy. Often an agency continued to provide the same services, but to different populations or on a different scale. For example, in San

Diego the local office of the state Employment Development Department, which had run job clubs for welfare recipients in the WIN program, was responsible for operating job clubs in the first of the two initiatives MDRC studied there. And the county's Department of Social Services, which had set up work experience positions for food stamp recipients, was responsible for operating that component of the new program.

Thus, many of the core staff and institutional relationships were in place at the outset, so the necessary service delivery capacity could be developed readily and the services themselves could be offered quickly. Often, too, organizations that did not have such experience referred welfare recipients to other agencies that did. In some programs, however, the agencies responsible for the initiatives had little or no pertinent in-house experience or had to develop new relationships with other organizations.

Involving the Caseload

A service delivery system is necessary but not sufficient to assure that potential participants become active. A program also needs a case oversight system—an organized way of tracking and handling each welfare case targeted by the program. Since case management was not a strength of WIN programs, WIN experience was not particularly useful in this regard.

Welfare employment programs have taken different approaches to case oversight. Some have used "generalist" case managers to handle the full array of oversight functions—conducting registration, making assessments, arranging support services, obtaining compliance with program participation requirements, initiating sanctions, and so forth—while others, particularly large or complex programs, have relied more on specialists. In the second program in San Diego, which required ongoing participation in a sequence of activities, all oversight functions requiring case contact were handled by case managers in the two agencies delivering the program services, while a separate unit monitored attendance and sent all notices to registrants. Other key differences in the seven programs studied included (1) the average number of cases assigned to each case manager, which ranged from about 50 to more than 250; (2) program rules and operating procedures (for example, approaches to granting deferrals from participation requirements for reasons such as illness and child-care problems);

and (3) the capabilities of the management information systems that supported case oversight efforts.

In general, the administrators of these new initiatives sought to increase participation over the levels obtained in their earlier WIN programs. However, they operated in a climate of substantial uncertainty. At that time—the early to mid-1980s—there was little reliable information on the feasibility of mandating participation or the level of activity that would reflect successful implementation of a participation mandate. The experiences of the seven programs—all of which were found to be relatively successful in reaching their targeted caseloads—provided new evidence of the potential for involving a population of AFDC single parents in employment activities.

The seven programs varied in the extent to which their services reached their targeted AFDC groups. Assessing this experience required considering the flow of welfare recipients through the program activities. While programs developed different procedures and sequences of services, several generic actions were common to virtually all of them—notably registration, orientation, participation by an individual in his or her first activity, participation in subsequent activities, and deregistration. These actions could be thought of as "milestones" in the movement of cases from registration to termination.

One way of assessing program participation was longitudinally, ascertaining the proportion of registrants who ever reached a given milestone within a specified period of time. (Longitudinal activity measures focused on the same cohort of registrants for the specified period.) Table 2 shows nine- or twelve-month activity indicators for the seven programs. The broadest indicator (column 1) shows that within nine (or twelve) months of registration, between 38 and 64 percent of all eligibles took part in a specific activity scheduled by the programs. The other figures show the specific components in which individuals participated. In all the program models except West Virginia and Baltimore, job search was the first component and work experience was the second. The table shows the pronounced dropoff that occurred in succeeding stages of the programs. For example, while half of all eligibles in the second San Diego initiative participated in job search, only one fifth participated in work experience.

It is important to recognize that achieving a 100 percent overall participation rate in these programs—or anything like it—was an unrealistic objective and that, whatever the overall rate, a smaller

TABLE 2

Summary of Participation and Other Program Outcomes
for AFDC Eligibles in Seven Welfare Employment Programs

Location	Participated in:				Deregistered for:	
	Any Activity	Job Search	Work Experience	Education and Training[a]	All Reasons	Sanction
Arkansas	38.0%	27.3%[b]	2.9%	n/a	57.5%	n/a
Baltimore	45.0	24.7	17.5	17.3%	37.6	n/a
Cook County	38.8	36.1	7.3	4.1	56.9	12.4%
San Diego I	46.4	44.1	13.0	n/a	60.6	8.0
San Diego II	64.4	50.6	19.5	24.3	61.5	10.6
Virginia	58.3	51.0	9.5	11.6	42.3	3.8
West Virginia	n/a	n/a	23.9	n/a	42.3	1.8

Source: MDRC reports.

Notes: All estimates are for the nine-month period following random assignment except those for Baltimore and San Diego II, which are for a twelve-month period.

As indicated in Table 1, estimates are for AFDC applicants and recipients in all locations except San Diego I, which included only applicants.

In Arkansas, San Diego II, and West Virginia, percentages are calculated using a base of all eligibles who registered in the program; in Baltimore, Cook County, San Diego I, and Virginia, the base includes nonregistrants.

[a] Includes only education and training that was either provided or approved and monitored by the program. Individuals in all seven programs also undertook other education and training.

[b] Participation in the individual Job Search component of the Arkansas demonstration is not included here.

proportion of eligibles would be involved at succeeding program stages. This occurred for several reasons. First, many cases were temporarily deferred from participation requirements because of part-time employment, illness, or other circumstances recognized by the programs; these situations could easily have lasted throughout the nine-month period under consideration. Second, normal welfare turnover meant that as time passed during the nine months cases left welfare or became ineligible for the program for other reasons. Indeed, to the extent that an early activity such as job search successfully moved people into jobs, the turnover increased. Table 2 indicates the proportion of registrants served by each program who deregistered from it because of a welfare departure or other change in status. Other data, not shown in Table 2, suggest that the programs in fact reached a very high proportion of those eligible. Within nine or twelve months of registration, typically between 75 and 90 percent of eligibles had, in some sense, satisfied the program mandate (if not through participation, then by getting a job or leaving the rolls) or had their welfare grant reduced.

Finally, the percentage of the targeted caseload that actively participated in a welfare employment program at any given point was even lower than these longitudinal rates suggest. In the second San Diego program, which achieved the highest longitudinal participation rate—64 percent—about one third of eligibles actively participated in the program during any given month and another one fifth were employed. While this may seem low, the evaluation concluded that it was probably the maximum proportion of the caseload that could have been active in the program and, consequently, that the program successfully implemented its ongoing participation requirement. (Participation might, in fact, have been lower if San Diego had not had a well-managed, experienced staff and favorable economic conditions.) The 50 percent activity rate did not mean that resources were spent on only half the caseload. On the contrary, to get that level of participation, the program had to work with a majority of those targeted in the caseload. Most of the people who did not participate during a given month were only temporarily inactive. They were deferred (for that month, which may or may not have been extended to the other months covered by the longitudinal measures) or they were waiting for service activities to begin. Only about 10 percent of eligibles in any month failed to participate without a program-approved reason. (As indicated in Table 2, the sanctioning process began for most of these cases.)

Program Impacts and Cost-Effectiveness

Planners and administrators of welfare employment programs want to know whether their efforts result in increases in employment and earnings or reductions in dependence on welfare, and the extent to which programs are cost-effective. While these appear to be straightforward questions, an extensive evaluation research literature suggests the difficulty of obtaining accurate answers. This section summarizes the available information from the 1980s experience with programs for the AFDC population, using information from the seven evaluations.[7] Before presenting the evidence, it is important to understand four issues that affect its interpretation.

Understanding Impacts

The Distinction Between Outcomes and Impacts. Administrators typically have information on the behavior of people who have participated in a program: for example, whether they entered jobs or left the welfare rolls. These "outcomes" may seem to provide an appropriate indicator of success, since they appear to measure exactly what the programs seek to achieve. However, extensive recent research has shown that many welfare recipients take jobs, get married, or move off the rolls—often quite rapidly—without special work mandates or program assistance.[8]

As a result, "gross" operating data on job placements or case closures inevitably overstate program achievements, since they count all positive changes, without identifying the extent to which they actually result from the employment program. The correct measure of a program's success is its "net" impact, which is the change in an outcome (for example, in the employment rate) that results only from the program. The challenge in estimating this is to distinguish accurately between program-induced changes and the normal dynamics of welfare turnover and labor market behavior of

---

[7] As indicated in Table 1, some of the programs also required participation of people in two-parent, AFDC-UP cases. Results for this primarily male population are not presented in this chapter.

[8] See, for example, Bane and Ellwood (1983) and Ellwood (1986).

the population. This requires a precise estimate of what would have happened to people in the program in the absence of any intervention.

The Role of Social Experiments. A number of recent studies and advisory panels point to the difficulty of developing a control group that accurately mimics the behavior of program enrollees. They urge the unique value of classical experiments using random assignment.[9] With random assignment, the control group is similar in all respects except access to program services and should not produce the biased estimates of program impact that have typically plagued studies in this area.

Because of uncertainty about the accuracy of quasi-experimental estimates, in this chapter we rely on the smaller number of studies in which welfare applicants or recipients were randomly assigned to a mandatory welfare employment program (the "experimentals") or to a control group excused from program requirements. Almost 35,000 people were randomly assigned to experimental and control groups in the seven MDRC studies discussed in this chapter. The behavior of these two statistically equivalent groups was tracked over time, using data from state unemployment insurance earnings records and state or county AFDC payment files. The activities of the control group provided a benchmark showing the extent to which experimentals would have become employed or left welfare without the program. The differences between the two groups provided unbiased estimates of net program impacts.

The Background of Other Services. Welfare employment programs were not the only service facing this population. They could also voluntarily participate in alternative employment and education programs offered by institutions as diverse as community colleges, Job Training Partnership Act (JTPA) providers, and the Employment Service. In fact, the studies that form the basis of this chapter indicate that a not inconsequential share of members of the control group received such services. As a result, the measured impacts show the added effect of the new welfare employment program over and above any underlying change that might have resulted from use of this broader network of services.

---

[9] See Betsey, Hollister, and Papageorgiou (1985); Job Training Longitudinal Survey Research Advisory Panel (1985); Burtless and Orr (1986); Ashenfelter (1987); and LaLonde and Maynard (1987) for discussions of the relative merits of experimental and quasi-experimental studies.

Estimating Impacts on Targeted Cases. The welfare employment programs of the early to mid-1980s were targeted at a specific segment of the welfare caseload, such as WIN-mandatory applicants (in the San Diego I demonstration) or all applicants and recipients (including women with children as young as age 3, in the Arkansas study). People in this eligible group might have been affected by actually participating in program services or by the threat of sanctions for not participating. (That is, nonparticipants might have been deterred from continuing their application for or remaining on welfare by the prospect of required participation or the actual application of sanctions.)

Because of this, studies of mandatory programs should estimate impacts across the full caseload that was targeted for program services, including people who may never actually have gotten on welfare or received program services. This is quite different from the more familiar procedure followed in the typical evaluation of voluntary employment and training programs, where impacts are estimated only for participants. Therefore, readers are cautioned in making comparisons between studies of these two types of programs.

Readers are also cautioned that, as in most evaluations of employment programs, impacts on earnings and welfare grants are estimated as averages that include nonearners as well as earners, those on welfare as well as those off the rolls. Thus, average earnings and earnings impacts may appear to be low and yet be relatively substantial if considered only for those individuals who were actually employed.

Program Impacts

The results from the seven studies show that in most cases the programs led to measurable increases in employment and earnings. Moreover, these positive impacts, in the three states for which longer-term estimates were available, were long-lasting. This was true both for the very low-cost job search/work experience programs in Arkansas and Virginia and for the more enriched (but still moderate-cost) multicomponent program in Baltimore.

Table 3 presents the findings, showing summary data for three years following random assignment in Arkansas, Baltimore, and

TABLE 3

Summary of the Impacts on AFDC Eligibles of Seven
Welfare Employment Programs

Location, Outcome and Follow-Up Period		Experimental Group Mean	Control Group Mean	Difference	Percentage Change
Arkansas					
Average earnings	Year 1	$ 674	$ 507	$167°°	33%
	Year 2	1180	957	223	23
	Year 3	1422	1085	337°°	31
Employed at end of	Year 1	20.4%	16.7%	3.7°	22%
	Year 2	23.9	20.3	3.6	18
	Year 3	24.5	18.3	6.2°°°	34
Average AFDC payments	Year 1	$ 998	$1143	−$145°°°	−13%
	Year 2	793	982	−190°°°	−19
	Year 3	742	910	−168	−18
On welfare at end of	Year 1	51.0%	59.1%	−8.1°°°	−14%
	Year 2	38.1	46.0	−7.9°°°	−17
	Year 3	32.8	40.1	−7.3°°°	−18
Baltimore					
Average earnings	Year 1	$1612	$1472	$140	10%
	Year 2	2787	2386	401°°°	17
	Year 3	3499	2989	511°°°	17
Employed at end of	Year 1	34.7%	31.2%	3.5°°	11%
	Year 2	39.5	37.1	2.4	6
	Year 3	40.7	40.3	0.4	1
Average AFDC payments	Year 1	$2520	$2517	$ 2	0%
	Year 2	2058	2092	−34	−2
	Year 3	1783	1815	−31	−2

TABLE 3 (*Continued*)
Summary of the Impacts on AFDC Eligibles of Seven
Welfare Employment Programs

Location, Outcome and Follow-Up Period		Experimental Group Mean	Control Group Mean	Difference	Percentage Change
On welfare at end of	Year 1	72.0%	73.3%	-1.4	-2%
	Year 2	58.7	59.0	-0.3	-1
	Year 3	48.2	48.4	-0.2	0
Cook County					
Average earnings	Year 1	$1227	$1217	$10	1%
Employed at end of	Year 1	22.6%	21.4%	1.3	6
Average AFDC payments	Year 1	$3105	$3146	-$40	-1
On welfare at end of	Year 1	78.9%	80.8%	-1.9**	-2
San Diego I					
Average earnings	Year 1	$2379	$1937	$443***	23%
Employed at end of	Year 1	42.4%	36.9%	5.5***	15
Average AFDC payments	Year 1	$2524	$2750	-$226***	-8
On welfare at end of	Year 1	45.8%	47.9%	-2.0	-4
San Diego II					
Average earnings	Year 1	$2029	$1677	$352***	21%
	Year 2	2903	2246	658***	29
Employed at end of	Year 1	34.7%	26.9%	7.7***	29
	Year 2	34.7	29.3	5.4***	18
Average AFDC payments	Year 1	$4424	$4830	-$407***	-8
	Year 2	3408	3961	-553	-14
On welfare at end of	Year 1	66.0%	72.4%	-6.4***	-9
	Year 2	51.3	58.7	-7.4***	-13

TABLE 3 (Continued)
Summary of the Impacts on AFDC Eligibles of Seven
Welfare Employment Programs

Location, Outcome and Follow-Up Period		Experimental Group Mean	Control Group Mean	Difference	Percentage Change
Virginia					
Average earnings	Year 1	$1352	$1282	$ 69	5%
	Year 2	2268	1988	280**	14
	Year 3[a]	2624	2356	268*	11
Employed at end of	Year 1	34.7%	31.0%	3.8**	12%
	Year 2	39.3	33.3	6.0***	18
	Year 3[b]	38.7	34.1	4.6***	13
Average AFDC payments	Year 1	$1961	$2029	-$ 69	-3%
	Year 2	1480	1516	-36	-2
	Year 3[a]	1184	1295	-111**	-9
On welfare at end of	Year 1	59.8%	59.4%	0.4	1%
	Year 2	44.0	44.9	-0.9	-2
	Year 3[b]	36.6	39.3	-2.6	-7
West Virginia					
Average earnings	Year 1	$ 451	$ 435	$ 16	4%
Employed at end of	Year 1	12.0%	13.1%	-1.0	-8
Average AFDC payments	Year 1	$1692	$1692	$ 0	0
On welfare at end of	Year 1	70.9%	72.5%	-1.5	-2

Sources: MDRC reports and unpublished estimates.

Notes: These data include zero values for sample members not employed and for sample members not receiving welfare. Estimates are regression-adjusted using ordinary least squares, controlling for pre-enrollment characteristics of sample members. There may be some discrepancies in experimental-control differences because of rounding.

TABLE 3 (*Continued*)

In all programs except the San Diego II program, year 1 begins with the quarter of random assignment. As a result, "average earnings" in year 1 may include up to two months of earnings prior to random assignment. In the San Diego II program, year 1 begins with the quarter following the quarter of random assignment.

"Employed" or "On Welfare" at the end of the year is defined as receiving earnings or welfare payments at some point during the last quarter of the year.

Earnings and AFDC payments are not adjusted for inflation.

[a] Annualized earnings and welfare payments are calculated from six to nine months of data, respectively.

[b] Percent employed and on welfare at end of 2½ and 2¾ years, respectively.

° Denotes statistical significance at the 10 percent level; °° at the 5 percent level; and °°° at the 1 percent level.

Virginia, and one or two years in the other locations.[10] Figures 1 through 4 show trends over time in key outcomes in Arkansas and Baltimore.

Five of the seven programs had statistically significant impacts on employment rates at the end of the first year after program enrollment. These gains ranged from 3.5 percentage points in Baltimore to 7.7 percentage points in the San Diego II program. For example, in San Diego I, 36.9 percent of the controls were employed at the end of the first year of follow-up compared to 42.4 percent of the experimentals, for a gain of 5.5 percentage points. As a result of this employment gain, during the full year, experimentals (including those who were and were not working) earned an average of $443, or 23 percent, more than the $1937 earned by controls. In the other four programs, first-year earnings were 5 to 33 percent above those for controls.

The longer-term follow-up available for three states indicates that these short-term earnings impacts persisted or grew over time, possibly reaching a peak around the end of the second or the beginning of the third year. Despite increases in the employment and earnings of controls over the three years (see Figures 1 and 2), experimentals continued to do better than controls. In Arkansas, by the end of year 3, the experimentals' employment rate was 6.2 percentage points above that for controls and they earned, over the year, an average of $337, or 31 percent, more than controls. In Baltimore, while there was no significant long-term difference in employment rates, experimentals in year 3 earned $511, or 17 percent, more than controls.

Impacts on AFDC dependence were smaller and less consistent than those on employment. As Table 3 shows, only two of the five programs with employment effects—Arkansas and San Diego II—resulted in statistically significant reductions in the welfare rolls in the first year after enrollment. Arkansas was unusual, with welfare dependence among the targeted WIN-mandatories reduced by a notable 8.1 percentage points in the first year and continuing to show similar impacts throughout the three years. (See Table 3 and Figures 3 and 4.) Over the full follow-up period, impacts on average

---

[10] The studies of Cook County (Illinois), San Diego I, and West Virginia show results for up to 18 months that are consistent with the shorter-term findings presented in Table 3.

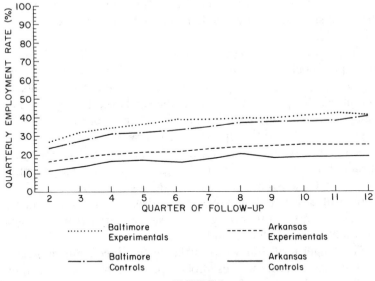

FIGURE 1

Trends in Average Quarterly Employment Rates in Arkansas and Baltimore

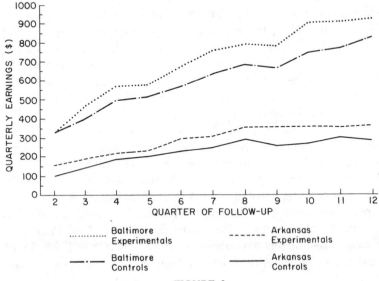

FIGURE 2

Trends in Average Quarterly Earnings in Arkansas and Baltimore

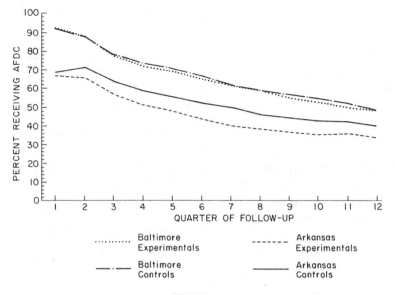

FIGURE 3

Trends in AFDC Average Quarterly Receipt in Arkansas and Baltimore

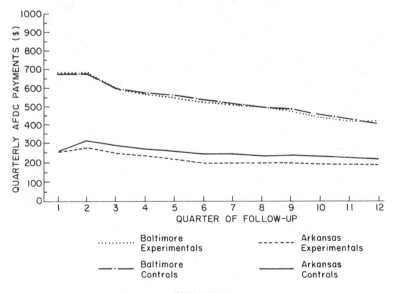

FIGURE 4

Trends in Average Quarterly AFDC Payments in Arkansas and Baltimore

annual welfare payments ranged from close to zero in Baltimore to $553, or a 14 percent saving, in the second year of the San Diego II program.

The findings from the two areas without statistically significant employment and earnings impacts provide important exceptions. In West Virginia, as programs planners foresaw, this probably resulted from the exceptional labor market conditions in a rural state with very high unemployment. While the program reinforced community preferences for work, kept job skills from deteriorating, and provided useful public services, it did not translate these gains into unsubsidized employment. The program in Cook County (Illinois) also resulted in no significant increases in employment and earnings, although there were small welfare savings. Here, part of the explanation may lie in the program design. The Cook County program, one of the two least expensive of those studied (averaging under $200 per experimental), mainly monitored people and sanctioned those who did not participate, providing little direct assistance even in its job-search component. These exceptions provide useful reminders of the importance of labor market conditions and, possibly, of the need to provide at least minimal assistance to get employment results (if not welfare savings).

A critical decision in the design of welfare employment initiatives is whether programs should try to reach the entire mandatory caseload or target specific subgroups—for example, potential long-term recipients. The programs summarized here can shed light on this issue because they were not narrowly targeted but, rather, tried to reach all welfare applicants and recipients meeting broad eligibility criteria.

An analysis of five of the programs showed that impacts were not evenly distributed across the eligible caseload (Friedlander, 1988b). The most employable people—for instance, women who were first-time welfare applicants and had been recently employed—showed below-average or no earnings impacts. While this group showed high program outcomes (as measured, for example, by employment rates), similarly high rates were also found for comparable people in the control group. That is, even without special assistance, many of these women stayed on welfare only for relatively brief periods. In contrast, more dependent groups— women with little or no recent work history—benefited more consistently from these programs, even though the programs offered only limited assistance and almost no intensive training. Despite the finding that more of these women remained on welfare after receiving services (that is, their measured "outcomes" were lower), their performance relative to similar people in the control group was more impressive. The study also, however, identified a third group—long-term welfare recipients with no recent employment—who did not show consistent earnings impacts. While this study provides strong evidence against "creaming"—that is, serving the most advantaged, who demonstrate high placement rates—it does not confirm narrow targeting of these low- to moderate-cost programs on the most disadvantaged.

These findings on the effectiveness of work programs for different subgroups of welfare recipients have implications for performance standards: that is, for the extent to which the use of certain standards would encourage programs to maximize long-term earnings gains and reductions in welfare dependence. Specifically, the lack of correlation between outcomes and impacts suggests that unweighted placement rates or case closings do not provide valid performance standards for this population (Friedlander, 1988b).

Cost-Effectiveness

An examination of these programs' effects on government budgets showed that, while programs required an initial investment, outlays were usually more than offset by projected savings over two to five years. For example, the San Diego I program had a net investment per eligible person in the caseload of approximately $640 (calculated as the cost per experimental, not per participant, minus the cost per control) and led to offsetting five-year savings from increased taxes and reduced AFDC, Medicaid, and other transfer payments of $1790, for a net gain of $1150 per experimental (or almost two dollars for each dollar of costs). The Arkansas, Virginia, and Cook County programs also resulted in estimated budget savings. The Baltimore program essentially broke even, and the West Virginia program incurred some net costs. In four of the states, more than half the savings went to the federal government. This provides a strong rationale for continued federal participation in the funding of such programs.

Benefits and costs can also be viewed from the perspective of the welfare recipients targeted for participation. For AFDC women, the projected earnings gains associated with the programs usually exceeded the estimated reductions in welfare benefits and losses in other transfer payments, such as Medicaid and food stamps.

Implications

Overall, these studies answer some key questions about the first-generation, low- to moderate-cost, mandatory welfare programs. First, with resources and time, such programs were successfully implemented and imposed obligations on a significant share of the welfare caseload. Second, even the relatively modest initiatives implemented in the early to mid-1980s—programs that consisted primarily of job search—led to a substitution of earnings for welfare, had durable impacts, and proved cost-effective.

Third, the earnings gains are particularly notable because they are averages that included all persons eligible for the programs, not just the approximately 50 percent who actually received services or the smaller percentage who worked during any three-month period. Moreover, average long-term annual earnings gains of $300 to $650 a year, or 10 to 30 percent across all people in the targeted share of the caseload, conceal wide variations. For the people who actually benefited from these programs through new jobs or higher earnings, the gains were much larger.

However, the results clearly also imply caution in what can be expected from this type of initiative. Alone, it does not offer an immediate cure for poverty or dependence. The impacts are modest, many people continue on welfare, and those who move off the rolls often remain poor.

Open Questions and Challenges

The Family Support Act of 1988 expresses what has often been called a new consensus about responsibilities and families. The key elements of this consensus are that parents—both fathers and mothers—should contribute to the support of their children and that government should assist and reward welfare recipients in obtaining employment. The Job Opportunities and Basic Skills Training (JOBS) program, complemented by other components of the bill—in particular, the provisions for strengthened enforcement of child-support collections, transitional Medicaid, and child-care benefits—provides the framework within which states will construct future welfare employment programs.

In many ways, the law builds on the state initiatives and the new federalism environment of the 1980s by establishing not a federal "program," but a structure for funding future state programs. In doing this, it goes substantially beyond WIN by extending mandatory participation to women with younger children, providing incentives for states to assure that a certain share of funds is spent on more difficult-to-serve clients, emphasizing and funding the provision of education and training services, including educational requirements for young school dropouts, and establishing monthly participation standards.

For many states, the road from their current, first-generation welfare employment programs to the full-blown JOBS vision is very long—and possibly unaffordable. For others, already embarked on second-generation efforts, it is more direct. All states, however, will face choices in heading down this path. The JOBS bill offers new federal money—and some mandates—as an incentive to the states to change and expand their welfare employment programs. But the amount of money available in each state, and thus the degree of change, will depend on how state legislators respond: on the extent to which they put up state funds to draw down matching federal resources and on the programs they design to put the JOBS message into practice.

The experience of the 1980s suggests that in all states new resources for these programs will not be sufficient to provide comprehensive employment and training services to everyone in the newly expanded JOBS-mandatory caseload. Given their own budget constraints, states will have to choose among the many design priorities noted earlier. While states can benefit from the lessons summarized in this chapter, they also face many unanswered questions.

The Return to Greater Investment in Education and Training

The first-generation initiatives discussed here had favorable impacts on the intended outcomes and were cost-effective, but they did not "solve" the problems of nonemployment, dependence, and poverty. The findings have generated mixed responses, reflecting different views on the causes of poverty and unemployment and the appropriate and feasible objectives of public policy. To some people, the findings suggest that proven, low-cost programs should be expanded to serve a greater share of the caseload. Others argue that larger changes are required and obtainable; they suggest a shift towards second-generation programs that provide greater investments in human capital development.

The most important unanswered question facing designers of welfare employment programs is whether greater investments in education and training services will result in greater success, particularly for the long-term dependent, who do not seem to benefit as much from low-cost services, and whether the additional gains will be large enough to justify the additional outlays. There is some evidence from small-scale, voluntary programs serving this group that more expensive services have higher returns per participant. However, differences in participation rates, the people served, the local economic conditions, and the voluntary/mandatory distinction make it difficult to draw conclusions from these results.[11] In particular, there is no evidence that intensive and expensive programs serving large numbers of mandatory recipients will have comparable results. Evaluations (planned or under way) of second-generation programs—particularly of California's GAIN program—should provide critical new information on the feasibility, cost, and long-term impact of the JOBS investment strategy, and especially the extent to which a greater initial investment will move more people out of poverty and off welfare permanently. The persistence of dependence for many—even after participation in first-generation programs—suggests the importance of future work in this area.

The Cost-Effectiveness of Programs for Mothers with Younger Children

The JOBS legislation extends mandatory participation to women with children 3 years of age or over and targets resources at young mothers, including those with even younger children. While some states have experimented with programs for this group, relatively little is known about the results. The evidence of long-term dependence for young, never-married mothers suggests the

---

[11] Studies of higher-cost, voluntary programs include the evaluations of intensive work experience. See Manpower Demonstration Research Corporation (1980) and Bell, Burstein, and Orr (1987). See Friedlander (1988a) for a discussion of why the available evidence does not support a strong conclusion on the relative return to high- and low-cost programs.

saliency of this issue and the need for careful review of program costs and the adequacy of child care. It will be particularly important to determine whether low-cost mandates are effective and feasible with this group, or whether very intensive services will be required to encourage and enable these young women to choose employment over long-term welfare.[12]

The Structure and Management of the Delivery System

The first-generation programs of the early and mid-1980s were relatively easy to implement. Even so, the states' newly responsible welfare agencies demonstrated highly varied capacity to provide employment services; the agencies also showed their need for time and commitment to improve management expertise. The newer, second-generation programs are much more complex, routinely involving extensive coordination among delivery systems: JTPA, adult education schools, community colleges, child-care agencies, and the welfare system. Determining the most appropriate division of labor, facilitating coordination, and managing the movement of welfare recipients into different services will require a new degree of expertise and systems support.[13]

Managing and Motivating the System

The 1980s were a period of exploration and decentralization in welfare employment programs. The Family Support Act brings new resources and new accountability; for example, the legislation calls for the eventual establishment of performance standards. The history of the WIN and JTPA programs suggests both the power of focusing staff on performance outcomes and the risk that this can steer them away from serving the very people most likely to benefit. A major challenge facing state and federal managers will be designing standards that direct the system towards making the greatest long-term difference in the lives of welfare recipients.

The Context of Broader Reform

The success of welfare employment programs is tied, to an

---

[12] Two current social experiments should provide important information on this question: the Teenage Parent Demonstration sponsored by the U.S. Department of Health and Human Services and MDRC's New Chance Demonstration.

[13] See JTPA-Welfare Linkages Workgroup (1989).

unknown degree, to larger issues in the economy and benefit structure. While the Medicaid and child-care provisions in the Family Support Act should help, for many welfare recipients realistic jobs will offer little or no economic gain over continued dependence. Despite this, many welfare recipients do take jobs and move off the rolls. But the choice for some is undoubtedly not an easy one, and for others it is compellingly negative. In practice, mandatory programs can make people participate, but have only a limited ability to require them to get or accept a job offer. There are two options to further tip the balance in favor of work: (1) make welfare even less attractive, and (2) further increase the rewards to work by raising the minimum wage, expanding the Earned Income Tax Credit, or effecting other changes (for instance, successfully increasing the collection of child-support payments, which would then be available to supplement earnings).[14] Given the realistic choices, actions that reward work will be an important complement to further expansion of the welfare employment system.

References

Ashenfelter, Orley. "The Case for Evaluating Training Programs with Randomized Trials." *Economics of Education Review* 6 (No. 4, 1987), pp. 333–38.
Bane, Mary Jo, and David T. Ellwood. *The Dynamics of Dependence: The Routes to Self-Sufficiency.* Report prepared for the Office of Income Security Policy. Washington: U.S. Department of Health and Human Services, 1983.
Bell, Stephen H., Nancy R. Burstein, and Larry L. Orr. *Overview of the Evaluation Results.* Evaluation reports of the AFDC Homemaker-Home Health Aide Demonstrations. Cambridge, MA: Abt Associates, 1987.
Betsey, Charles L., Robinson G. Hollister, Jr., and Mary R. Papageorgiou, eds. *Youth Employment and Training Programs: The YEDPA Years.* Washington: National Academy Press, 1985.
Burtless, Gary, and Larry L. Orr. "Are Classical Experiments Needed for Manpower Policy?" *Journal of Human Resources* 21 (Fall 1986), pp. 606–39.
Ellwood, David T. *Poor Support: Poverty in the American Family.* New York: Basic Books, 1988.
————. *Targeting "Would-Be" Long-Term Recipients of AFDC.* Princeton, NJ: Mathematica Policy Research, 1986.
Friedlander, Daniel. "Comparative Effectiveness of Low- and High-Intensity Interventions in the Welfare Employment Demonstrations." Paper presented at the Annual Meeting of the American Economic Association, New York, December 28–30, 1988a.
————. *Subgroup Impacts and Performance Indicators for Selected Welfare Employment Programs.* New York: Manpower Demonstration Research Corporation, 1988b.
Gueron, Judith M. *Reforming Welfare with Work.* New York: The Ford Foundation, 1987.
Gueron, Judith M., and Richard P. Nathan. "The MDRC Work/Welfare Project: Objectives, Status, Significance." *Policy Studies Review* 4 (February 1985), pp. 417–32.

---

[14] For further discussion of this issue, see Ellwood (1988).

Job Training Longitudinal Survey Research Advisory Panel. "Recommendations of the Job Training Longitudinal Survey Research Advisory Panel." Report prepared for the Office of Strategic Planning and Policy Development, Employment and Training Administration. Washington: U.S. Department of Labor, 1985.

JTPA-Welfare Linkages Workgroup. *Working Capital: Coordinated Human Investment Directions for the 90's—JTPA-Welfare Linkages: A Subpart of the Final Report of the Job Training Partnership Act (JTPA) Advisory Committee.* Washington: U.S. Department of Labor, July 1989.

LaLonde, Robert, and Rebecca Maynard. "How Precise Are Evaluations of Employment and Training Programs: Evidence from a Field Experiment." *Evaluation Review* 11 (August 1987), pp. 428-51.

Manpower Demonstration Research Corporation, The Board of Directors. *Summary and Findings of the National Supported Work Demonstration.* Cambridge, MA: Ballinger, 1980.

Mead, Lawrence W. *Beyond Entitlement: The Obligations of Citizenship.* New York: Free Press, 1986.

Mitchell, J. J., et al. "Implementing Welfare Employment Programs: An Institutional Analysis of the Work Incentive (WIN) Program." Working paper. Washington: Urban Institute, October 1979.

Nightingale, Demetra Smith. *Federal Employment and Training Policy Changes During the Reagan Administration: State and Local Responses.* Washington: Urban Institute, 1985.

Nightingale, Demetra Smith, and Lynn C. Burbridge. *The Status of State Work-Welfare Programs in 1986: Implications for Welfare Reform.* Washington: Urban Institute, 1987.

Rein, Mildred. *Dilemmas of Welfare Policy: Why Work Strategies Haven't Worked.* New York: Praeger, 1982.

Wolfhagen, Carl, with Barbara S. Goldman. *Job Search Strategies: Lessons from the Louisville WIN Laboratory Project.* New York: Manpower Demonstration Research Corporation, 1983.

Chapter 8

Uncle Sam's Helping Hand: Educating, Training, and Employing the Disadvantaged

Sar A. Levitan and Frank Gallo*
George Washington University

The federal government is no stranger to supporting efforts for improving the skills of the workforce. The 1787 Northwest Ordinance authorized land grants to establish schools, and four score years later the Morrill Act provided land grants for agricultural and mechanical colleges and universities. Congress enacted a general vocational rehabilitation program for the handicapped in 1921. During the Great Depression, with a quarter of the labor force unemployed, the Roosevelt administration inaugurated several massive public employment programs. Since their primary purpose was employment rather than training, the programs were dismantled when full employment was achieved during World War II. In contrast, federal involvement since the early 1960s originated because of widespread concerns about continued poverty despite economic growth. Although the federal commitment slackened considerably during the 1980s, new laws and the promise of additional funding at the decade's end provided some hope of reinvigorating assistance to those in need.

The Need for Intervention

Millions of Americans who are poor, unemployed, and deficiently educated in good as well as bad times justify a strong government role in employment and training. The erosion of the traditional family structure within the past quarter century, and sluggish income growth and scant increases in productivity since

* This study was prepared under an ongoing grant from the Ford Foundation to the Center for Social Policy Studies of The George Washington University. In line with the Foundation's practice, responsibility for the contents of the study was left with the Center director.

1973 have strengthened this need since the programs began. Because the private sector and state and local governments have failed to furnish much help, the federal government has assumed primary responsibility for employment and training assistance.

Despite dramatic improvements in educational attainment, large numbers of Americans remain functionally illiterate. Most adults now possess a high school education, and about half of young adults have been exposed to at least a smattering of "higher" education. The proportion of Americans over age 24 with high school or college degrees has more than tripled over the past half century (U.S. Bureau of the Census, April 1989, p. 22).

	1940	1988
High school degree	24%	76%
College degree	4	20

However, 13.6 percent of 18–21-year-olds have left school prior to completing a high school education (U.S. Bureau of the Census, August 1988, Tables 14 and 15, pp. 49, 54–55). Even 12 years of formal schooling is no guarantee that a student can adequately perform in today's labor market. Some 13 percent of Americans were judged functionally illiterate in the most recent Bureau of the Census survey, including 6 percent of high school graduates (Werner, 1986).

Other examinations of educational ability provide further grounds for concern. The latest national reading assessment of students found "precipitous declines" characterized by the Educational Testing Service as "simply not believable" (Applebee, Langer, and Mullis, 1988, p. 57). Half of 17-year-old students could not calculate percentages, determine the area of a rectangle, or solve simple equations (Dossey et al., 1988, p. 39). Two-thirds did not know that the Civil War occurred between 1850 and 1890 (Applebee, Langer, and Mullis, 1987, p. 9). Almost 30 percent of adults do not know that the earth revolves around the sun ("Poll Finds . . .," 1988). International comparisons of industrialized nations in math, science, and geography rank American students last or very close to it (International Association for the Evaluation of Educational Achievement, 1988, p. 3; Redd and Riddle, 1988, pp. 53–61).

Although the unemployment rate in mid-1989 was lower than at any time since 1974, historical and international comparisons indicate that the economy can do much better. Despite increasing work effort—primarily due to the influx of women into the workforce—real median family income has increased little since 1973. An increasingly skewed income distribution system has meant that low-income families have obtained a progressively smaller share of the pie.

Slowing productivity growth impedes real income gains and underlines the need for employment and training programs. Labor productivity growth in the business sector was impressive in the immediate post-World War II period, but has slackened considerably since 1973 (U.S. Bureau of Labor Statistics, February 1989):

	Increase	Average annual increase
1960–73	42.5%	3.3%
1973–88	16.9	1.1

Poverty trends have closely followed economic and income patterns. Counting only cash income, the poverty rate dropped from 34 percent in 1949 to 11 percent in 1973. The official rate remained in the 11–12 percent range for the remainder of the 1970s, although increasing subsidies for in-kind assistance (food stamps, medical care, and housing not counted as cash income) reduced deprivation further. But after six years of economic recovery, the poverty rate was higher in 1987 than in 1979, however it is measured (U.S. Bureau of the Census, August 1988, Table B, p. 5):

	1979	1987
Cash income only (official definition)	11.7%	13.5%
Plus food, housing, and medical benefits (market value)	7.0	8.5

In the last quarter century the breakdown of the traditional family stucture has increasingly exacerbated poverty and educational deficiencies. The number of single parents as a proportion of both poor families and all families has increased alarmingly since the 1960s. Single mothers (who constitute nine of ten single parents) have always stood a much greater risk of impoverishment than other family heads. Children of single parents exhibit more behavioral problems, do more poorly in school and have a lower educational attainment, and earn less money than children of intact families. A large part of these difficulties is attributable to poverty (Levitan, Belous, and Gallo, 1988, pp. 117–20).

The failure of private business and state and local governments to address these critical problems has provided a continuing impetus for federal intervention. Employers do what comes naturally and hire applicants they consider the best qualified, extending opportunities to those with unimpressive backgrounds who nevertheless might become productive workers only when other alternatives are unavailable. Even when provided subsidies to hire, train, and retain the disadvantaged, employers will if possible select individuals they would have hired in any case. While some states and localities have raised funds and introduced innovative programs to help the disadvantaged, the federal government has led the way in promoting employment and training assistance.

Those in Need

The poor, the jobless, the deficiently educated, and the handicapped are the primary targets of federal employment and training efforts. Minorities, single mothers and their families, and young people are especially likely to face employment difficulties (U.S. Bureau of Labor Statistics, January 1989; U.S. Bureau of the Census, August 1988). The incidence of black unemployment and poverty is more than twice that of the rest of the population. While not quite as bleak, Hispanic unemployment and poverty also far exceed that of the total population. Of all age groups, youth are the most vulnerable to unemployment. The level of teenage joblessness is about three times that of adults, and that of young adults, ages 20–24, is about twice as high. Black youth joblessness is especially severe: in 1988 only four of ten black teenagers were in the labor force, and less than three of ten were employed. Unemployment in female-headed families is double that in married-couple families, and the poverty rate is over five times higher. In recent years the problems of workers dislocated by foreign economic competition or technological change have gained increasing attention, although worker dislocation has subsided in the late 1980s.

A large proportion of the working age population is potentially in need of job-related assistance, including, with substantial over-lap:

- 19 million persons unemployed at some time during 1987
- 18 million working-age individuals poor during 1987
- 12 million persons who worked part time involuntarily in 1987
- 6 million single mothers living in their own households, and another 2 million living with relatives or friends
- 4 million full-time workers who earned less than $6700 in 1987—minimum-wage earnings for a full year of work
- nearly 3 million workers dislocated through plant closings or major layoffs in 1987

The diverse characteristics of the poor, jobless, and deficiently educated require different strategies to improve their employability, productivity, and earnings. Young people who have mastered the three Rs but have little labor market experience may benefit from learning basic job-search skills. Disadvantaged youth without adequate skills can profit from programs providing a high school equivalency degree or vocational training. The discrimination often faced by minorities may be overcome by partially subsidizing employers for on-the-job training costs and by vigorous enforcement of equal opportunity laws. Women who maintain families frequently require child-care assistance to successfully complete a training course.

The poor not infrequently face multiple problems simultaneously, including joblessness, insufficient education, welfare dependency, poor health, family violence or break-ups, out-of-wedlock births, poor housing, crime, drug or alcohol abuse, and limited access to transportation. Depending on the problem, heads of poor families with children are three to thirty times as likely to face readily quantifiable obstacles to self-sufficiency as nonpoor families (Figures 1 and 2). Achieving self-sufficiency may necessitate ameliorating a variety of family difficulties simultaneously, with employment and training assistance as only one essential component of a comprehensive attack on poverty (Levitan, Mangum, and Pines, 1989).

Educational Assistance

To qualify even for entry occupations, a job applicant must master the three Rs. A clear dividing line cannot be drawn between

FIGURE 1

The Incidence of Joblessness, Deficient Education,
Disability, and Single Parenthood Is Much More Common
Among the Poor Than Among Middle-Class Families
(1986)

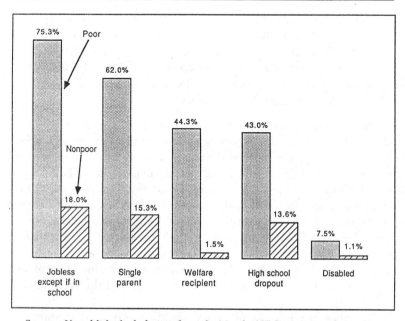

Source: Unpublished tabulations from the March 1987 Current Population Survey
provided by Andrew Sum, Northeastern University.

education and employment and training programs, which are often
identified as "second chance" education programs. Total public
education expenditures, and even federal education spending alone,
dwarf the federal training investment. This distribution is
appropriate because learning rates are highest during childhood,
and those who fail in or are failed by the schools frequently benefit
only marginally from the assistance provided later in life.

Traditionally, provision of tuition-free education for elementary
and secondary students has been the responsibility of local and state
governments. Major federal investments in education began in the
mid-1960s because most state and local governments were unable or
unwilling to offer the necessary assistance, especially in poor
neighborhoods where schools are typically deficient in resources,

TRAINING THE DISADVANTAGED   231

FIGURE 2

If Any Proof Were Needed, the Poor
Face Many More Obstacles to Self-Sufficiency
Than Middle-Class Families (1986)

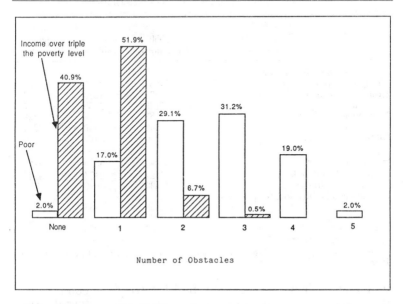

Note: Obstacles are listed in Figure 1.

Source: Unpublished tabulations from the March 1987 Current Population Survey
provided by Andrew Sum, Northeastern University.

facilities, and personnel. The federal government has developed a
variety of supportive services to help poor, deficiently educated,
and handicapped preschool to college-age youngsters mature into
independent adulthood.

Federal education funding peaked at the end of the 1970s.
Congress appropriated $21.8 billion in fiscal 1989 for the Depart-
ment of Education (which oversees most federal assistance), a 7.7
percent decrease after adjustment for inflation since 1980. The bulk
of federal funding assists low-income, academically deficient, and
handicapped students, although college financial aid is available to
a broader clientele (Table 1).

Elementary and Secondary Education

Assistance to poor children should start early because by the time

TABLE 1

Major Federal Education Programs
Prepare Children and Youth to Compete
in the Labor Market
(1980 Appropriations in Estimated 1989 Dollars)

	1980 (millions)	1989 (millions)	Partici-pants (thousands)
Elementary and Secondary			
Compensatory education	$4851	$4570	5200
Education of the handicapped	1508	1996	4470
Head Start	1109	1235	447
Vocational education	1183	918	NA
Native Americans	346	340	284
Bilingual education	240	197	230
Postsecondary			
Pell grants	3682	4484	2861
Guaranteed student loans	2427	3174	3548
College work study	830	610	753
Supplemental educational opportunity grants	558	438	720
Trio programs	223	219	525
Perkins loans	454	205	880

Source: Congressional Research Service (September 22, 1988); Lewis (September 1988).

they reach school age they may find it difficult to compete with their peers from more affluent homes. Hence, since 1965 the Head Start program has provided child care and education to 3- to 5-year-olds from poor families. The available funding permits assistance to only one in five poor children. Nevertheless, Head Start remains the nation's largest public child-care and early education program. Longitudinal evaluations of Head Start and similar programs indicate that they improve school performance, and employability in later life, in a cost-effective manner. Head Start children, compared with a control group, were more likely to graduate from high school and to find work (59 percent employed, compared with 32 percent of the control group) (Committee on Children, Youth, and Families, 1988, pp. 39–46; Gramlich, 1986).

Federal aid to elementary and secondary students continues with the compensatory education program (Chapter 1 of the Elementary and Secondary Education Act). Although the law targets areas where poverty is concentrated, the program serves educationally deficient children regardless of family income. Compensatory education funds may be used up to the 12th grade, but three-quarters of enrollees are in kindergarten or elementary school. Evaluations indicate that compensatory education improves students' reading and mathematics performance. However, because of limited funds, older children who require continuing assistance often do not receive it and tend to lose ground. Another problem is that since many schools pull enrollees out of their regular classes for compensatory education, total instructional time may not be significantly increased (Congressional Research Service, January 1987, pp. 2:34–37).

Federal support for vocational education, dating back to 1917, primarily assists high school students (U.S. Department of Education, September 1988, p. 2:6). Current federal appropriations account for about a tenth of the estimated $9 billion devoted to vocational education in public schools. The program serves primarily noncollege-bound students; a minority of the funds are set aside for the disadvantaged and the handicapped. Minimal data collection precludes estimates of the number of students enrolled or their characteristics.

Handicapped, immigrant, and Native American children benefit from targeted federal assistance in addition to the help they receive from the Head Start and compensatory education programs. Aid to the handicapped has mushroomed within the past decade and a half, and Congress considerably expanded eligibility by including children with emotional and psychological problems and learning disabilities such as dyslexia. Handicapped persons regardless of family income need early assistance to function in or out of the labor market. Since 1975 the federal government has sought to ensure that all handicapped young people aged 3 to 21 receive a tuition-free education in the least restrictive environment. States are eligible to receive up to 40 percent of the national average expenditure per pupil for every handicapped child enrolled. The Education Department estimates that current federal appropriations pay for about a tenth of the excess costs incurred in educating handicapped children (Congressional Research Service, April 1988. pp. 38–39). Efforts to aid Native Americans have traditionally been the responsibility of the federal government since the end of the 19th century. Most of the students taught through bilingual education programs are the offspring of poor Hispanic immigrants. Bilingual education progams have engendered heated controversy, and as a result Congress expanded the authority of local schools to use other means than bilingual education—such as immersion in English classes—to teach students with limited English skills (U.S. General Accounting Office, March 1987). Special programs for students from disadvantaged backgrounds (commonly called Trio programs) provide a variety of services through grants to colleges and other agencies. These programs target students from low-income families who represent the first generation to attend college. The assistance includes basic skills instruction, personal and academic counseling, stipends, and help with obtaining financial aid.

Post-Secondary Education

Major federal investment in college programs for the poor expanded in the early 1970s, based on the sound principle that possessing a sheepskin opens doors in the labor market. Less than one of eight 18- to 24-year-olds from families with annual incomes less than $10,000 attended college in 1986, compared to over half of those from families making $50,000 or more. Almost all federal post-secondary assistance is provided directly to students through grants or loans focused on those from families with annual incomes below $30,000. The college work-study program supplements federal grants and loans. It reimburses educational institutions for 70–80 percent of wages paid to students working at mostly low-wage jobs on or off campus.

Because of rapidly rising post-secondary tuition and other expenses and relatively high real interest rates, federal appropriations for higher education have exceeded the overall inflation rate, yet have fallen progressively further behind college costs. In the 1980s, public higher education costs have increased twice as much as overall inflation, and private college costs have risen even more (Schenet, October 1988, pp. 12–13). Estimated average 1987-88 annual tuition and fees were (Congressional Research Service, October 1988, p. 21):

	Public	*Private*
Two-year college	$ 687	$4,058
Four-year college	1,359	7,110

The Reagan administration also shifted assistance to loans rather than outright grants. Although federal grants and loans have not kept pace with rising expenses, they can still meet a large share of college costs at public institutions (Lewis, September 1988, p. 10):

Program	Maximum grant or loan	Estimated 1987-88 average
Pell grants	60% of education costs, but not exceeding $2200 annually	$1306
Guaranteed student loans (main component)	$17,250 for undergraduate years	2530
Supplemental educational opportunity grants	$4000 annually	600
Perkins loans	$9000 for undergraduate years	1048

The 1944 G.I. bill was a landmark in providing educational opportunities for half of the 14 million veterans discharged after World War II, and in stimulating the growth of the American college and university system. In 1989 the federal government provided $598 million for a variety of veteran education, training, and vocational rehabilitation programs. These benefits are available to veterans regardless of income. Veterans used most of the benefits to finance college costs.

Rapidly rising college costs, declining federal aid, and sluggish family income growth have made it increasingly difficult for middle and working class families to put their children through college, and undoubtedly discouraged many poor youth from even attempting to enroll. Consequently, minority enrollment has dropped during this decade. Exorbitant inflation in post-secondary tuition and expenses should prompt a search for alternatives to federal reliance on grants and loans, which may feed inflation in the same manner that Medicare encouraged higher health-care costs.

Military Training and Adult Education

Military training represents a potentially important but widely fluctuating source of support for training the disadvantaged. During the Vietnam War and much of the 1970s a large proportion of military draftees and recruits were poor and/or members of minority groups. The military undoubtedly provided a career ladder for many of these individuals, some of whom might not have been able to land jobs in civilian life. Because of the rising educational attainment of recruits in the 1980s, however, the military has become a less important source for training the disadvantaged: 93 percent of new enlistees in 1987 possessed high school diplomas, compared to 61 percent in 1974. The services accept only 42 percent of official applicants, and thousands more prospective but unqualified applicants are discouraged from applying by recruiters (Office of the Assistant Secretary of Defense, August 1988, pp. 2:10, 20). The Defense Department operates a small basic functional skills program for an estimated 65-70,000 new service personnel annually who lack the fundamentals necessary to begin specific training for military assignments, and subsidized high school equivalency courses for another 13,000 in 1987.[1]

Federal assistance for adult education began with the 1964 Economic Opportunity Act, but has remained woefully inadequate. Within the past two years Congress has increased adult education appropriations by 50 percent, to $162 million for fiscal 1989. States and localities contribute another estimated $175 million annually. The federal Education Department estimates that 17 to 21 million adults are functionally illiterate, but only about 3.2 million were served in adult education programs in 1987. About one in four participants received English as a second language instruction (Congressional Research Service, January 1987, pp. 9:17-23). Other programs and agencies—including the Job Training Partnership Act, vocational education, and the Defense Department—provide supplementary adult basic education. The Education Department has not evaluated adult education efforts during this decade and collects very little information on the program.

Employment and Training

Despite substantial investments in education, millions of Americans are not adequately prepared for the workforce, or experience poverty or unemployment. Federal job-training programs for the disadvantaged began with a $10 million appropriation as part of the 1961 Area Redevelopment Act, rising more than a thousandfold within two decades. The second major step was the 1962 enactment of the Manpower Development and Training Act, originally intended for workers displaced by automation, but quickly redirected toward the needs of the impoverished. President Johnson's antipoverty efforts experi-

---

[1] Phone conversations with Lenore Saltman and Colonel David Bergman, U.S. Department of Defense, November 22, 1988.

mented with a wide variety of training programs, most of which Congress consolidated—along with MDTA programs—under the Comprehensive Employment and Training Act in 1973. CETA's largely undeserved disrepute led to major reforms in 1978 and to its replacement in 1982 by the current Job Training Partnership Act. The federal government provides employment and training assistance for individuals with employment difficulties through a variety of programs, the largest being JTPA (Table 2).

TABLE 2

Federal Employment and Training
Assistance Is Fragmented Into
Over a Dozen Separate Programs

Program	1989 Appropriation (millions)	1987 Enrollees (thousands)
Total	$6911	22,155
JTPA total	3728	2101
Title IIA adults and youth	1788	1094
Title IIB youth in summer jobs	709	640
Title III dislocated workers	284	183
Title IV federally administered programs		
Job Corps	742	104
Migrant and seasonal farmworkers	69	47
Native Americans	59	33
Veterans	10	NA
Technical assistance, research, and pilot projects	69	—
Vocational rehabilitation	1668	917
Employment service	815	18,439
Senior community service employment program	344	100
Targeted jobs tax credit	240 (1988)	598
Training for food stamp recipients	116	NA

Source: Congressional Research Service (September 27, 1988); unpublished data from the program year 1987 JTPA annual status report, U.S. Department of Labor, Employment and Training Administration.

During the past three decades a multitude of programs have proliferated and withered, but five major issues have persisted:

- How much money should be spent?
- Who should be helped?
- What services should be provided to enrollees?
- Who should administer the programs?
- How can the programs best be evaluated?

The Rise and Decline of Federal Spending

Federal employment and training financing expanded almost continually between 1961 and the late 1970s (Figure 3). A negative image and growing concern about federal budget deficits caused

FIGURE 3

Federal Employment and Training
Financing and Services Have Fluctuated Dramatically
Over the Past Two Decades
(July 1989 dollars)

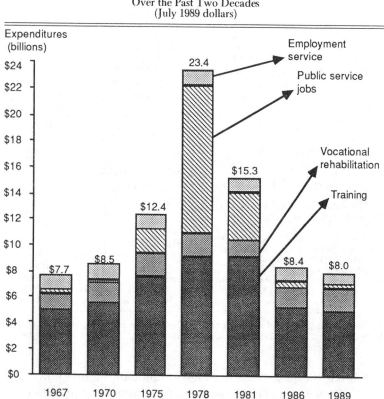

Sources: U.S. Office of Management and Budget, Budget of the U.S. Government, various years; and U.S. Congressional Research Service.

Congress to scale back employment and training funds. President Reagan carried these reductions much further, cutting employment and training programs more than any other social program (U.S.

Congressional Budget Office, August 1983, p. vii). Employment and training funding has declined by over two-thirds since 1978. Only vocational rehabilitation financing has kept pace with inflation; Congress in 1986 required that appropriations be adjusted annually for inflation. Due to limited funds, JTPA can enroll no more than about one in fifteen working-age, low-income individuals even if participants are provided only cursory assistance. In fact, funding cutbacks have put pressure on administrators to reduce services in order to maintain enrollment levels.

Congress has increased appropriations for selected employment and training programs in the late 1980s, but overall spending continues to decline in inflation-adjusted dollars. Opinion polls indicate that nearly three of four Americans regard support of education and training as the best means to combat poverty, but advocates possess virtually no lobbying network and have failed to press Congress for increased assistance (Sundquist, 1986, p. 521). Whether support will increase in President Bush's "kinder, gentler nation" remains to be seen.

Who to Help?

During the past three decades there has been a continuous debate over which groups federal employment and training programs should target for assistance: all low-income persons, youth, welfare recipients, the unemployed, high school dropouts, and workers displaced by foreign economic competition or technology have represented the principal target populations. Started initially to aid technologically displaced workers, Congress soon redirected employment and training programs toward the needs of the poor. Assigning priority to poor youth was based on the belief that by breaking the "cycle of poverty," the federal government could ameliorate what many observers erroneously believed to be a prevalent transmission of destitution from one generation to another. In the 1970s the federal government targeted unemployed individuals—sometimes irrespective of income—for assistance. The underlying notion was to establish a federally enforced right to employment. The result was the 1978 Full Employment and Balanced Growth Act—essentially a restatement of the 1946 Employment Act. Both acts proclaimed noble sentiments, but were ignored by successive Republican and Democratic administrations and Congress.

Toward the decade's end, President Carter favored substantially increased training and employment assistance for welfare recipients and poor youth, although only the latter endeavor received funding. Increased foreign economic competition and major layoffs and plant closings in manufacturing industries in the late 1970s and early 1980s prompted Congress to implement a small new program for dislocated workers at the same time that it drastically reduced other employment assistance. Congress authorized a tripling of the dislocated worker program in 1988, but did not appropriate the funds. In the same year, Congress authorized additional funding for training welfare recipients.

In the course of three decades of changing priorities in assisting the poor and disadvantaged, only poor youth and the disabled have been consistently served in greater numbers than their proportion in the eligible population. Many policymakers believe that assisting young people will reap a greater net long-term impact than aid to adults, but this assumption rests largely on faith. Because of rapid job turnover among youth, occupational training may in fact be more useful for adults, who have a clearer sense of their interests and abilities.

Eligibility for current employment and training programs is generally confined to individuals from poor or low-income families, except for the employment service which is open to all but mostly serves the unemployed, vocational rehabilitation projects devoted to the handicapped, and dislocated worker programs for those laid off and unlikely to return to their previous occupation or industry. Major programs for which data are available serve different, although somewhat overlapping, populations (Table 3). The summer youth employment program and the Job Corps are restricted to youth, and 60 percent of individuals certified for the targeted jobs tax credit are young people.

Whatever the group served, tension exists between assisting the most and the least job-ready applicants. The two largest programs—JTPA and vocational rehabilitation—statutorily require administrators to give priority to individuals most in need of assistance. However, program operators face pressures from businesses who favor individuals they would like to hire, from community leaders to enroll the largest number of applicants, and from federal performance standards emphasizing high job-placement rates at low costs. All of these influences, together with administrators' desires to look good on paper, often lead local programs to select the most employable individuals presumably within the eligible population. This practice is known as "creaming."

Every case study of JTPA has found evidence of creaming in the major training programs, but federal administrators have done nothing to restrict this practice (Levitan and Gallo, 1988, pp. 58–60; Arthur Young with Training Research Corporation, September 1988, pp. 4:31–32). Local administrators and training contractors tend to weed out the functionally illiterate, applicants with unsatisfactory work histories or skills, and older individuals. For example, high school dropouts make up an estimated 40 percent of jobless individuals eligible for JTPA Title IIA, but only 27 percent of program enrollees.[2] When the least job-ready individuals are enrolled, they paradoxically also tend to receive less intensive assistance than more qualified participants.

TABLE 3

Characteristics of JTPA Enrollees (1987)

Characteristic	Adults and Youth (IIA)	Summer Youth (IIB)	Dislocated Workers (III)	Job Corps (IV)
Male	48%	51%	62%	60%
White	49	31	73	30
Black	33	41	17	55
Hispanic	14	24	9	10
Other	4	4	2	5
14-15	4	38	—	—
16-21	42	62	4	99
22-54	53	—	88	—
Over 54	2	—	8	—
High school dropout	27	4	15	82
High school student	19	86	1	—
High school graduate	54	10	84	18
Single parent	20	2	12	NA
AFDC recipient	22	NA	4	22
Limited English	5	11	3	1
Handicapped	11	13	3	NA

Source: Unpublished data from the program year 1987 JTPA annual status report, U.S. Department of Labor, Employment and Training Administration.

The introduction of cost and job-placement performance standards, severe restrictions on stipends and support services, reduced funding, and an expanded business role have made

[2] Unpublished back-up data from Sandell and Rupp (February 1988).

creaming common under JTPA. Selecting the most employable applicants helps guarantee "success" because employers normally hire the most qualified individuals. Such practices may, however, undermine the mission of employment and training programs to serve those who most require help. Moreover, this politically safe policy may be economically inefficient, as well as inequitable, because job-training programs produce the greatest *net* impact by serving individuals with greater labor market handicaps (Gueron, March 1986, p. 21).

Training, Employment, and Other Services

Views about how best to improve the employability of the poor, deficiently educated, and handicapped have shifted dramatically during the past three decades, reminiscent of alchemists searching for the proper solvent to turn base metal into gold. The popularity of a given service has depended much more upon administrative convenience or changing ideological winds than upon research or experience. During the 1960s most occupational training occurred in the classroom. However, because many believed that the best training was having a job, the federal government subsidized jobs in both the public sector (work experience and public service employment programs) and the private sector (on-the-job training programs). The Reagan administration's emphasis on private-sector solutions and public-sector retrenchment led to the increased use of on-the-job training and brief courses teaching enrollees how to find a job. In addition to training or employment services, employment and training programs historically have provided stipends or support services such as transportation assistance or child care to varying degrees.

Basic Education and Classroom Training. Despite the educational deficiencies of many eligible for employment and training assistance, few programs have provided basic education assistance to enrollees. Remedial training has been distinctly downplayed during the 1980s. In CETA's final year, 14 percent of enrollees received education assistance, compared to 7 percent of JTPA Title IIA enrollees three years later. Even among dislocated worker program participants, generally considered to be relatively advantaged compared to the poor, a fifth of enrollees did not complete high school and observers reported that many graduates required remedial education. However, only one in twenty participants received even minimal remedial help.

Unlike other federal efforts, the Job Corps provides its enrollees—who enter the program on average reading at the sixth grade level—with approximately equal doses of educational and occupational training. Congress in 1986 also required summer youth programs to operate at least some educational programs. As a result of this minimal requirement, the programs more than doubled their investment in education from 1986 to 1987, devoting an average of 12 percent of program funds to educate a fifth of enrollees. Pilot summer education programs indicate that such efforts prevent participants from losing ground relative to more advantaged students over the summer months, and in some cases narrow the achievement gap (Berlin and Sum, 1988, pp. 45–46; U.S. General Accounting Office, September 1988, pp. 15–16; Public/Private Ventures, Summer 1988, pp. iii–viii).

Because of the limited availability of remedial education and lack of funds or interest to provide sequential assistance—remedial education followed by skill training—many programs reject applicants without basic skills. Deficiently educated applicants who are recruited undoubtedly cannot fully benefit from occupational training because they lack prerequisite skills. Relatively less-educated participants also tend to be placed in quickie job-search courses with little potential to enhance long-term employability (U.S. General Accounting Office, June 1989, p. 37).

Quality classroom training has a proven track record for cost-effectively improving participants' long-term job prospects, as indicated by analyses of CETA and the impact of the Job Corps, which emphasizes relatively lengthy classroom training (seven months on average) (Taggart, 1981, pp. 62–66; Westat, Inc., December 1984, p. 7:9; Mathematica Policy Research, Inc., September 1982, pp. 111, 118, 121, 157, 177–79). Classroom training remains the single most common form of assistance, but only a third of JTPA Title IIA participants are enrolled in this type of training, for an average of 415 hours. Inadequate training is largely responsible for the fact that only half of subsequently employed classroom trainees found work related to their training.[3]

Subsidizing Private-Sector Jobs. On-the-job training programs typically reimburse firms for half of the employee's wage costs, for

---

[3] Testimony of Gerald Peterson, Office of Inspector General, U.S. Department of Labor, before the House Education and Labor Committee, September 29, 1988, p. 5.

an average of 435 hours in JTPA Title IIA programs. One of every four participants are enrolled in OJT. Theoretically, payment is made to reimburse employers for additional training costs and to induce firms to hire individuals who might not otherwise be considered. However, absent monitoring, OJT as administered under JTPA may in fact be providing windfall benefits to employers who take advantage of the subsidy for individuals they would have hired in any case. About 60 percent of the employers who receive JTPA OJT subsidies stated that they would have hired the same individual even without the inducement (Office of Inspector General, January 1988, p. 63). The General Accounting Office found numerous examples of individuals assigned to OJT who already possessed experience in the field, and of contracts providing full-time subsidies for nearly 3.5 months on average for rudimentary jobs such as food service worker, laborer, or custodian.[4] In addition to JTPA, Congress has appropriated $206 million since 1983 to subsidize OJT slots for 58,000 veterans through the Veterans Job Training Act. Although the law remains on the books, Congress has not appropriated new funding for the program since fiscal 1987.[5]

Most classroom and on-the-job training under JTPA Title IIA is for low-skilled jobs, and ten occupations account for half of all occupationally-specific training:[6]

Office clerk/typist, secretary, or word processor	18.5%
Assembler (predominantly electronic assembly)	8.0
Machinist or machine operator	6.6
Custodian or maintenance person	3.2
Nurse's aid	3.0
Salesperson	2.9
Licensed practical nurse or registered nurse	2.6
Accounting clerk or bookkeeper	2.2

---

[4] "JTPA Programs . . .," April 29, 1988, pp. A2–4; testimony of Lawrence Thompson, U.S. General Accounting Office, before the House Education and Labor Committee, September 29, 1988, pp. 11–12.

[5] Phone conversation with John Pearson, Veterans Administration, November 7, 1988; Centaur Associates (September 24, 1986).

[6] Phone conversation with Thomas Medvetz, U.S. General Accounting Office, October 26, 1988.

Food service worker   2.0
Computer operator or programmer   1.9

The targeted jobs tax credit (TJTC), enacted in 1978, provides subsidies to employers who hire 16- to 22-year-olds living in low-income households, welfare recipients, and handicapped individuals undergoing vocational rehabilitation, among other groups. Due to negligent oversight and supervision by Congress and the executive branch, it has been impossible to assess TJTC's worth. Although there is some evidence that the tax credit has had a positive impact, problems have also become apparent. Similar to problems with OJT subsidies, a significant proportion of the employees hired under the program would have been employed without TJTC, providing windfall profits to employers (Lorenz, November 1988; Levitan and Gallo, October 1987).

Subsidizing Public-Sector Jobs. Work-experience programs are based on the notion that the best form of training is by doing, while public-service employment aims to add jobs to the economy to further full employment goals. Whatever the rhetoric associated with their purposes, participants in both programs work at government or nonprofit agencies. Public employment fell into disfavor in the 1980s. Following a careful evaluation which concluded that work experience improved long-term employability only for welfare recipients—who tended to have limited résumés—Congress strictly limited the use of work experience for adults enrolled in JTPA programs (Manpower Demonstration Research Corporation, 1980, pp. 5-9). Consequently, the proportion of enrollees in work-experience programs declined from 29 to 7 percent from CETA's last year to 1987 under JTPA Title IIA. However, most JTPA summer youth program enrollees participate in work-experience jobs for seven weeks at the federal hourly minimum wage of $3.35.

Because of adamant opposition by the Reagan administration to what it considered "make work" public jobs, Congress prohibited most JTPA programs from funding public-service employment. The law did not preclude the use of dislocated worker program funds for subsidizing public jobs, although Labor Department regulations banned the practice. Congress specifically permitted the Indian training program to provide public employment, and projects enroll a third of Indian participants in work-experience or public-service job slots.

The senior community-service employment program, designed to alleviate joblessness among the poor aged 55 or older, is the only remaining adult public-service jobs program. The law requires the Labor Department to distribute 78 percent of the funds to eight national contractors (the largest being Green Thumb, Inc., and the National Council of Senior Citizens), and the remaining 22 percent to the states. The majority of participants work in recreation centers and parks, social service agencies, schools, and nutrition agencies for the elderly. Apart from their experiences on the job, few enrollees receive any form of training. In 1987 hourly wages averaged $3.50 for about a 20-hour workweek. The median length of stay in the program is almost a year, but because some participants remain for much longer, the mean is nearly two years (Centaur Associates, Inc., July 1986, pp. 4:11–13, 5:3, 8:3, 10, 9:4, 11).

Public-service employment should play an important role in programs aimed at ameliorating the lot of the unemployed. By mid-1989 after six and a half years of economic recovery, 1.3 million persons—one of every five unemployed—remained idle for more than 15 weeks. Evaluations of CETA indicate that public-service employment effectively created new jobs which provided valuable services to communities (Cook et al., 1985, pp. 125–31).

Job-Search Assistance. Established in 1933, the federal-state employment service attempts to match employers with job seekers—mostly unemployed or poor—through a nationwide network of over 2000 public employment offices. Changing congressional mandates have pulled the service in a variety of directions since the 1960s. Severely deficient funding combined with competing pressures to assist unemployment insurance recipients, employers, the poor, veterans, welfare clients, food stamp beneficiaries, and other groups has often precluded the employment service from doing more than playing catch-up. By 1982 the employment service was attempting to fulfill responsibilities to 17 different programs, many unrelated to its original labor exchange role. In that year Congress stipulated that the employment service could perform activities for other agencies unrelated to its labor exchange mission only if it was fully reimbursed.

The most recent evaluation concluded that program benefits exceeded costs by two to one. However, earning gains were concentrated only among women (SRI International, June 1983).

Jobs garnered through the employment service tend to pay low wages, largely reflecting the fact that roughly a quarter of the service's clientele are disadvantaged. In filling about 7 to 8 percent of all job openings annually, the employment service represents one of the largest single sources of job placements outside of individual contacts and newspaper ads. About 20 million individuals apply for employment services annually; many—including unemployment insurance and public assistance recipients—are required to do so.

Job-search training, designed to hone participants' job-hunting skills, is usually taught through group workshops or individual counseling. Job-search assistance usually lasts no longer than two weeks, often no more than a few days. Most federal support for job-search assistance is provided through the employment service, although a significant minority of JTPA Title IIA enrollees and two-thirds of dislocated worker program participants receive job-search training. Job-search assistance should be provided to program entrants already possessing the job skills necessary for their chosen occupation, or as an adjunct service to participants who have completed classroom or on-the-job training.

Virtually every study of job-search assistance has concluded that while the training has clear short-term benefits, the impact dissipates within one to two years because job search does nothing to increase educational or occupational skills (Betsey, Hollister, and Papageorgiou, 1985, pp. 137–74; Gueron, March 1986, pp. 15, 17). Nevertheless, job-search assistance as a substitute for rather than an adjunct to skill training has become increasingly common in the 1980s. Job-search and other assistance accounts for a third of JTPA Title IIA training, primarily because it produces positive results on paper at extremely low costs. Selecting more qualified applicants for brief job-search courses has been facilitated by expanding employment opportunities since the last recession ended in 1982.

Stipends and Supportive Services. Paying stipends to trainees was an essential component of training programs in the 1970s, on the assumption that the poor could not pursue sustained training without income support. However, the Reagan administration argued that stipends turned training programs into welfare programs and strictly limited their use. Statutes or regulations prohibit many programs from devoting more than 15 percent of their budgets to stipends or support services such as transportation assistance or child care. These rules preclude many individuals lacking independent financial support from either entering the programs or receiving anything other than the briefest training assistance. Moreover, local officials generally spend even less on support services than the law permits. For example, less than one in seven Title IIA participants receive stipends, averaging $35 per week. Interviews with local administrators indicate that because of niggardly support service policies, JTPA enrolls more employable applicants and operates shorter training courses than did similar CETA projects.

Who's in Charge?

No issue in employment and training programs has been more contested than responsibility for the administration of the programs. During the past three decades administrative authority has shifted back and forth among the three levels of government and the private sector. Initially federal officials designed the programs and attempted to directly supervise them. In 1973, with the passage of CETA, the watchword was decentralization, resulting in expanded authority for local governments. In response to high unemployment and instances of fraud and waste, the federal government reasserted its authority. Because of the Reagan administration's denigration of federal competence and its abiding faith in the business community, JTPA radically overhauled program administration. The law greatly expanded the oversight role of state governments and business representatives, previously minor actors in employment and training efforts. Going well beyond the law's intent, the Reagan administration also virtually abdicated the federal role in overseeing JTPA and the employment service. After failing to convince Congress to either abolish or turn over employment and training efforts to the states, the administration acted unilaterally, ignoring congressional intent.

The conclusion that all wisdom resides in state houses and private business offices and that the federal government can do little, if anything, right is grounded in ideology rather than knowledge gained from research or experience. Although the Reagan administration severely limited the federal role, most states have continued to passively wait for federal instruction rather than forging ahead on their own (Arthur Young with Training Research Corporation, September 1988, pp. 8:14–15). State contributions for federal training programs are negligible, and the states spend about

$150 million annually on their own training programs (Ganzglass and Heidkamp, December 1987, pp. 17–20). Ironically, federal programs designed to demonstrate the potential of state leadership have instead indicated that a strong federal presence is necessary to administer effective training programs for the poor, unskilled, and deficiently educated. Stricter federal oversight and monitoring will not impede activist state leadership dedicated to improving programs.

An enhanced business role has significantly helped to bolster the public's image of employment and training programs, but there is no persuasive evidence that employer involvement has improved program operations. The increased business role may have contributed to diminished services to the most needy individuals.

Turf battles among congressional committees, executive branch departments, and the three levels of government as well as the private sector have also produced an extremely fragmented employment and training system. The most egregious example of wasteful administrative duplication occurs in training programs for welfare recipients. Although two-fifths of JTPA enrollees receive public assistance (in cash or in food stamps), Congress has within the past several years enacted two other separate training programs for AFDC and food stamp recipients. Two separate programs exist for older individuals: the senior community service employment program and the 3 percent set-aside for older workers under JTPA Title IIA. Two separate programs also exist to train dislocated workers, JTPA's Title III and a smaller training program under the trade adjustment assistance program. The employment service exists to place unemployed job-seekers, but most JTPA programs have little faith in public employment offices and consequently establish their own placement efforts. The federal government has made feeble attempts at promoting coordination between programs, to little effect (National Alliance of Business, 1987, p. 15). A wag commented that the federal attempt to coordinate training efforts at the local level is tantamount to requiring the commitment of an unnatural act among unconsenting adults.

Measuring Effectiveness

Three decades of experience with employment and training programs has yet to result in satisfactory techniques to assess program effectiveness. Initially, employment and training programs were widely considered, like general education, to be a self-evident good. However, dissatisfaction with CETA led Congress in 1978 to require the Labor Department to develop performance standards to assess program effectiveness. Performance standards have particularly appealed to policymakers in the 1980s as a supposedly reliable means to boost results without costly, detailed oversight. The most common performance standards measure the proportion of program terminees who find work, hourly wages, and the cost per job placement (usually defined as total outlays divided by the number of individuals employed). The Labor Department defined "positive terminations" to include activities that enhance future employability but may not directly result in a job—such as returning to school or successfully completing a basic education course.

Performance standards, if appropriately implemented, could potentially improve the effectiveness of job training programs. However, to achieve *reported* success, the Labor Department places far too much reliance on the standards, to the exclusion of other means of improving program quality. The job placement standards allow equal credit for all jobs, whether they are permanent, temporary, or part-time positions. Where indicators exist, reported performance has generally exceeded both the performance standards and CETA's results (Table 4).

TABLE 4
Reported Performance Under Major
JTPA Programs (1987)

	Adults (IIA)	Youth (IIB)	Dislocated Workers (III)	Job Corps (IV)
Entered employment rate	72%	54%	71%	62%
Positive termination rate	NA	80%	NA	76%
Hourly wage	$5.15	$4.25	$7.10	$4.34
Cost per placement	$2775	$3825	$1925	$16,653

Source: Unpublished data from the U.S. Department of Labor, Employment and Training Administration.

However, there are good reasons to believe that reported performance is exaggerated. For example, a fourth of JTPA Title IIA trainees employed at termination lost their jobs within four months. Trainees below age 22 and those 22 to 34 found jobs paying more than they made before entering (40 and 83 cents per hour more, respectively), but older trainees who found work suffered pay cuts (36 cents per hour for 35- to 44-year olds and $1.35 per hour for those 45 and older). The proportion of adults receiving public assistance dropped by only five percentage points after leaving JTPA, and youth recipiency did not decline at all (Office of the Inspector General, January 1988, pp. 25, 29, 31, 33). Widespread anecdotal reports indicate that many localities manipulate enrollment and termination practices. For example, a quarter of the service providers examined in Illinois did not officially enroll individuals until training was under way to avoid counting early program dropouts who were less likely to find work (Orfield and Slessarev, 1986, p. 190). Because federal, state, and local authorities do little monitoring, results are vulnerable to flagrant abuses in reporting.

Needed Reforms

Basic education and job training programs enhance participants' employability, but there remains considerable room for improvement. The plethora of existing programs should be consolidated, but Congress is likely to move on this with deliberate speed, if at all. In the meantime, much could be accomplished with a renewed sense of mission by the Labor Department. The following steps could be accomplished administratively:

1. Congress directed JTPA to serve the individuals who are "most in need" of assistance.[7] Past research suggests that training programs can make the greatest impact by aiding individuals who are relatively more disadvantaged. To effectively implement the law, the Labor Department should require local project administrators to test applicants' reading and math skills and consider their income, employment history, and educational attainment in order to screen in rather than screen out those most in need of help.

2. The demonstrably effective curricula of the Job Corps should be tested at selected localities and adapted to other training programs to enhance the quality of education and training. Program administrators need to recognize that the public would be better served if training provided more than a lick and a promise. Current

---

[7] Job Training Partnership Act, Section 141(a).

claims that millions are being helped serves only press release scribblers and program administrators.

3. The Labor Department should conduct spot-check audits of reported contractor performance to ensure the integrity of the performance standards system. The department should also set uniform standards for the content of competency-based programs, for without enforced standards superficial courses produce the best results on paper at minimal costs.

Selected statutory changes, augmented by congressional financial support and constructive oversight, are also needed to improve training programs. Some changes that Congress might consider follow:

1. The poor cannot eat training. Strict limitations on stipends and support services prevent poor individuals from enrolling in or completing training programs. Congress should liberalize the current limits on support service expenditures to allow stipends on a broader basis, scaled to the income and financial resources of the enrollee's family, and mandate the Labor Department to promote their increased use.

2. Congress should reconsider rejected 1986 amendments to the summer youth employment program requiring that a fourth of the funds be spent on basic education. While providing job opportunities may be necessary to entice disadvantaged youth to enroll in a summer educational program, work experience alone—especially the payment of the hourly minimum wage to 14- and 15-year-olds— is not the best investment of almost three-quarters of a billion dollars annually.

3. During the past two reauthorizations, Congress has increasingly limited the targeted jobs tax credit, and most recently extended it for a single year, until the end of 1989. Congress should extend the program for a longer period, but only if the Labor Department takes steps to promote TJTC more vigorously and collects the information necessary to evaluate its effectiveness. Subsidies to employers for employees who have already been hired should be barred, and the tax credit should be restructured to encourage employers to hire individuals for better-paying jobs and to retain them for longer periods. The current credit unduly rewards industries with large numbers of low-wage, high-turnover occupations.

4. While job training programs have enhanced the employability

of enrollees, training by itself cannot ameliorate job shortages. During the seventh year of the economic recovery, unemployment in one of every eight metropolitan areas and in five states remained at recession levels. Public-service employment projects in areas with job deficits are needed to expand employment opportunities.

5. Government antipoverty funds, including employment and training assistance, could be used more effectively by consolidating them into a comprehensive family investment initiative. In this program the family, the locus of and a potential solution for a variety of problems, would be assisted in appropriate cases rather than individuals in isolation. For example, enrollees often report that they quit training courses because of pressing family obligations that training administrators cannot address because the needed assistance is controlled by other agencies and/or programs. Uniform eligibility rules and centralized access centers would reduce duplicative administrative costs while making it considerably easier for the poor to obtain help. A case manager would guide the family through the program and would require continued progress and good faith effort as a condition of support.

Improving training quality, targeting the most disadvantaged clientele, expanding the use of stipends, and providing public-service jobs will increase the costs, but also the effectiveness of the federal investment. In addition, adequate monitoring and technical assistance are not possible without funds for more federal personnel. Increased expenditures are also necessary because only about one in fifteen eligible persons can be assisted with the present funding. Even more than doubling the current appropriations would fall short of the 1980 funding level in inflation-adjusted dollars.

To reap the optimum benefits and to avoid the administrative difficulties, expansion should be phased in gradually. Increases will be difficult to achieve given present federal budget deficits. However, prudent public policy should not ignore the costs of forced idleness and poverty.[8] Continuing national concern over the problems of dislocated workers, welfare recipients, and the deficiently educated may facilitate budget increases for employment and training programs.

---

[8] Brenner (June 15, 1984); Gordus and McAlinden (June 15, 1984). Both studies were prepared for the U.S. Congress, Joint Economic Committee.

Postscript

After more than seven years of JTPA, the Bush administration and Congress have taken some halting steps to strengthen the legislation. While the bills introduced in 1989 by Senator Paul Simon (S543), Representative Augustus Hawkins (HR2039), and the administration (HR2803) differ over some details, they share common provisions by: (1) targeting eligibility toward relatively more disadvantaged applicants; (2) adding performance standards to measure enrollees' acquisition of basic skills; (3) loosening current restrictions on support services and administrative costs; (4) revising the funding allocation formula to emphasize the low-income population JTPA is designed to assist, rather than the current stress on unemployment rates; and (5) in a tacit criticism of state management, redirecting funding from the states to local training agencies.

In sum, after nearly a decade of floundering, the employment and training system appears to be moving in a more positive direction. The Labor Department's new attitude is characterized by, "We weren't creaming before, and we're not going to do it again." However, whether Congress and the executive branch will back up the needed reforms with equally needed financing is doubtful. The Bush administration has not recommended additional funds, and the increased financing envisioned in the congressional proposals would barely cover the losses from inflation since 1984.

In utter disregard for IRRA scheduling, Congress has failed to come up with a final bill as this volume is being readied for press.

References

Applebee, Arthur, Judith Langer, and Ina Mullis. *Literature and U.S. History.* Princeton, NJ: Educational Testing Service, October 1987.
————. *Who Reads Best?* Princeton, NJ: Educational Testing Service, February 1988.
Arthur Young with Training Research Corporation. *Final Report on a Coordination Study of SJTCC and JTPA.* Sacramento, CA: Arthur Young, September 1, 1988.
Berlin, Gordon, and Andrew Sum. *Toward a More Perfect Union: Basic Skills, Poor Families, and Our Economic Future.* New York: Ford Foundation, 1988.
Betsey, Charles, Robinson Hollister, Jr., and Mary Papageorgiou, eds. *Youth Employment and Training Programs: The YEDPA Years.* Washington: National Academy Press, 1985.
Brenner, M. Harvey. *Estimating the Effects of Economic Change on National Health and Social Well-Being.* S. Prt. 98-198. Washington: U.S. Government Printing Office, June 15, 1984.
Centaur Associates, Inc. *Evaluation Study of the Senior Community Service Employment Program Funded Under Title V of the Older Americans Act.* Washington: Centaur Associates, Inc., July 25, 1986.

_____. *Supplementary Report: Evaluation of the Veterans' Job Training Program.* Washington: Centaur Associates, Inc., September 24, 1986.

Committee on Children, Youth, and Families. *Opportunities for Success: Cost Effective Programs for Children.* Washington: U.S. Government Printing Office, 1988.

Congressional Research Service. *Education Funding Issues for FY89.* Washington: Congressional Research Service, September 22, 1988.

_____. "Education: The Challenge." *Review* (October 1988).

_____. *Federal Assistance for Elementary and Secondary Education: Background Information on Selected Programs Likely to be Considered for Reauthorization by the 100th Congress.* 87-330 EPW. Washington: Congressional Research Service, January 27, 1987.

_____. *Job Training: FY89 Budget and Legislative Issues.* IB88027. Washington: Congressional Research Service, September 27, 1988.

_____. *U.S. Department of Education: Major Program Trends, Fiscal Years 1980–1989.* 88-330 EPW. Washington: Congressional Research Service, April 15, 1988.

Cook, Robert, Charles Adams, Jr., V. Lane Rawlins, and Associates. *Public Service Employment.* Kalamazoo, MI: W. E. Upjohn Institute for Employment Research, 1985.

Dossey, John, Ina Mullis, Mary Lindquist, and Donald Chambers. *The Mathematics Report Card.* Princeton, NJ: Educational Testing Service, June 1988.

Ganzglass, Evelyn, and Maria Heidkamp. *State Strategies to Train a Competitive Workforce: The Emerging Role of State-Funded Job Training Programs.* Washington: National Governors' Association, December 1987.

Gordus, Jeanne Prial, and Sean McAlinden. *Economic Change, Physical Illness, and Social Deviance.* S. Prt. 98-200. Washington: U.S. Government Printing Office, June 15, 1984.

Gramlich, Edward. "Evaluation of Education Projects: The Case of the Perry Preschool Program." *Economics of Education Review* 5, 1 (1986), pp. 17–24.

Gueron, Judith M. *Work Initiatives for Welfare Recipients.* New York: Manpower Demonstration Research Corporation, March 1986.

International Association for the Evaluation of Educational Achievement. *Science Achievement in Seventeen Countries: A Preliminary Report.* New York: Pergamon Press, 1988.

"JTPA Programs Tending Toward Placements in Low-Wage, Low-Skill Jobs, GAO Finds." *Daily Labor Report.* Washington: Bureau of National Affairs, April 29, 1988.

Levitan, Sar, Richard Belous, and Frank Gallo. *What's Happening to the American Family?* Baltimore, MD: Johns Hopkins University Press, 1988.

Levitan, Sar, and Frank Gallo. *A Second Chance: Training for Jobs.* Kalamazoo, MI: W. E. Upjohn Institute for Employment Research, 1988.

_____. "The Targeted Jobs Tax Credit: An Uncertain and Unfinished Experiment." *Labor Law Journal* (October 1987), pp. 641-49.

Levitan, Sar, Garth Mangum, and Marion Pines. *A Proper Inheritance: Investing in the Self-Sufficiency of Poor Families.* Washington: Center for Social Policy Studies, July 1989.

Lewis, Gwendolyn. *Trends in Student Aid: 1980 to 1988.* Washington: College Board, September 1988.

Lorenz, Edward. *The Targeted Jobs Tax Credit in Maryland and Missouri: 1982-1987.* Washington: National Commission for Employment Policy, November 1988.

Manpower Demonstration Research Corporation. *Summary and Findings of the National Supported Work Demonstration.* Cambridge, MA: Ballinger Publishing Co., 1980.

Mathematica Policy Research, Inc. *Evaluation of the Economic Impact of the Job Corps Program: Third Follow-Up Report.* Princeton, NJ: Mathematica Policy Research, Inc., September 1982.

National Alliance of Business. *JTPA Operations at the Local Level: Coordination or Discord.* Washington: NAB, 1987.

Office of the Assistant Secretary of Defense (Force Management and Personnel). *Population Representation in the Military Service, Fiscal year 1987.* Washington: U.S. Department of Defense, August 1988.

Office of the Inspector General. *Audit of JTPA Participant Training and Services: Report 1—Participant Training and Employment.* Washington: U.S. Department of Labor, January 25, 1988.

Orfield, Gary, and Helene Slessarev. *Job Training Under the New Federalism.* Chicago: University of Chicago, 1986.

"Poll Finds Americans Are Ignorant of Science." *The New York Times,* October 25, 1988. P. C10.

Public/Private Ventures. *Summer Training and Education Program: Report on the 1987 Experience.* Philadelphia: Public/Private Ventures, Summer 1988.

Redd, Kenneth, and Wayne Riddle. *Comparative Education: Statistics on Education in the United States and Selected Foreign Nations.* Washington: U.S. Congressional Research Service, November 14, 1988.

Sandell, Steven, and Kalman Rupp. *Who Is Served in JTPA Programs: Patterns of Participation and Intergroup Equity.* Washington: U.S. National Commission for Employment Policy, February 1988.

Schenet, Margot. *College Costs: Analysis of Trends in Costs and Sources of Support.* 88-694 EPW. Washington: U.S. Congressional Research Service, October 26, 1988.

SRI International. *A National Evaluation of the Impact of the United States Employment Service, Final Report.* Menlo Park, CA: SRI International, June 1983.

Sundquist, James. "Has America Lost Its Social Conscience—And How Will It Get It Back?" *Political Science Quarterly* 4 (1986).

Taggart, Robert. *A Fisherman's Guide.* Kalamazoo, MI: W. E. Upjohn Institute for Employment Research, 1981.

U.S. Bureau of the Census. *Estimates of Poverty Including the Value of Noncash Benefits: 1987.* Technical Paper 58. Washington: U.S. Government Printing Office, August 1988.

————. *Money Income and Poverty Status in the United States: 1987.* Current Population Report, Series P-60, No. 161. Washington: U. S. Government Printing Office, August 1988.

————. *Population Profile of the United States, 1989.* Current Population Report, Series P-23, No. 159. Washington: U.S. Government Printing Office, April 1989.

————. *School Enrollment—Social and Economic Characteristics of Students: October 1986.* Current Population Report, Series P-20, No. 429. Washington: U.S. Government Printing Office, August 1988.

U.S. Bureau of Labor Statistics. *Employment and Earnings.* Washington: U.S. Department of Labor, January 1989.

————. "Productivity and Costs." Press release USDL 89-57, February 6, 1989.

U.S. Congressional Budget Office. *Major Legislative Changes in Human Resources Programs Since January 1981.* Washington: CBO, August 1983.

U.S. Department of Education. *Second Interim Report from the National Assessment of Vocational Education.* Washington: Department of Education, September 1988.

U.S. General Accounting Office. *Bilingual Education: A New Look at the Research Evidence.* PEMD-87-12BR. Washington: GAO, March 1987.

————. *Job Training Partnership Act: Services and Outcomes for Participants with Differing Needs.* HRD-89-52. Washington: GAO, June 1989.

————. *Summer Youth Jobs Program.* HRD-88-118. Washington: GAO, September 1988.

Werner, Leslie Maitland. "13% of U.S. Adults Are Illiterate in English, a Federal Study Finds." *The New York Times,* April 21, 1986. P. A1.

Westat, Inc. *Continuous Longitudinal Manpower Survey Follow-Up Report No. 13.* Rockville, MD: Westat, Inc., December 1984.

CHAPTER 9

Elements of a
National Training Policy

PAUL OSTERMAN*
Massachusetts Institute of Technology

Training is a prominent item on both public and private policy agendas. Concern with dislocated workers and disruptions caused by trade led to infusions of funds into worker assistance programs. At the other end of the labor market, a central premise of welfare reform is heightened commitment to training, and recent legislation requires states to establish education and training efforts aimed at moving welfare recipients into private jobs.

Training has also emerged as a policy issue in the private sector. A common explanation of poor American productivity growth relative to international competitors is a general deficiency in American human resources policies. Skill development ranks high on the list of problem areas. The diffusion of information technologies has also increased interest in training since they require both new skills in data manipulation and that employees obtain a broad view of the production process. Indeed, although much of the popular discussion about jobs has emphasized growth in low-wage/low-skill sectors, the consensus of experienced observers is that skill requirements will rise, not fall, over time.

This resurgence of interest in training is welcome, but it also embodies risks. This is not the first era of enthusiasm. In the early 1960s concern over structural unemployment led to the enactment of the Manpower Development and Training Act, and soon thereafter the War on Poverty transformed much of the public training system into an antipoverty effort with special emphasis on youth. Although these efforts performed better than the popular press and political critics often credit, they nevertheless proved a

---

* Lisa Lynch and the volume editors provided helpful comments.

disappointment. More seriously, their legacy is a delivery system that embodies certain presumptions regarding the organization of training. The danger is that we will, without thinking too much about it, simply increase the level of resources devoted to efforts similar to those in the past and channel these efforts through the existing structure. This risks falling short of our goals and losing the chance to establish an active and effective employment and training policy in this country.

In this chapter I will raise some basic questions about how best to organize training. I will try to view the American training system as a whole and ask about the strengths and weaknesses of how it is organized. The focus will be on the broad choices that are available, and I will reach some judgment about the best path to follow.

The American Training System

The American training system is large and diverse. This is true even ignoring, as I do throughout this chapter, professional and technical training. A minimum list of its public components would include high school vocational education, community colleges (which, as noted below, are largely vocational), and numerous federal/state efforts such as the Job Training Partnership Act and the California Employment and Training Panel. Private training includes apprenticeship, private for-profit training schools (ranging from barbers to aircraft repair), and the extensive, though poorly measured, formal and informal programs of employers.

I argue below that resources devoted to training are inadequate and that many of these components perform well below expectations. Nonetheless, the array of institutions is impressive. Indeed, what often appears to outside observers as a deficiency of the system—the complex and poorly connected training mechanisms— is in fact a strength. The system is very much driven by individual initiative, and a person who wants to change careers or gain new skills can find numerous ways to do so. Unlike systems in some European nations and in Japan, early choices are not binding and the system provides chances (for those with the resources) to start over or change direction.

A sense of this diversity can be gained by seeing how many different ways people enter the same occupation. In a survey in which workers were asked where they received training for their jobs, 5 percent of technicians reported high school vocational training, 21 percent post-high school vocational training, 20 percent community colleges, 24 percent colleges, 14 percent formal firm-based training, and 32 percent informal firm-based training (U.S. Department of Labor, 1985, p. 36). This range is mirrored in most other occupations and illustrates the numerous entry routes and the impossibility of arriving at a simple characterization of the training system.

The Rationale for Change

Given the size and diversity of the American training system why the concern? Despite these positive aspects, there is good reason to consider improving the system. The reasons are:

- America undertrains its labor force compared to other nations, particularly those with whom we compete in the international economy.
- Demographics are shifting in a direction which makes renewed investment in training more important.
- The current system for serving the disadvantaged is isolated from the mainstream of the labor market and tends to stigmatize its clients.

America Undertrains Its Labor Force

Undertraining is especially a problem for blue-collar employees, a group whose skills tend to be undervalued by American employers. Most of the often noted extensive private-sector training is aimed at white-collar and managerial employees. The Conference Board surveyed large employers and found that 60 percent of firms provided managerial employees off-the-job training and only 11 percent did so for blue-collar workers (Lusterman, 1985, p. 50). In another survey the Bureau of National Affairs found that 60 percent of firms provided training courses to managers, 50 percent to professional and technical workers, yet only 18 percent to nonexempt employees (Bureau of National Affairs, 1985, p. 37). Additional evidence is provided by a content analysis of training courses offered to companies by outside training vendors. Only 14 percent of the more than 1500 courses surveyed claimed to serve other than clerical or managerial employees (Sonnenfeld, 1985, p. 302).

Additional evidence of the shortfall in American training comes from comparing the practices of foreign firms to American ones in similar industries. For example, Japanese-owned auto firms located in the U.S. provide much more training than do American-owned firms (Shimada and MacDuffie, 1986). In addition, entry-level training is more extensive elsewhere. In Germany, more than 80 percent of youth go through a broad vocational training curriculum and on-the-job training experience before entering the labor force. While there are no hard data to exactly compare training efforts across nations, examples like these could be easily multiplied, and most observers would accept the truth of the observation.

Undertraining is a problem because the nature of the demand for labor is shifting. Jobs employing modern information technology require higher skill levels than in the past. The reasons for this are complex, but can be summarized as follows (Osterman, forthcoming). Modern production processes shift skill from manual dexterity to data manipulation and pattern recognition. Employees need to have a broader view of the production process than required in the past, and they need to be able to respond to events that are recorded in data, not necessarily through the senses. In addition, computer-based systems lead to a tighter integration of production and more rapid speeds, and both of these characteristics place a premium on error-free operation. In new systems errors can propagate and have large-scale consequences. The role of workers is increasingly exception-handling, and this requires ability to understand and respond to unexpected and atypical situations. These reasons, taken together with the size of capital investment, are leading firms to seek a higher skilled labor force.

The demands of new technologies are one reason why undertraining is a problem. The second reason is broader and concerns efforts by firms to achieve more flexible internal labor market systems. American firms are seeking to shift their internal labor market systems away from the traditional narrow job definitions and rigid workrules and towards much more flexible arrangements. Indeed, the United States is an outlier with respect to both Europe and Japan in terms of the rigidity of its shop-floor systems.

What often stands in the way of achieving more flexible internal labor markets is workers' quite reasonable fear of the extremely adverse consequences of job loss. Workrules which appear inefficient and obsolete are often viewed by employees as a protection against arbitrary management behavior and as a way of maintaining employment levels or, at the least, of determining who gets laid off if it comes to that. If these rules are to be altered, short of aggressive unilateral management action, then a strong employment and training system has a role to play. By expanding training opportunities for employed workers and, hence, making them more employable both elsewhere in their current firm and in other firms, and by easing the consequences of job loss (through training or through the labor exchange), the stage can be set for more flexible and more productive employment systems. Indeed, one of the lessons that the United States can learn from other nations is that there is a link between flexible internal labor market systems and the existence of an active employment policy and a deeply trained labor force.

Demographics

The American workforce is going to grow slowly—at a rate of 1 percent a year in the 1990s, compared to the 2.9 percent a year rate in the 1970s. The average age of the workforce will rise as the number of 16-24-year old workers falls 2 million by the year 2000; between now and then minorities will account for 29 percent of all new entrants, twice their current share of the labor force, and nearly two-thirds of all new entrants will be women. The shrinking labor force creates an opportunity for lower unemployment rates. However, these developments also place a heavy burden on the education and training system to provide the skills the economy will need. Given that groups which have historically had difficulty in the labor market (minorities and women) will account for such a large share of new entrants, the burden on the training system will be all the heavier.

Training for the Disadvantaged

There is a vast literature evaluating employment and training programs—a literature which varies in its coverage and sophistication. The results of all these evaluations are not, of course, identical. However, taken as a whole a clear message does come through. Employment and training programs raise annual earned income by somewhere between $500 and $1500 per year.[1] A similar conclusion

---

[1] There are numerous reviews of the evaluation literature. See, for example, Betsey et al. (1985), Barnow (Spring 1987), Bloom (Fall 1984), Bassi and Ashenfelter (1986).

emerges from studies of employment subsidies such as the Targeted Jobs Tax Credit (Bishop and Hollenbeck, 1985).

Gains of this magnitude are (given typical program costs) large enough to justify the programs on a cost/benefit basis. However, these results raise questions about whether the programs achieve their central goal. A person entering a program most likely has experienced a sporadic work history and employment in a low-wage and dead-end job. Program participation does not change these facts. The modest earnings gains are generally due to longer hours, not higher wages, and in any case do not suggest that an individual's life circumstances have changed in any fundamental way. The participants in these programs remain at the bottom of the income distribution, and there is no evidence that they have been placed upon a new trajectory with respect to lifetime earnings.

Some readers may, however, feel that the standard against which the previous paragraphs judge programs is unduly harsh. There is some justice to this complaint. After all, the programs do raise earnings somewhat. They also may provide other benefits such as increased literacy and higher self-esteem. These results are valuable. Furthermore, many people would quite reasonably argue that, given the limited resources expended, little more could be expected. For example, in New York in 1986 an average of $2984 was spent per participant in adult JTPA training programs, and the typical youth program expended less than half that amount. By contrast, the public schools spent on average $4587 per pupil (Bailey, 1987).

Put differently, most trainees spend less than half a year in employment programs, and why should we expect that much can be achieved in this period? While it is certainly the case that better results would flow from increased resources, it does not follow that merely expanding programs without other changes would produce results that would change the central conclusion. Evaluations of several expensive programs support this view.[2]

---

[2] The most carefully evaluated program which expends substantial resources is the Job Corps, a year-long residential job training and remedial education program for youth which spent (in 1980) over $6800 per trainee. The program received one of the most careful evaluations in the literature, and it was found to be fully justified in cost/benefit terms once reduced crime and welfare payments were considered. Nonetheless, the average earnings gain was only $600 per year and was essentially double that if only program completers are considered.

Another expensive program for which we have good evaluation results is Supported Work. This program provided work experience and some remediation to four groups—youth, drug addicts, individuals involved in the criminal justice system, and welfare mothers. The only group for which there were positive results were welfare mothers, and those results were within the range we have described.

In my view, the poor performance of the employment and training system is because it has been explicitly limited to the bottom of the labor market. The targeting isolates and stigmatizes the system and its clients. Another way of making the same point is to note another characteristic of the programs: their uncertain identity as between an element of labor market policy or a part of the larger transfer (welfare) system. On its face the system is a labor market program aimed at providing skills and finding jobs for its clients. Set against this is the fact that the system has consistently been used as an adjunct of the welfare system. In part this occurred when (as is no longer possible) stipends for training were sufficiently attractive that people enrolled in training simply to receive the cash. Under these circumstances the training programs were literally welfare and transfer programs.

The connection of employment and training to the welfare system extends beyond direct transfer. Growing public concern about the legitimacy of welfare has meant that participation in training is often a requirement for receipt of transfer payments. This trend began in the 1960s with the Work Incentive Program (WIN), continues under that rubric today and in various "workfare" programs passed at the state level, and has recently been made into a centerpiece of federal welfare reform. Commendable as this may be from the perspective of the welfare system and even in terms of the mission of many job-training programs (which, after all, are intended to help people escape poverty), these efforts reinforce the view that job training and welfare are parts of the same overall system for dealing with a particular segment of the population. Under these circumstances it is hard to argue with the view that training is really an element of the welfare system, and it is not surprising that the employer community views the system with suspicion.

The fact that a narrowly targeted training program defeats its own purpose, via stigmatization, is one element in a larger argument that it is important to broaden the base of the employment and training system. There are more positive reasons for doing this, but the self-defeating nature of the present structure should stimulate reform.

Formulating an Employment Policy

The foregoing developed a rationale for an expanded American employment policy which included, but went beyond, distributional concerns. When turning to design issues it is useful to frame the discussion in functional terms by identifying categories of training that most societies find it necessary to provide. There appear to be three such categories: entry, further, and remedial training.

Entry training obviously concerns efforts to inculcate job skills into new labor market entrants. Normally, these are young people who are leaving school and the training occurs either in school (for example, vocational education) or via initial training provided by firms.

In most economies the level of training provided at the entry level does not fully prepare people for a lifetime of productive work and additional, or further, training is necessary. Hence, further training is typically job-related, aimed at deepening skills. The bulk of this training occurs on the job and is provided by firms. Community colleges and proprietary schools also play an important role. Further training is less formally organized than entry training and is therefore more difficult to define and measure. It might, for example, range from a one- or two-day typing course to advanced electronics training.

Finally, in all economies some individuals lack the basic skills to compete even at the entry level and have fallen so far behind that they need extra help. Remedial training is necessary to enable these people to compete in the labor market. Firms are reluctant to provide this training (although in very tight labor markets they may do so) and, hence, remedial efforts are typically organized and funded by the public sector.

The Location of Training

It is worth noting at the outset one question or theme which will run through the discussion—the proper balance between publicly and privately provided training. Should training occur inside the firm and be under the control of the private sector, or is it best accomplished via public funding and in public institutions? How does the weight of different considerations change depending upon the type of training, who is receiving it, and our analysis of the strengths and weaknesses of the current system?

This choice between public and private training can quickly be motivated by considering the vocational training systems of

Germany and Japan. The comparison is apt because both nations are often held up for emulation, at least in the United States, as producers of high-quality export products and possessors of skilled and committed labor forces able and willing to adapt quickly to the demands of the most advanced technologies. Yet if the outcome for the two nations is similar, the path by which they arrived there is quite different. As is well known, Germany has an extensive vocational education system through which more than 80 percent of each cohort passes.[3] Training takes place largely in firms and students prepare for one of roughly 400 occupations whose training requirements are uniform nationally. Although a federal agency oversees the system, the business community plays a dominant role in terms of daily supervision and administration of the final examination. Employment and career advancement is crucially dependent upon successful completion of this program.

The Japanese system is in sharp contrast to the German model. Japanese high schools have a strong anti-vocational-education bias (Rohlen, 1983). Recent observers note that "despite the government's relatively early attempts to institute systematic vocation-oriented schooling beyond the elementary level, these efforts proved to be limited and ad hoc" (Levine and Kawada, 1980, p. 284). It is therefore not surprising that another scholar commented that "Japanese public vocational education seems to have played a surprisingly small part in the process of rapid industrialization, and in the structural change of industries" (Umetani, 1980, p. 34).

Instead, Japanese firms (or at least the large ones) provide considerable internal training. New hires at all levels experience extensive initial training and are systematically rotated through a series of jobs to broaden their skills. In a sense this is like the German model in that training is firm-based. However, whereas a minority of German youth remain with the firm in which they are trained,[4] the Japanese norm is that training and continued employment occur in one firm. The key to the clearly successful training of the Japanese labor force lies in the extensive training inside the firm, in the internal labor market.

---

[3] Participation data on the dual system are based on the 1954–56 birth cohort and are estimated from the Qualification and Occupation Survey conducted by the Federal Institute of Vocational Training. See Blossfeld (July 1987).

[4] The small firm sector's share of training slots considerably exceeds their share of employment.

The lesson to draw from these two cases is that there are alternative ways to accomplish the same economic goal of developing a trained labor force adaptable to new demands. A key dimension is whether training is provided externally or inside the firm. It is important to understand the strengths and weaknesses of the alternative approaches and under what conditions one strategy is more desirable than another.

Entry Training

It is important to be cautious in generalizing about the nature and content of American vocational education because, like everything else in the American education system, there is considerable local control and, hence, widespread variation. Although the federal government spends about $1 billion in support of high school vocational programs, this accounts for a small fraction of total local vocational education expenditures; thus, federal leverage is limited. References to high school vocational education may refer to students who have taken a single course (a typing course, for example), students who have completed a vocational program which is offered in a comprehensive high school (that is, a school which also offers college preparation), or a student who has attended a vocational high school dedicated to specific categories of training. Even within these categories there is considerable quality variation.

These caveats suggest caution about interpreting evaluation results, but the fact remains that there have been numerous evaluations of American programs and the results are reasonably consistent—and discouraging. Students who participate in vocational education programs appear to do no better, and frequently worse, than comparable nonparticipants in terms of wages. Furthermore, with the exception of a few fields, there is little relationship between the skills studied in high school and those required on the job held after graduation.[5] There is evidence that in recent years vocational education programs have improved (Bishop, 1988), but at the minimum we must remain agnostic about their value.

There are a number of reasons to expect school-based vocational

---

[5] A recent summary of this literature is provided by the National Research Council (1984). See also Grasso and Shea (1979).

education programs to perform poorly. Schools make considerable investment in capital equipment and in staff with a particular set of skills, but both the physical and human capital can quickly become obsolete. Because of the investment, the schools often maintain enrollment, and the system can become supply- rather than demand-driven. Even ignoring this problem, it is very difficult for schools to maintain up-to-date knowledge of actual production technologies, and there are reasons to believe that on-the-job training is simply more effective than classroom work in most areas.

These arguments represent the conventional critique of vocational education, but are not entirely persuasive. The great potential advantage of school-based training is that it is likely to be more general than training provided in firms. Firms face strong incentives to render training as company-specific as possible in order to assure that they can capture the investment without risk of turnover. For similar reasons, firms often truncate training, limiting employees to narrow skill ranges (for example, training programs to maintain a specific accounting package rather than in more general skills). By contrast, school-based training is general and, hence, trainees simply enjoy greater opportunities for mobility. Indeed, it is arguments of just this sort that have led to considerable reluctance, particularly on the part of unions, to entrust training to firms.

Furthermore, the United States has a strong postsecondary layer of school-based training which, in contrast to high school vocational education, seems to perform well. These community colleges (which are typically financed by state governments) offer a two-year degree program after high school and have experienced explosive growth in the past two decades. Between 1960 and 1980 enrollment increased from 650,000 to 4 million. In 1960 they accounted for 16 percent of all higher education enrollments; by 1983 that figure had risen to 38 percent.[6] Along with this growth came a substantial change in the schools' mission: they shifted from institutions intended to help students transfer to four-year colleges to largely self-contained vocational institutions. While 13 percent of all community college enrollment in 1965 was in vocational programs, by 1984 that figure was 66 percent. The majority of these courses are school-designed and school-based programs aimed at

---

[6] The data in this paragraph are taken from Pincus (1985). I am grateful to Norton Grubb and Jerry Karabel for sharing with me drafts of their work on community colleges.

general preparation for a broad class of occupations. Thus, for example, a community college might offer a two-year degree with a specialty in office skills, health areas, or electronic technology.

Community colleges tend to be more flexible and entrepreneurial than the secondary school system. The student body is older and should enjoy more direct contact with employers. For these reasons one must expect the performance of community colleges to exceed that of vocational schools. The anecdotal evidence seems to support this view; however, hard research evidence on this point is much weaker than one would like.[7]

Finally, it is important to embed any effort to understand the success, and failure, of high school vocational programs in the context of an understanding of the American youth labor market. That labor market is chaotic by international standards.

As we have already seen, there are numerous routes into occupations rather than one or a few that are generally accepted. The wide variety in entry experiences is mirrored in the actual operation of the American youth labor market.[8] Most noncollege youth who leave school, either graduating or dropping out, do not move quickly into the job that will eventually become their "career" job (assuming that they are fortunate enough to eventually find such a job). Rather, they go through a period of casual work in so-called "secondary labor market jobs," that is, in firms which do not offer stable employment, well-developed internal labor markets, or a significant degree of training. Aging, marriage, and peer pressure lead the youth to settle down eventually into "primary" firms that do offer training and at least the prospects of stable employment. Other youth may enter another training institution such as the community colleges we have discussed. The consequences of this initial "moratorium" period is that specific skills learned in school are likely to be attenuated by the time the youth is ready to settle

---

[7] A recent review of the literature concludes that "no-one seems to know whether or not programs are effective." This particular paper takes a negative view, but shares in common with the rest of the literature several weaknesses. The analysis is based on a simple comparison of outcomes of community college graduates and college graduates. The sophisticated controls common in the literature on vocational education are absent, but, more to the point, the wrong comparison is made. The proper comparison is between youth who go from high school directly into work and those who attend community colleges. The comparison with four-year colleges is a red herring. See Pincus (August 1980); the quote above is from p. 347. Another widely cited study that shares the same problems is Wilms and Hansell (Spring 1982).

[8] The arguments that follow are developed in detail in Osterman (1980).

into a career job, and any relationship between that job and the vocational training taken in school is likely to be coincidental.

In summary, publicly provided vocational education has not worked well in the United States at the high school level. This, however, does not translate into a general indictment of such efforts, as the community college case makes clear. The failure at the high school level has to be understood in the context of the operation of the U.S. youth labor market. In principle there are advantages to public vocational entry training, and many of these do, in fact, appear to be reaped by other institutions aimed at older students.

Reforming Entry-Level Training

The specific proposal which seems to generate the greatest interest is a move towards the German apprenticeship model. That model seemingly offers the opportunity to deepen general skills, reduce youth unemployment, and link training more closely to employment practices within firms.

There is considerable irony to the current interest in the German model. A heated debate raged in the United States during the first two decades of the 20th century concerning the desirability of emphasizing vocational training and establishing separate vocational schools. The rationale for two tracks was that technologies were changing, the U.S. labor force lacked adequate skills, the role of schools was to prepare youth for work, and efficiency and equality of opportunity required a separate track for the "vocationally inclined." The irony is that then, as now, Germany was the model. The Chicago Superintendent of Schools, who was the major advocate of the plan, had developed his ideas after a trip to Germany. Business support for the effort was also derived from the German model. Consider the following comments by a Chicago businessman, comments which could easily be mistaken as excerpts from the current debate:[9]

> There is perhaps no greater object lesson of the possibilities of vocational training than the phenomenal industrial advance of Germany during the last generation. . . . This

---

[9] The quote is from Theodore Robinson, first vice-president of the Illinois Steel Company, and was delivered in 1913 to the American Steel Institute. It is taken from Wrigley (1982), p. 69.

has been accomplished primarily because forty years ago German statesmen were sufficiently farsighted and progressive to inaugurate the comprehensive system of vocational education by which German youth acquire a better training for their life's work than youth of any other nation.

The Chicago proposal led to a bitter battle as unions and progressive reformers fought the plan on the grounds that it would enshrine class distinctions, remove education from democratic control, and place it in the hands of business. The plan was defeated and, indeed, this very struggle over the proposal to create a dual system was one of the key events in the formation of the current structure of American education.[10] Perhaps ironically, unions did nonetheless support establishment of vocational tracks (or lines) within comprehensive high schools, and in the end these became both ineffective and stigmatizing.

If the prospect of transplanting the German system raised such opposition in the past, what is the point of reconsidering the issue now? It is clear, for example, that a strict adoption of the model is out of the question: Americans would never accept the tracking implicit in assigning youth to career tracks as early as the ninth or tenth grades. However, the difficulties are even deeper than this. American education is highly decentralized, with the federal government exerting minimal control, state governments having modest influence, and the greatest power being at the community level. However, the credentials which are granted by this system have to be understood nationally by both higher education and employers. This context makes it difficult to imagine as broad a shift in content of high school programs as would be required by adoption of an apprenticeship model.

The more plausible reform lies in organizing a more formal post-high-school graduation year of vocational training and apprenticeship. Schools or public-private partnerships might organize training placements for high school graduates who do not continue to college. These placements might resemble the German model in that most time is spent in firms, but a given portion is spent off the job in classroom training.

In order for this model to work well, it is important that care be

---

[10] For additional material, see Lazerson and Grubb (1974).

given to the selection and supervision of the training placements in firms. These positions should involve real skill acquisition and the training should be as general as possible. The danger is that without oversight and a serious commitment from employers the placements will simply provide low-wage labor. It is also important to carefully design the educational component. Past experience suggests that the most promising venue would be community colleges. Finally, supportive services need to be provided for those who require special assistance.

Further Training

The second functional requirement facing all economies is to deepen the skills of the incumbent labor force. This is not necessary for all employees; there are now and will continue to be jobs for which the skill level provided by entry training is adequate. Nonetheless, for a substantial fraction of the labor force further training is necessary. The training can be required to increase performance on the current job, to prepare for additional jobs within the same firm, or to enhance the prospects of successful mobility.

For entry training in the U.S., resources and opportunities for policy intervention are fairly evenly balanced between the two venues, public and private. This is not the case for further training, which is very heavily tilted towards provision in the context of internal labor markets. As a result, any analysis of issues underlying further training as well as any policy effort must be oriented towards understanding and altering patterns of behavior within firms.

As noted earlier, in the U.S. there appears to be an underprovision of further training relative to the levels achieved by many nations which are competitive with us. The explanation lies in the distinctive nature of the American internal labor market system.

Most blue-collar work in the U.S. is organized along the lines of what I have termed the "industrial" model (Osterman, 1988). Work is divided into relatively narrow jobs, and employees do not cross these boundaries to perform other duties. The consequence is that there is little premium, for either firms or workers, to engage in broad training.

A striking illustration of this point was provided by two scholars who studied Japanese auto firms in the U.S.:

Training is another factor which Japanese companies in the U.S. emphasize greatly. Training provided to workers is an intensive and long-lasting process. . . . Training is given in several forms: preliminary vocational training, orientation training, introduction to Japanese "mother" plants, and on-the-job and off the job training. Since the entire production system depends so heavily on human resources effectiveness, unlike the conventional American production system, Japanese companies need to be extraordinarily sensitive to personality, preparedness, attitude, and participation by workers. (Shimada, and MacDuffie, 1986, pp. 57, 60)

The logic of production limits training in American firms, but so does a related aspect of the system—managerial attitudes or culture. American managers have been schooled to distrust employees and the essentially adversarial nature of the production system reinforces this view. Because there is little expectation that employees can or should contribute to production, the need for training is limited. In part this view derives from Tayloristic production systems which were organized to restrict employee involvement, and in part from the absence of a tradition of labor-management cooperation in production. In other nations, even in countries with strong political conflict between labor and management, at the shop-floor level there is more cooperation and trust and, as a result, a greater incentive to increase training.

A final reason why training is underprovided in American internal labor markets is the standard human capital concern that workers will quit and firms will lose their investment. Why should this be more of a problem in the United States than in other nations? It would appear that, at least in large firms, mobility rates are lower in nations such as Japan and Germany than here. This point can be exaggerated, and recent evidence suggests that roughly 40 percent of the U.S. labor force will hold jobs that will eventually last 20 years or more (Hall, 1982). Nonetheless, what comparative data there are on job tenure as well as accounts by observers suggest that employees in Japan and Germany remain with their firms longer (Hashimoto and Raisian, 1985). At the minimum, the assumption, at the beginning of employment with a large "core" employer, that the worker will stay is stronger abroad than here. Ironically, the benefits—in terms of training—of this stable employment relationship is often overlooked in discussions of the rigidity of foreign labor markets compared to the U.S.

If U.S. firms do undertrain relative to those of other nations, and if the reason lies in the dynamics of the firms' internal labor markets, what does this imply about policy? In the case of entry training there is a clear case for public involvement since no private party bears responsibility. Similarly, as we shall see, there is a strong case for public involvement in remedial training. However, with respect to further training the issue is more complicated. If there is a problem, and if the problem impedes the firm's productivity, then we should expect the firm to remedy the situation. If the firm does not act, then the reasonable inference is that the problem is not serious enough to justify additional resources, either financial or organizational.

For these reasons the case for policy is not self-evidently strong, but neither is it nonexistent. One justification rests on the issue of unemployment and mobility. Firms might be expected to act in their own self-interest, but there is no reason to expect them to provide training that was beneficial only to employees. However, in an era of demand-side shocks, worker dislocation will be a continuing problem and employees with broad skills will find better jobs more rapidly than those without such training. Operators of dislocated worker training programs believe that training is provided much more effectively in the context of current employment than in after-the-fact worker dislocation programs. Given that wage rigidities and other internal labor market arrangements prevent workers from "buying" their training from their employer, it would be desirable to encourage firms to augment training provided to incumbent workers.

Another justification emphasizes the difficulties firms have in transforming their internal labor market systems. If more flexible (or what I have termed "salaried" in contrast to "industrial") internal labor markets are more productive, then it is in the national interest to move in that direction. However, any individual firm may have problems making the transition. These problems may result from simple uncertainty about what kinds of arrangements work well with respect to pay, work organization, or training. The problems might also flow from a history of adversarial labor-management relations which is difficult to overcome. Uncertainty about how to proceed may be exacerbated by the relative paucity of visible examples of other firms undertaking similar efforts. Training can encourage more flexible internal labor markets both because the employees can be more flexibly deployed and because training enhances their chances in the external labor market; hence their willingness to provide internal flexibility. In these circumstances there may be a case for a national policy that emphasizes technical assistance, demonstration programs, and diffusion of best practices.

Finally, small firms may face special problems. Not only do they lack resources and managerial "slack" for training, but they also confront higher rates of turnover and hence higher risks of losing whatever investments they do make to other firms which are "free riders." Thus, for small firms there are positive externalities for a public authority which arranges training and finds a way to "tax" each small employer for its fair share of costs. Various kinds of consortia arrangements fit this description.

There is, therefore, an argument for policy with respect to further training, although the case is less compelling than in other areas. The issue becomes even murkier when we consider the range of possible policy. The problem is that we lack a good understanding of how best to influence private decisions concerning employment practices. We lack good models other than coercion, as in equal employment opportunity, or direct regulation, as in occupational health and safety, and obviously neither of these is appropriate here.

It is also important to note that public policy in this area will run up against a central tension between firms' desire to offer specific training and the labor forces' interest in more general training. Firms want to make training as specific as possible because such training will seem the most productivity-enhancing strategy. Employees will seek general training because this will offer them the most options in the external labor market and, hence, will increase their market power. In settings where decisionmaking over training is formalized—for example, in Germany—these conflicts have been explicitly played out as unions and firms have struggled over training content (Streeck et al., 1987). In the U.S. context the public authorities will need to be aware of the issues at stake.

As for policy options, financial incentives are a possibility, and there is often discussion of a training tax which would be rebated to firms, provided they met certain target levels of training. However, this scheme (variants of which are employed in France and Ireland) runs up against severe problems of implementation. A proposal along these lines would require clear definitions of what kinds of training would qualify, baseline measurement of the amount of training currently under way, and measurements of additions to training efforts.

Short of a tax scheme, there appears to be two broad choices. The first is to rely on a package of modest ventures aimed at increasing training. These would include technical and financial support to existing and potential joint union-management training efforts of the sort initiated in the automobile and telecommunications industries. Another option is modest support to firms, union and nonunion, which want to expand training, particularly in areas in which shortages can be documented.

Another useful initiative would be programs directed to small firms. An example of a useful program is assistance in establishing a training consortium, with a community college acting as the central training facility. Indeed, the general area of assistance to small firms is one that is often overlooked, yet holds great promise.

The second strategy is to embed the training issue in broader human resources reforms. Observers concerned with remedying the weakening employee representation system in the United States, and achieving more competitive use of human resources, have suggested movement towards a modified works council system in which a range of issues would be considered jointly by employers and employees (Kochan and McKersie, 1989). Such a "human resources council" could operate in both union and nonunion settings. In such a framework, training would clearly be an important item on the agenda, and this would provide a natural framework for steps aimed at expanding training efforts.

In many ways the human resources council approach is the more satisfactory strategy since it naturally embeds discussions of training in a wider context and, once such councils are in place, it is much easier to envision ways to encourage employers to expand general training. However, establishing such councils and convincing firms to provide them with any real authority is a daunting proposition. Presumably this would happen incrementally, with councils created or required around particular concerns, such as health and safety, and then gradually enlarged in scope.

In summary, the case for expanded training within firms is strong, but the case for public intervention is somewhat weaker.

When it comes to actual policies, a series of small steps seems plausible, but none promises to address the issue in a large-scale or convincing way. It may be consoling to know that other nations, even those with well-established entry training and remedial systems, have similar problems deploying public policy to expand training within the firm.[11]

Remedial Training

As we have seen, the remedial training system in the U.S. suffers because it is stratified by income and isolated from the mainstream of the labor market. The central policy issue is how to remedy this problem. Put differently, in the past the system was the preserve of narrow target groups. These were the groups most in need and who had a legitimate claim to resources. However, the nature of the system left it unable to work effectively with firms and to place clients in good jobs. This both reduced its effectiveness and left it vulnerable to budget-cutting. The objective should now be to find ways to broaden the system's appeal and, by doing so, to better serve traditional as well as emerging needs.

In thinking through the shape of policy, two major issues emerge: the institutional structure in which that policy is embedded and the programmatic content of the policy. In fact, it is more important to focus upon the creation of a credible system than upon specific programmatic interventions. There are two reasons for this. The first is the relatively obvious one that the needs of individuals are too varied to admit a single category of intervention. The issue then is whether a system can be put into place which is flexible enough to shape programs to particular circumstances.

There are, in addition, a series of tasks appropriate to an employment and training system which can be accomplished only by an ongoing administrative entity. Such an agency should work with local economic development officials to use training as a tool for job creation. When faced with the threat of a plant closing or large-scale layoff, it should bring training, mediation, and technical assistance to bear in an effort to ward off the problem or to mitigate its effects. It should be able to work with other agencies, such as the

---

[11] Sweden, for example, has tried to implement what is termed "bottleneck training" which is aimed at assisting firms to upgrade current employees. This has run into considerable criticism that it simply represents windfall gains for employers with very little public benefit.

school system, to address the problems of youth and the needs of the firms in the community. These and other tasks can only be achieved through a strong, ongoing system.

There are, it is true, current discussions of programs—for example, Individual Training Accounts—which bypass this question by simply making funds available to people to purchase their own training. In addition to being poorly targeted and, hence, wasteful (a substantial fraction of the funds would go to people who do not need them), the idea raises serious issues of quality control (consider scandals regarding proprietary schools). Such a plan also provides no method for maintaining any ongoing responsibility for individuals, either while they are "spending" their vouchers or after their training is completed. Without an organizational structure with a goal and accountability as well as specific program components (counseling and placement, for example), it is hard to believe that a program can deliver quality results.

Program Eligibility

We have already described the consequences of an employment and training system which is means-tested. It becomes perceived as part of the welfare system, and mere participation has the effect of stigmatizing clients. Furthermore, firms, interested in recruiting people with a broad range of characteristics, will avoid the system or treat it as a charity.

It is clear, therefore, that a remedial employment policy should be embedded in a broader system. As a practical matter, however, this does not mean universal coverage. The training system for high-level personnel appears to perform well, and there is no reason to expect that any new policy can or should supplant it. Indeed, the public employment policies of even the most activist European nations still do not extend into the top half or so of the occupational distribution. One conclusion is that, in the U.S., means-tested eligibility should be eliminated, and we should expect that the system will touch upon noncollege-level occupations and perhaps a bit further. Even this more modest objective will greatly extend the system and make it a far more attractive instrument for the private economy.

What about poor people? Is it not a perverse set of priorities to broaden the system, given the substantial needs at the bottom of the labor market? The answer goes to results. The current system "belongs" to poor people, but it does not (as we have shown) serve them well. A different system may have a broader constituency, but if the system as a whole is more effective, then it will serve poor people better. The basic idea is that a set of institutions provides training for a wide range of people and the governmental (regulatory) authorities assure that the poor are included. The "graduates" of such training would not be stigmatized, due to the broad client base. Poor people would blend in and, at the next step in the system, be treated no differently than anyone else.

There are practical objections to this scenario, the most serious of which is that many disadvantaged labor force participants require remedial services, especially basic education, which "mainstream" institutions either may be loath to offer or will provide in a set of tracks that have the effect of restratifying the system. It is here that there remains a continuing role for the range of community-based institutions which in the past have served as the backbone of the old employment and training system. It would be undesirable for these institutions to retain their training and placement functions since, by their very nature, they signal employers about the nature of their clients. However, they may effectively serve as preparatory institutions for the broader employment and training system that we envision.

Given the organizational structure outlined above, the training system could engage in a wide variety of activities (many of which it already does). These include organizing remedial and basic education programs (for clients ranging from welfare recipients to employed workers in need of such assistance), training and drop-out prevention programs for high school students, organizing the apprenticeship effort outlined earlier, skills training for adults, and programs aimed at training and placing dislocated workers.

As the above list makes clear, it is important that the public training system engage in as wide a range of activities as possible and that whenever possible it reach beyond its traditional constituency of poor people. This means that policymakers should not create new administrative structures for programs (as was done with the recent dislocated workers legislation), but should rather seek to broaden and strengthen the existing system. It is also important to build up as strong and visible a system as possible, and this also requires channeling all training through the same infrastructure, a policy which was not fully adhered to in the recent welfare reform legislation.

Conclusion

A strong and effective training system delivers benefits beyond the private ones accruing to individuals who participate. Deeper training can assist American companies as they seek to transform their internal labor markets in the direction of the more productive and flexible "salaried" systems. Higher skilled workers can more quickly adopt and work effectively with new techniques. In addition, expanded training can ease the consequences of restructuring and dislocation and, hence, reduce resistance to new work systems. These benefits are in addition to the more conventional, and still important, argument that we all gain from a society with more equal distribution of earnings and security and that training is an important tool for achieving this.

If we accept this general case for training, then we need to think carefully about the organization of the three kinds of training—entry, further, and remedial—which are identified in this chapter. There are important differences among these with respect to public and private responsibilities, the appropriate mix between general and specific training, and the extent to which the existing infrastructure is adequate. The most important lesson is that we should step back and view the training system as a whole. We should not accept the current institutional structure as a given; rather, we need to see how the pieces fit together and to understand how the system fits with the other major pieces of the labor market. This style of analysis can move us in the direction of a system that is at once more equitable and more effective.

References

Bailey, Thomas. "An Assessment of the Employment and Training System in New York City." In *Setting Municipal Priorities, 1988,* eds. Charles Brecher and Raymond Horton. New York: New York University Press, 1987.

Barnow, Burt. "The Impact of CETA Programs on Earnings: A Review of the Literature." *Journal of Human Resources* 22, 2 (Spring 1987), pp. 157-93.

Bassi, Laurie, and Orley Ashenfelter. "The Effect of Direct Job Creation and Training Programs on Low-Skilled Workers." In *Fighting Poverty,* eds. Sheldon Danziger and Daniel Weinberg. Cambridge, MA: Harvard University Press, 1986. Pp. 133-51.

Betsey, Charles, et al. *Youth Employment and Training Programs, The YEDPA Years.* Washington: National Research Council, 1985.

Bishop, John. "Vocational Education for At-Risk Youth: How Can It Be Made More Effective?" Working Paper 88-11, Center for Advanced Human Resource Studies. Ithaca: New York State School of Industrial and Labor Relations, Cornell University, 1988.

Bishop, John, and Kevin Hollenbeck. *The Effects of TJTC on Employers.* Columbus, OH: National Center for Research on Vocational Education, November 1985.

Bloom, Howard. "Estimating the Effect of Job Training Programs Using Longitudinal Data: Ashenfelter's Findings Reconsidered." *Journal of Human Resources* 19, 4 (Fall 1984), pp. 545–55.

Blossfeld, Hans-Peter. "Labor Market Entry and the Sexual Segregation of Careers in the Federal Republic of Germany." *American Journal of Sociology* 93, 1 (July 1987).

Bureau of National Affairs. *Personnel Policies Forum Report*, No. 140. Washington: BNA, 1985.

Burtless, Gary. "Are Targeted Wage Subsidies Harmful? Evidence from a Voucher Experiment." *Industrial and Labor Relations Review* 39, 1 (October 1985), pp. 105–14.

Grasso, John, and John Shea. *Vocational Education and Training: Impact on Youth.* New York: Carnegie Foundation for the Advancement of Teaching, 1979.

Hall, Robert. "Lifetime Jobs in the U.S. Economy." *American Economic Review* 72 (September 1982), pp. 716–24.

Hashimoto, Masanori, and John Raisian. "Employment Tenures and Earning Profiles in Japan and the United States." *American Economic Review* 75 (September 1985), pp. 721–25.

Kochan, Thomas, and Robert McKersie. "Future Directions for American Labor and Human Resources Policy." *Relations Industrielles* 44, 1 (1989), pp. 224–48.

Lazerson, Marvin, and W. Norton Grubb. *American Education and Vocationalism.* New York: Teachers College Press, 1974.

Levine, Solomon B., and Hisashi Kawada. *Human Resources in Japanese Industrial Development.* Princeton, NJ: Princeton University Press, 1980.

Lusterman, Seymour. *Corporate Training.* New York: The Conference Board, 1985.

National Research Council. *High Schools and the Changing Workplace.* Washington: National Research Council, 1984.

Osterman, Paul. *Getting Started: The Youth Labor Market.* Cambridge, MA: MIT Press, 1980.

_____. *Employment Futures: Reorganization, Dislocation, and Public Policy.* New York: Oxford University Press, 1988.

_____. "New Technology and the Organization of Work, A Review of the Issues." Washington: U.S. Department of Labor, forthcoming.

Pincus, Fred. "The False Promise of Community Colleges: Class Conflict and Vocational Education." *Harvard Education Review* 50, 3 (August 1980), pp. 332–61.

_____. "Customized Contract Training in Community Colleges: Who Really Benefits." Paper presented to the American Sociological Association, Washington, 1985.

Rohlen, Thomas P. *Japan's High Schools.* Berkeley: University of California Press, 1983.

Shimada, Haruo, and John Paul MacDuffie. "Industrial Relations and 'Humanware': Japanese Investments in Automobile Manufacturing in the United States." Working Paper No. 1855-86. Cambridge, MA: Sloan School of Management, MIT, December 1986.

Sonnenfeld, Jeffrey. "Demystifying the Magic of Training." In *HRM Trends and Practices*, eds. Richard Walton and Paul Lawrence. Cambridge, MA: Harvard Business School Press, 1985.

Streeck, Wolfgang, Josef Hilbert, Karl-Heinze van Kevelaer, Friederike Maier, and Hajo Weber. "The Role of the Social Partners in Vocational Training and Further Training in the Federal Republic of Germany." Working Paper. Brussels: European Center for the Promotion of Vocational Training, October 1987.

Umetani, Shun'ichiro. "Background Paper for Japan/ARSDEP Study Tour on In-Plant Training." Tokyo: Gakugei University, October 1980. Mimeo.

U.S Department of Labor. *How Workers Get Their Training.* Bull. 2226. Washington: U.S. Government Printing Office, February 1985.

Wilms, Wellford, and Stephen Hansell. "The Dubious Promise of Postsecondary Vocational Education: Its Payoff to Graduates and Dropouts in the U.S.A." *International Journal of Educational Development* 2 (Spring 1982), pp. 43-60.

Wrigley, Julia. *Class Politics and Public Schools.* New Brunswick, NJ: Rutgers University Press, 1982.

CHAPTER 10

The Evolution of Worker Training: The Canadian Experience

NOAH M. MELTZ[*]
University of Toronto

In the late 1960s, Canada's adult training programs represented ". . . a very substantial undertaking in international terms, second only to that of Sweden . . ." (Economic Council of Canada, 1971, p. 104). In the two decades that followed there have been a number of major changes in government funding of training, culminating in the Canadian Jobs Strategy, which represents a shift away from pure training toward a combination of training and work experience. This examination of the evolution of worker training in Canada will consider two sets of issues. The first is the role of training in the effort to achieve economic growth, equity, and stability. The second is the question of institutional versus industrial training. Both sets of issues are relevant in considering the challenge of training in the 1990s.

This chapter begins with a brief consideration of the role of training in relation to labour markets and economic development. This is followed by a description of the division of responsibilities for training in Canada between the federal government and the provinces and then a review of the development of the labour market in the past three decades. The next section presents an overview of training versus immigration as sources of supply of skilled persons. The evolution of public and private support for training is divided into three perspectives: a federal perspective, a

[*]The author would like to acknowledge the assistance received from Denise Beauvais, J. S. Blain, Peter Hicks, Georges Latour, and Richard Monette of Employment and Immigration Canada; Ieva Kravis, William G. Wolfson, and Helmut Zisser of the Ontario Ministry of Skills Development; the staff and library of the Centre for Industrial Relations, University of Toronto; and helpful comments from Roy Adams, Morley Gunderson, and Craig Riddell. Financial support for the research was provided by the Humanities and Social Sciences Committee of the University of Toronto.

provincial perspective, and a perspective on employer-sponsored training. Issues for the future are explored in the final section.

The Role of Training in the Labour Market

In economic terms, both education and training represent investment in human capital. That is, both denote the acquisition of skills that enable people to enhance their stream of future earnings by acquiring the ability to perform a wider range of occupations, including more highly paid occupations. The distinction between education and training is accepted, but it is somewhat blurred. Education is viewed as acquiring general and theoretical knowledge, while training is thought to be job-focused—that is, rendering an individual skillful or proficient, such as in a particular trade. In practice the distinction means separating university and liberal arts college education, on the one hand, from technical school, community college (in Canadian terms), and apprenticeship programs. While such a distinction is artificial from a labour market perspective, the approach is long standing in practice.[1] This chapter will focus on the acquisition of skills in Canada, outside of the university system, where the purpose is to enhance job-related proficiency.

In a labour market context, training has implications for the economy as a whole, for employers, and for the employees themselves. For the economy, training not only provides a means of filling vacant jobs that require particular skills, but also may enhance capacity for workers to be innovative and responsive to changing technology and market demands. This is the role of training in promoting economic growth. It is not possible to have an advanced technical industrial society with an untrained and uneducated workforce. For employers (whether private or public sector), an available supply of trained persons means being able to produce the goods and services in demand. If the employers are in sectors with above-average productivity, then training will promote economic growth. If the sectors have below-average productivity, then training may add to the total output of the economy, but it may

---

[1] The only case for a distinction between education and training would be that training includes practice whereas education does not. For example, apprenticeship training requires working in the field—for example, tool and die making—whereas in acquiring a degree in economics a student is not required to work for an economist. The fine line breaks down in the case of some professional degrees where work experience or internship may be a prerequisite.

not enhance growth so much as producing stabilization (additional jobs) if it occurs during a period of recession. For individual workers, training means the possibility of greater job security, enhanced income prospects, along with prospects of greater job mobility. Here training plays the role of promoting equity and, if the economy is slack, stabilization as well.

In the Canadian context, public policy toward training has consciously linked growth, stabilization, and equity. As a result, although the focus of this chapter is on training, the analysis will consider the relationship between training and job creation/work experience, where the latter was undertaken by the Department of Employment and Immigration.

Constitutional Division of Responsibilities for Training

Canada's first constitution, the British North America Act of 1867, as well as the Constitution Act of 1982 gave the provinces responsibility for education. Training for employment has been interpreted as being a shared jurisdiction because the federal government has responsibility for the general state of the economy. As a result, both the federal government and the provinces are free to engage in training. In addition, unlike in the United States, the national employment service (Canada Employment Centres) and the Unemployment Insurance Commission are entirely federally run and financed. Quebec is the only province that also has its own separate employment service.

In practice, the bulk of public expenditures on training have come from the federal government, initially in the first half of the 1960s on a shared-cost basis with the provinces. While negotiations with the provinces have often produced major confrontations, especially over the role of the provinces as exclusive brokers for the institutional portion of training (Dupré et al., 1973), compromises have been reached.

Trends in the Canadian Economy

To provide a context for discussing the evolution of training in Canada, we will briefly indicate the major developments in the Canadian economy during the period 1959 to 1989. Canada's population and its economy are approximately one-tenth those of the United States. Because of the close economic links between Canada and the U.S., their economic cycles have been very similar.

The recession at the end of the 1950s was followed by prolonged growth in the first half of the 1960s, slower growth in the late 1960s and early 1970s and a slowdown in the mid-1970s, moderate growth in the late 1970s, and a deep recession from 1981 to 1983.

Canada's labour force has grown at a faster rate than the U.S. labour force and, partly related to this, the unemployment rate, on average, has been slightly above that in the U.S. In the post-1983 period, the gap between the unemployment rates widened to the greatest extent ever. In 1988 Canada's unemployment rate was 7.8 percent compared with 5.5 percent in the U.S. At the start of the recession in 1981, the unemployment rates in the two countries were identical at 7.5 percent. Half of the gap between the rates is the result of more rapid employment growth in the U.S. and half is due to the greater increase in Canada's labor force (Gower, 1988).

Training vs. Immigration as Sources of Skilled Workers

Canada has always relied on immigrants to provide a significant portion of its skilled manpower and, to a lesser extent, its professional manpower. While there was a major expansion in the education and training facilities of the country beginning in the 1960s, immigrants still make up between a fifth and a third of the most skilled trades such as those in construction and machining.

Although there has been public pressure to increase the role of training to enhance domestic supply, the periodic skill shortages that have regularly appeared during the peak growth phases in the economic cycle (e.g., 1965-66, 1972-73, 1979-80, 1987-88) have been followed by an expansion in immigration. It would be desirable to attempt to measure the specific contribution of immigration versus training to employment in skilled jobs, but this is beyond the scope of this chapter.

An Overview of Training in Canada

Table 1 provides an overview of the amount of expenditures on training and the number of participants in various programs from 1961-62 to 1987-88. Also included in the table are expenditures on and participants in job-creation and work experience/training programs. It should be noted that these statistics have been pieced together from a number of sources. Details on the sources and methodology are presented in Appendix 1. Job-creation and work experience programs are included along with training because

TABLE 1

Federal Government Funding of Training,
Job Creation, and Combined Work Experience/Training Projects,
Canada, Operating Expenditures and Participants[a]

Year	Operating Expenditures ($ millions)				Participants (thousands)			
	Trng	Job Creation	Work Exp. & Trng	Total	Trng	Job Creation	Work Exp. & Trng	Total
1987-88	945.2	257.4	553.0	1,755.6	218.7	110.1	97.8	426.5
86-87	998.2	241.2	536.9	1,776.3	223.5	100.8	109.9	434.2
85-86	1,054.2	472.1	140.1	1,666.4	239.7	181.5	49.5	470.6
1984-85	1,089.8	809.1	7.0	1,905.9	267.5	253.2	3.3	524.0
83-84	1,021.3	810.2		1,831.5	282.0	321.9		603.8
82-83	925.9	385.4		1,311.3	295.3	179.5		474.8
81-82	829.8	340.4		1,170.2	292.7	103.6		396.3
80-81	770.0	265.0		1,035.0	307.8	81.5		389.3
1979-80	672.9	248.6		921.5	309.0	72.0		381.0
78-79	637.4	323.6		961.0	286.5	96.8		383.3
77-78	572.2	291.6		863.8	299.4	113.2		412.6
76-77	547.7	225.6		773.3	297.3	63.7		361.0
75-76	506.6	176.1		682.7	274.6	71.4		346.0
1974-75	401.2	120.3		521.5	291.6	59.8		351.4
73-74	363.2	75.3		438.5	319.7	32.1		351.8
72-73	343.5	164.3		507.8	316.2	88.8		405.0
71-72	328.5	200.0		528.5	308.2	136.4		444.6
70-71	289.6			289.6	344.8			344.8
1969-70	245.0			245.0	304.9			304.9
68-69	190.0			190.0	301.2			301.2
67-68	190.7			190.7	293.6			293.6
66-67	85.3			85.3	338.0[b]			338.0[b]
65-66	48.6			48.6	222.6[b]			222.6[b]

TABLE 1 (*Continued*)
Federal Government Funding of Training,
Job Creation, and Combined Work Experience/Training Projects,
Canada, Operating Expenditures and Participants[a]

Year	Operating Expenditures ($ millions)				Participants (thousands)			
	Trng	Job Creation	Work Exp. & Trng	Total	Trng	Job Creation	Work Exp. & Trng	Total
1964-65	44.4			44.4	205.9[b]			205.9[b]
63-64	34.5			34.5	139.3[b]			139.3[b]
62-63	28.4			28.4	86.4[b]			86.4[b]
61-62	17.8			17.8	55.2[c]			55.2[c]

Source: See Appendix 1.

Note: Numbers may not add to total due to rounding.

[a] Data for 1982-83 to 1987-88 are for new starts and carry over and exclude part-time trainees. Earlier participant data are for new trainees only and exclude carry-overs.

[b] Excludes vocational high school students (see Table 4).

[c] Excludes vocational high school students and several other categories (see Table 4).

federal Canadian policy has consistently combined both training and job creation/work experience in dealing with issues of economic growth and stabilization.

Table 1 indicates that total federal Canadian government expenditures on training (both institutional and industrial) increased over time to 1984-85 and then decreased. In real terms, there was no change in the constant dollar expenditures on training in 1971-72 and 1987-88. The $945.2 million 1987 dollars would represent $285.8 million in 1971 dollars compared with the actual expenditures of $289.6. On the other hand, the number of participants in training programs has fallen by over a third since 1971-72 (when the Economic Council of Canada offered much praise for the Canadian program). This decline in number of trainees was almost offset by an increase in the number of participants in job-creation and work experience/ training programs. As a proportion of the labour force, the number of persons in all forms of federal government-sponsored training fell sharply from 5.1 percent in 1971-72 to 3.3 percent in 1987-88. It should be noted that the number of participants or enrollees is a very rough measure of the extent to which persons are involved in training. A better measure would be person-weeks or full-time equivalents. Unfortunately, data for only some of the programs show average weeks worked or full-time equivalents.[2]

The long-term pattern seems to be a decline in pure training and an increase in job creation and the combination of work experience/training. However, the participant and expenditure data show that there has been a great deal of volatility in the job-creation programs. This volatility is linked to fluctuations in the unemployment rate. The biggest leap in the job-creation program, by almost half a billion dollars and over 200,000 persons, occurred during the depth of the 1981-1983 recession when unemployment rose from 7.5 to 11.9 percent.

---

[2] There are also differences between data on the numbers of trainees started and figures on carryover plus new starts. The participant figures in Table 1 up to 1981-82 are for new starts, including persons enrolled in institutional part-time training. The figures from 1982-83 to 1987-88 are for carryover plus new starts excluding part-time participants. The differences in totals are small. For example, the Annual Report of the Department of Employment and Immigration reports a total of 277,340 trainees started in 1983-1984 (including part-time), while the figure for the same year from a special Departmental tabulation gives a total of 281,965 (including carryover and excluding part-time). Institutional training according to the Annual Report is 8,412 more than that for full-time, including carryover, while industrial training is lower by 13,036. For a comparison, see the participant data from 1982-83 to 1984-85 in Tables 1 and 2.

The newest development, associated with the Canadian Jobs Strategy introduced in 1985, is to combine work experience with training. Expenditures on these programs are now twice that of job creation, with roughly the same number of people. The purpose is to enhance the long-run ability of persons to acquire skills and enter or re-enter the workforce. The implications of this change in direction will be considered in the final section of this chapter.

Within the training component there was a shift toward and then away from training in industry. In 1971 the Economic Council of Canada called for a shift away from institutional training toward training in industry. At that time (1970-71), persons enrolled in industrial training programs represented 7 percent of the total number of trainees. By 1980-81 the proportion of industrial trainees had risen to 27 percent, but by 1987-88 the proportion had fallen to 15 percent (see Table 2). Offsetting the decline has been the enrollment in combined work experience/training programs. Expenditures on industrial training followed a similar pattern, rising to 22 percent of the total federal training budget in 1984-85 and then declining to 8 percent in 1987-88 (see Table 3).

Federal Support for Training

There were four federal program initiatives in the period 1959–1989: the Technical and Vocational Training Act (TVTA) of 1960, the Adult Occupational Training Act (AOTA) of 1967, the National Training Act (NTA) of 1982, and the Canadian Jobs Strategy (CJS) of 1985. Each of these initiatives was preceded by a significant economic event: two were recessions and two were shortage situations. Each of these programs will be outlined in light of the events which preceded the change in programs and each will be considered from the perspective of growth, equity, and stabilization. This discussion will form the basis for the concluding consideration of issues for the 1990s.

The Technical and Vocational Training Act of 1960

The most serious recession to that point in the post-World War II period occurred in the years 1957-1962. Not only did unemployment rise to levels above 7.0 percent, but there was a public discussion as to whether automation had produced a structural shift in the economy toward higher skilled jobs for which many youths were unsuited through lack of training (Winder, 1968; Economic

TABLE 2

Number of Participants Under Federal Government
Training Programs, Canada (thousands)

Year	Institutional Training							Industrial Trng.	Total
	Skill	Lang.	BTSD	Apprentice-ship	Other[a]	Part-time	Total		
1987-88				42.9			185.2	33.5	218.7
86-87				42.7			196.4	27.1	223.5
85-86				42.1			210.9	28.8	239.7
1984-85	57.5	13.9	21.2	46.7	14.3	63.2	216.8	42.6	259.4[b]
83-84	61.1	12.4	20.7	56.5	12.3	68.2	231.2	46.1	277.3[a]
82-83	63.6	13.2	20.2	65.9	11.4	60.5	235.0	36.8	271.8[a]
81-82	59.6	10.8	21.1	60.3	10.8	56.8	219.5	73.2	292.7
80-81	64.1	15.8	24.8	58.2	7.8	51.3	223.8	84.0	307.8
1979-80	72.1	11.4	29.6	55.5	7.8	49.1	225.6	83.3	309.0
78-79	65.0	5.7	31.4	51.4	8.6	45.4	207.6	78.9	286.5
77-78	70.0	7.9	44.0	57.4		50.4	229.7	69.7	299.4
76-77	69.7	8.0	44.9	54.7		59.1	236.5	60.8	297.3
75-76	70.0	10.1	45.9	49.6		37.6	213.2	61.4	274.6
1974-75	136.1	8.4	50.6	46.5		[c]	241.6	50.0	291.6
73-74	170.4	9.9	55.6	40.7		[c]	276.6	43.1	319.7
72-73	163.7	10.9	60.7	40.4		[c]	275.7	40.5	316.2[d]
71-72	143.8	12.5	74.1	46.2		[c]	276.6	31.5	308.2[e]
70-71	155.7	13.2	97.1	53.9		[c]	319.9	24.9	344.8[f]
1969-70				57.0			269.9	35.0	304.9
68-69				54.0			266.2	35.0	301.2
67-68				49.9				35.5	293.6[g]
66-67				38.0				39.2	338.0[h]

Source: See Appendix 1.

TABLE 2 (*Continued*)

Note: Lang. = Language training; BTSD = Basic training for skill development. Numbers may not add to total due to rounding.

[a] Other includes Job readiness training, Work adjustment training, and Occupational orientation training.

[b] Data for 1982-83 to 1984-85 are from Employment and Immigration Canada Annual Report for new trainees only, which differ slightly from the figures shown in Table 1. See footnote a to that table.

[c] Part-time and full-time were combined.

[d] Includes 746 in supplementary training program for unemployed.

[e] Includes 13,229 in supplementary training program for unemployed.

[f] Includes 26,118 in supplementary training program for unemployed.

[g] Combines training under AOTA and TVTA programs.

[h] Excludes vocational high school students (see Table 4).

TABLE 3

Federal Government Institutional
and Industrial Training Expenditures, Canada
(millions)

Year	Institutional Training				Indus-trial Training	Total Trng. Costs
	Purch.	Allow-ances	UI	Total		
1987-88	464.0	176.1	226.8	866.9	78.3	945.2
86-87	487.2	184.3	233.5	905.1	93.1	998.2
85-86	521.0	165.8	234.5	921.4	132.8	1054.2
1984-85	511.8	117.8	217.5	847.2	242.6	1089.8
83-84	516.0	115.8	221.4	853.3	168.0	1021.3
82-83	482.4	109.1	206.0	797.4	128.5	925.9
81-82	419.9	105.7	166.5	692.1	137.7	829.8
80-81	395.0	103.6	157.8	656.4	113.6	770.0
1979-80	345.9^c	84.3^d	140.7	570.9	102.0	672.9
78-79	331.7	117.0	102.7	551.4	86.0^b	637.4
77-78	302.2	190.8	^{c}	493.0	79.2	572.2^c
76-77	285.3	200.2		485.5	62.2	547.7
75-76	269.4	186.3		455.6	51.0	506.6
1974-75	252.5	148.7		401.2	(37.3)	401.2
73-74	215.5	147.7		363.2	(14.6)	363.2
72-73	197.3	146.2		343.5	^{a}	343.5
71-72	167.1	161.3		328.4	^{a}	328.4
70-71	133.0	156.6		289.6	^{a}	289.6
1969-70	113.9	131.2		245.0	^{a}	245.0
68-69	81.7	108.3		190.0	^{a}	190.0
67-68						190.7
66-67						85.3

Source: See Appendix 1.

Note: Numbers may not add to total due to rounding.

[a] Included with institutional training.

[b] Training Improvement Fund.

[c] Includes program administrative costs.

[d] Includes CMTP and trainee travel allowances.

[e] $19 million was also provided by UI, but it is not included in the total.

Council of Canada, 1971; Meltz, 1974). To meet this challenge, the federal government launched the shared (federal-provincial) cost program known as the Technical and Vocational Training Act (TVTA). The act was administered by the federal Department of Labour which at that time was responsible for training. The program represented a quantum leap in expenditures and in the number of persons participating in training. TVTA not only included funds for operating expenditures, but also provided 75 percent of capital costs. By the time the capital portion of the program was ended in the early 1970s, the federal government had spent $1.1 billion. The province of Ontario used TVTA as the basis for the introduction of an alternative postsecondary school system of community colleges, the purpose of which was to train enrollees for jobs through diploma programs which were alternatives to, but not linked with, university degree programs.

The objectives of TVTA were a combination of stabilization and economic growth. The program was mainly aimed at reducing the high levels of unemployment of manual and primary-sector workers. It also had a growth-oriented component because the objective was to increase the skill levels of youth who were about to enter the workforce as well as increase the skills of workers who were already unemployed. Table 4 shows that this dual emphasis was borne out in the pattern of expenditures. Program 5, Training of the Unemployed, was the largest of the ten programs between 1961-62 and 1967-68, followed by Program 3, Trade and Occupational Training, and Program 2, Technician Training. The pattern for enrollment is even more heavily biased in favour of the unemployed. It should be noted that the huge number of persons indicated under vocational high school training represent enrollees in provincial vocational high schools to which the federal government contributed. On a per trainee basis, for 1965-66, the federal government contributed $11 to vocational high schools, compared with $296 for each unemployed trainee, $256 for each person in trade and occupational training, $222 for each technical and vocational teacher, and $200 for each disabled trainee. The number of trainees in the latter two groups was very small. The apprenticeship program (excluding high school students) was second in number of enrollees to the training of the unemployed, but the funds for it were small. Class time of apprenticeships was included in Program 3, but separate figures on the amount spent for apprentices are not available.

While TVTA succeeded in raising the nation's consciousness about the need for enhanced training, the federal government became increasingly frustrated with the shared cost arrangements which placed it in the role of banker while the provinces assumed the initiatives. This frustration was intensified by the economic developments in the mid-1960s and led to a change in the federal training program.

TABLE 4

Operating Expenditures (millions) and Enrollments (thousands)
by Type of Training Program Under the Technical
Vocational Training Act (TVTA) 1961-62 to 1967-68

Program Year	Total	1 School	2 Technician	3 Trade/ Occupational	4 In Coop- with Industry	5 Unemployed	6 Disabled	7 Technical & Vocational Teacher	8 Employees of Government Agencies	9 Student Aid	10 Appship. Super.[b]
Expenditures											
1967-68	85.6										
1966-67	85.3	1.6	6.2[c]	18.7	1.2	54.2	.8	1.1	.1	.2	1.2
1965-66	48.6	2.3	3.9	15.4	.6	24.0	.8	.4	.1	.2	.9
1964-65	44.4	3.6	10.2	14.4	.3	13.6	.6	.6	.1	.3	.7
1963-64	34.5	2.8	7.1	10.3	.1	10.5	.6	.4	.1	.3	2.3
1962-63	28.4	1.9	6.8	8.2	.1	7.8	.8	.2	⊙	.3	2.2
1961-62	17.8	2.0	3.4	5.4	⊙	3.9	.4	.2		.3	2.2
Enrollments											
1967-68	110.1										
1966-67	578.5	240.5	27.7	75.8	39.2	150.0	4.6	.6	.7	1.3[a]	38.0
1965-66	438.0	215.4	21.7	60.1	20.1	81.0	4.0	1.8	1.2	.9[a]	31.8
1964-65	406.2	200.3	19.6	57.4	9.2	59.8	4.0	3.1	1.4	24.7	26.7
1963-64	303.7	164.4	13.9	27.4	7.8	49.0	3.5	.7	1.2	16.7	19.1
1962-63	198.5	112.1	11.1	6.3	3.8	38.4	3.0	.6	.4	4.7	18.1
1961-62	NA	NA	NA	NA	1.7	26.9	2.8	1.2	NA	4.1	18.5

Source: Department of Labour, Canada, Annual Reports, and Department of Manpower and Immigration Canada, Annual Reports for 1966-67 and 1967-68.

Note: Numbers may not add to total due to rounding.

TABLE 4 (*Continued*)

NA = Not available.

° Less than $50,000.

ᵃ No awards in Quebec. In 1964-65 there were 21,281 in Quebec. In 1963-64 the total for Quebec was 13,138.

ᵇ Classroom supervision of apprenticeship is included with Program 3.

ᶜ Estimated by subtracting the sum of the other programs from the total expenditures indicated on page 14 of the 1966-67 Annual Report.

The Adult Occupational Training Act of 1967

The lengthy period of economic growth in the early and middle 1960s produced a low unemployment rate (3.4 percent by 1966), labor shortages, and active recruitment of immigrants abroad. In 1967, 223,000 immigrants entered Canada, a number exceeded only in 1907 and from 1910 to 1913. While inflation had remained low during the early stages of the economic recovery, there were fears that the tight labour market, especially for skilled workers, would result in cost-push inflation. Labour market policies, particularly the training of skilled workers and increased mobility, were seen as the most important economic tools to maintain economic growth and prevent a surge of inflation (Economic Council, 1964, 1965). However, the shared-cost arrangement under TVTA was seen as limiting possible federal initiatives to meet the need for an enhanced role for labour market policy, especially training. In addition, in 1966 a new federal department had been created to administer manpower policies—the Department of Manpower (now called Employment) and Immigration—combining the training activities and the employment service from the Department of Labour with Immigration, which was in a separate unit.

The result was the Adult Occupational Training Act (AOTA) of 1967, following by one year the creation of the new federal department. The AOTA was to concentrate exclusively on the training of adults, defined as persons one year past the school-leaving age and out of school for one year. This was done so that the federal government could proceed unilaterally in an area under its jurisdiction—that is, one that was not exclusively a provincial jurisdiction as was the case with education.

The AOTA represented a phasing out of the capital grants introduced under TVTA and the introduction of a training seat purchase arrangement with the provincial training authorities (see Adams, 1987). AOTA expenditures were to be guided by a system of labour market information enhanced by a job-vacancy survey (Meltz, 1974) and COFOR (the Canadian Occupational Forecasting System). In addition, the criteria for immigration were to be determined by labour market needs through a point system. As a result, the existence of a shortage as determined by the job vacancy survey and labour market information analysis would stimulate two responses: an increase in training and an increase in immigration. Since the response time is much shorter for immigration than for training, the labour market adjustment system was inherently biased in favour of immigration.

In the decade after the introduction of AOTA, the unemployment rate gradually increased and pressure was removed from the growth-oriented aspect of training toward stabilization and equity objectives. The results are shown in Table 1. While the number of trainees gradually drifted downward, a major job-creation program was put in place, equal to over 40 percent of the number of trainees in years when the unemployment rate rose sharply (1971-72, 1977-78). The job-creation projects included the Local Initiatives Program (LIP), the Local Employment Assistance Program (LEAP), and Opportunities for Youth (OFY). More job-creation programs were added over time. By 1987-88 more than 30 different job-creation programs had been introduced at one time or another (see Appendix 1).

In 1979 and 1980 a new economic development occurred—the emergence of skill shortages throughout the country. The result was a series of public examinations of the problems of skill shortages and the effectiveness of the training system in Canada (Dodge, 1981; Allmand, 1982; Meltz, 1982a). Unfortunately for Canada, the skill shortage occurred just after the cancellation of Statistics Canada's Job Vacancy Survey (JVS) (Meltz, 1982b). The JVS was a major component of the labour market information system to determine both training and immigration needs. The combination of the skill shortage, dissatisfaction with the training system, and weakness in the labour market information system led to the National Training Act of 1982.

The National Training Act of 1982

The National Training Act (NTA) as intended to provide employers ". . . with needed skilled workers and [to help] adults acquire the skills required for more remunerative and satisfying jobs" (Employment and Immigration Canada, 1983, p. 23). Following the proclamation of the act, new three-year federal-provincial/territorial agreements were signed with all provinces and the two territories (Yukon and Northwest Territories). The NTA continued occupational training and general industrial training and added a new component—Critical Trade Skills Training (CTST), the latter a part of the new concept of national occupations in the training program. The purpose was to meet the likely skills needs of the 1980s, and the intention was to introduce more flexibility in the training program and ". . . to make training more relevant to the needs of the labour market . . . by directing the purchase of courses towards higher demand occupations" (Employment and Immigration Canada, 1983, p. 23).

While the intention may have been to increase industrial training, the statistics in Table 2 show that the number of participants between 1982-83 and 1984-85 was actually below the levels in 1981-82 and earlier. It is also difficult to determine the degree of success of the institutional portion. The number of institutional trainees declined during the NTA. In the meantime the economy had experienced the worst recession since the depression of the 1930s. The result was the emergence of a new approach to training.

The Canadian Jobs Strategy, 1985

In 1985 there was more revamping of the training and job-creation programs with the introduction of the Canadian Jobs Strategy (CJS). The objective was a complete redesign of the federal government's labour market program to link ". . . training with ongoing economic activity and real jobs" (Employment and Immigration Canada, 1986, p. 18). The new programs were directed toward the long-term unemployed, young people out of school and unable to find work, women entering or reentering the labour market, workers needing skills training to avoid layoffs, employers needing assistance to train employees in skills for which there was an existing or anticipated shortage, communities suffering severe economic decline, and innovative pilot projects. Included in the new programs were cooperative education, small business training, extended training leave, self-employment incentives, business development centres, relocation and exploration assistance, and summer employment experience. A number of these programs, such as summer employment for students, had been introduced in the early 1970s, but the overall emphasis now was different.

Table 1 shows that while the pure training component declined under CJS, this was more than offset by the introduction of combined work experience/training programs. Total expenditures and participants in training plus work experience/training expanded somewhat. In 1984-85 this total was 270,800 persons, while in 1987-88 it was 316,500.

At the same time, both the funding of and enrollment in pure job-creation programs contracted. The overall result was a decline in expenditures and participants from the peaks under the National Training Act.

There has also been an effort to direct a greater proportion of training funds to enhance equity. By equity we mean increased training and work experience for designated groups: women, visible minorities, the disabled, and native people. Training programs in Canada have always included the disabled (see Table 4). The difference under CJS is that the list of target groups has been expanded in line with groups identified in need of enhanced employment equity (affirmative action) as set out in the Abella Report (1984) and the federal Employment Equity Act of 1986.

How successful is the Canadian Jobs Strategy? Critics complain that CJS is creating bottlenecks in crucial industries because the total expenditures and number of pure training positions have declined (Rowan, 1988). The criticism arises at a time of a booming labour market in central Canada, particularly the province of Ontario, and the emergence of skill shortages which CJS was supposed to avoid (*Financial Post*, 1989). Without much more detail than is regularly published, it is difficult to determine the degree of success of the work experience/training programs, the major new feature of CJS.

Provincial Training Programs

As indicated earlier, federal-provincial negotiations over cost-sharing of training have been sources of tension and contention over the years. While the author had hoped to develop data on the provincial expenditures, on the basis of the information available it is difficult to determine the precise amount of provincial spending on training. At the present time it appears that the federal government is still the major provider of funding for training in Canada.

Employer-Sponsored Training

In addition to government-sponsored training, there is also training sponsored by employers. It has been estimated that in 1984, in the largest province of Canada, Ontario, approximately 27 percent of all establishments conducted formal training programs (Ontario Manpower Commission, 1986). While these programs included an estimated 22 percent of all full-time permanent employees, only 2.7 percent received formal qualifying or upgrading training that lasted two weeks or more.

If these figures are representative of all full-time employment, then 785,000 of Ontario's 3.5 million full-time employees would have received some employer-sponsored training, of whom 96,363 would have received some formal training from employers; these figures may be compared with the 69,411 who were in federal government-sponsored training (Employment and Immigration Canada, 1985). Excluding the 13,203 apprentices in full-time institutional training in Ontario in 1984, there were 14,814 persons in industrial training who would also have been included among the 96,363 employer-sponsored trainees. In terms of numbers, it would appear that employers are training more persons than the federal and provincial governments. However, when the duration of training is taken into consideration, there is a dramatic difference in the training efforts. The median amount of long-term employer-sponsored training is 3.5 weeks compared with 26 weeks for government-sponsored training. The result is an estimate of time spent in training showing government-sponsored training exceeding employer-sponsored training by a factor of five.[3]

The Ontario Manpower Commission (1986) survey also found that 80 percent of all establishments did not sponsor qualifying or upgrading programs. Even for those establishments which were doing some training, ". . . the vast majority . . . were not aware of the major training-assistance programs of the federal and Ontario governments. Of establishments with formal training programs, only about 12 percent participated in a government assistance program during 1984" (Ontario Manpower Commission, 1986, p. 3). In this survey of employer-sponsored training, responses were received from 4200 of the 9050 establishments contacted. Readers of the survey report are cautioned that the responses may be

---

[3] The estimates of time spent in training were calculated as follows: The number of employees who received formal qualifying or upgrading training lasting two weeks or more was estimated as 2.7 percent of all full-time employees—that is, .027 × 3,569,000 = 96,363. Since 14,814 were in industrial training programs, we have subtracted them from both the employer-sponsored and government-sponsored trainees. This leaves 81,549 at 3.5 weeks, the median amount of training = 285,422 weeks. If 41,814 is subtracted from the 69,411 government-sponsored trainees, the remaining 54,597 persons at 26 weeks of training = 1,419,522 weeks, five times the amount of employer-sponsored training. Even if the other persons who received less than two weeks of training were included, government-sponsored training would still exceed employer-sponsored training. If the remainder averaged one week, the government/employer ratio would still be 2:1.

inflated since it is expected that employers who offer formal training programs were more likely to respond than those who did not (see also Harvey, 1980). It seems reasonable to conclude that governments are sponsoring far more training than are employers.

Training Issues for the 1990s

The preceding analysis has indicated that the federal government has played a dominant role in funding worker training in Canada and that the emphasis of the funding has alternated between growth and stabilization. The major determining factor seems to have been the state of the economy. The severe recessions of 1957–1962 and 1981–1983 prompted major revisions in training programs which emphasized training or job creation for the unemployed, while the strong economic upswings in the 1960s and, to a lesser extent, in the late 1970s led to more emphasis on providing skills to reduce labour shortages. The rise in unemployment at the beginning of the 1970s led to the introduction of job-creation programs which fluctuated with the other economic cycles and have remained a part of the federal government's labour market programs.

The introduction of the Canadian Jobs Strategy in 1985 seems to have been both a response to the recession of 1981–1983 and an attempt to chart a new course by combining training with work experience. While the objective is admirable, there was a growing criticism of the implementation of the new program in 1988 and 1989 (see Ontario Ministry of Skills Development, 1989; Crane, 1989; Gibb-Clark, 1989; Rowan, 1988; Yalnizyan and Wolfe, 1989). The criticism centred on the reductions in federal spending on training, as indicated in Table 1 above.

The issues for the future of training in Canada deal with both the level and direction of expenditures. To discuss these issues we return to the multiple objectives of growth, stabilization, and equity. While there has been a recent commitment to enhanced equity in the training programs (particularly for women, native peoples, the disadvantaged, and visible minorities), the primary objectives seem to swing between growth and stabilization. The recent emphasis on the combination of work experience and training may have been a way to reduce the swings by looking to a more long-term strategy.

The difficulty with the Canadian Jobs Strategy in the late 1980s is that the changes in direction, on balance, were reducing the support for the growth objective while at the same time reducing the stabilization component of job creation. The latter seemed to be reasonable since the economy was expanding, while the former seemed less reasonable.

To focus the discussion on issues of the future, we will consider apprenticeship programs. Much of the criticism of the Canadian Jobs Strategy was on the inadequacies of skill training in Canada. While many of the shortage occupations that were identified fall into the apprenticeship category (Ontario Ministry of Skills Development, 1988), the actual number of apprentices has declined significantly since the time of the National Training Act of 1982 (see Table 2). In 1987-88, a year of severe labour shortage, 42,900 apprentices started full-time training, compared with 65,900 in 1982-83. The current apprenticeship levels are the lowest in 20 years. Since Canada is intent on enhancing its technological capability, the role of the apprenticeship system and the level of its support must be considered.

A related issue for Canada is the imbalance between job vacancies for skilled and professional jobs in general and the continuing high rate of unemployment. The fact that there are both a significant number of job vacancies and an unemployment rate above that at the start of the 1981–1983 recession raises serious policy considerations. In its conception, the Canadian Jobs Strategy would seem to be an ideal vehicle to reduce the imbalance between vacancies and the unemployed. For some reason this has not happened (see Canadian Labour Market and Productivity Centre, 1988). This would seem to be an appropriate time for an examination of the functioning of the CJS in relation to this imbalance.

The direction of training between institutional and industrial forms has always been an issue in Canada. The recent swing away from industrial has been associated with the rise of the combination of work experience and training, which blurs the distinction. It is beyond the scope of this chapter to comment on how successful the CJS has been in combining the approaches, but it is something that needs to be examined.

The relationship between the federal government and the provinces in relation to training has been an old and continuing theme in Canada. Clearly, a central concern for the country is how the two jurisdictions jointly deal with the responsibility (Canadian Labour Market and Productivity Centre, 1989; Crane, 1989; Solomon, 1989). Unfortunately, the current lack of data and the complexity of the issue make this a subject appropriate only for future research.

A final issue is the role of employer-sponsored training. Earlier research has indicated that this has tended to focus on short-term programs and to be limited in scope. In spite of recommendations that efforts be made to increase the scope and level of private training (Adams, Draper, and Ducharme, 1979), little has changed. The relationship between government funding of training (both federal and provincial) and private efforts will be another major issue for the 1990s, especially with the pressures to decrease government spending in order to reduce the deficit.

Appendix 1
Sources of Data

The data in the tables were obtained from the annual reports of the federal department of Labour and Manpower (Employment) and Immigration. In addition, special tabulations of expenditures and participants in training, job creation, and work experience/ training programs from 1982-83 to 1987-88 were provided by Employment and Immigration Canada (EIC).

The grouping of data into the three categories of training, job creation, and work experience/training was prepared by the author based on the categories for the 1982-83 to 1984-85 period as provided by EIC, taking into consideration the primary objective of the various programs as indicated in EIC's annual reports. The groupings of various programs are shown in Appendix Table 1. The author would like to acknowledge the advice and assistance received from Georges Latour of Employment and Immigration Canada in preparing these groupings, and to acknowledge the assistance of Richard Monette of Employment and Immigration Canada in providing the special tabulations for 1982-83 to 1987-88.

APPENDIX TABLE 1

Training, Job Creation, and Combined
Work Experience/Training Programs in Canada

Training

1. Institutional
      Coordinated groups
      Direct purchase option
      Direct purchase—allowances
      Grants to provinces
      Skills Growth Fund
      Travel and relocation assistance

2. Industrial
      Critical Trade Skills Training (CTST)
      General Industrial Training (GIT)
      Skill Investment (except for the direct purchase option)
      Skill shortages (except for the direct purchase option)

Job Creation
      Canada Community Development Projects (CCDP)
      Canada Community Services Projects (CCSP)
      Canada Employment Centres for Students and Native Internship
      Canada Manpower Training-on-the-Job Program (CMTJP)
      Career Access
      Community Employment Program (CEP)
      Community Employment Strategy (CES)
      Community Futures
      Employment Creation
      Employment Tax Credit Program (ETCP)
      Immediate Employment Stimulation
      Innovations
      Job Corps
      Job Exploration by Students (JES)
      Job Experience Training (JET)
      Local Economic Development Assistance (LEDA)
      Local Employment Assistance Development (LEAD)
      Local Employment Assistance Program (LEAP)
      Local Initiatives Program (LIP)
      New Employment Expansion and Development (NEED)
      New Technology Employment Program (NTEP)
      Opportunities for Youth (OFY)
      Portable Wage Subsidy Program (PWS)
      Program for Employment Disadvantaged (PED)
      Special Response Feature
      Summer Employment/Experience Development (SEED)
      Summer Job Corps
      Student Business Loan (SBL)
      Student Summer Employment and Activities Program (SSEAP)
      Unemployment Insurance Job Creation—UI 38 (now 25)
      Work Experience Workshop (WOW)
      Young Canada Works (YCW)

Combined Work Experience/Training
1. Job Development
      Subsidized Projects General
      Subsidized Projects General—Social Assistance Recipients (SAR)
      Individually Subsidized Jobs

APPENDIX TABLE 1 (*Continued*)

Training, Job Creation, and Combined
Work Experience/Training Programs in Canada

2. Job Entry
    Cooperative Education
    Entry Option
    Entry Option—Social Assistance Recipient (SAR)
    Re-entry Option
    Re-entry Option—SAR
    Subsidized Projects—Severely Employment Disabled (SED)
    Subsidized Projects—SED, SAR

Source: Employment and Immigration Canada, Annual Reports.

References

Abella Report, Judge Rosalie Silberman Abella. *Report of the Commission on Equity in Employment*. Ottawa: Supply and Services Canada, 1984.

Adams, Roy J. "An Overview of Training and Development in Canada." In *Canadian Readings in Personnel and Human Resources Management*, eds. Shimon L. Dolan and Randall S. Schuler. St. Paul, MN: West Publishing Co., 1987. Pp. 279–88.

————. *Skills Development for Working Canadians—Towards a National Strategy*. Ottawa: CEIC Task Force on Skill Development Leave, 1983.

————. "Towards a more competent labour force: A training levy scheme for Canadians." *Relations Industrielles* 35, 3 (1980).

Adams Roy J., P. Draper, and Claude Ducharme. "Education and Working Canadians." Report of the Commission of Inquiry on Educational Leave and Productivity. Ottawa: Labour Canada, 1979.

Allmand Report. *Work for Tomorrow*. Report of the Parliamentary Task Force on Employment Opportunities for the 80's. Ottawa: House of Commons, 1982.

Canadian Labour Market and Productivity Centre. *Focus on Adjustment*. Ottawa: 1989.

————. *Labour Market and Productivity Review* (Winter 1988).

Crane, David. "Recent layoffs reveal urgency for federal training programs." *The Toronto Star*, February 25, 1989.

Dodge Report. *Labour Market Development in the 1980s*. Report of the Task Force on Labour Market Development. Ottawa: Employment and Immigration Commission Canada, 1981.

Dupré, J. Stefan, David M. Cameron, Graeme H. McKechnie, and Theodore B. Rotenberg. *Federalism & Policy Development: The Case of Adult Occupational Training in Ontario*. Toronto: University of Toronto Press, 1973.

Economic Council of Canada. *Eighth Annual Report*. Ottawa: Information Canada, September 1971.

————. *Second Annual Report*. Ottawa: Queen's Printer, December 1964.

Employment and Immigration Canada. *Annual Report 1985-86*. Ottawa: Minister of Supply and Services, Canada, 1986.

————. *Annual Report 1984-85*. Ottawa: Minister of Supply and Services Canada, 1985.

————. *Annual Report 1982-83*. Ottawa: Minister of Supply and Services Canada, 1983.

The Financial Post. "Job training is an urgent priority," editorial, February 13, 1989.

Gibb-Clark, Margot. "Social body slams job training policies." *The Globe and Mail*, February 23, 1989.

Gigantes Report. *In Training Only Work Works*. The Report of the Sub-Committee on Training and Employment of the Standing Senate Committee on Social Affairs, Science and Technology. Ottawa: Supply and Services Canada, 1987.

Gower, David. "The Labour Market in the 80s: Canada and the United States." *The Labour Force* (71-001), Statistics Canada, June 1988, pp. 87-113.

Harvey, E. B. *Barriers to Employer-Sponsored Training in Ontario*. Toronto: Ministry of Colleges and Universities, 1980.

Meltz, Noah M. *An Economic Analysis of Labour Shortages: The Case of Tool and Die Makers in Ontario*. Toronto: Ontario Economic Council, 1982a.

_____. "Labour Market Information in Canada: The Current Situation and a Proposal." *Relations Industrielles* 37, 2 (1982b), pp. 431-37.

_____. "Implications of Manpower and Immigration Policy." In *Issues in Canadian Economics*, eds. L. H. Officer and L. B. Smith. Scarborough, Ont.: McGraw-Hill Ryerson, 1974. Pp. 245-57.

Ontario Manpower Commission. *Training in Industry: A Survey of Employer-Sponsored Programs in Ontario*. Toronto: 1986.

Ontario Ministry of Skills Development. *Building a Training System for the 1990's: A Shared Responsibility*. Toronto: 1989.

_____. *Adjusting to Change: An Overview of Labour Market Issues in Ontario*. Toronto: 1988.

Rowan, Geoffrey. "Skimping by Ottawa in job-training programs decried." *The Globe and Mail*, August 3, 1988.

Solomon, Hyman. "Business, labor talk sense on training." *The Financial Post*, February 13, 1989.

Weiermair, Klaus. "Industrial training in Canada: An international perspective." *International Journal of Social Economics*, 9, 2 (1982).

Winder, John W. L. "Structural Unemployment." In *The Canadian Labour Market, Readings in Manpower Economics*, eds. Arthur Kruger and Noah M. Meltz. Toronto: Centre for Industrial Relations. University of Toronto, 1968. Pp. 135-220.

Yalnizyan, Armine, and David Wolfe. *Target on Training. Meeting Workers Needs in a Changing Economy*. Toronto: Social Planning Council of Metropolitan Toronto, 1989.

Chapter 11

Intermediate Level Vocational Training and the Structure of Labour Markets in Western Europe in the 1980s[*]

DAVID MARSDEN
London School of Economics and
Laboratoire d'Economie et de Sociologie,
Aix-en-Provence

PAUL RYAN
Kings College, University of Cambridge

Training of both young people and adults has been a major item on the policy agenda of most West European countries since the early 1970s. Its importance has increased because of concern about youth unemployment, which rose steeply in the 1970s in Europe as compared with the U.S., and about international competitiveness. It was also seen as a way to industrial restructuring where the emphasis has been mostly on adults and on retraining. Additional concerns have been the adequacy of the link between training and skilled jobs, and with equity arising as an issue since some groups have had better access to training than others. The latter consideration may become more important as greater emphasis is placed on private provision of training by employers.

Although employers usually have a free hand in the numbers and qualifications they recruit, their freedom is much more constrained when it comes to utilisation of these skills within the enterprise. In West Germany, for example, the institutions of codetermination

---

[*] We would like to express our thanks to the Rowntree Memorial Trust for funding part of our work, and to Alain d'Iribarne for valuable comments on an earlier draft.

give employees considerable powers over internal training and upgrading. In Britain, workplace custom often defines who may undertake craft work, and in France, longstanding company practices of upgrading on seniority determine the paths along which externally qualified workers should pass in order to reach skilled positions. Thus, whereas governments can decide how much is to be spent on national training programmes and how many people may be admitted, the subsequent access of trainees to suitable skilled jobs rests on a delicate balance of institutional forces representing employer, union, and worker interests. Hence, some understanding of the differences in labour market structure and institutions between the various West European countries is necessary to understand the different problems faced by national training programmes and the policies they have developed in consequence.

This chapter then starts by identifying two major and contrasted types of labour market organisation in Western European economies and then proceeds to survey the problems of vocational training in recent years. A central argument is that certain types of training systems are suited to certain types of labour market structure, and that lack of adaptation between these two is one of the main difficulties facing training policy in several West European countries. The nature of labour market structures can also be a serious constraint on the reform of training systems.

Labour Market Structures in Western Europe

Sectoral labour markets are dominated, broadly speaking, by one of three types: (1) occupational, (2) internal, and (3) unstructured or secondary labour markets. The first type is particularly widespread in West Germany and, for skilled manual workers, in Britain. In contrast, internal labour markets provide the predominant model in France and Italy, and in many countries for managerial employees. We take an occupational market to relate to persons endowed with a particular skill or qualification, validated by a diploma or by the opinion of their peer group. An internal labour market may be said to exist for a particular job when an employer regularly fills vacancies for that job from among existing employees.

Typically, the occupational model rests on a set of transferable skills and fairly standardised job descriptions (otherwise there is little market for transferable skills). Concentrating investment in such skills early in a person's working life will increase the period over which the return can be earned, so that methods of training such as apprenticeships would seem to be particularly appropriate to this kind of labour market structure. In the standard human capital analysis, the trainee should bear the cost of training for skills in the form of a trainee wage below the value of his or her output. Ryan (1987) suggests that this solution is particularly fragile in an environment in which skilled adult workers fear substitution by cheap trainee labour. Consequently, in practice, employers frequently bear a large part of the costs of such training, thus creating scope for free-rider problems which, if unchecked, can undermine the supply of skilled labor and break up the occupational market as employers devise ways of restricting skilled mobility (Marsden, 1986). For this reason, Marsden and Ryan (1988) argue that the institutional framework for such markets is essential to their long-run viability and has proved a major policy problem in Britain, and also in France.

Internal labour markets, in contrast, rest on skills which, for technical and institutional reasons, are not transferable, and because of the lesser risk of wastage by skilled workers, employers have greater freedom in how they organise training and the build-up of work experience. But once workers have invested in such skills, they too may fear substitution from outside, and thus will seek to ensure that the rules by which they reached their skilled status apply to subsequent new entrants into the firm.

The third type, that of unstructured labour markets, typically involves little training or skill beyond the general skills provided by basic secondary education. In recent years, such labour markets have, to some extent, been favoured indirectly by public policies seeking to reduce youth unemployment, as these have sought to "price" certain categories of workers back into jobs either by lower pay or by exclusion from certain levels of employee protection.[1] Although the special training and employment measures for young workers, which have often involved employers taking on young

---

[1] An example would be the British Young Workers' Scheme which provided a marginal employment subsidy to employers of young unemployed people provided that they were engaged at below a particular level of pay. The philosophy of the scheme was to price young workers back into employment, but this would inevitably be low-wage employment.

people outside the normal employment relationship, have improved youth access to jobs and training places, at the lower end of the quality spectrum, they have also boosted secondary labour market conditions.

There is now quite a body of evidence suggesting that one or other of these models prevails over large sectors of employment in various EEC countries. The comparison of a matched sample of manufacturing plants in France and West Germany by Maurice et al. (1978, 1986) showed clearly the influence of internal enterprise norms on skill acquisition and skill organisation in France, compared with that of the apprenticeship-based organisation of skilled work in the German firms. This work has been extended by plant-level studies to Britain (Maurice, Sorge, and Warner, 1979), and using a broad range of aggregate statistical indicators, Marsden (1990) has shown that for industrial workers, the internal market model predominates in France and Italy and the occupational model in West Germany and Britain. The extent to which the two models can coexist within the same sector is limited by the fact that using an occupational market for skilled labour effectively truncates upgrading possibilities for unskilled and semiskilled workers. Moreover, the dependence of occupational markets on a strong institutional framework implies high fixed costs in their establishment, and so limits the number of such markets in an economy.

Sweden provides a particularly interesting hybrid case as it appears to offer a picture of interfirm mobility in the absence of occupational markets. However, a proportion of labour mobility there is managed through the training and retraining components of that country's active manpower policy, which is run on tripartite lines. In addition, it should be noted that, at least until the 1970s, an important part of the Swedish "accord" underlying the industrial relations system was that the unions accepted a particularly strong version of management prerogative in the enterprise, and thus would have given little support to attempts to press occupational specific demands. Moreover, from early on, Swedish unions dropped ideas of occupational organisation in favour of industry lines.[2]

---

[2] Although the organisational policies of unions are important in determining patterns of workplace action, there are limits, as is illustrated by the recent experience of both French and Italian unions of the emergence of "corporatist" demands, pressed by individual occupational groups, such as air traffic controllers or train drivers.

Vocational Training Systems in Western Europe

Intermediate-level vocational training in Western Europe falls into three broad categories: off-the-job training in specialised vocational schools, mixed on-the-job and off-the-job training in the form of apprenticeships, and simple on-the-job training. These can be found in varying mixes in most EEC economies. For example, apprenticeship training, albeit of varying degrees of quality, can be found in the small firm sectors and in construction in most of the countries, even those in which it will later be shown that on-the-job training and internal labour market conditions prevail in most of the industrial sector. One of the big users of intermediate-level vocational training in specialised schools is France in which the role of the Certificat d'Aptitude Professionnelle (CAP) and the Brevet des Etudes Professionnelles (BEP) has greatly expanded over the past 15 years. The biggest user of apprentice training in manual employment, and practically the only one in nonmanual employment, is West Germany. In Britain, for a broad range of (male) industrial skills, apprenticeship is used, but for other types of similarly skilled work, little more than on-the-job experience is used, as tends to be the case also in Italy.

School-Based Vocational Training

A quantitative overview of the various mixes is given in Tables 1 and 2 showing, respectively, the rates of enrollment by age in full-time off-the-job education, and the proportion of workers classed as apprentices or full-time trainees in the enterprise in industry in various countries. The concentration of intermediate-level vocational education within the state educational system in France is highlighted by the relatively high enrollment rates of teenagers, both male and female. For 17-year-olds, these rates are higher than the rates ten years earlier—by about 12 points for males and more than 20 for females. Somewhat larger increases for the same age group can be found in Italy, indicating a serious effort by the Italian government to raise the level of education. The predominant school-based vocational qualifications in France are the intermediate-level CAP and BEP, mostly lasting two years, and the various streams of the technical baccalaureat, which provides the backbone of technician training. The volume of all these has increased over the past 15 years, that of the CAP and BEP now running at over 150,000 a year (Mouy, 1983).

TABLE 1

Percentage Enrollment in Full-Time Education, 1982-83[a]

Age	France	Italy	West Germany[b]	United Kingdom
		Males		
15	97.1	78.4	94.9	100.0
16	73.0	70.3	59.1	48.3
17	56.6	59.9	41.4	30.3
18	38.8	49.6	28.1	17.8
		Females		
15	98.9	82.3	96.9	100.0
16	84.8	72.1	65.9	57.6
17	70.6	65.1	48.4	36.9
18	50.1	51.1	33.7	16.8

[a] Pupils and students enrolled at public- and private-sector establishments incorporated in the school and university system. Out-of-school education, such as television and correspondence courses and adult education are excluded. Data provided by national education authorities, except for Italy, based on Labour Force Survey estimates.

[b] Federal Republic of Germany, 1981-82.

Source: Eurostat, Education and Training, 1985.

In Italy, vocational training institutes for the industrial and artisan sectors provide the main body of intermediate-level qualifications (about half a million places over three years in 1985-86 [Margirier, 1988]). Since 1972 these have increasingly been complemented by the regionally organised vocational training centres which offer both basic vocational training and a chance for adults to add to their existing skills; however they are believed to have been less than successful in the second of these functions. Being regionally based, they offer a flexible response to local labour market needs, but this also means that their training and qualifications lack national homogeneity.

Enterprise-Based Training and Apprenticeship

The strength of apprenticeship training in West Germany (Table 2), which being within the enterprise is excluded from the school enrollment rates, accounts for the lower rates of enrollment among teenagers, both males and females. In Britain, apprenticeship has also been the main form of institutionalised training for intermediate skills in industry, but the absence of apprenticeships from certain industries and from nearly all services means the relatively

TABLE 2

Apprentices and Trainees
in Industry and Construction, 1978-84

	Belgium	France	West Germany	Italy	Nether-lands	United Kindom
Manual apprentices and trainees as percent of manual workers						
			Industry			
Number	3,839	18,925	401,866	34,615	—	236,702
Percent	0.6	0.5	6.5	1.3	—	4.6
Manual and nonmanual apprentices and trainees as percent of all workers						
			Industry			
Number	5,906	19,556	516,533	35,470	10,336	276,782
Percent	0.7	0.4	5.9	1.1	0.9	3.7
		Wholesale and Retail Distribution				
Number	43	5,918	192,513	4,787	357	37,497
Percent	0.0	0.5	9.6	1.3	0.1	1.5
		Credit Institutions, 1981				
Number	—	7	45,382	—	7	1,028
Percent	—	0.0	5.5	—	0.0	0.3

Note: Apprentices are defined by Eurostat as all employees who do not yet fully participate in the production process and work either under a contract of apprenticeship or in conditions in which vocational training predominates over productivity. Employers are asked to provide apprentices' earnings and social security contributions and other related costs separately from those of other employees. In the table we use the expression "apprentices and trainees" rather than Eurostat's term "apprentices." Establishments with 10 or more employees.

Source: Eurostat, Labour Cost Survey.

low enrollment figures of Table 1 also signify low rates of education. This applies even more strongly to teenage women who are more or less excluded from apprenticeship, except in hairdressing. For more recent years, the Youth Training Scheme (YTS), which would also be excluded from the enrollment figures, has extended training opportunities for school-leavers.

In both Britain and West Germany apprenticeship training underwent reform and modernisation between the late 1960s and early 1970s. In both countries the reforms sought to increase the amount of theoretical training in schools, in the belief that this led to higher quality and provided a more adaptable skill for the future. In West Germany, although employers and unions retained control over the apprenticeship system, the state intervened by boosting the provision of special vocational schools which dispense the theoretical training. Despite the poor press of British apprenticeships, similar moves were undertaken in certain industries, notably the engineering industry, greatly increasing the amount and quality of theoretical instruction to British engineering apprentices (Venning et al., 1980), but not all of the sectoral training boards were as farsighted or as successful (one reason for the abolition of the majority of industrial training boards after Mrs. Thatcher's election).

Apprenticeship in France and Italy accounts for a fair volume of training. In France in 1981-82 there were about 220,000 apprentices (Combes, 1988a), and in Italy in 1984 about 550,000 (Garonna, 1986), but it is mainly confined to artisan workshops and construction, and particularly in Italy its quality is very low. A survey of industry-level apprentice agreements (ISFOL, 1982) revealed the short duration of most apprenticeships, and another survey by ISFOL confirmed the small amount of monitoring of the quality of training. In France, in contrast, the reform of apprenticeship in 1971 treated it as one of the paths by which young workers could obtain their CAP, the other being through vocational schools. Consequently, apprenticeship training is only recognised by employers if it has led to successful completion of the CAP exams, and it has tended to be the least favoured route among young people and the one with the highest failure rate. Subsequent legislation in 1987 has sought to open up higher level diplomas to those following an apprenticeship (Combes, 1988b).

Reliance Upon Private Training Provision by Individual Employers

The degree of reliance upon individually organised employer training provision has varied considerably between countries. During the rapid industrial growth in France and Italy in the 1950s and 1960s, great reliance was placed upon on-the-job training organised either formally or informally by individual employers. This has been one of the reasons for the strength of internal labour markets in these countries. In both countries, the problems of industrial restructuring highlighted the problems of nontransferable skills, and some of the public policies of the 1970s and 1980s can be understood as attempts to create more adaptable skills.

In all countries there are signs that, in recent years, employers have sought to increase the volume of company-level training, to rely less upon the old informal methods of on-the-job training, and to be more systematic in training for nontransferable skills. One influence has been the experience of enterprise restructuring during the late 1970s and early 1980s in which retraining was seen as one of the keys to enhanced workforce flexibility (Atkinson and Meager, 1986). A second has been the spread of new technology and the accompanying increase in the demand for both quantity and quality of skilled labour. A third has been the spread of the popularity among managers of "Human Resource Management" which places a greater emphasis upon training as a key to quality in production than in the past (Guest, 1987).

The Changing Mix of Training Methods

During the 1970s and 1980s, two of these countries have greatly boosted vocational training: France, by the expansion of training in state vocational schools, and West Germany, by the expansion of apprenticeship training from an already high base in the early 1970s. Neither Britain nor Italy have been so successful, and both have been sliding toward greater reliance upon private provision by individual employers, as both the British YTS and the Italian CFL leave a lot of autonomy to individual employers as to training design and levels.

The rise of "alternance training," especially in France, has been an element in this changing mix as countries have sought to supplement school-based training with spells of enterprise-based training and experience. A major force behind this has been the belief that school-based training is too academic and too distant from the needs for firms, so that qualified young people experience considerable difficulty in making the transition from school to work. There has also been a belief, more controversial, that secondary schools have long been hostile to the values of private industry and hostile to "vocationalism" in education. This has been a long-standing issue in Britain, as in some other countries, and is partly a question of educational values and partly also one of the opportunities for social mobility. For example, the British Trades Union Congress has long been leery of vocationalism in secondary education on the grounds that it closes off opportunities to bright working class children who might otherwise go to university.

The Unqualified

One of the serious failings of most countries' educational and training systems, with the exception of West Germany and Sweden, is the high percentage of young people with neither educational nor vocational qualifications. In Britain and France, for example, the figure is about 40 percent. Such people are almost entirely dependent upon what they can learn on the job, which is usually not transferable. In France, the strong position of internal labour markets and the practice of upgrading does at least provide a limited second chance (those with the CAP or BEP have a much higher probability of such upgrading), whereas in Britain the more limited use of upgrading in many major sectors leaves them with little more than the prospect of a life of largely unskilled work.

Causes of the Link Between Training Systems and Labour Market Structures

The causes of the relationship between training systems and labour market structure can best be understood from an appreciation of the difficulty of sustaining stable occupational labour markets in the absence of an institutional underpinning. Without such an underpinning, there are few restraints that would serve to construct barriers to substitution among workers and to free-riding among employers. It can be shown that the first of these causes employers to bear a considerable part of the net cost of training for transferable skills, which thus creates an incentive to free-riding (Marsden, 1986; Marsden and Ryan, 1988). Because such an institutional framework is hard to establish, occupational markets tend to be the exception rather than the rule, and the more usual position is that of internal labour markets in which employers seek to reduce the potential mobility of their more highly skilled employees. Thus, internal labour markets generally provide an unfavourable environment for general skills developed within the educational system. Equally, occupational labour markets provide somewhat rigid occupational boundaries so that the slots into which skills developed within the educational system would have to fit are not easy to change.

As Lorenz's (1987) study of the British and French shipbuilding industries in the first part of this century suggests, reliance on one or other type of labour market structure is long-standing, and given the institutional dependence of occupational labour markets, it would seem that the predominance of one or other type of labour market structure in major sectors and in particular countries is historically contingent. In other words, internal labour markets have tended to predominate in France and Italy almost by default because of the absence of occupational labour markets. Indeed, in the 1930s the French government tried to set up a German-style apprenticeship system, but it failed, in part because of the lack of suitable jobs (Maurice, Sellier, and Silvestre, 1978).

Individual provision by employers has been much smaller in West Germany, and to some extent also in Britain, than in France or Italy. In Germany the long-standing commitment to apprenticeship has provided individual employers with a set of training norms which both their peers and their employees thought worth defending. Moreover, the viability of external labour markets for skilled labour meant that employers could usually draw on these without having to anticipate future needs in the way necessary with internal labour markets. In addition, through much of the period of rapid growth in West Germany, skilled labour markets were topped up with a supply of skilled emigrants from East Germany who would have been trained to the same kind of norms.

In industry in Britain, the strong position of skilled workers in most firms has meant that they could prevent employers from upgrading workers who had not served an apprenticeship.[3] This limited the rewards employers could offer semiskilled workers in return for accepting on-the-job training, and so inhibited the growth of this kind of training.

Sweden provides an interesting case in that it has apparently achieved a fair degree of interfirm skilled mobility without the existence of established occupational labour markets. This can be partly explained by the strong tripartite commitment to a system of highly institutionalised labour mobility in which people trained off-the-job are accepted by skilled workers in employment. One feature of the Swedish "accord" between labour and employers, at least until the mid-1970s, was that the unions, particularly LO, were strongly committed to economic growth through rising productivity, and thus accepted a high degree of management prerogative in

[3] For recent evidence of the small amount of upgrading and additional training to skilled jobs, see Millward and Stevens (1986) and the Warwick Survey (Brown, 1981).

the enterprise in exchange for a high degree of public support for mobility and retraining. Thus the unions had little sympathy with attempts to mobilise around demands for special treatment of occupational groups.

Finally, one of the big problems faced by both the successful and the less successful countries has been that of matching the supply and demand sides of skilled labour markets in qualitative terms especially.

Getting ahead of the argument, one might say that West Germany alone has succeeded in matching the two. France has fought hard to reconcile two basically contradictory systems. In Britain and Italy, the governments have sought to delegate more and more control of training to individual employers, but because in neither country do employers have the collective organisation of German employers, private provision is likely to enhance the role of internal labour markets, laying in store severe problems of labour market adaptation for the future and creating skilled workforces of a very heterogeneous quality.

Problems of Vocational Training
in the Late 1970s and the 1980s

International Competition, New Technology, and the
Increased Interest in Vocational Education and Training

In many EEC countries increased and improved vocational education and training have been seen as one response to the apparent slowness with which European firms have been responding to challenges of new technology and increased competition in all markets. There has been widespread concern that skill shortages, in terms of both quality and quantity, have hampered adoption of new technology. Fleck (1983) reported that slow rates of diffusion and high rates of equipment failure in Britain were due to shortages of both workers with relevant maintenance skills and more general skills, and Cross (1983) reported similar views of a sample of British managers concerned with technical innovations in process industries—that shortages of trained staff were a major barrier to innovation. However, some recent research suggests that providing extra training is only part of the solution and that quality and the ability of firms to utilise the trained staff they have are equally important.

The problems are best illustrated by two countries in which there has been acute awareness of the difficulties, namely Britain and France. In both cases the state can do most on the supply side, but it is likely to find its policies foundering on the demand side.

A number of studies have attributed a significant part of Britain's relatively poor economic performance to inadequacies of training. Detailed comparisons by the National Institute for Economic and Social Research have shown that, in Britain, both the content of intermediate vocational diplomas and the level of attainment in mathematical and linguistic skills of the kind of school-leavers likely to enter upon intermediate vocational training are lower than in France and especially in West Germany (Prais, 1981; Prais and Wagner, 1988; Steedman, 1987a, 1987b, 1988). These studies show the considerable strength of the German system of technical education, especially as compared with Britain, and echo the warnings issued as long ago as the turn of the century (Marshall, 1920). The Finniston Report (1980), set up by the Department of Industry, drew similar conclusions from international comparisons for higher level engineering training in Britain, as did a report by the National Economic Development Office (NEDO, 1984) in relation to Japanese and American industry.

Low rates of training may arise out of an interaction between the supply and demand sides of labour markets, constituting something of a "low skill equilibrium" out of which it is hard to break (Finegold and Soskice, 1988). The problem is particularly well illustrated by the British case, but it is of wider relevance. An important feature of British manufacturing is that, although similar in industrial composition to that of West Germany, the British firms tend to be concentrated among the low value-added activities, while those of West Germany are more commonly found among the high value-added ones (Saunders, 1978). Low value-added activities tend to rely on more repetitive and less skilled work, and so give rise to a smaller demand for skilled labour. This, in turn, leads to less openings for qualified workers and discourages the supply side. The problem is particularly well illustrated in a comparison of training, work organisation, and type of product market in the British and West German kitchen furniture industries (Steedman and Wagner, 1987). Under such conditions, governments may try to increase the input of qualified labour supply into the system, but the labour will be poorly utilised.

Poor utilisation of highly qualified manpower in British industry has also been highlighted in a recent study of the careers of young engineers in Britain and Japan (Thurley, Lam, and Lorriman, 1988), and by evidence presented by some of the associations of professional engineers to the Finniston Report on the engineering profession (Finniston, 1980) that the management of many firms did not know how to utilise their engineering staff fully, nor did they know how to select them or manage their early careers in the firm.[4]

Part of the problem seems to arise from the integration of most longer service engineers into internal labour markets (Mace, 1979), whereas the training system is oriented towards occupational markets, with the result that young engineers face poor integration into their firms and experience high turnover rates (Thurley, Lam, and Lorriman, 1988). Indeed, the recommendations of the Finniston Report recognized the same problem and urged a strengthening of the professional status of engineers.

In France, the major effort to improve vocational training since the early 1970s has been motivated by the need to modernise French industry, diagnosed, in part, as an excessive reliance on skills from manual to managerial levels developed by practical experience rather than theoretical training.[5] The policy of successive governments (both Gaullist and Socialist) has been to improve the responsiveness of the state vocational training system to the needs of employers, a problem encountered in different forms in many countries.

The causes of this are twofold and long-standing. The first relates to the difficulty of integrating general qualifications into a labour market organised on enterprise lines, and the second, to contrasting philosophies of education and training between employers and the state educational system. The long-standing

---

[4] "A significant proportion of engineering graduates are engaged in work appropriate to technician engineers. This is sometimes because employers do not, or cannot, provide opportunities for promotion of young engineers who have the capacity to undertake responsibilities appropriate to chartered engineers. In such cases the employers are not exploiting the full potential of their young engineers." (Finniston, 1980, p. 58, Evidence from the Institution of Mechanical Engineers).

"We were, however, even more concerned by the charge that all too few job descriptions bear real comparison with the actual task—the successful candidate finds himself given work quite different from that which he is led to expect. At best, this suggests an inability on the part of the personnel managers to define a vacancy or to specify and recognise the type of engineer to match it." (Finniston, 1980, p. 58, Evidence from the Institution of Mechanical Engineers).

[5] See, for example, Preamble to the Ninth Plan 1984-88, Journal Officiel 13.5.93.

nature of the first problem is illustrated by the failure of French attempts to create a West German style apprenticeship system in France in the 1930s (Maurice, Sellier, and Silvestre, 1978). Creating a new qualification without simultaneously creating a corresponding set of job vacancies was bound to make such training unattractive to young people. This problem has persisted in recent years, taking the form of the "occupational downgrading" experienced by young workers holding state vocational qualifications, as they take unskilled or semiskilled positions before subsequent upgrading to skilled jobs several years later (Marsden and Germe, forthcoming). Evidence from the cohort studies of the CEREQ and from the French Labour Force Surveys shows that such "occupational downgrading" is common for qualified young workers (Table 3) and that only after a period of five to ten years of activity do they eventually emerge into skilled positions (Capdeville and Grapin, 1975; Coeffic, 1987).

The second, the clash of educational philosophies, is also long-standing. The educational system also contributed to undermining the attempted apprenticeship system because of the high prestige of the general as compared with the vocational streams. The institutional strength of the teaching unions within the educational system has also militated against educational policies which limit young people's opportunities by dividing some of them off into vocational streams with limited chances for upward social mobility, a point also raised on many occasions by British trade unions with regard to British educational policy. In France, the educational system remains the key to the top administrative and many of the top established business positions. In more recent times the problem has persisted, and despite considerable innovations in technical education (for example, the development of more vocational technical streams in the Baccalaureat), it has proved difficult to gain acceptance for a mixture of theoretical training in schools and practical training in the enterprise.

In West Germany, the strength and technical sophistication of the economy has meant that competitive disadvantage due to inadequate training has been less of an issue. Nevertheless, a major preoccupation has been the rigidity of the apprenticeship system of occupational licencing. Until the reform of the late 1960s and early

TABLE 3

France, Young Workers in 1984 Who Were Still at School in 1983

	Bacca-laureat and Higher	CAP or BEP	No Quali-fications or Brevet des Colleges	Total
	Males (000)			
Skilled	3.9	11.6	5.4	21.7
Semiskilled and unskilled	2.0	14.0	15.6	31.9
All occupations	49.0	35.0	30.0	114.0
	Females (000)			
White-collar				
Administrative	37.1	12.8	8.9	58.8
Other	5.1	7.5	11.9	24.2
Blue-collar				
Skilled	—	1.5	1.7	3.5
Semiskilled and unskilled	1.4	4.9	5.9	12.1
All occupations	111.0	29.0	33.0	173.0

Source: Coeffic (1987). Based on the Enquête sur l'Emploi.

1970s (mostly implemented by negotiation, but boosted by the 1969 law on vocational training, the Arbeitsförderungsgesetz), this was exacerbated by the large number of different trades to which young workers could be apprenticed. One of the objects of the reform was to increase adaptability by greatly reducing the number of recognised trades and simultaneously broadening their base, so that workers' skills would be less exposed to technical obsolescence. A key to the West German success lies in the consensus of support for apprenticeship among employers, unions, and the government authorities, although negotiations of the reforms required the resolution of a number of conflicting interests (Streeck, 1985), notably between industrial and artisan employers.

The problems of skill supply, especially as concerns new technology, have stimulated a number of major employers to develop their own initiatives (OECD, 1988, Ch. 4). Recently some big firms such as General Motors and Lucas, not previously reputed for their policies on training, have launched major training initiatives. In Britain, Ford has recently allocated $34 million for the establishment of training and education centres in all its 22 British plants (IDS, 1988). In the past such initiatives have often been undermined by "beggar-thy-neighbour" reactions of other employers who have sought to entice away the newly trained personnel, but there have also been some recent examples of interfirm cooperation. In early 1988, four major employers of graduate software specialists agreed on an industry-wide scheme for workplace training involving inspection and certification. Among British travel agents there have been moves to agree on industry norms for training. In France, the system of continuing training (see the section on Adult Training below) encourages employers to cooperate in the formation of locally based training facilities (the FAFs). Although these initiatives fall short of the degree of interemployer cooperation institutionalised in the West German chambers of industry and commerce, they may represent a new direction.

The Rise in Youth Unemployment

Unlike in the United States where youth unemployment has been high throughout the 1970s, young workers in Western Europe were one of the main groups to suffer the brunt of the increase in unemployment in the late 1970s. By 1981 male teenage unemployment rates were mostly in the region of 20 percent except in West Germany, where they remained under 5 percent, and in Sweden. For females, in several countries they rose to over 30 percent (notably in Belgium, France, and Italy), and to about 20 and 15 percent, respectively, in Britain and the Netherlands. In all of these European countries, teenage unemployment rates were at least double the aggregate rate (Table 4).

Youth unemployment as a social and human problem. In several countries the state took the lead either in direct support measures for young people or through measures taken through employers, but resting heavily on government finance. The main exception was West Germany where the predominant action was by private employers using increased apprentice intake as the means of absorbing the fall in demand for youth labour (and its increased supply), although more recently this has been supplemented to help workers unable to get an apprenticeship place (Schober and Wadensjö, forthcoming).

In Britain, France, and Italy, the state has played a major role in organising employment and training contracts for young workers, usually supported by marginal employment subsidies. In Britain these took the form of the Youth Opportunities Programme (YOP), and more recently the Youth Training Scheme (YTS), in which the

TABLE 4

Unemployment Rates by Sex and Age, 1979-1985

	Males			Females		
	14–19	20–24	All Ages	14–19	20–24	All Ages
			France			
1979	18.4	10.0	4.6	40.4	17.5	10.2
1981	23.2	10.2	5.3	43.4	19.7	12.1
1983	24.1	12.9	6.1	38.9	18.9	10.5
1985	32.1	19.9	8.5	46.9	23.5	12.6
			West Germany			
1979	4.5	3.2	2.3	6.8	4.5	4.2
1981	5.0	4.4	2.8	7.3	5.5	4.6
1983	10.3	10.2	5.8	13.3	9.6	7.5
1985	9.0	8.9	5.8	12.5	9.8	8.5
			Italy			
1979	25.1	20.6	5.3	40.1	26.0	13.3
1981	27.6	19.9	5.6	41.0	29.2	5.1
1983	30.2	20.7	5.7	45.1	29.6	14.4
1985	32.8	22.9	6.2	47.2	34.2	15.0
			United Kingdom			
1979	15.3	6.4	4.6	16.3	7.9	6.0
1981	27.7	16.1	10.5	26.6	13.1	10.0
1983	27.7	19.1	12.0	23.4	13.2	9.8
1985	21.4	18.5	11.8	19.4	14.6	11.0

Note: Based on enlarged concept of labour force (including nonactive persons seeking paid employment). 1983 enlarged concept adapted slightly to ILO concept.

Source: Eurostat Labour Force Sample Survey.

training element is much more important than in its predecessor. In France there were various forms of employment and training contracts (contrats emploi-formation, CEF, started in 1975), and in Italy the contratti formazione lavoro, CFL, begun in 1977.

The increased private employer apprentice intake in industrial and commercial enterprises in West Germany was particularly striking. Between 1978 and 1985 it rose by a quarter for males to just under half a million, and by 30 percent for females (Statistisches Jahrbuch). Over the same period, and under similar cost pressures, British employers reduced their apprentice intake. The process by which this came about owes much to the corporatist organisation of West German employers and to the discount on apprentice employment (which we argue later is itself dependent upon a similar institutional structure). Streeck (1985) described this process for the construction industry. There, the employers, who are organised into chambers of industry and commerce with extensive supervisory powers over employer-based vocational training, and into industry employers' associations, agreed with the construction union on a programme of reform and modernisation of apprenticeship training (introducing a system of training by stages) and a system of privately organised training levies. The importance of sustaining these private relations is illustrated, in Streeck's account, by the use of the threat of state intervention when agreement seemed to elude the partners. The effectiveness of the German system seems to lie in the ability of employers' associations to control free-riding by individual employers (despite the discount on apprentice employment, employers pay a considerable share of the net costs of apprentice training [Noll et al., 1984]). Unlike in internal labour market systems, all employers in a particular sector may benefit from a well-stocked occupational market, so there is an element of collective self-interest in ensuring a strong entry into apprenticeship.

Youth unemployment and interrupted skill formation. The high level of unemployment among young people has been seen as a problem in itself, but equally important is the interruption which unemployment at this stage of a person's working life makes in the national training effort. In a period of recession employers are often under pressure to cut private training, and in internal labour markets the presumption of long-term employment may be an incentive to cut youth recruitment. Hence, the increased emphasis of the more recent youth unemployment schemes on a training component, and it has been in France that there has been the greatest effort to link training policies with a research-based diagnosis of the problems.

In France, the transition from school vocational training to skilled work was already delicate before the rise of youth unemployment. As a result, the state has felt the need to intervene more, notably with supplementary training and experience schemes to help bridge the gap.

Vocational skills produced in the educational system commonly lack an important component of work experience which would make them immediately applicable. Provision of such experience is costly, and as Germe (1986) has argued, the experience is sufficiently transferable to make individual employers unwilling to provide it. As a result, qualified young workers have tended to start their careers in low-paid sectors, small firms, and unskilled or semiskilled jobs, and to wait until opportunities become available in their preferred firms. Even then they may have to take a semiskilled job and await upgrading to a skilled job; thus the occupational downgrading mentioned earlier has been compounded by a form of sectoral downgrading similar to the "moratorium period" experienced by young workers in the U.S. (Osterman, 1980). This is part of a wider phenomenon of labour market segmentation, accentuated when unemployment rises. In all the European Community countries discussed in this chapter, young workers were concentrated in low-paid (for adults) industries (Marsden and Ryan, 1988).

Several of the French youth employment and training schemes have been aimed at bridging this gap, notably the training and adaptation contracts which are designed to supplement the school-based vocational qualifications already held. The evidence so far suggests that their success has been mixed, largely because even though they may subsidise the provision of practical experience, they still do not tackle the other aspects of internal labour market logic, notably that relating to the fears more senior adult workers have of substitution if job progression is undermined. It would seem to be a result of this that take-up of these schemes has been greatest in small firms and in some services sectors (Guasco, 1985).

The Rise of "Alternance" Training

One of the strengths of the West German apprenticeship system since reforms of the early 1970s has been the mix of theoretical and practical training which it has provided. As a result, on graduating, a former apprentice is immediately attractive to potential employers, requiring little more than some additional practice. Since the 1969 reform, German apprenticeships generally consist of a first year in which a great deal of time is spent in special schools, the ratio of practical to theoretical training increasing as the apprentice moves towards his or her third year. Similar moves occurred in Britain, for example under the auspices of the Engineering Industry Training Board (Venning et al., 1980), but these have been more sectorally specific than the changes in Germany.

Recognising that school-based training needs a big complement of practical experience in the enterprise, both French and Swedish, and to some extent also British, training policy has sought to complement school training with a period of work experience and further training as part of the transition from school to adult status work. Indeed, in a recent comparison of training in the construction industry in four countries, Campinos and Grando (1988) and Moebus and Grando (1988) argue that the French policy of "alternance" has meant that in terms of the *content* of training, as distinct from its labour market links, the French system was moving strongly in the direction of that in Germany.

The British Youth Training Scheme, instituted in 1981, has some potential as a vehicle for alternance as school leavers can supplement their general school education with up to two years of training and experience within the enterprise, leading to a recognised vocational qualification. However, what it lacks in relation to the French system is the quality school-based vocational training provided by the CAP, the BEP, and other technical diplomas as a basis on which to build, and in relation to the German system it lacks the quality of organised theoretical training provided within the apprenticeship (Marsden and Ryan, 1990).

Adult Training and Retraining

Adult training and retraining has been most developed in France, Germany, and also in Sweden where it has played a key role in the active manpower policy. In West Germany, a framework for further training after the apprenticeship has long existed in the possibilities of taking further exams to graduate to "Meister" or foreman level, the Meister being the traditional master craftsman who is entitled to set up his own handicraft enterprise or to manage the work of apprentice-trained skilled workers on behalf of a nonapprentice-trained employer.

In West Germany, further training beyond the apprenticeship (zusätzliche Berufsausbildung and Weiterbildung) has a long history. In the plant-level comparisons of French and German enterprises in the middle 1970s (Maurice et al., 1978), whereas in France the decisions on further training and promotion are largely taken by management (subject to the growing importance of "formation permanente" [see below]), in West Germany gaining a further diploma, within limits, entitled the employee to promotion, so that such training was often undertaken on the employee's own initiative. In West Germany, further training was encouraged by the

1969 law on training, and it was given a special role in the 1979 special labour market programme for regions with major problems of industrial restructuring (Bosch et al., 1984). In both instances the works councils have had a major role to play, training decisions by the enterprise being subject to consultation as to strategy and form, and codecision (obligatory agreement) as to their implementation in the enterprise.

As an illustration of the extent of this kind of training in Germany, Maurice et al. (1978) found that in their sample of firms in the early 1970s, the percentage of white-collar employees who had obtained their highest vocational diploma *after* entering full-time employment was about 50 percent in the German firms, compared to about 15 percent in the French ones. In the German firms these diplomas were mostly those of foremen (Meister), technicians, and graduate engineers (graduierte ingenieur) (Maurice et al., 1978, Table 42). Obtaining these diplomas was often linked with changing enterprise, again illustrating their recognition across occupational labour markets.

The development of continuing training ("formation permanente" or "continue") in France has been one of the most original developments in adult training in Western Europe, offering a system well adapted to supplementing training within internal labour markets. The system was launched in 1971, generalising a national agreement between the unions and the employers reached in 1970. A training fund was created,[6] financed by a payroll tax (set initially at 0.8 percent of the total wage bill in 1971) on employers, to be managed by the employer in consultation with and under the supervision of the bipartite enterprise committee. The law gave individual workers the right to leave for training purposes. This could be on full pay, on a state grant, or unpaid, so clearly the highest rate of take-up would be either where the employer and employee agree on what training is needed or where the employer decides to send employees to training courses (Dupeyroux, 1973). Thus, an important part of the underlying philosophy of both the national agreement and the law was that, apart from providing an opportunity for individual advancement, continuous training should

---

[6] These funds, the Fonds d'Assurance Formation (FAF), can be set up also by groups of employers or groups of employers and unions, thus maintaining the philosophy that, as far as possible, continuous training should be run on voluntaristic lines (Belorgey, 1973).

also serve as an instrument of personnel management. Its use has perhaps been favoured by the fact that the law built on the national agreement rather than seeking to impose some alternative design. In this respect, too, it represented something of a departure from the traditional state-led approach to education and training.

Spending by firms on continuing training in 1985 amounted to 2.3 percent of the wage bill, up from 1.5 percent in 1972 (Géhin, 1989), but varied considerably between sectors. It was highest in the sectors with greatest state involvement, such as electricity (7 percent), and least in some of the traditional low-wage industries such as textiles and clothing, which also employ large numbers of women and young workers. Géhin's study showed several important developments, notably that continuing training has increased most in sectors seeking to adapt to new technology, such as electrical engineering, electronics, and automobiles, suggesting that the programme has been successful in assisting industrial adjustment. In these branches the greatest effort has gone into training the more highly qualified groups. In earlier years, heavier use was made by industries undergoing major restructuring, such as coal and iron and steel (see Villeval and Mehaut, 1986), where training could be used to help those leaving find other employment, but also to train remaining employees in more advanced skills. Another important development has been the gradual shift towards use of external training centres rather than relying on internal training. This may signal a shift to better quality training and reflect the needs of smaller enterprises, but it may also be the result of training for new technology, for which firms cannot rely on the existing stock of skills they hold.

The greater flexibility of the programme makes it appear well adapted to the needs of firms operating with internal labour markets. However, the programme has important limitations, notably that many firms still undertake very little training, and averaged across all employees, the actual amount of training is small compared with the size of changes facing the French economy (averages of six hours a year for unskilled workers to 21 hours for supervisors) (Géhin, 1989).

Use of the continuing training as a means of individual advancement has perhaps proved the more problematic objective because, unlike in Germany where the reward for training is to some extent institutionalised, entitling workers to upgrading, in

France, in private industry at any rate, it has been more the practice for employers to decide who should be upgraded and then to give the necessary training (Maurice, Sellier, and Silvestre, 1978), and, as mentioned earlier, the employer is not obliged to pay the person's salary for training which has not been agreed.

In the area of enterprise restructuring, continuing training has been boosted by a number of other complementary training initiatives, some of which have attracted additional government support. This helps to explain the view of the French national employers' confederation that the system of continuing training has been an important factor in easing the problems of restructuring enterprises as it gave workers an opportunity to gain new skills when they would otherwise have had to seek a new job with only nontransferable internal labor market skills to offer.

Future Concerns

Access to Training

Many of the established forms of intermediate-level vocational training, such as apprenticeships and private employer-based training, pose problems of access. Indeed, one important characteristic is that they may be used to regulate entry into occupational and internal labour markets.

In the case of unqualified young workers, the elimination of large areas of unskilled employment, plus the raising of requirements for skilled employment, have closed off many of the traditional ports of entry into industrial employment (Roberts et al., 1987). In times of high unemployment, employers have, in any case, been less interested in hiring young workers, adding to the disadvantages faced by the unqualified young. To some extent, public employment policies, such as the British Youth Training Scheme, have sought to redress the balance by aiming to provide subsidised training places to all young school leavers without a job, and thus make some provision for the most disadvantaged young people. The argument about access has been taken further, suggesting that all young people should have a right to a period of vocational training, as expressed in the declaration adopted in 1982 by EEC political leaders in favour of a social guarantee of a two-year course of continuing training for all young people (Sellin, 1983). Although disadvantaged young workers may still not gain access to the best training opportunities, without such measures they might gain nothing at all.

In the case of adult workers, access to training is often difficult because conditions have been tailored to young workers. The development of continuing training in countries such as France has improved the situation somewhat, but it can still prove difficult for adults to gain access to training institutions and to obtain employer support and finance. This has led to modest take-up rates of such rights in France, reflecting the loss of income and of employer approval which may often follow (Jallade, 1982; Géhin, 1989). Unemployed adults especially have difficulty gaining access to these schemes because of their emphasis upon decisions within companies. The declining number of young people entering the labour market, expected for demographic reasons, may lead to greater interest among employers in such training.

Workplace training has often been criticised for inequity because it goes to employees who already show the most promise and is concentrated on what Atkinson and Meager (1986) characterised as the "core" workforce. If, as seems possible, a polarisation develops between a core workforce with high skills and employed under favourable conditions and a periphery with low skills and unstable employment, as was indicated by the intentions expressed by a number of the firms interviewed by Atkinson and Meager, then access to skilled jobs for young workers, for women, and also for the unemployed adult males could become more difficult.

In the case of women, a notable feature of many of the employer-based training systems, such as apprenticeships, is the virtual exclusion of women from a large number of types of specialisation, the exception being personal services and white-collar apprenticeships. In both Britain and West Germany, very few women undertake apprenticeships for skilled occupations in industry. Young women have fared much better in the state educational system, even in vocational streams, although access to the work experience necessary for entry to skilled jobs, for example in France, has not proved easy, leaving young women concentrated in a smaller number of skilled occupations than are men (Pohl and Soleillhavoup, 1981).

Thus, for all three groups—unqualified young workers, displaced males, and females—there remain important problems of inequity posed by intermediate vocational training systems and their links with jobs.

1992: Is There Convergence to a Single European Model of Vocational Training?

The creation of the Single Market of 1992 is likely to have a considerable effect on national vocational training systems, particularly if the more optimistic forecasts of the economic changes to follow materialise (such as those of the Cecchini report, 1988). A number of influences can be identified: enhanced competition and increased capital integration, highlighting existing weaknesses in national vocational training; the move towards harmonisation and mutual recognition of national qualifications; the possibility of bargaining over intermediate skills; and the longer-run moves to improve language teaching in schools which could facilitate mobility of the skilled categories of labour which in the past have tended to be among the least mobile.

One of the provisions of the Treaty of Rome, founding the European Community, is that there should be free mobility of labour between member countries, but so far only limited mobility has occurred among qualified workers because of the large number of obstacles posed by differences in training systems and in the balance between school and enterprise-based training. In recent years the Community has devoted considerable effort to remove some of these obstacles. It has adopted three main approaches: the directive approach, the comparability approach, and the development of "occupational profiles" (Sellin, 1989). The first is illustrated by the 1988 directive for the recognition of regulated (licenced) occupations such as lawyers and teachers, and the second by the 1985 directive currently pursued for nonregulated occupations, notably those of hotel, restaurant and catering, motor vehicle repair, construction, agricultural, and electrical trades. The comparability exercises have been conducted jointly with government, employer, and worker organisations so that, in theory, the conclusions should be tantamount to the establishment of agreed criteria for mutual recognition. Work on level two, roughly the intermediate vocational qualifications discussed in this chapter, is scheduled to be completed by 1996 (CEDEFOP, 1988). The third approach, still to be clarified, has been proposed for occupations whose structure is heavily determined by internal labour market conditions. Although the diversity in many areas remains great, as Steedman (1986) has argued, the state of flux of vocational training in some countries, such as Britain, creates opportunities for establishing national standards which are closer to those of their EEC neighbours.

Although the competitive pressures of 1992 are likely to be similar to those experienced in the latter 1970s and early 1980s, the monetary changes may have a profound influence. If governments surrender a significant degree of independence over exchange rates and national monetary policy, such as might follow with European Monetary Union, and also give up some autonomy over taxation (as free movement of goods, services, and savings is likely to bring taxes on consumption and saving more into line), then national governments will find that the range of instruments for acting on relative unit labour costs will be reduced. Wage controls will be one possible instrument, and competitive reduction of labour standards ("social dumping") another. Policies to raise efficiency, including by better training, may well provide a third and more socially desirable form of adjustment.

If the move is towards better training, the evidence presented in this chapter suggests that it will be the similarities in or differences between European labour markets after 1992, more than policy pronouncements, that will determine the nature of the training involved.

References

Atkinson, J., and N. Meager. *Changing Patterns of Work*. London: National Economic Development Council, 1986.

Belorgey, J. M. "Les fonds d'assurance formation." *Droit Social* 36, No. 9-10 (September-October 1973), pp. 73–82.

Bosch, G., H. Seifert, and B-G. Spies. *Arbeitsmarktpolitik und gewerkschaftliche interressenvertretung*. Koln: Bund Verlag, 1984.

Brown, W., ed. *Changing Contours of British Industrial Relations*. Oxford: Blackwell, 1981.

Campinos, M., and J. M. Grando. "Formation professionnelle ouvrière: trois modèles européens." *Formation Emploi* 22 (June 1988), pp. 5-29.

Capdeville and Grapin. "L'insertion professionnelle à la sortie du système scolaire: quelques exemples sur la période récente." *Economie et Statistique* 81-82 (1975), pp. 57-72.

Cecchini, P. *The European Challenge: The Benefits of a Single Market*. Aldershot: Wildwood House, 1988.

CEDEFOP (European Centre for the Development of Vocational Training). "Comparability of vocational training qualifications." *CEDEFOP Flash*, 1/88, Berlin (1988).

Coeffic, N. "Le devenir des jeunes sortis de l'école." *Données Sociales*, INSEE, Paris, 1987.

Combes, M-C. "L'apprentissage en France." *Document de Travail CEREQ* 33, Paris (March 1988a).

————. "La loi de 1987 sur l'apprentissage." *Formation Emploi* 22 (April-June 1988b), pp. 83–100.

Cross, M. *Changing Requirements for Craftsmen in the Process Industries*. Interim report. London: Technical Change Centre, 1983.

Dupeyroux, J. J. "Le droit à la formation: le congé de formation." *Droit Social* 36, No. 9-10 (September-October 1973), pp. 7-27.

Finegold, D., and D. Soskice. "The failure of training in Britain: analysis and prescription." *Oxford Review of Economic Policy* 4, No. 3 (1988), pp. 21-53.

Finniston. "Engineering our Future: Report of the Committee of Inquiry into the Engineering Profession." Cmnd 7794. London: HMSO, 1980.

Fleck, V. "Robotics in manufacturing organisations." In *Information Technology in Manufacturing Processes*, ed. G. Winch. London: Rosendale, 1983.

Garonna, P. "Youth unemployment, labour market deregulation and union strategies in Italy." *British Journal of Industrial Relations* 24, No. 1 (March 1986).

Garonna, P., and P. Ryan. "Youth labour, industrial relations and deregulation in advanced economies." *Economia e Lavoro* 20, No. 1 (October-December 1986), pp. 3-19.

Géhin, J-P. "L'évolution de la formation continue dans les secteurs d'activité (1973-1985)." *Formation Emploi* 25 (March 1989), pp. 19-38.

Germe, J. F. "Employment policies and the entry of young people into the labour market in France." *British Journal of Industrial Relations* 24, No. 1 (March 1986).

Guest, D. "Human resource management and industrial relations." *Journal of Management Studies* 24, No. 5 (September 1987).

IDS (Incomes Data Services). 1988. IDS Report.

ISFOL. "L'apprendistato in Italia: problemi attuali e prospettive." *ISFOL Quaderni di Formazione* 80 (May-June 1982).

Jallade, J-P. *Alternance Training for Young People: Guidelines for Action*. Berlin: CEDEFOP, 1982.

Jones, I. "Skill formation and pay relativities." In *Education and Economic Performance*, by G. D. N. Worswick. London: Gower, 1985.

Lorenz, E. "Les chantiers navals en France et en Grande-Bretagne, 1890-1970." *Le Mouvement Social* 138 (January-March 1987), pp. 21-44.

Mace, J. "Internal labour markets for engineers in British industry." *British Journal of Industrial Relations* 17, No. 1 (March 1979), pp. 50-63.

Margirier, G. "Les métiers du batiment dans les systèmes de formation: Italie: le déclin de la formation sur le tas." *Formation Emploi* 22 (June 1988), pp. 46-57.

Marsden, D. W. *The End of Economic Man? Custom and Competition in Labour Markets*. Brighton: Wheatsheaf, 1986.

—————. "Institutions and labour mobility: occupational and internal labour markets in Britain, France, Italy, and West Germany." In *Labour Relations and Economic Performance*, eds. R. Brunetta and C. Dell'Aringa. London: Macmillan, 1990.

Marsden, D. W., and J. F. Germe. "Young people and entry paths to long term jobs and occupations in France and Great Britain." In *The Problem of Youth: The Regulation of Youth Employment in Advanced Economies*, eds. P. Ryan, P. Garonna, and R. Edwards. London: Macmillan, forthcoming.

Marsden, D. W., and P. Ryan. *Youth Labour Market Structures and the Quality of Youth Employment in Major EEC Economies*. Report for the Joseph Rowntree Memorial Trust, August 1988.

—————. "Apprenticeship and labour market structure: UK youth employment and training in international context." *British Journal of Industrial Relations*, forthcoming 1990.

Marshall, A. *Principles of Economics*, 8th ed. London: Macmillan, 1920.

Maurice, M., F. Sellier, and J. J. Silvestre. *Production de la hiérarchie dans l'entreprise: recherche d'un effect sociétal France-Allemagne*. Mimeo. Aix-en-Provence: Laboratoire d'Economie et de Sociologie du Travail, 1978.

—————. *The Social Foundations of Industrial Power, A Comparison of France and Germany*. Cambridge, MA: MIT Press, 1986.

Maurice, M., A. Sorge, and M. Warner. "Societal differences in organising manufacturing units. A comparison of France, West Germany and Great Britain." International Institute of Management Working Paper IIM/79-15, Berlin, 1979.

Millward, N., and M. Stevens. *Workplace Industrial Relations: 1980-1984*. Aldershot: Gower, 1986.

Moebus, M., and J-M Grando. "Les métiers du bâtiment dans les systèmes de formation: la RFA: le monopole du système dual." *Formation Emploi* 22 (April 1988), pp. 30-45.

Mouy, P. "La formation professionnelle initiale des ouvriers et l'evolution du travail industriel." *Formation Emploi* 1 (January-March 1983), pp. 52-70.

National Economic Development Office. *Competence and Competition*. London: HMSO, 1984.

Noll, I., U. Beicht, G. Boll, W. Malcher, and S. Wiederhold-Fritz. *Nettokosten der betrieblichen Berufsbildung*. Schriften zur Berufsbildungforschung, Band 63. Berlin: Beuth Verlag GMBH, 1984.

OECD. *New Technologies in the 1990s: A Socioeconomic Appraisal*. Paris: OECD, 1988.

Osterman, P. *Getting Started*. Cambridge, MA: MIT Press, 1980.

Pohl, R., and J. Soliellhavoup. "Entrées des jeunes et mobilité des moins jeunes." *Economie et Statistique* 134 (June 1981), pp. 85-108.

Prais, S. "Vocational qualifications of the labour force in Britain and Germany." *National Institute Economic Review* 98 (1981), pp. 47-59.

Prais, S., and K. Wagner. "Productivity and management: the training of foremen in Britain and Germany." *National Institute Economic Review* 123 (February 1988), pp. 34-46.

Roberts, K., S. Dench, and D. Richardson. *The Changing Structure of Youth Labour Markets*. Research Paper No. 59. London: Department of Employment, 1987.

Ryan, P. "Job training, employment practices, and the large enterprise: the case of costly transferable skills." In *Internal Labor Markets*, ed. P. Osterman. Cambridge, MA: MIT Press, 1984.

————. "Trade unionism and the pay of young workers." In *From School to Unemployment: The Labour Market for Young People*, ed. P. N. Junankar. London: Macmillan, 1987.

————. "Youth interventions, job substitution and trade union policy in Great Britain, 1976-1986." In *The State and the Labor Market: Employment Policy, Collective Bargaining and Economic Crisis*, ed. S. Rosenberg. New York: Plenum, 1988.

————. "Trade union responses to special employment and training measures in Great Britain: regulated inclusion or exclusion?" In *The Problem of Youth: The Regulation of Youth Employment in Advanced Economies*, eds. P. Ryan, P. Garonna, and R. Edwards. London: Macmillan, forthcoming.

Ryan, P., P. Garonna, and R. Edwards, eds. *The Problem of Youth: The Regulation of Youth Employment in Advanced Economies*. London: Macmillan, forthcoming.

Saunders, C. T. *The Engineering Industries in Great Britain, France, and West Germany*. Sussex European Papers. Brighton: University of Sussex, 1978.

Schober, K., and E. Wadensjö. "Contrasting forms of youth training and employment in Sweden and West Germany." In *The Problem of Youth: The Regulation of Youth Employment in Advanced Economies*, eds. P. Ryan, P. Garonna, and R. Edwards. London: Macmillan, forthcoming.

Sellin, B. "The development of alternance training for young people in the European Community." *Vocational Training* 12 (September 1983), pp. 73-83.

————. *The Recognition and/or Comparability of Non-University Vocational Training Qualifications in the Member States of the European Communities*. Interim Report prepared by Burkhart Sellin. Berlin: CEDEFOP, 1989.

Social Europe. "The Social dimension of the internal market (interim report of the internal working party)." Special issue. Bruxelles: Commission of the European Communities, 1988.

Steedman, H. "Qualifications pour les activités administratives et commerciales au Royaume Uni, en France et en République Fédérale d'Allemagne," *Document CEDEFOP* (Centre Européen pour le Développement de la Formation Professionnelle). Luxembourg: Office des Publications Officielles des Communautés Européennes, 1986.

Steedman, H. "Vocational training in France and Britain: office work." *National Institute Economic Review* (May 1987), pp. 58–70.

———. "Vocational training in France and Britain: mechanical and electrical craftsmen." *National Institute Economic Review* 126 (November 1988), pp. 57–70.

Steedman, H., and K. Wagner. "The kitchen furniture industries in Britain and West Germany." *National Institute Economic Review* 122 (November 1987).

Streeck, W. *Die reform der beruflichen Bildung in der westdeutschen Bauwirtschaft 1969–1982.* Berlin: WZB, 1985.

Thurley, K., C. L. Lam, and P. Lorriman. *The development of electronics engineers: a Japanese/UK comparison. A preliminary report.* Discussion paper CIR/88/179, STICERD, London School of Economics, 1988.

Venning, M., O. Frith, and C. Grimbley. *The Craftsman in Engineering.* Watford, Engineering Industry Training Board, 1980.

Villeval, M-C., and P. Mehaut. "Les congés de formation-conversion et la gestion des mobilités: une étude de cas dans la sidérurgie." *Formation Emploi* 16 (October–December 1986), pp. 59–69.